The Continuity of Feudal Power

The Continuity of Feudal Power is an analytic study of a family of the Neapolitan aristocracy during the early modern period, with particular focus on the time of Spanish rule (1503–1707). The Caracciolo marquis of Brienza were a branch of one of the oldest and most powerful clans in the kingdom of Naples, and they numbered among the hundred wealthiest feudal families throughout the early modern period. Professor Astarita reconstructs the family's patrimony, administration, and revenues, its relationship with the rural communities over which it had jurisdiction, its marriage and alliance policies, and the relations between the aristocracy and the monarchical government. His emphasis is on the continuing importance of feudal traditions, institutions, and values both in the definition of the aristocracy's status, and in its success in insuring the persistence of its wealth and power within the kingdom.

T0371191

CAMBRIDGE STUDIES IN EARLY MODERN HISTORY

Edited by Professor J. H. Elliott, University of Oxford,
Professor Olwen Hufton, Harvard University, and
Professor H. G. Koenigsberger

The idea of an "early modern" period of European history from the fifteenth to the late eighteenth century is now widely accepted among historians. The purpose of Cambridge Studies in Early Modern History is to publish monographs and studies which illuminate the character of the period as a whole, and in particular focus attention on a dominant theme within it, the interplay of continuity and change as they are presented by the continuity of medieval ideas, political and social organization, and by the impact of new ideas, new methods, and new demands on the traditional structures.

For a list of titles published in the series, please see end of book

The Continuity
of Feudal Power

The Caracciolo di Brienza in Spanish Naples

Tommaso Astarita

Assistant Professor of History, Georgetown University, Washington DC

The right of the
University of Cambridge
to print and sell
all manner of books
was granted by
Henry VIII in 1534.
The University has printed
and published continuously
since 1584.

CAMBRIDGE UNIVERSITY PRESS

Cambridge
New York   Port Chester
Melbourne   Sydney

PUBLISHED BY THE PRESS SYNDICATE OF THE UNIVERSITY OF CAMBRIDGE
The Pitt Building, Trumpington Street, Cambridge, United Kingdom

CAMBRIDGE UNIVERSITY PRESS
The Edinburgh Building, Cambridge CB2 2RU, UK
40 West 20th Street, New York NY 10011–4211, USA
477 Williamstown Road, Port Melbourne, VIC 3207, Australia
Ruiz de Alarcón 13, 28014 Madrid, Spain
Dock House, The Waterfront, Cape Town 8001, South Africa

http://www.cambridge.org

First published 1992
First paperback edition 2004

A catalogue record for this book is available from the British Library

Library of Congress cataloguing in publication data

Astarita, Tommaso
The continuity of feudal power: the Caracciolo di Brienza
in Spanish Naples / Tommaso Astarita
p. cm. – (Cambridge studies in early modern history)
Based on the author's thesis (Ph.D.) – Johns Hopkins University, 1988
Includes bibliographical references and index
ISBN 0 521 40474 6 hardback
1. Naples (Kingdom) – History – Spanish rule, 1442–1707
2. Caracciolo family. 3. Feudalism – Italy – Naples (Kingdom) – History
I. Series
DG848.1.A88 1992
945′.7 – dc20   91-3024 CIP

ISBN 0 521 40474 6 hardback
ISBN 0 521 89316 X paperback

Contents

Illustrations

Tables

Acknowledgments

I thank the staff of the Archivio Storico del Banco di Napoli (in particular Eduardo Nappi and Giuseppe Zevola), of the Archivio Segreto Vaticano, and of the Archivio di Stato di Potenza for their assistance. I wish to thank dottoresse Azzinnari, Belli, Esposito, and Nicodemo of the Archivio di Stato di Napoli for their help and patience. I thank Señora Gloria Tejada of the Archivo General de Simancas for her kind assistance in providing me with microfilms. I also have to thank the staff of the Biblioteca Nazionale di Napoli (in particular the Sezioni Manoscritti and Napoletana), of the Milton S. Eisenhower Library of The Johns Hopkins University (in particular the Inter-Library Loan Department), and of the Wright State University and Georgetown University Libraries.

I am grateful to the Department of History of The Johns Hopkins University and to the Charles S. Singleton Center for Italian Studies for generously supporting my doctoral studies, during which I completed most of the research for this book. My thanks also to my readers and editors at Cambridge University Press.

By working in two continents and two cultures one develops debts of gratitude to many people. In Europe I owe thanks to Count Giovanni Caracciolo di Brienza, Alberto Cutillo, Carlo de Conciliis, Antonio Delfino, Filippo Faes, Luigina Mattioli, Giovanna Moracci, Giovanni Muto, Anna Maria Rao, Marco Rapetti, Crispin Robinson, Renato Ruotolo, and Hartwin Spenkuch. In the United States I received the support and assistance, in various ways, of Laurent Cartayrade, Thomas Cole, William Connell, Andy Federer, Alison Games, Julie Hardwick, William Kuhn, Silvana Patriarca, Michael Schaffer, Kathy and Peter Taylor, and Wendy Thompson. On both sides of the Atlantic I have benefited from the help and advice of John Marino and Thomas Willette.

The late Rosa Pannain, the late Olga Staro, Isa Proto Pisani, and Massimo Lojacono encouraged and supported my early interest in history and in teaching. Mario del Treppo, Giuseppe Galasso, and the late Ettore Lepore nurtured and deepened that interest.

My colleagues and friends at Georgetown University have been generous with their support. I am especially indebted to Jim Collins, John McNeill, Howard Spendelow, and Steve Tamari. Many of my students at Wright State and Georgetown have unknowingly helped me write this book by strengthening my

Acknowledgments

love for history and teaching. My professors at Johns Hopkins taught me in their courses and through their example most of what I know about my work. I thank John Baldwin, Richard Kagan, Orest Ranum, and Mack Walker for their kind advice over the years. I am indebted to Elborg and Robert Forster for their warm support. I am deeply grateful to Richard Goldthwaite for his constant encouragement and for the generosity of his supervision of my doctoral work.

I am deeply indebted to Scott Spector for our long discussions and for his example; to John Garrigus for his patient and gracious work on my written English; to Trevor Burnard for our arguments and for his unfailing warmth; to Robert Jenner for his help during the epilogue of this book's story; and to Alessandra Galizzi Kroegel for often saving me from despairing of more than this book. My gratitude for their help is matched only by my gratitude for their friendship. Finally, this study of a Neapolitan family could not have been written without the support of my own Neapolitan family.

Questo libro è dedicato alla cara memoria di mio nonno, Vincenzo Giuliani.

Note on abbreviations and measurements

The following abbreviations have been used:

ACB	Archivio privato Caracciolo di Brienza (in ASN)
AGS	Archivo General de Simancas
ASBN	Archivio Storico del Banco di Napoli
ASCL	*Archivio Storico per la Calabria e la Lucania*
ASI	*Archivio Storico Italiano*
ASN	Archivio di Stato di Napoli
ASP	Archivio di Stato di Potenza
ASPN	*Archivio Storico per le Province Napoletane*
ASV	Archivio Segreto Vaticano
MEFRM	*Mélanges de l'Ecole Française de Rome. Moyen Age et Temps Modernes*
QS	*Quaderni Storici*
RSI	*Rivista Storica Italiana*

The Neapolitan ducat (*ducato*) was divided into five *tarì*, each consisting of twenty *grani*. At times the ducat was divided into ten *carlini*, each worth ten *grani*.

The following measurements were used in early modern Naples:

tomolo (for surfaces)	=	0.33 ha.
tomolo (for capacity)	=	0.55 hl.
soma (for wine)	=	58.16 l.
libbra (pound)	=	0.32 kg.
rotolo (for weights)	=	0.89 kg.
cantaro (for weights)	=	89.09 kg.

Introduction

From all parts of the castle, the lord enjoys the happiest view of the countryside, dominating from it his entire village.

(From a 1625 description of Brienza)

The view of Southern Italy and Sicily held by educated Italians and Europeans is heavily shaped by literary images, ancient and modern. It is hard, perhaps pointless, to escape the suggestions of Carlo Levi's memoirs, of Verga's novels, of Lampedusa's *Gattopardo*, not to mention rural sociologists, who depict a world of millennial traditions, of immobile, proud backwardness, of resigned and internalized hostility to, and alienation from, public authority. Still today, many parts of the rural South appear to have changed but little in centuries, whatever the signs of modernity one sees everywhere. Leaving behind the highway in the Vallo di Diano, one reaches the village of Brienza much more easily than did its masters and visitors of old; but the village itself those masters would still recognize. The ruined medieval castle hovers over the remains of the old village, uninhabited after the earthquake of 1980, and climbing on its walls, one visually dominates vast fields, hills, and pastures. The way to the neighboring villages is harder, as it climbs over hills and mountains. The few remains of the feudal castle in Sasso, "on a raised height of a rocky mountain" according to a 1625 description, still command a domineering and impressive view of the village and of the surrounding countryside, which appears harsh and ungenerous. The people of the village, though far from exhibiting the violence described by early modern bishops, still seem to regard outside visitors with curiosity mixed with suspicion.

This was the world of the Caracciolo Brienza, the noble family that ruled Brienza and its neighboring villages for over three centuries. They owned land there, they levied fees, they administered justice, they controlled local trade, they were involved in every aspect of the life of their subject population. Though their rule, privileges, and power continued for centuries, they did not, however, do so without undergoing changes and adaptations. Political, economic, and social changes in the South of Italy and in Europe as a whole affected the world of the Caracciolo Brienza, and the family, like other aristocrats, was able to react and adapt to evolving circumstances in all aspects of its life and behavior.

What were the relations of the early modern aristocracy with the monarchical state on the one hand, and with the rural communities on the other? What difficulties were associated with the preservation and transmission of the patrimony, particularly in the face of the conflicting claims of family members? How did the amount and composition of aristocratic revenues evolve over time, and what strategies were devised to protect and increase them? In the case of the kingdom of Naples, as for most of Western Europe, to attempt to answer these questions is to look for the key to aristocratic survival into recent times: to what extent, and how, did the aristocracy succeed in parrying or accommodating economic, social, and political change?

The present work suggests ways to answer these questions based on the study of a Neapolitan aristocratic family, the Caracciolo Brienza, from the mid-sixteenth to the early eighteenth century.[1] Although a quarter century has passed since Stuart Woolf's ground-breaking book on the Piedmontese aristocracy, monographs on Italian aristocratic families remain very few.[2] This situation can be ascribed to a lack of sources and to the Marxist-inspired lack of interest in the elite that prevailed in Italian academic circles in the 1960s and 1970s; but the resulting gap in our understanding of the social and economic life of early modern Italy is substantial. In particular, there is no modern book-length study of any aristocratic family of the kingdom of Naples.

The South of Italy has traditionally been seen as a backward area, far behind the North of the peninsula in economic, cultural, and political terms. Whatever the validity of such a characterization for the present time, its projection onto the past can lead to a failure of historical analysis, and to the neglect of an opportunity to enrich our understanding of past societies. However weak its economy, the early modern kingdom of Naples participated fully in Western European political, social, and cultural developments, and the study of its society can illuminate those developments from the perspective of one of the many parts of the continent that historians have perhaps been too quick to consign to the dustbin of historiographical marginality.

EUROPEAN ELITE GROUPS AND THE PRESERVATION OF STATUS, WEALTH, AND POWER

In 1942, Lucien Febvre called for historians to apply the methods of social history to the study of aristocratic families and patrimonies. In the ensuing decades, many have studied the European aristocracies, and there is now a rich

---

[1] The adjective "Neapolitan" refers both to the city of Naples, and to the whole kingdom of that name; in this work I have tried to use it only in the latter sense, specifying explicitly when I refer simply to the capital city.

[2] S. J. Woolf, *Studi sulla nobiltà piemontese nell'epoca dell'assolutismo* (Turin, 1963). G. Montroni, "Alcune riflessioni sulle storie di famiglia in età contemporanea" *Studi Storici* 27 (1986), pp. 901–13, discusses monographs on modern Italian families.

literature on the subject, both comparative and monographical.[3] Recently, Michael L. Bush has been able to draw on works devoted to almost all areas of Europe in two stern volumes on noble privilege and noble wealth.[4] I hope that the present case-study may enrich our understanding of the problems that faced Western European aristocrats and of the solutions that they found, or failed to find, in order to preserve their privileged position in their societies.

The institutional and political framework of the various early modern states in Western Europe has obviously influenced the issues addressed by modern historians. While the historiography of Northern Italian elite groups focusses on urban patrician oligarchies, primarily of mercantile origins, for instance, historians of absolutist France are more concerned with great landowning courtiers or with the development of the robe nobility; historians of the English nobility discuss the degree of adaptability of landed magnates in the face of political upheaval and commercial expansion.[5] Yet, all European aristocracies shared a preoccupation with the acquisition, and especially the preservation, of pre-eminent status and vast power, and of wealth sufficient to uphold them. In order successfully to maintain their position, aristocrats had to devise effective policies concerning inheritances and marriages; they had to learn to manage their revenues so as not to jeopardize the sources of their income while permitting the high levels of consumption that were an essential element of aristocratic identity; they needed to maintain their ties with the state without, on the other hand, losing too much of their social and economic power; and they had to preserve the paternalism and deference that traditionally bound the landowning aristocrats in particular to the rest of the population. The privileges, customs, and behaviors associated with these pursuits were, or became, the very definitions of aristocratic status.[6]

[3] L. Febvre, "Ce que peuvent nous apprendre les monographies familiales" *Annales d'histoire sociale* 4 (1942), pp. 31–34, later in Febvre, *Pour une histoire à part entière* (Paris, 1962), pp. 404–9; surveys of the history of European aristocracies include A. Goodwin, ed. *The European Nobility in the Eighteenth Century* (New York, 1967; first edit. London, 1953); J. Meyer, *Noblesses et pouvoirs dans l'Europe d'Ancien Régime* (Paris, 1973); J.-P. Labatut, *Les noblesses européennes* (Paris, 1978); and R. Vierhaus, ed. *Der Adel vor der Revolution* (Göttingen, 1971). On trends in family history, L. Stone, "Family History in the 1980s: Past Achievements and Future Trends" *Journal of Interdisciplinary History* 12 (1981), pp. 51–87.

[4] M. L. Bush, *The European Nobility*, I, *Noble Privilege* (New York, 1983), and II, *Rich Noble, Poor Noble* (Manchester, 1988). See also the much slimmer survey by J. Powis, *Aristocracy* (Oxford, 1984).

[5] The historiography of Italian elite groups will be discussed below; for France see, for example, R. Forster, *The House of Saulx-Tavanes. Versailles and Burgundy, 1700–1830* (Baltimore, 1971), and J. Dewald, *The Formation of a Provincial Nobility. The Magistrates of the Parlement of Rouen, 1499–1610* (Princeton, 1980); for England the many books of L. Stone, more recently Stone and J. C. Fawtier Stone, *An Open Elite? England 1540–1880* (Oxford, 1984), and J. V. Beckett, *The Aristocracy in England, 1660–1914* (New York, 1986); on the German world, H. Rössler, ed. *Deutscher Adel, 1430–1740*, 2 vols. (Darmstadt, 1965).

[6] All these issues will be addressed in the following chapters; I will, on the other hand, give little space to the issue of the definition and perception of the aristocracy, for which see Bush, *Noble Privilege*, C. Donati, *L'idea di nobiltà in Italia (secoli XIV–XVIII)* (Bari, 1988), and for France,

Aristocratic family policy strove to ensure the continuation of the family name through the male line while preventing the patrimony from divisions at each generation which would make it impossible to support an aristocratic lifestyle. This goal was achieved through the limitation of marriages (only much later also of births) and through various forms of entails. In Catholic countries the religious career was the easiest and cheapest method to dispose of excess progeny, while the growing armies and bureaucracies of the modern state provided employment for, and often encouraged the celibacy of, the male offspring of aristocrats across the religious division of the continent. Roman legal traditions over much of the continent, and the feudal nature of much noble property, also allowed aristocratic fathers to limit the shares of most of their children.[7]

Beginning in some areas of Europe in the late fifteenth century, aristocrats also often acquired the privilege of entailing their estates. Entails, which guaranteed the succession through the male line of undivided patrimonies, took many forms: they were at their strictest in Spain, where the shackles of the *mayorazgos* forced the aristocracy into a larger dependence on the crown for favors. The restrictions were fewer in Italy and France, while the strict settlement in England gave a maximum of flexibility and adaptability. The strict settlement protected the patrimony from irresponsible heirs, and yet allowed the family to sell its lands if needed, and was therefore one of the major reasons why the English aristocracy was able to preserve its social status and its landed wealth.[8]

Coupled with family policy and entails, but also with the management of revenues, was the concern of nobles with *dérogeance*, or the loss of noble status through the exercise of activities defined as "vile" by their society. In general, historians have perhaps exaggerated the actual weight of *dérogeance* rules: when economic conditions favored aristocratic involvement in business those rules were often ignored or circumvented. But rules and customs there certainly were, and they differed from country to country: as with entail policies they were strictest in Spain, where by the seventeenth century reformers had identified them as one of the main causes of Spain's economic decline. The acceptability of

E. Schalk, *From Valor to Pedigree. Ideas of Nobility in France in the Sixteenth and Seventeenth Centuries* (Princeton, 1986), and R. Moro, *Il tempo dei signori. Mentalità, ideologia, dottrine della nobiltà francese d'Antico Regime* (Rome, 1981).

[7] On these issues see chapter 5, and J. P. Cooper, "Patterns of Inheritance and Settlement by Great Landowners from the Fifteenth to the Eighteenth Century" in J. Goody *et al.*, eds. *Family and Inheritance. Rural Society in Western Europe, 1200–1800* (Cambridge, 1976), pp. 192–327.

[8] Cooper, "Patterns"; L. Stone, "Inheritance Strategies among the English Landed Elite, 1540–1880" in G. Delille and F. Rizzi, eds. *Le modèle familial européen; normes, déviances, contrôle du pouvoir* (Rome, 1986), pp. 267–290; G. Montroni, "Aristocrazia fondiaria e modelli di trasferimento della ricchezza in Inghilterra tra XVII e XIX secolo: lo 'Strict Settlement'" *Studi storici* 30 (1989), pp. 579–602; for Spain, most recently I. Atienza Hernandez, *Aristocracia, poder y riqueza en la España moderna. La casa de Osuna, siglos XV–XIX* (Madrid, 1987).

certain clerical and commercial activities was hotly debated in France as well, where the debate had a bearing on the status of the robe nobility. In Northern Italy *dérogeance* became an issue of major concern by the sixteenth century, as the old patrician elite of commercial origin acquired many of the trappings of courtiers and landowners. In England, noble status and its privileges were more limited than on the continent; therefore it was possible for the younger sons of the aristocracy to engage in most activities without endangering the status of their families. English cadets could and did engage in liberal professions, in trade, and in industrial enterprises without causing scandal, though landowning remained the foundation of aristocratic prestige.[9]

Economic historians have long blamed early modern aristocrats, especially landowners, for their failure to adopt management methods aimed at maximizing profits and increasing productivity. This criticism has been particularly severe in the case of the commercial and industrial elite, for example in Northern Italy, who, with the land they purchased, seemed to acquire also the traditional absentee management style typical of aristocratic landowners throughout most of Western Europe. Considering, however, that aristocrats showed as much financial ability as any other group with regard to movable investments or to urban properties, such criticism seems based on a misunderstanding of the economic and social priorities of early modern elite groups.[10]

When the needs of the early modern state led to a huge growth in the public debt, many aristocrats invested heavily in this very profitable field, which also strengthened a *rentier* mentality already associated with the concern to avoid *dérogeance*. Many an aristocratic fortune throughout Europe was made or consolidated through shares of government taxes, newly awarded jurisdictional powers, or public offices, to name a few of the forms these investments could take: from those of the Osuna family in Spain, through those of many a cardinal in the papal states, to those of the Cecil family in Tudor and Stuart England.[11]

Land offered a lower rate of return than any other investment. It also offered, however, security, prestige, and the pleasures of a paternalistic relationship with the local community – whether or not the landowner also enjoyed the jurisdictional powers of lordship. Such a relationship, even when landowners resided

---

9 On *dérogeance*, Bush, *Rich Noble*, chapters 4 and 5; R. B. Grassby, "Social Status and Commercial Enterprise under Louis XIV" in R. F. Kierstead, ed. *State and Society in Seventeenth-Century France* (New York, 1975), pp. 200–32 (originally in *Economic History Review* 13 (1960–61)); Donati, *L'idea*; J. Heers, *Le clan familial au Moyen Age* (Paris, 1974), pp. 36–38; G. E. Mingay, *The Gentry. The Rise and Fall of a Ruling Class* (London, 1976), pp. 116–17; Schalk, *From Valor*, pp. 157–59, 214–19; Moro, *Il tempo*, especially chapter 10.

10 The situation is different for Eastern European aristocratic landowners, with their commercially-oriented estates employing servile labor; see the relevant chapters in the cited surveys by Goodwin, Meyer, and Bush.

11 Atienza Hernandez, *Aristocracia*, chapter 5; V. Reinhardt, *Kardinal Scipione Borghese (1605–1633)* (Tübingen, 1984), especially chapter 5; Stone, *Family and Fortune. Studies in Aristocratic Finance in the Sixteenth and Seventeenth Centuries* (Oxford, 1973), part I.

only irregularly on their lands, offered psychological gratifications, especially to poorer nobles, that urban living rarely afforded. As will be discussed in chapter 4, these ties with the rural population also translated into an economic advantage, however unquantifiable, in that they facilitated the continuation of traditional social structures, thereby supporting the status of the landowners. Land was, in short, a special commodity, closely linked to aristocratic status, and landownership – even more so lordship – was an essential component of aristocratic definition.

Aristocratic traditional management of landed patrimonies was based on a system of leases and on rudimentary accounting and administrative techniques. Some historians have recognized that the stable, reliable revenues, and the very limited expense guaranteed by such a system, answered to a common need of the aristocracy: the need for predictable, unencumbered income to use for family and prestige expenses. This need was shared by aristocrats high and low all over Western Europe, and it made them wary of any costly investment: the Tuscan aristocrat Gabriello Riccardi wrote to his brother in 1637 that, in response to an agent who had recommended some profitable investment, "I told him that we do not care to enrich ourselves"; when a later member of the family was confronted with the need to economize he urged his administrators to "restrain internal expenses, of which the public is not aware, and [to] maintain exterior appearances."[12]

Even where economic innovation entered the lands of the aristocracy (as it did in parts of England and more rarely on the continent), the significance of the local presence and role of noble landowners and lords was rarely reduced to purely economic relationships. Whether as Justices of the Peace in England, or as holders of jurisdictional rights or monopolies through most of Western Europe, noble landowners remained consequential authority figures for much of the rural population. As such they could support and help as well as exploit and abuse. The significance of traditional feudal powers for the revenues and the privileges of the aristocracy varied substantially from country to country, and tended to be very limited in large areas of Northern Italy, France, and England. Yet the aristocracy remained immensely influential at the provincial and local level, and its authority was not negatively affected by the growth of the institutions of the modern state. In fact, historians have pointed to the close

---

[12] The quotes in P. Malanima, "Patrimonio, reddito, investimenti, spese di una famiglia dell'aristocrazia fiorentina nel '700" in M. Mirri, ed. *Ricerche di storia moderna*, II, *Aziende e patrimoni di grandi famiglie (secoli XV–XIX)* (Pisa, 1979), pp. 225–60, on p. 255 and p. 260 respectively (all translations from sources and literature are my own, unless otherwise indicated); for the psychological pleasures of country living see Donati, *L'idea*, pp. 160–61. English landowners were the first to adapt more accurate and thorough accounting methods, see Stone, *Family and Fortune*. For aristocratic economic priorities, most clearly S. J. Woolf, "Prefazione" to T. Davies, *Famiglie feudali siciliane. Patrimoni redditi investimenti tra '500 e '600* (Caltanissetta, 1985), pp. 7–11, and the discussion in K. Pomian's review of A. Manikowski's study of the patrimony of Lorenzo Strozzi (1595–1671), in *Annales ESC* 44 (1989), pp. 1153–55.

"connection between the creation of the absolutist state and the predominance of the aristocracy."[13]

The development of stronger central governments in Western Europe represented one of the new challenges aristocrats had to face in the early modern period. The traditional feudal powers of the aristocracy were often eroded by the action of these governments as well as by changing economic conditions; the ascent of new families through government service, and the expanded powers of royal tribunals, forced the high landed aristocracy all over Western Europe to move to the cities, to adopt a less bellicose, and more expensive, lifestyle, and to devise ways to deal with the presence of new wealthy groups in positions of power. But the financial needs of governments, the attraction of aristocratic values and behaviors, the deep roots of aristocratic power in the countryside, and the limits of early modern economic development, all contributed to the preservation and even the reinforcement of aristocratic social and political status.[14] Early modern Italy, with its regional variations, offers good examples of such processes.

ITALIAN ARISTOCRATS: NORTHERN PATRICIANS AND SOUTHERN FEUDATORIES

Until not too long ago, Italian early modern historiography, especially in the English-speaking world, was influenced by a long tradition of attention to what was perceived as Italy's most glorious contribution to the modern world, the Renaissance, dated usually from the time of Dante to the sack of Rome in 1527. This led to an overwhelming focus on Florence and Venice, and to an insistence on the predominantly urban character of Italian history, and on Italy's peculiar path to the modern state. In their concentration on city-states, historians have given much space to the study of elite groups as the key to the political and economic structure and the social functioning of urban societies. These ruling groups were also the segment of society most heavily involved, as patrons or practitioners, in the artistic and cultural developments that are, after all, the major reason why most people are interested in Renaissance Italy.[15]

---

[13] Woolf, "Prefazione," p. 8; on agricultural innovation in Northern Italy, see E. Roveda, "Una grande possessione lodigiana dei Trivulzio tra '500 e '700" in Mirri, ed. *Ricerche*, pp. 25–139; on the Justices of the Peace, see Mingay, *Gentry*, chapter 5; see below, chapter 4, for extensive discussion of rural paternalism; see also Moro, *Il tempo*, chapter 2, and for a later period in Germany, G. W. Pedlow, *The Survival of the Hessian Nobility, 1770–1870* (Princeton, 1988), chapter 5. A survey of these issues is in F. Billacois, "La crise de la noblesse européenne (1550–1650), une mise au point" *Revue d'histoire moderne et contemporaine* 23 (1976), pp. 258–77.

[14] On these issues, see in particular P. Anderson, *Lo stato assoluto* (Milan, 1980; English edit. 1974), especially pp. 17–56, 202–14, and 355–84.

[15] This lopsided situation has been partly corrected in recent years; its most insistent critic was Eric Cochrane, whose posthumous *Italy, 1530–1630* (New York, 1988) repeats once more his old appeal to study the "forgotten centuries."

The continuity of feudal power

These studies have focused on a relatively small set of problems: whether urban elite groups originated as inurbated feudal magnates or as upstart merchants and entrepreneurs; when and how the extended kinship group of the late Middle Ages – which dominated the life of entire neighborhoods, managed vast patrimonies, acted as a unified force in communal politics, and controlled networks of friends and clients – broke down into more isolated nuclear families, each with its own economic interests and political goals; whether, when, and to what extent the ruling groups switched from trade, banking, or manufacturing to absentee landownership (the Braudelian "treason of the bourgeoisie"); how important careers in government were for the elite, in economic terms, and in terms of the very definition of elite status. Historians saw landed properties, in this context, primarily as the source of income spent elsewhere. In short, the history of Italian elite groups has often been a history from the top up, the study of how the urban elite became more aristocratic.[16]

The two major narrative and analytical formats used by historians of the Florentine and Venetian elite, as is also true for the history of European aristocracies in general, have been the family monograph and the study of a group of families, united by membership in the same neighbourhood or communal institutions. The family monograph obviously emphasizes the precise reconstruction of patrimonies and strategies, while the group study presents statistical data and generalizations on the ties of the elite with other urban groups.[17]

Given the influence of this historiography, many studies of other areas of Italy, especially Northern Italy, have been used as ways to test hypotheses formulated in studies of Florence and Venice. The study of other Italian elite groups, however, can and does serve a more valuable purpose, in that it offers an opportunity to recognize and understand alternative forms of social organizations and their contributions, responses, and adaptations to the developments of European society. This is particularly true in the case of the Neapolitan kingdom. The South of Italy participated to a large extent in the historical

[16] For example, P. Jones, "Economia e società nell'Italia medievale: la leggenda della borghesia" in *Storia d'Italia Einaudi. Annali I Dal feudalesimo al capitalismo* (Turin, 1978), pp. 185–372; R. A. Goldthwaite, *Private Wealth in Renaissance Florence. A Study of Four Families* (Princeton, 1968); F. W. Kent, *Household and Lineage in Renaissance Florence* (Princeton, 1977); M. Berengo, *Nobili e mercanti nella Lucca del '500* (Turin, 1965); a survey of the issue of the "return to the land" is in F. Angiolini, "Le basi economiche del potere aristocratico nell'Italia centrosettentrionale tra XVI e XVIII secolo" *Società e storia* 1 (1978), pp. 317–31; an attempt at definition and comparison is in A. F. Cowan, *The Urban Patriciate, Lübeck and Venice, 1580–1700* (Köln, 1986); similar themes appear in studies of German patriciates, see H. Rössler, ed. *Deutsches Patriziat, 1430–1740* (Limburg, 1968).
[17] Two examples by the same author are J. C. Davis, *The Decline of the Venetian Aristocracy as a Ruling Class* (Baltimore, 1962), and *A Venetian Family and its Fortune 1500–1900: The Donà and the Conservation of their Wealth* (Philadelphia, 1975); for European elite groups, see the two studies by J. Dewald, *The Formation of a Provincial Nobility*, and *Pont-St-Pierre 1398–1789. Lordship, Community, and Capitalism in Early Modern France* (Berkeley–Los Angeles, 1987).

8

Introduction

developments of the rest of the peninsula: Naples was the largest city in Italy and its culture, lifestyle, and traditions had much in common with those of Northern and Central cities. According to some historians, even the Neapolitan aristocracy, notwithstanding its feudal and military origins, differed but little in culture, interests, and economic behavior from Northern elite groups. Yet a closer look at the kingdom's aristocracy shows that the difference was indeed great, and that its study enriches our picture of Italian early modern society.[18]

This work will underline the great importance of the feudal character of the Neapolitan aristocracy in determining its income, its political role, its self-perception, its family strategies, and its relationship with the rural population of the kingdom. Even after the establishment in the mid-sixteenth century of a solid royal administration on the part of the Spanish viceroys, the aristocracy dominated Neapolitan economy and society. Feudal laws, traditions, and institutions were used or adapted by the aristocracy to protect its patrimonies from dispersal or diminution. Feudal traditions and values were crucial in determining the status of a family within the aristocracy in general, and therefore in shaping its alliance policy. The old feudal clans played an important political role in the life of the city of Naples and of the kingdom as a whole. Income from feudal sources not dependent on the ownership of land remained a substantial element of aristocratic income well into the eighteenth century. Feudal traditions and conceptions shaped the aristocracy's ties with its subject peasant population, and played an essential role in strengthening aristocratic control of the provincial life of the kingdom.

Chapter 2 includes a closer discussion of what the feudal system meant in the early modern kingdom of Naples, but a brief definition is necessary here. The term "feudal" was used until the early nineteenth century in the kingdom to describe the structure of power and lordship in the countryside. This structure was characterized by the traditional rights and monopolies of the rural seigneurie, common throughout Western Europe, and also by a large amount of rights that the landlord enjoyed over the resident population of his lands. Neapolitan landlords continued to exercise remarkable judicial and administrative powers that in other parts of Europe had become the prerogative of public officers. Though the specific ways in which these powers were exercised, their impact on the landlords' revenues, and the structure of land management differed substantially in the different regions of the South of Italy, and no model fully describes or explains these regional variations, the use of the term

[18] On the culture, see E. Gothein, *Il Rinascimento nell'Italia meridionale* (Italian transl. Florence, 1915); and J. H. Bentley, *Politics and Culture in Renaissance Naples* (Princeton, 1987); "Florentine patricians and Neapolitan barons are old accomplices" according to R. Romano, *Tra due crisi: l'Italia del Rinascimento* (Turin, 1982; first edit. 1971), p. 203; Giovanni Muto is currently working on an analysis of the common culture of Southern and Northern Italian aristocrats.

9

"feudal" to describe the social and economic structure of the kingdom seems both appropriate and useful.[19]

That Neapolitan history in general offers many contrasts with the history of Northern Italy has been emphasized in much of the historiography devoted specifically to the South of Italy. Interpretations of these peculiarities have been of two kinds. On the one hand, scholars native to the South from Croce onwards have stressed how Naples contributed to, and partook of, Western European history and culture – from Aquinas to Vico to Croce himself. The conditions of its economy and society are then due to "backwardness" or "delay," seen either from a Marxist or a Crocean idealist point of view. Within this school of interpretation, debate focuses therefore on the causes of that delay and especially on how and why it became irreversible. This literature is obviously closely tied to the tradition of *meridionalismo*, as the critical study of the economic and social problems of the South was called at the time of the great statistical investigations of the late nineteenth century.[20]

Other scholars, primarily French, have applied anthropological concerns to their study of the South and emphasized the "otherness," the profound, innate difference of Neapolitans from other Europeans. In the preface to his important recent book, Gérard Delille, for instance, felt the need to say that

this work ... has also been to some extent the result of a process of "deculturation"; in order to "understand," we have had, beforehand, to cease understanding, to forget what we had learned, to forget that we were in Europe, very close to the heart of Christendom, to forget that our documents carried dates and geographic indications.

And Gérard Labrot, though less given to rhetorical flourishes, concludes his survey of aristocratic palaces in Naples with the observation that, with the arrival of the Bourbons in 1734, Neapolitan aristocrats began behaving like aristocrats all over Europe, and thereby their residential patterns lost "their 'ethnological'

---

[19] Two models that have been considered applicable to various degrees to the kingdom of Naples are G. Bois, *The Crisis of Feudalism. Economy and Society in Eastern Normandy, c. 1300–1550* (Cambridge, 1984; French edit. 1976), and W. Kula, *Teoria economica del sistema feudale. Proposta di un modello* (Turin, 1980; Polish edit. 1962). They are discussed in A. Lepre, *Storia del Mezzogiorno d'Italia* (2 vols.; Naples, 1986), I, pp. 165–81; M. Aymard, "L'Europe moderne: féodalité ou féodalités?" *Annales ESC* 36 (1981), pp. 426–35, and Aymard, "La transizione dal feudalesimo al capitalismo" in *Storia d'Italia Einaudi. Annali I Dal feudalesimo al capitalismo* (Turin, 1978), pp. 1131–92. Aymard tends to focus exclusively on the areas of the kingdom and of Sicily characterized by commercially-oriented large estates. On these issues, see also Anderson, *Lo stato*, pp. 17–56 and the conclusions.

[20] B. Croce, *Storia del regno di Napoli* (Bari, 1931; first edit. 1924); examples of the debate abound in the many works of G. Galasso, R. Villari, and A. Lepre cited in the following chapters and in the bibliography. Cochrane, "Southern Italy in the Age of the Spanish Viceroys: Some Recent Titles" *Journal of Modern History* 58 (1986), pp. 194–217, assesses recent historiography on Naples. A brief introduction to *meridionalismo* is in F. Barbagallo, *Mezzogiorno e questione meridionale (1860–1980)* (Naples, 1980); an anthology of texts is in R. Villari, ed. *Il Sud nella storia d'Italia*, 2 vols. (Bari, 1974; first edit. 1961); see also the inspired pages of U. La Malfa, "Mezzogiorno nell'Occidente" in *Nord e Sud* 1 (1954), pp. 11–22.

extraneousness, and therefore their power to fascinate." This insistence on the alleged fundamental "otherness" of Naples is obviously even more pronounced in the anthropological literature.[21]

It is, however, altogether more fruitful to see Neapolitan society and history, for all their peculiarities, as endowed with inner coherence and rationale rather than as simply the expression of a backward or alien land. The kingdom was on the whole economically less advanced than Northern Italy, but this "delay" should not lead us to conceive of only one inevitable model of development, and especially should not blind us to what made Neapolitan society acceptable and functional for many of its members. The feudal characteristics of Neapolitan society were not simply anachronisms, but, if properly understood on their own terms, they offer a key to the social functioning of many neglected and provincial areas of Western Europe, often seen only as backward and therefore irrelevant. In a reversal of historical practice, the study of the most feudal area of Italy might also shed light on the behavior of Florentine and other Northern Italian elite groups. Cultural imitation in attitudes and lifestyle did not after all travel in only one direction, and, especially by the late sixteenth century, the influence of Spanish (and Neapolitan) customs on the Northern Italian elite is undoubted. A clear picture of what it meant to be a feudal lord in the South will therefore also help us to understand the motivations of the Northern patricians' "return to the land."[22]

The need for unprejudiced assessment of seemingly backward societies has been forcefully stated in recent historical works on Italy. Giovanni Levi has pointed to the need for historians not to read peasant history solely as an account of passive resistance to a process of modernization defined elsewhere, but rather to identify the autonomous rationale, the creative mechanisms, and the contributions of the peasant world to the wider society. His words can be applied to the study of the aristocracy. Seemingly obsolete social and economic structures must be analyzed on their own terms, in order to understand the benefits that they

---

[21] G. Delille, *Famille et propriété dans le royaume de Naples (XVe–XIXe siècles)* (Rome, 1985), p. 2 (see also his "L'ordine dei villaggi e l'ordine dei campi. Per uno studio antropologico del paesaggio agrario nel regno di Napoli (secoli XV–XVIII)" in *Storia d'Italia Einaudi. Annali* VIII *Insediamenti e territorio* (Turin, 1978), pp. 499–560, in which he notes that, though Naples gave birth to Aquinas, Vico, and Croce, its early modern agrarian structures can be described with anthropological techniques usually applied to the study of "primitive" societies – as if this were not the case for most of early modern Europe); G. Labrot, *Baroni in città. Residenze e comportamenti dell'aristocrazia napoletana, 1530–1734* (Naples, 1979), p. 140 (on which, see the comments of G. Galasso in his preface to Labrot's book); T. Belmonte, *The Broken Fountain* (New York, 1989; first edit. 1979) speaks of his stay in Naples as an "immersion in otherness" and an exploration of an "ethnographic frontier" (preface); for comments on the eternal theatricality of life in Naples, see P. Burke, *The Historical Anthropology of Early Modern Italy* (Cambridge, 1987), especially chapter 14, which first appeared in *Past and Present* 99 (1983), pp. 3–21 (and on which, see Villari, "Masaniello: Contemporary and Recent Interpretations" *Past and Present* 108 (1985), pp. 117–32). This romanticization has obvious literary parallels, some of which I have mentioned at the beginning of this introduction.

[22] Donati, *L'idea*, is the most recent discussion of these influences.

offered to most of those who participated in them, and therefore the profound reasons for their longevity. John Marino's global and unprejudiced reconstruction of the pastoral economy of the kingdom of Naples, for instance, has allowed him to avoid futile condemnations of an apparently archaic system. He has instead illuminated the rewards and significance that system held for all involved, and thereby contributed to a real explanation of its mechanisms and resistance to reform and change. I have attempted to approach the study of the aristocracy on similar bases.[23]

For a study of the aristocracy, a family monograph is the research and narrative format most conducive to the approach outlined above. While my goals here include the study of the economic and political position of the Neapolitan aristocracy and of its involvement in social conflict, a family monograph makes it also possible to investigate the importance of community ties, networks of obligations and symbols, attitudes, and beliefs. In order to gain a fuller understanding of the actions and motivations of the aristocrats who form the object of this study, I have tried to see both the feudal clan and the feudal village as communities bound together not only by economic and political ties, but also by symbolic and reciprocal obligations. These obligations played, in some instances, much the more important role in preserving the social order and in legitimating it in the eyes of all of its participants.[24]

OVERVIEW OF NEAPOLITAN HISTORY

Today the front of the royal palace built in Naples by the Spanish viceroys at the beginning of the seventeenth century is adorned with the statues of the eight most prominent kings of Naples: founders of dynasties, conquerors, powerful monarchs. None of them, from Roger the Norman to Charles of Anjou, from Charles V to Victor Emanuel II, was native to the kingdom, nor did any of them speak the local vernacular. The foreign character of many of the kingdom's sovereigns helps explain the aristocracy's success in remaining the dominant force in Neapolitan society. In the eyes of the population, especially of the peasants, the traditional, native lords must have appeared endowed with more permanence and legitimacy than the various tax-hungry governments – than the fellows in Naples, to paraphrase Carlo Levi's memoirs.

A brief overview of Neapolitan history is necessary to an understanding of the characteristics of Spanish rule over the kingdom of Naples in the sixteenth and

---

[23] G. Levi, *L'eredità immateriale. Carriera di un esorcista nel Piemonte del Seicento* (Turin, 1985); J. Marino, *Pastoral Economics in the Kingdom of Naples* (Baltimore, 1988). Understanding, of course, does not imply nostalgia or rehabilitation.

[24] I have discussed some of the content of these pages in talks I gave at the Miami Valley European History Seminar at Wright State University, Dayton, in February 1989, and at the annual meeting of the Ohio Academy of History in Columbus in April 1989; I thank the participants for their comments.

Introduction

seventeenth centuries. Few regions of Europe underwent such frequent changes of political regime as did the South of Italy; the Spanish were perhaps the most incisive and effective of its many rulers, but even they failed to achieve many of their goals in the Mezzogiorno. The Southern monarchy was established in 1130 by the Norman King Roger, and in the following four centuries it was ruled by the Norman dynasty, the German Hohenstaufen emperors, the French Anjou, and the Aragonese. The kingdom was the object of conflict between France and Spain in the early phase of the Italian wars, until in 1503 Gonsalvo de Córdoba – the "Great Captain" – secured it for King Ferdinand of Aragon. From him Naples, like all Aragonese possessions, passed to his grandson Charles V of Habsburg. Though it had been conquered by arms, the kingdom of Naples, like those of Sicily and Sardinia, was held as a hereditary possession by the house of Austria, so that its union with Spain was purely dynastic. As with all other parts of Charles V's European inheritance, the Neapolitan kingdom preserved its traditional privileges and institutions.[25]

The kingdom of Naples was ruled by the kings of Spain through officials called viceroys. The kingdom's most important function within the Spanish imperial system was to administer to the needs of Charles' Mediterranean policies. Until the battle of Lepanto in 1571, Naples remained the bulwark of Christianity against the Turks. With the 1570s the kingdom became a source of supplies, money, and men for the defense of Milan and Flanders. It remained a Spanish possession until 1707, save for the brief period when the French Duke of Guise led an ill-fated revolutionary Republic, following the so-called revolt of Masaniello, in 1647–48. From 1707 to 1734, as a result of the War of the Spanish Succession, the kingdom was under Austrian control, until it fell to the army of Charles of Bourbon, son of Philip V of Spain. From 1734 to 1806 Naples and Sicily were ruled by a resident branch of the Spanish Bourbons. The continental kingdom was then conquered by French troops and became one of Napoleon's satellite kingdoms. In 1815 the Bourbons were restored and ruled what was known as the Kingdom of the Two Sicilies until Italian unification in 1860.

The Spanish period, which lasted from 1503 to 1707, is the main setting for this study. During the two centuries in which Southern Italy was tied to Spain, the region's economic and social history was closely connected to developments in the Iberian peninsula. Government fiscal pressure increased as much in the kingdom of Naples as in Castile, at least until the mid-seventeenth century. Genoese merchants and financiers played as prominent a role in the Neapolitan economy as they did in that of Spain, and probably for a longer time. Close

---

[25] A general history of the kingdom – though particularly of its capital – is in E. Pontieri, ed. *Storia di Napoli* (10 vols.; Naples, 1967–72; second edit. 1975–81); the planned sixteen volumes of G. Galasso and R. Romeo, eds. *Storia del Mezzogiorno* began to be published in Naples in the late 1980s; for the early modern period, see Lepre, *Storia*.

13

integration with the Spanish economy meant that the kingdom of Naples experienced a more severe inflation than other parts of Italy. The kingdom's economy was always primarily agricultural, and by the late sixteenth century its exports were almost wholly in grain, oil, and wine, while its textile production declined sharply. The economic difficulties that began in the 1590s led to serious economic problems in the 1620s, which were worsened by the government's misguided fiscal pressure and monetary policies. Although after the 1647–48 revolt taxation declined considerably, in 1656 a plague killed a large part of the population of the kingdom (including possibly up to half the inhabitants of Naples, at the time one of the three largest cities in Europe), and this disaster delayed economic recovery until the 1680s or 1690s. In the eighteenth century, attempts at reforms met with similar limitations and obstacles in Naples and Castile.[26]

After 1530, the establishment and consolidation of the Spanish administration in Naples brought about a significant increase in the central government's power in the kingdom. Historians credit Spain for developing the institutions and apparatus of a modern state in the Mezzogiorno. In a marked shift from the time of the earlier sovereigns, the government's relations with various social groups were modified in that the monarchy could now use its external forces to solidify its position within the kingdom. The stronger Spanish government was able to place limits on the political power of the Neapolitan aristocracy. Moreover, in order to meet its own financial and administrative needs, the monarchy favored the social ascent of new families, mostly of Neapolitan, Genoese, or Iberian origins, who made their fortune in official positions, in finance, or in trade.

Yet the Spanish government did not pursue any conscious policy of social and economic change in the kingdom, especially outside of the capital, and was willing to leave to the Neapolitan feudal aristocracy its old powers and privileges. Indeed, these privileges were even allowed to increase significantly, so long as the kingdom fulfilled the tasks assigned to it within the Spanish imperial system. Thus the feudal aristocracy was able to maintain its social status and economic position within the kingdom until the end of the Spanish rule, and indeed in many ways until the end of the old regime in 1806. I will examine closely the ways in which the old Neapolitan aristocracy protected and preserved its wealth, status, and power over three centuries. A nineteenth-century German historian called the two centuries of Spanish rule over Naples a "melancholy period," but

---

[26] Bibliographical references have been kept to a minimum in this introduction; the relevant literature will be cited in the following chapters. For the demography of Naples, see C. Petraccone, *Napoli dal '500 all''800, problemi di storia demografica e sociale* (Naples, 1974); G. Delille, *Agricoltura e demografia nel regno di Napoli nei secoli XVIII e XIX* (Naples, 1977). For an introduction to the social and economic history of Spain, see J. Vicens Vives, ed. *Historia social y económica de España y América* (5 vols.; Barcelona, 1957; new edit. 1971); V. Vazquez de Prada, *Historia económica y social de España*, III, *Los siglos XVI y XVII* (Madrid, 1978).

Introduction

from the point of view of the local aristocracy this was a time of continuity, and even of social and economic success.[27]

While all aristocracies, as mentioned above, aspire to the conservation of their social and economic position, this family study will allow us to stress the feudal nature of the early modern Neapolitan aristocracy, a characteristic that distinguishes it from most other Italian aristocracies. The Caracciolo Brienza were a branch of an aristocratic clan dating back to the tenth and eleventh centuries that had held feudal lordships in the kingdom since at least the thirteenth century. Up until the abolition of the feudal regime in 1806, the most powerful Neapolitan aristocrats were distinguished, perhaps more than anywhere else in Western Europe, by their feudal character. Feudal laws regulated or influenced family policy, feudal revenues constituted often the largest share of aristocratic income, and the relations with the rural communities were marked by expectations and behaviors associated with the vassal–lord bond.

OUTLINE OF THE WORK

Most existing studies of the Neapolitan aristocracy are based on fiscal sources, in particular the records of the *relevi*, or feudal succession tax. These records tend to underestimate a family's revenues and to concentrate on the landed properties. This study is based primarily on the Caracciolo Brienza family archive, which consists mostly of notarial acts, copies of government records, a few accounts, and trial records. These sources, together with fiscal and other public documents, allow us to reconstruct a more complete picture of aristocratic wealth, one which can serve as a setting for a clearer understanding of aristocratic family policy and relations with the rural communities and the government. To this end, it is also necessary to take into account the importance of regional variations within the kingdom.[28]

The choice of the Caracciolo Brienza from among the many aristocratic families whose papers lie in the Naples state archive is due to a number of reasons: they belonged to the old aristocracy whose fortune in the kingdom was made long before the fifteenth century. Moreover, their archive is of manageable size, and its inventories, thanks to the foresight of a late-eighteenth-century marquis, are quite accurate and organized. The archive contains as many or more economic records than other comparable Neapolitan collections, enough

[27] A. von Reumont, *The Carafas of Maddaloni, Naples under Spanish Dominion* (London, 1854; German edit. 1850), preface. No full study exists of the numbers of the Neapolitan aristocracy; according to Bush, *Rich Noble*, pp. 7–29, the percentage of nobles in the entire population of Naples and Sicily was about one percent, that is lower than the two percent of France and the substantially higher percentages of some areas of Spain.

[28] On the importance of regional variations within the kingdom, as well as on the marginalized position of the Cilento, the area near the Caracciolo Brienza's fiefs, see A. Musi, "Regione storica, provincia e società nel Mezzogiorno moderno" *Quaderni sardi di storia* 1 (1980), pp. 83–100.

to allow the researcher to reconstruct the core patrimony of the family. The family owned some of its fiefs for a long time, thus allowing an analysis of changes in management and attitudes. None of these characteristics is unique to this archive, and in fact a few others would have offered similar advantages.

The main bias implicit in the archive papers is that all the documents in the family archive were collected by the family itself for the purpose of litigation (real or potential). This has been taken into account when necessary, and documents originating from other sources have been used whenever possible. It must be said, in any case, that documents damaging to the family's interests can also be found in the archive (for instance, the judicial allegations of the opposite parties in any litigation).[29]

This study is organized in six chapters, arranged thematically rather than chronologically. Chapter 1 situates the Caracciolo Brienza within the Neapolitan aristocracy and provides a brief overview of the family's history. The following two chapters examine the family's patrimony: chapter 2 discusses the various components of an aristocratic patrimony (fiefs, real estate, credit, other assets) and the family's attempts to achieve a balance between its feudal and allodial assets, while chapter 3 analyzes in particular the administration and revenues of the fiefs. The Caracciolo Brienza's fiefs were in a relatively poor and isolated region, and this has to be taken into account in explaining why few changes took place in the way in which the family's revenues were managed. The same traditionalism characterized the family's relations with its vassals, which is the subject of chapter 4; the villages' ancient institutions were preserved to the end of the old regime, and the Caracciolo lords, especially after the mid-seventeenth century, stressed the paternalistic nature of their feudal position.

The last two chapters focus on the aristocracy in the city of Naples, rather than in the provinces, as it responded to the challenges posed by the ascent of new families and by the increase in power of the government. Chapter 5 discusses how, after the early sixteenth century, family policy adapted to the new political situation under Spanish rule by moving away from the division of inheritances through the limitation of marriages to one son in each generation. Throughout the Spanish period, the aristocracy found in its old clans the main source of its identity and an essential basis for solidarity, mutual support, and assistance in its family alliances. Chapter 6 examines the ways in which the aristocracy was able to take advantage of the Spanish government's needs and policies, and to contain the control that the monarchy tried to impose on aristocratic privileges and powers.

The choice of the mid-sixteenth century as the beginning point of this study

[29] The Appendix on sources at the end of this work provides a thorough description of the documents used. There were, I confess, two other minor reasons for selecting this family: I had a personal introduction to present members of the family, which I thought might be useful; I also discovered from the archive inventory that the family had long lived half a block from my own family's home.

calls for little explanation. The consolidation of Spanish rule in Naples led to political, social, and economic changes in Neapolitan history that affected the aristocracy as all other social groups. The decision to end this study with the first quarter of the eighteenth century is also determined, at least in part, by a political event, namely the end of the viceroyal period with the establishment of the resident Bourbon monarchy. The economic history of the family and of the kingdom as a whole further suggests that the 1720s marked the end of a cohesive historical period. Some sections of the work pursue the family's history to the end of the old regime in the early nineteenth century; but by the 1720s the Caracciolo Brienza's patrimony had definitely weathered the economic difficulties that had afflicted it in the central decades of the seventeenth century. By that time, their feudal rule was also again on firm foundations. In the following six or seven decades the family would not have to meet significant challenges to its economic and social position.

However rich it may be, the documentation that originates from a family archive cannot cover all aspects of aristocratic life. Records of expenses are very rare, and only for the mid-eighteenth century would it be possible to reconstruct patterns of consumption and material culture. The Caracciolo Brienza, alas, like most of their peers, did not leave behind any letters, memoirs, or diaries, so that one rarely hears their voices. Similarly, books and chronicles written in Spanish Naples on the aristocracy focus on its glorious genealogies (and especially on its military traditions) rather than on a more theoretical definition or legitimation of noble status, perhaps because the social position of the Neapolitan aristocracy seemed more self-evident and less threatened than was the case for some Northern Italian patriciates. My discussion of motivations or "mentality" is therefore based primarily on inferences from the specific economic, social, and public behavior I have been able to document.[30]

---

[30] Two recent introductory works on Spanish Naples that reached me too late for full consideration are A. Calabria and J. Marino's introduction to their *Good Government in Spanish Naples* (New York: Peter Lang, 1990) (a collection of essays by Neapolitan historians), and G. Muto, "Il regno di Napoli sotto la dominazione spagnola" in *Storia della società italiana*, XI, *La Controriforma e il Seicento* (Milan: Teti, 1989), pp. 225–316. Muto calculates the number of nobles in the kingdom of Naples in the seventeenth century at approximately 15,000, or slightly less than one percent of the total population, and he proposes a division of the entire nobility into four categories, depending on residence, possession of a title, and membership of the Naples patriciate.

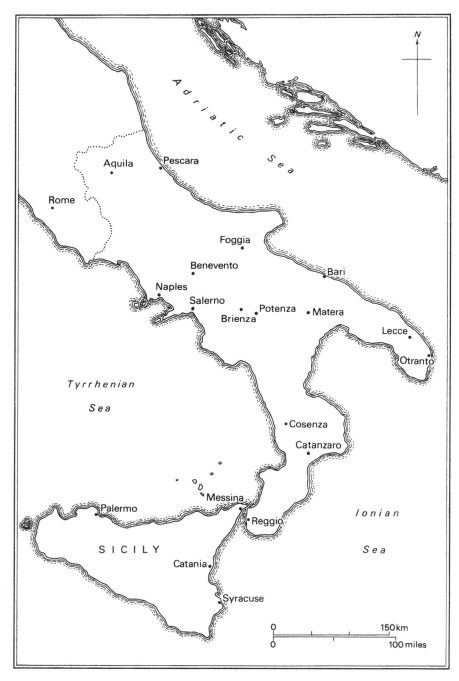

Map 1 The kingdom of Naples

18

The Caracciolo di Brienza

I can trace my ancestry back to a protoplasmal primordial atomic globule.
Consequently, my family pride is something inconceivable

The Mikado

The early modern Neapolitan aristocracy shared many characteristics with its
Northern Italian and European counterparts. It acknowledged the superior
political authority of a government that in turn recognized the aristocracy's
predominant social role. It was the wealthiest group in society and the source of
its wealth lay primarily in its landed patrimony, as was becoming increasingly
true of most Northern Italian patriciates. Though it did not always reside in the
capital, to a large extent the Neopolitan aristocracy shared in the urban culture
and lifestyle common among Venetian or Florentine patricians. Finally, it
occupied a preeminent share of the military and bureaucratic offices the early
modern states needed to man.[1]

But the aristocracy of the kingdom of Naples was considerably different from
the Venetian or Florentine patriciates, as well as from other Italian and Western
European nobilities, in its feudal character. Although there were feudal lands,
which endowed their owners with feudal rights and exemptions, in all the Italian
states, in none of them were feudal institutions and powers so widespread,
pervasive, and influential as in the three kingdoms among them – Naples, Sicily,
and Sardinia. In the kingdom of Naples throughout the early modern period,
between two-thirds and three-fourths of the population – and much more of the
land – was subject to feudal jurisdiction. This percentage was even higher than
in Spain, where in the late eighteenth century only about one third of the cities
and villages were under feudal jurisdiction; in Old Castile the King had direct
control over forty-one percent of the land and fifty percent of the population.
Moreover, though feudal lands were relatively common in some other Italian
states, such as Piedmont or the papal territories, nowhere did feudal rights

---

[1] All these issues will be addressed in the following chapters. Most recently on Florentine patricians,
see R. B. Litchfield, *Emergence of a Bureaucracy: The Florentine Patricians 1530–1790* (Princeton,
1986); on Venice, for an earlier period, see D. E. Queller, *The Venetian Patriciate. Reality versus
Myth* (Urbana–Chicago, 1986), and D. Romano, *Patricians and Popolani. The Social Foundations of
the Venetian Renaissance State* (Baltimore, 1987).

extend so far in scope, and grant to their holders so much power, status, and income as in the Southern Italian kingdoms.[2]

The Spanish government in Naples sold titles, fiefs, and jurisdictions, and made it possible for Neapolitan, Spanish, and other – especially Genoese – bankers, financiers, lawyers, or magistrates to enter the ranks of the aristocracy. The old feudal aristocracy, however, retained its preeminent position in the kingdom's society. By the early sixteenth century, the closed patriciate that dominated the city of Naples and the powerful provincial barons – always tied to each other by family connections – began to unite in a single elite: most of the more powerful baronial families were, or became, members of the city patriciate, and most patrician families acquired fiefs. This group remained the dominating force in the kingdom's economy and society even after the end of the Spanish rule over Naples: as late as the end of the eighteenth century most of the eighty or so families that had jurisdiction over more than 10,000 vassals – for a total of almost two million people, or about two fifths of the kingdom's entire population – traced their roots to the old feudal clans of the centuries preceding the Spanish rule. The few exceptions were Genoese aristocratic families, such as the Doria, the Grimaldi, or the Serra, who had obtained fiefs and titles in the kingdom mainly in the second half of the sixteenth century.[3]

The continuity of the social and economic power of the old feudal aristocracy, and the persisting importance of its feudal character, are the subject of this book. The Caracciolo Brienza belonged to one of the oldest and noblest clans in the kingdom, and its history will be briefly presented in this chapter. The importance of the Neapolitan aristocracy's feudal and military past can also be seen in the strength of its clan solidarity. In order to locate the Caracciolo Brienza in the

[2] G. Anes, *El Antiguo Régimen. Los Borbones* (Madrid, 1975), chapter 2; in Sicily, the percentage of the population subject to feudal jurisdiction was forty-four percent in 1583, fifty percent in 1652, and fifty-nine percent in 1748, see D. Ligresti, *Sicilia moderna: le città e gli uomini* (Naples, 1984), p. 85; on Sardinia, see B. Anatra, "I rapporti tra corona e ceti privilegiati nella Sardegna del XVII secolo" in S. di Bella, ed. *La rivolta di Messina (1674–78) e il mondo mediterraneo nella seconda metà del Seicento*, acts of the conference held in Messina in October 1975 (Cosenza, 1979), pp. 71–80; Anatra *et al.*, *Problemi di storia della Sardegna spagnola* (Cagliari, 1975). Very little work has been done on the papal states, see P. Hurtubise, OMI, *Une famille-témoin: les Salviati* (Vatican City, 1985); G. Pescosolido, *Terra e nobiltà: i Borghese (secoli XVIII e XIX)* (Rome, 1979); in Piedmont in the early eighteenth century, seven percent of the land was feudal, though the aristocracy also owned much allodial land, see S. J. Woolf, *Studi sulla nobiltà piemontese nell'epoca dell'assolutismo* (Turin, 1963), introduction. Though the extension of feudal land in Lazio surpassed even that of the kingdom of Naples, feudal rights do not seem to have been nearly as extended or widespread in Lazio as in the Mezzogiorno, see P. Villani, *Mezzogiorno tra riforme e rivoluzione* (Bari, 1973; first edit. 1962), pp. 188–99, and Villani, "Ricerche sulla proprietà e sul regime fondiario nel Lazio" *Annuario dell'Istituto Storico Italiano per l'età moderna e contemporanea* 12 (1960), pp. 97–263. On Tuscany and the Veneto, see G. Pansini, "Per una storia del feudalesimo nel granducato di Toscana durante il periodo medieceo" *QS* 7 (1972), pp. 131–86, and G. Gullino, "I patrizi veneti di fronte alla proprietà feudale (secoli XVI-XVIII), materiale per una ricerca" *QS* 15 (1980), pp. 162–93.

[3] Villani, *Mezzogiorno*, pp. 188–99, and "La feudalità dalle riforme all'eversione" *Clio* 1 (1965), pp. 599–622.

context of the Neapolitan feudal aristocracy it is therefore first necessary to discuss their clan affiliation and their origins.[4]

"L'ECCELLENTISSIMA CASA": THE CARACCIOLO CLAN

When in 1774 Litterio Caracciolo, tenth marquis of Brienza, sixth prince of Atena, lord of Pietrafesa and Sasso, entrusted his newly-formed family archive to Michelangelo Pacifici, he also commissioned Pacifici to write a genealogical treatise on his family. Both men intended, and believed, this work to be a glorification of the Brienza family. Pacifici might have been painfully aware of the difficulty of finding deeds worthy of exaltation in the history of the Brienza alone; it is, however, in itself a measure of the attachment felt as late as the end of the eighteenth century for the clan, and of its importance, that the treatise is mainly concerned with a reconstruction of the genealogy of the whole of the Caracciolo clan, from its mythical Byzantine beginnings on, through many of the foremost branches and individuals, to the 1770s.[5]

In a later chapter we will analyze more specifically what the relations were between clan and family in Spanish Naples. It is, however, necessary to offer here a preliminary definition. A Neapolitan aristocratic clan (the most common Italian word is *casata*) consisted of all the individuals who could trace back their origins to common ancestors. All members of the clan lived, originally, in the same district of the city and, even when – by the sixteenth century – some of them had moved to other districts, they retained until 1800 their membership in the same aristocratic organizations that participated in the government of the city. A clan had several member families. When used in opposition to clan, family (*famiglia*) refers to successive divisions of a clan into several lines, taking their origins from some distinguished member of the clan. Although in the Angevin period (late thirteenth to early fifteenth centuries) there were families who took their identification from the name of a specific ancestor, by the late fifteenth and especially sixteenth centuries, families were associated with a specific fief, in most cases a titled fief, which remained in the same hands for many generations. The family of the Caracciolo Brienza consisted, therefore, of the successive marquis of Brienza with all their male descendants, all of whom were at the same time members of the Caracciolo clan. Family is by the Spanish period almost equivalent to titled line. Because of the limitation of sons' marriages, each family usually consisted of only one line of descent. In rare cases, however, when a cadet son had descendants, we can speak of a new branch within a family. Were

---

[4] Clan solidarity was stronger in Naples than elsewhere in Italy or Western Europe, see chapter 5.
[5] ACB 1.1, the ms. genealogical treatise.

Plate 1 Porta Capuana, Naples

that new branch to acquire fiefs, titled or not, with which it came to be identified, then it would become a new family.[6]

The Caracciolo were, throughout the history of the kingdom of Naples, one of the most important and powerful aristocratic clans. Their origins were "buried in the very dark abyss of many hundreds of years,"[7] but men with the Caracciolo name owned lands and houses in Naples as early as the tenth century. By the mid-thirteenth century, twenty-five Caracciolo had lordships over several

[6] On the predominance of clans at all levels of Neapolitan society, see G. Delille, *Famille et propriété dans le royaume de Naples (XVe–XIXe siècles)* (Rome, 1985).

[7] F. de Pietri, *Cronologia della famiglia Caracciolo*, second edit. annotated by Ferrante della Marra (Naples, 1803; first edit. 1605), p. 1. The main genealogical works on the Caracciolo, and the basis for this chapter, are, in addition to de Pietri and Pacifici, F. Fabris, *La genealogia della famiglia Caracciolo*, revised by A. Caracciolo di Torchiarolo (Naples, 1966; originally in P. Litta, *Famiglie celebri italiane* (Milan, 1819 on)); A. Caracciolo di Torchiarolo, *Una famiglia italianissima: i Caracciolo di Napoli* (Naples, 1939); the ms. genealogies in ASN Carte del marchese Livio Serra di Gerace, and Archivio Serra Gerace, ms. 73; C. A. Pacca, *Historia della famiglia Caracciola*, BNN ms. San Martino 379 (c. 1580–85). Information on the Caracciolo appears also in the several genealogical works on the Neapolitan aristocracy, especially in Biagio Aldimari, *Memorie historiche di diverse famiglie nobili* (Naples, 1691); Scipione Ammirato, *Delle famiglie nobili napoletane* (Florence, 1580; second vol. 1651); C. Borrelli, *Vindex Neapolitanae Nobilitatis* (Naples, 1653); Carlo de Lellis, *Discorsi delle famiglie nobili del regno di Napoli* (3 vols.; Naples, 1654–1671; reprint Bologna, 1968); D. Confuorto, *Il torto o vero il dritto della nobiltà napoletana*, BNN ms. X-A-25 (1690s). I have also used the *Dizionario biografico degli Italiani*.

Plate 2 Coat of arms of the Caracciolo

communities in the kingdom. At least some members of the clan remained centered in Naples, where a section of what was to become the *Seggio* of Capuana was known as the *Vico dei Caraccioli* (Road of the Caracciolo).[8]

The city of Naples was traditionally divided in several administrative districts, known as *Seggi* or *Sedili*. The term referred both to topographical sections of the city, and to the councils or clubs governing the districts that were composed of all the prominent families residing there. In the course of the fourteenth century these were consolidated into five. Since 1339, King Robert of Anjou had recognized the superior prestige of the two *Seggi* of Capuana and Nido, and these two always comprised the largest number of aristocratic families, while the *Seggi* of Porto, Portanova, and Montagna had fewer members and less influence with the kings. The superiority of Capuana and Nido was even recognized by the rebels in 1647. Membership in the *Seggi* was reserved to the aristocracy residing in Naples, and by the late fifteenth and early sixteenth centuries they all enacted rules rendering the aggregation of new families very difficult. Attempts on the part of non-*Seggio* aristocratic families to open up the five *Seggi*, or to establish new ones, were thwarted in the sixteenth century, and beginning in 1559 any application needed the preliminary approval of the king. After that, the only aggregations occurred on a case-by-case basis.[9]

Every year, each *Seggio* elected one of its members to serve as its representative (*Eletto*). The five *Eletti* of the aristocratic *Seggi*, together with the *Eletto* of the *Seggio del Popolo* (*Seggio* of the People), established in 1495, constituted the city government of Naples, known as the Tribunal of Saint Lawrence (*Tribunale di San Lorenzo*) from the church in which it had its meetings. The *Eletti* controlled the grain provisions of the town, under the direction of the *Grassiero*, an aristocrat chosen by the viceroy, and they formed the main city tribunal. After 1642, when the last General Parliament of the kingdom was convened, the *Eletti* of the *Seggi* of Naples also served as the kingdom's only representative institution, voting taxes and grants to the king in the name of the whole kingdom. The *Seggi* elected several committees that controlled the administration of buildings, fountains, and streets, or ensured that the city's privileges be

---

[8] Throughout their history, the Caracciolo were particularly present in the streets around the church of San Giovanni a Carbonara, see L. de la Ville sur-Yllon, "La strada di San Giovanni a Carbonara" *Napoli nobilissima* 15 (1906), pp. 17–23. Borrelli, *Vindex*, pp. 170–79, reports a 1239 list of barons that includes several Caracciolo.

[9] A. Cernigliaro, *Sovranità e feudo nel regno di Napoli 1505–1557* (2 vols.; Naples, 1983), especially pp. 267–75; G. Muto, "Gestione del potere e classi sociali nel Mezzogiorno spagnolo" in A. Tagliaferri, ed. *I ceti dirigenti in Italia in età moderna e contemporanea* (Udine, 1984), pp. 287–301; Muto, "Gestione politica e controllo sociale nella Napoli spagnola" in C. de Seta, ed. *Le città capitali* (Bari, 1985), pp. 67–94; I. del Bagno, "Reintegrazione nei Seggi napoletani e dialettica degli 'status' " *ASPN* 102 (1984), pp. 189–204; G. Vitale, "La nobiltà di Seggio a Napoli nel basso Medioevo: aspetti della dinamica interna" *ASPN* 106 (1988), pp. 151–69. On the 1647 episode, see A. Musi, *La rivolta di Masaniello nella scena politica barocca* (Naples, 1989), pp. 166–67. On an attempt to obtain aggregation, see the documents published by F. Palermo, ed. "Narrazioni e documenti sulla storia del regno di Napoli dall'anno 1522 al 1667" *ASI* 9 (1846), pp. 147–90.

observed, and the *Seggi* alone could send an official envoy to the king to plead in the name of the city. The *Eletti* also had limited power over the city police. All of these powers the *Seggi* and *Eletti* kept until their abolition in 1800. Belonging to a *Seggio* was therefore crucial if a family was to play any significant role within the political and social elite of the kingdom, and the discontent of excluded aristocratic families grew during the Spanish period.[10]

The *Seggio* of Capuana was the only one to have internal subdivisions: it consisted of three branches, and the honors and offices pertaining to the *Seggio* were equally distributed between the three. The Caracciolo clan alone constituted formally one third of the *Seggio* of Capuana, the other two being represented by the Capece clan and by the so-called Aienti, a denomination which included all the other members. The Carafa, who were most likely a branch of the Caracciolo originating in the mid-thirteenth century, formed the largest clan in the *Seggio* of Nido.[11]

The Caracciolo clan itself was so large as to create internal subdivisions. At the end of the thirteenth century, the brothers Gualtiero and Giovanni Caracciolo began what were to be the two major subdivisions of the clan, known

10 Most of the documents relating to the *Seggi* in ASN were destroyed in 1943, see F. Trinchera, *Degli archivi napoletani relazione* (Naples, 1872), and J. Mazzoleni, *Guida dell'Archivio di Stato di Napoli* (2 vols.; Naples, 1972). The main source on the *Seggi* is still Camillo Tutini, *Del origine e fundatione de' Seggi di Napoli* (Naples, 1644), on which see G. Galasso, "Un'ipotesi di 'blocco storico' oligarchico–borghese nella Napoli del '600: i *Seggi* di Camillo Tutini tra politica e storiografia" *RSI* 90 (1978), pp. 507–29; see also F. Imperato, *Discorso politico intorno al regimento delle piazze della città di Napoli* (Naples, 1604; the term *piazza* was equivalent to *Seggio*); C. A. Pacca, *Discorso circa li seggi di questa città di Napoli*, BNN ms. San Martino 73 (late sixteenth century); F. Capecelatro, *Origine della città e delle famiglie nobili di Napoli* in vol. II of Capecelatro, *Istoria della città e del regno di Napoli detto di Sicilia* (Naples, 1769; written in the 1630s); L. Contarino, *Dell'antiquità, sito, chiese, corpi santi, reliquie et statue di Roma, con l'origine e nobiltà di Napoli* (Naples, 1569); and the rather vacuous L. de Lutio di Castelguidone, *I Sedili di Napoli* (Naples, 1973). Information on the *Seggi* appears in all the histories and descriptions of the city and kingdom published in the early modern period: see S. Mazzella, *Descrittione del regno di Napoli...* (Naples, 1601; reprint Bologna, 1981; first edit. 1586; there is a fascinating English edition of Mazzella titled *Parthenopoeia or the history of the most noble and renowned kingdom of Naples...* (London, 1654)); P. Collenuccio, M. Roseo, T. Costo, *Compendio dell'historia del regno di Napoli...* (Venice, 1591; second edit. 1613); O. Beltrano, *Breve descrittione del regno di Napoli diviso in dodici provincie...* (Naples, 1646; second edit. 1671; reprint Bologna, 1969); H. Bacco Alemanno, *Il regno di Napoli in dodici provincie...* (Naples, 1609; second edit. ed. C. d'Engenio, 1620); G. C. Capaccio, *Il forastiero dialogi* (Naples, 1634); G. A. Summonte, *Historia della città e regno di Napoli* (6 vols.; third edit. Naples, 1748–50; first edit. 1599 on). All these texts (with the exception of Summonte and Capaccio) are congeries of all sorts of data, and were published several times during the seventeenth century with small variations. John Marino is preparing a study of the membership and functioning of the *Seggi*.
11 On the prominent role of the *Seggi* of Capuana and Nido, and of the Caracciolo and Carafa respectively within them, see Galasso, "Ideologia e sociologia del patronato di San Tommaso d'Aquino su Napoli (1605)" in Galasso and C. Russo, eds. *Per la storia sociale e religiosa del Mezzogiorno d'Italia* (2 vols.; Naples, 1980–82), II, pp. 213–49; Capecelatro, *Origine*, pp. 95–135, relates all the major disputes between the *Seggi* in the late medieval period; Vitale, "La nobiltà," stresses the importance of the large clans within the *Seggi*: the *Seggio* of Nido, for instance, had statutes that barred more than one member of each clan from participation in important *Seggio* organs.

25

respectively as the Caracciolo Pisquizi or Squizzari, and the Caracciolo Rossi. Both gave origins to many families that acquired titled fiefs. De Pietri (1605) and Aldimari (1691) counted fifty titled Caracciolo families, including, according to Aldimari, nine princely, ten ducal, and nineteen marchional families. If one counts nineteenth-century titles, members of the clan received, in its long history, thirty-two titles of prince, fifty-six of duke, forty-three of marquis, and thirty-three of count, and they had lordship over 558 villages and towns in the kingdom of Naples and elsewhere. In the Spanish period, the Caracciolo ruled over several communities in each of the twelve provinces of the kingdom.[12]

The many Caracciolo families distinguished themselves in the traditional fields of aristocratic involvement, especially in the military and in the Church. The feudal aristocracy dominated the upper levels of the Neapolitan Church, and at the end of the seventeenth century, Francesco D'Andrea, a noted lawyer, discouraged his nephews from entering an ecclesiastic career because, he claimed, men of their origin could not in practice aspire to occupy the top positions. If not so prominent as the Carafa, who gave the Church a pope (Paul IV), seven cardinals, and seven archbishops of Naples, the Caracciolo still had their share of ecclesiastic preferments. Their only taste of the papacy came with Boniface IX, whose mother was a Caracciolo, but by the end of the seventeenth century that had included among their numbers five cardinals, ten archbishops (one of Naples), a Grand Master of Rhodes, and one of the Templars; these numbers would grow in the eighteenth and nineteenth centuries. Francesco Ascanio Caracciolo (1563–1608) gained religious merits of a different sort and was canonized in 1807; he has recently been declared the patron saint of cooks, an unreservedly worthy calling. Caracciolo families received the French Order of Saint Michel, the Golden Fleece, and several Spanish grandeeships. At different times they held all of the seven traditional Grand Offices of the Neapolitan monarchy, and in the seventeenth century the princes of Avellino were the Grand Chancellors of the kingdom. Galeazzo Caracciolo, marquis of Vico, had the peculiar distinction of being the most socially eminent member of the Calvinist government of Geneva, and the only first cousin of a pope to have converted to Calvinism.[13]

Most Caracciolo who were not in the Church fought in the armies of the king of Naples and of other European states. Four Caracciolo were marshals of Naples, one of France, and more than twenty became generals in the Spanish

---

[12] Besides the works cited in footnote 7, I rely here on an examination of the inventories of the various series of feudal documents in ASN.

[13] His father obtained from Charles V that his fiefs be passed to his grandson, Galeazzo's son; Galeazzo divorced his Neapolitan wife and remarried in Geneva, see B. Croce, "Il marchese di Vico Galeazzo Caracciolo" in Croce, *Vite di avventure, di fede, di passione* (Bari, 1936); on St. Francesco Ascanio Caracciolo, see the *Enciclopedia Italiana Treccani, sub voce*; D'Andrea, *I ricordi di un avvocato napoletano del '600*, ed. N. Cortese, (Naples, 1923; originally published in *ASPN* 44–46 (1919–21) as "Avvertimenti ai nipoti").

armies. At the end of the seventeenth century, a series of biographies of celebrated Neapolitan aristocratic generals of the century included five Caracciolo among its fifty-five subjects.[14] The Aragonese and Spanish governments also offered many opportunities for careers in administration, and many Caracciolo were provincial governors or ambassadors: one was governor of Milan for Charles V, one was viceroy of Peru in the early eighteenth century, and Domenico Caracciolo was one of Ferdinand IV's ministers. With the admiral Francesco Caracciolo Brienza, who was executed in 1799 for his role in the Jacobin Republic, the Caracciolo could also offer a martyr for freedom to their patriotic nineteenth- and early twentieth-century eulogists.

ORIGINS OF THE BRIENZA FAMILY

The Angevin and Aragonese monarchs employed the Neapolitan aristocracy in prominent positions both within and outside the kingdom. The entrance of the kingdom of Naples into the Spanish imperial system further increased the opportunities for aristocratic advancement. The Caracciolo Brienza family originated from royal service at the highest level. At the end of the fifteenth century, Domizio Caracciolo Rosso, whose grandfather Nicola had been viceroy in Provence, ambassador to France, and Captain General of the pope, and whose father Ciarletta Viola had been lord of Monteleone, governor of the castle of Sant'Elmo in Naples, and royal vicar in the provinces of Basilicata and Principato Citra, died, leaving at least four sons to consolidate his family's fortunes, Giovan Battista, Marino, Antonio, and Scipione.

Marino Caracciolo (1469–1538) sought his fortune as a follower of Cardinal Ascanio Sforza, and in 1505 he received an abbey in Emilia. He then turned to a diplomatic career and was orator for Milan in Rome in 1513, nuncio in Austria in 1517, and nuncio to the newly elected Charles V in 1520. In 1523 he passed to imperial service, and was rewarded in 1524 with the bishopric of Catania in Sicily, which he passed to his brother Scipione, and, at Scipione's death in 1529, to his nephews Luigi (d. 1536) and Nicola Maria, who "for his good qualities died in odor of cardinalhood" in 1567.[15] From 1526, Marino was Charles V's representative in Milan. In 1529 he received the abbey of Sant'Angelo a Fasanella, near Salerno, which was also to remain in his family for a long time, and in 1530 the Duke of Milan bestowed on him the county of Gallarate, which included at least thirteen communities. In 1535 he became a cardinal, and in 1536 he was chosen as imperial governor of Milan, where he died two years later. His tomb is in the cathedral of Milan.[16]

[14] Raffaele Maria Filamondo, *Il genio bellicoso di Napoli* (Naples, 1694).
[15] Ammirato, I, p. 129 ("in concetto di cardinale").
[16] See the genealogical works cited, and A. Caracciolo di Torchiarolo, "Un feudatario di Gallarate: il cardinale Marino Caracciolo," offprint from *Rassegna Gallaratese di storia e d'arte* 12 (1953). On

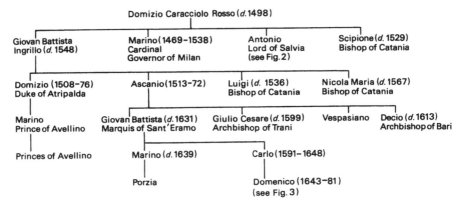

Figure 1 Descendants of Domizio Caracciolo Rosso (d. 1498). Like Figures 2 and 3, this
Figure is a simplified genealogy. It excludes most women and a few men.

Marino's spectacular career created the basis for his brothers' ascent. As we
shall see in a later chapter, the central years of the sixteenth century were the last
period in which it was both possible and advisable for an aristocratic family to
expand its numbers through a policy of frequent marriages and acquisitions of
lands. The two Brienza lines both began in the 1550s. After that, for about two
centuries, new branches would only be the rare result of accidents or conflicts
within an aristocratic family, and in general cadet sons would never marry unless
their elder brothers failed to produce a male heir. We shall here examine the
origins of the second Brienza line before those of the first one.[17]

Giovan Battista Caracciolo, called Ingrillo (d. 1548), married Beatrice,
daughter of Giovanni Gambacorta lord of Celenza, and inherited the county of
Gallarate. His first son Domizio (1508–76) exchanged Gallarate with the town
of Atripalda near Naples, on which he obtained the title of duke in 1572. His son
Marino became, in 1589, prince of Avellino, and his remained the most
prestigious and wealthy Caracciolo family in the Spanish period, giving origin
later to the titled families of Torchiarolo, Torella, and Parete.

Domizio's brother Ascanio (1513–72), as many a second son, followed a
career in the royal service. He fought at Tunis in 1535, in Flanders in 1538, and
at Algiers in 1541. In the 1550s he was ambassador to Urbino and Siena. In 1556
he pleaded before Philip II for the confirmation of Naples' privileges. In 1557 he
was made Cavallerizzo Maggiore (Master of the Royal Stables), an office which
remained in his family for several generations. In the years 1558–61 he was in
Rome, to act as Philip II's agent in the king's contrasts with the Carafa pope and

the bishopric of Catania to the Caracciolo, see the bulls and concessions in ACB 1.16, 18, 19, 22,
23 (19 consists of nine documents). See Figure 1.

[17] Chapter 5 discusses the changes in family structure in the mid-sixteenth century.

his family. In 1561 Ascanio and his brother-in-law Marino Caracciolo, marquis of Bucchianico, cruelly repressed the Waldensian insurrection in Calabria, where the latter was royal governor. In 1562–63 Ascanio was in Spain to accompany the young Francesco de'Medici. He spent his last years in Naples, where he and his wife Aurelia Caracciolo Bucchianico – whom he had married in 1540 – bought, in 1567, a chapel in the church of San Giovanni a Carbonara in the district of Capuana, which was to be the family chapel of the new line.[18]

Ascanio left ten children, among them four surviving sons, only one of whom married. Giulio Cesare (d. 1599) was archbishop of Trani, and Decio (d. 1613) was archbishop of Bari, while Vespasiano, knight of Calatrava since 1591, went to serve the della Rovere as soldier and diplomat and became count of Feniglia, near Urbino, in 1625, a title which would pass through his nephew to the Brienza family. The eldest son, Giovan Battista (d. 1631), became marquis of Sant'Eramo in Puglia through his marriage to Porzia Carafa, and transmitted his title to his son Marino. Giovan Battista's other son, Carlo (1591–1648), was destined to an ecclesiastic career, but later inherited his uncle Vespasiano's title, and, when his brother died in 1639 leaving only one daughter, the office of Cavallerizzo Maggiore. He married Cornelia Caracciolo Celenza, and his son Domenico (d. 1681) became, through marriage, the seventh marquis of Brienza.[19]

The last brother of Marino and Giovan Battista Ingrillo Caracciolo, Antonio, married Giovanna Gesualdo, daughter of the count of Conza, but little is known about him. Through the intercession of his powerful brother Marino, he became lord of Salvia, in the province of Principato Citra, in 1522.[20] His son Giulio Cesare (d. 1544) inherited the fief, while his three brothers did not marry and followed military or ecclesiastic careers. Giovan Francesco was abbot of Sant'Angelo a Fasanella after his uncle Marino, Baldassarre served in the Spanish army in Flanders, and so did Ottaviano. Giulio Cesare married Ippolita, daughter of Giovan Battista Filomarino prince of Rocca, of a very old and wealthy family. Ippolita disposed of a considerable fortune that she employed in 1557 in buying the fiefs of Brienza and Pietrafesa from Ferdinando Giovan Battista Caracciolo, duke of Martina, for 22,500 ducats. She then transferred the two fiefs, located next to one another in the provinces of Principato Citra and

---

[18] On Ascanio, in addition to the cited bibliography, see Cernigliaro, *Sovranità*, pp. 541–60. On his mission to Rome, see ACB 1. 25–31. On the repression in Calabria, see the documents published by Palermo, ed. "Relazioni varie dall'anno 1561 al 1596" *ASI* 9 (1846), pp. 193–99; E. Pontieri "A proposito della 'Crociata' contro i Valdesi della Calabria nel 1561" in Pontieri, *Nei tempi grigi della storia d'Italia* (Naples, 1966; first edit. 1949), pp. 159–96. On the chapel, see R. Filangieri di Candida, "La chiesa e il monastero di San Giovanni a Carbonara" *ASPN* 48 (1923), pp. 5–135.

[19] ACB 2 consists mostly in documents pertaining to Ascanio's line (notarial acts and reports of the central government organs to the viceroy). See Figure 1. Vespasiano's request for a knighthood in AGS Secr. Prov. Nápoles, leg. 219, of 30 August 1589.

[20] The royal privilege granting Salvia to Antonio and his wife is in J. E. Martinez Ferrando, *Privilegios otorgados por el emperador Carlos V en el Reyno de Nápoles* (Barcelona, 1943), p. 52, no. 447.

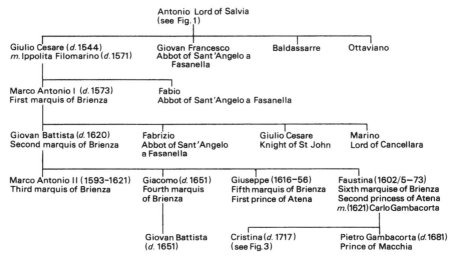

Figure 2 The first marquis of Brienza

Basilicata, to her first son from Giulio Cesare, Marco Antonio Caracciolo, who in 1569 became the first marquis of Brienza. In 1571 Ippolita bought also Atena, near Brienza in Principato Citra, from Scipione Carafa, duke of Morcone, for 10,000 ducats. At her death later that year, Atena and all her other rights on Brienza and Pietrafesa passed to her son, who was just returning from the battle of Lepanto.[21]

HISTORY OF THE FAMILY

The new marquis of Brienza, Marco Antonio Caracciolo, married two women of the Caracciolo clan, first Diana, daughter of his cousin Domizio, duke of Atripalda, and, at her death, Giulia, daughter of the heretic Galeazzo, marquis of Vico. His only brother, Fabio, was in his turn abbot of Sant'Angelo a Fasanella. Marco Antonio extended his possessions, and at his death in 1573 he left to his many children Brienza, Pietrafesa, and Atena acquired by his mother, Salvia – which had already belonged to his father – and the neighboring town of Sala, in

---

[21] ACB 1.3, a memoir written in 1655 for Giuseppe Caracciolo, marquis of Brienza. Ottaviano was a soldier in Flanders according to some genealogies, and an abbot of Sant'Angelo according to others. The origin of Ippolita's fortune is not documented; the purchase of Brienza and Pietrafesa is confirmed in AGS Titulos y privilegios Nápoles, S. P. 118, fols. 90vff., of 26 January 1558. See Figure 2. The Caracciolo counts of Brienza, of a different branch, had been prominent in the political life of the late Aragonese kingdom.

addition to some annuities. His estate, at its division in 1584, was valued at ducats 189,426.3.10, with liabilities of 81,575.4.02.[22]

Marco Antonio's widow, Giulia, and his brother, Fabio, divided the estate in 1584 among the seven surviving children. The three daughters were later married, the second son Fabrizio was abbot of Sant'Angelo a Fasanella, while the third, Giulio Cesare, was a knight of St. John, and fought in the Spanish infantry and cavalry as a captain. The fourth son, Marino, fought in the Spanish infantry in Flanders, and was a captain of cavalry in the duke of Parma's army when it entered Paris. He later married an aristocratic widow and became lord of Cancellara in Basilicata, but had no legitimate children. Marco Antonio's first son, Giovan Battista, inherited the titles, fiefs, and bulk of the estate, to which his mother Giulia had added the fief of Sasso, near Pietrafesa, bought in 1580 from Cesare Piscicelli for 15,000 ducats. Because of Marco Antonio's extensive purchases, and of the expenses involved in placing his six siblings, Giovan Battista's wealth declined. The 1590s marked the beginning of economic hard times for the kingdom of Naples, and Giovan Battista had to sell Salvia and Diano, the latter of which his mother had bought in 1592. From then on, the four fiefs of Brienza, Pietrafesa, Atena, and Sasso remained the only ones continuously in the hands of the family, and all later acquisitions were short-lived.

Though not comparable to the 150,000 ducats the Sanseverino princes of Bisignano collected from their fiefs in 1590, the Caracciolo Brienza's revenues of about 10,000 ducats a year in around 1600 placed them among the fifty wealthiest titled families in the kingdom; in 1605, when the *Seggio* aristocracy taxed itself to pay for the ceremonies celebrating the naming of St. Thomas Aquinas as the eighth patron of Naples, the six ducats contributed by Giovan Battista Caracciolo, marquis of Brienza, placed him in the top fourth among the city aristocracy. Though relatively low for families of marquis in contemporary Castile, the Caracciolo Brienza's revenues would have placed them among the ninety wealthiest Castilian titled families around 1600.[23]

In the early seventeenth century, however, the family entered a phase of severe financial difficulties. In 1590 Giovan Battista married Diana, daughter of Giacomo Caracciolo, duke of Sicignano, in whose veins ran some distant drops of Aragonese royal blood. Her large dowry of 33,000 ducats, though very useful

---

[22] The memoir in ACB 1.3 attributes the title of marquis to Marco Antonio's performance at Lepanto, but the title was awarded two years before the battle (Marco Antonio's presence at Lepanto is documented in Collenuccio *et al.*, *Compendio*, part III, book II). The evaluation of the estate is in ACB 9.8.

[23] On the Sanseverino, see G. Galasso, *Economia e società nella Calabria del Cinquecento* (Milan, 1975; first edit. Naples, 1967), pp. 3–17. On the relative status of the Caracciolo Brienza, see M. A. Visceglia, "Formazione e dissoluzione di un patrimonio aristocratico: la famiglia Muscettola tra XVI e XIX secolo" *MEFRM* 92 (1980), pp. 555–624, p. 574; Galasso, "Ideologia," p. 223 and tables; B. Bennassar, *Il secolo d'oro spagnolo* (Milan, 1985; French edit. 1982), pp. 195–99. In 1586, Giovan Battista, marquis of Brienza, solicited a knighthood in the order of Santiago, which seems to have been granted, AGS Secr. Prov. Nápoles, leg. 219, of 28 March 1586.

The continuity of feudal power

in future legal disputes to protect the family's patrimony, did not rescue Giovan Battista from his economic decline. He had several harsh lawsuits with his vassal communities; he bought lands in his fiefs extensively and spent most of his life there, in part, according to one source, to mark his discontent with the viceroyal government. When he died in 1620, Giovan Battista left debts amounting probably to more than the total value of his estate. Two of his three daughters became nuns, while the third, Faustina, married in 1621 Carlo Gambacorta, later prince of Macchia and marquis of Celenza. His first son, Marco Antonio, died little more than a year after his father, leaving to his brother Giacomo the additional burden of paying two succession taxes.[24]

According to the rules regulating aristocratic dowries, Giovan Battista's widow Diana had a right to receive her entire dowry plus the counterdowry her husband had pledged to her. In 1623, therefore, Diana came to an agreement with her son Giacomo which recognized her claims to 54,000 ducats on her deceased husband's estate. Being obviously unable to meet her demands, Giacomo gave his mother the fiefs of Atena and Sasso, which she later passed to her youngest son Giuseppe. Brienza and Pietrafesa were then sequestered by the government in order to be rented out to satisfy Giovan Battista's many creditors, though the Caracciolo managed to rent them themselves until 1684 and thus keep the continuity of their rule on the fiefs. Atena and Sasso, on the other hand, though the object of a fierce, century-long lawsuit, remained freely in Giuseppe's power, and indeed he obtained the title of prince of Atena in 1636.[25]

Giacomo and Giuseppe, as well as their cousin Carlo Caracciolo di Sant'Eramo, were prominent in the defense of Viceroy Arcos in the early days of the 1647 revolt, and Giuseppe led a small army in Atena to repress – most cruelly, according to his vassals – the revolt there, and especially to punish the seizing of princely goods and revenues. Giuseppe spent most of his time in Naples, had a visible role among the opponents of the government in the General Parliament of 1642, and, even after succeeding his brother as marquis of Brienza in 1651, remained mostly in Naples, where he died in the plague of 1656 while serving on the *Deputazione della Salute* for the city.[26]

Giuseppe's only heir was his sister Faustina, widow of Carlo Gambacorta.

[24] Chapter 2 will analyze in detail the formation and evolution of the Brienza patrimony. The source on Giovan Battista's discontent is a Florentine report to the Grand Duke, published in G. Ceci, "I feudatari napoletani alla fine del secolo XVI" *ASPN* 24 (1899), pp. 122–38. On the 1590s, recently Peter Burke, "Southern Italy in the 1590s: Hard Times or Crisis?" in Peter Clark, ed. *The European Crisis of the 1590s. Essays in Comparative History* (London, 1985), pp. 177–90.
[25] The whole troubled story of the passage of Atena and Sasso to Giuseppe and his heirs is the object of a large part of the documents in ACB, and will be closely analyzed in chapters 5 and 6.
[26] Capecelatro, *Diario 1647–1650*, ed. A. Granito di Belmonte, (3 vols.; Naples, 1850–54) (Capecelatro was a personal friend of Giuseppe's, but his testimony is reinforced by other sources, for example, ACB 1.3 and 2.7); G. Carignani, "L'ultimo Parlamento Generale del Regno di Napoli nel 1642" *ASPN* 8 (1883), pp. 34–57. Giuseppe's death of the plague and his membership in the Committee on Public Health are reported by the nuncio, ASV, SS. Napoli, vol. 55, fols. 272v and 643r (my thanks to James Clifton for this last reference).

32

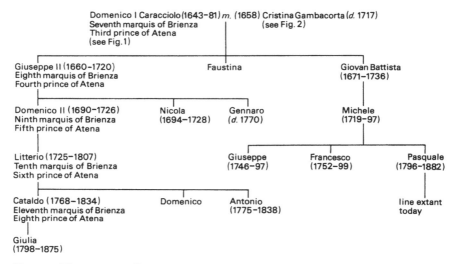

Figure 3   The marquis of Brienza after the mid-seventeenth century. My thanks to Count Giovanni Caracciolo di Brienza for kindly clarifying the genealogy of the family over the last 150 years.

Giuseppe's will enjoined her to pass his entire estate to Domenico, first son of their cousin Carlo Caracciolo Sant'Eramo. Faustina married her daughter Cristina (d. 1717) to Domenico in 1658, giving her Atena as part of the dowry, and at her death in 1673 a lawsuit ensued between her son Pietro Gambacorta and her son-in-law Domenico Caracciolo, which ended in 1681 with the death of the childless Pietro, followed shortly by Domenico's death, when the titles and lands of the Brienza passed to Giuseppe (1660–1720), first son of Domenico and Cristina.[27]

In 1684 Giuseppe came to an agreement with Francesco Maria Campione, a nobleman from Savona, agent in Naples for marquis Francesco Balbi of Genoa. Campione had bought from creditors of the Caracciolo several claims on Brienza and Pietrafesa, and Giuseppe now agreed to renounce his own claims in favor of Campione, making it possible thereby for the latter to purchase the two fiefs. Giuseppe would then rent them from Campione and would be free to buy them from him at a price 10,000 ducats lower than that paid by Campione. Following the agreement, Campione bought Brienza and Pietrafesa for 80,994 ducats, which went to satisfy some of the most persistent creditors of the Caracciolo. In 1688 Giuseppe married Teresa Pinto (d. 1755), of a wealthy Portuguese family recently come to Naples where it had amassed a large fortune,

---

[27] See Figures 2 and 3.

33

mainly through the management of taxes and the purchase of lucrative public offices. Teresa received a very large dowry of 50,000 ducats, most of which was paid in cash. This good example of alliance between sword and robe enabled Giuseppe to buy back the two old fiefs of his family in 1690.[28]

Giuseppe had only one sister, Faustina, who married Orazio Tuttavilla, duke of Calabritto, and one brother, Giovan Battista, who, quite late in life, and, according to one genealogist, in rather awkward circumstances, married the daughter of a minor aristocrat, and began a junior branch of the Brienza family which still exists in Naples, and of which Admiral Francesco Caracciolo was a member.[29] Of Giuseppe's seven surviving children, the four daughters married in the Neapolitan aristocracy (one married a Pinto cousin, by now prince of Ischitella), while the two younger sons entered the clergy. Domenico (1690–1726), the first son, inherited the patrimony, and in 1722 married Imara, only child of Francesco Ruffo di Bagnara, a junior member of the old and powerful Sicilian and Calabrian family of the Ruffo, and of Teodora Alberti, of a family claiming descent from Leon Battista, heiress in her own right to the marquisate of Pentidattilo in Calabria.

This marriage brought to Domenico's only son and heir, Litterio Giuseppe Caracciolo (1725–1807), first his mother's properties in Messina at her death in 1754, and then the marquisate of Pentidattilo itself at his grandmother's death in 1758. Litterio immediately sold Pentidattilo to Lorenzo Clemente, marquis of San Luca, for 68,000 ducats, which served to pay the Caracciolo's remaining debts. With their family fiefs and about 15,000 vassals, the Caracciolo Brienza were in the later eighteenth century one of the eighty-four families in the kingdom who ruled over more than 10,000 vassals, although they were far from possessing the wealth and power of the eighteen families who ruled over more than 30,000. In 1806, Litterio donated all his properties and rights to his eldest surviving son, Cataldo (1768–1834), who fought long bitter disputes with the new Communes of his four ex-fiefs after the abolition of feudalism in 1806. At his death the still healthy fortune of the Caracciolo passed to his only child, Giulia (1798–1875), wife of Marzio Carafa, prince of Colubrano. She died childless, leaving all her fortune to her sister-in-law's son and heir, baron Luigi

---

[28] The marriage contract is an ACB 3.(2).7 (this bundle is practically, though not formally, divided in two sections, the first containing baptism certificates, the second marriage contracts). In 1686, under the strict rule of Viceroy Carpio, Giuseppe had spent some time imprisoned in the old Norman castle in Naples, due, presumably, to his involvement with bandits, Galasso, *Napoli spagnola dopo Masaniello* (2 vols.; Florence, 1982; previously in Pontieri, ed. *Storia di Napoli*), I, p. 278.

[29] Giovan Battista is said to have married Candida Grassi to achieve reconciliation with her family after he had killed her brother in a duel. See Caracciolo, *Una famiglia*, pp. 159–60, who does not quote his source for this story, nor for others he mentions. The admiral was Giovan Battista's grandson. This line obtained a ducal title on the surname in the mid-eighteenth century. See Figure 3.

Barracco, whose family later donated the Brienza archive to the Società Napoletana di Storia Patria.[30]

At the end of the eighteenth century, with 15,000 vassals and annual revenues slightly over 10,000 ducats, the Caracciolo Brienza were not on a par with the few wealthiest, most powerful families, such as the Pignatelli dukes of Monteleone with their over 70,000 vassals, or the Caracciolo princes of Avellino with their annual revenues of well over 50,000 ducats.[31] But their relative status within the kingdom's aristocracy was the same as two centuries before, and they – like many of their peers – had well weathered the social and economic turmoil of the seventeenth century. The Caracciolo Brienza were, at the end of the old regime, among the wealthier one hundred families of the kingdom; they belonged to one of the oldest and most prestigious clans, a fact from which they did not fail to reap remarkable benefits in their social status and in their marriage policy; they were the peacefully recognized lords of vassals whom they had governed for over two hundred years with powers that no royal government had so far been willing or able seriously to challenge or limit. It is the aim of this study to illustrate and discuss how this position was achieved and maintained through almost three centuries.

[30] A. Massafra, "Un problème ouvert à la recherche: la 'crise' du baronnage napolitain à la fin du XVIIIe siècle" in *L'abolition de la féodalité dans le monde occidental*, Actes du colloque international, (Toulouse, November 1968), I, pp. 245–62.

[31] Massafra, "Un problème"; Massafra, "Fisco e baroni nel regno di Napoli alla fine del secolo XVIII" in *Studi storici in onore di Gabriele Pepe* (Bari, 1969), pp. 625–75, p. 632, footnote 16, for the Caracciolo Avellino. No Neapolitan family could equal the patrimonies of some Spanish aristocrats: the dukes of Infantado, for instance, already around 1600 ruled over 85,000 vassals and 620 villages, see J. H. Elliott, *Imperial Spain, 1469–1716* (New York, 1977; first edit. 1963), pp. 309–10.

2

Structure and evolution of an aristocratic patrimony

> It gives one position and it prevents one from keeping it up. That's all that
> can be said about land.
>
> (Wilde, *The Importance of Being Earnest*)

It was through the acquisition of a fief, and later of a title, that the Caracciolo
Brienza established themselves as a new, separate family within the Caracciolo
clan. As late as the Aragonese period (1442–1503), many families and clans of
undisputed nobility, including several members of the Caracciolo clan, did not
own fiefs and were content with the ownership of allodial land in or near the city
of Naples where they resided. By the mid-sixteenth century, however, the old
urban patriciate and the provincial baronage had become much more integrated;
many barons moved to Naples and managed to enter the *Seggi* before their
closure, while the increased commercialization of fiefs, encouraged by the
Aragonese and Spanish kings, led to greater availability of fiefs for both new and
old aristocratic families. The fief, and especially the titled one, became,
therefore, an essential element of the aristocratic patrimony, both for its
economic value and for the status and powers it conferred. By the late sixteenth
century, and until the abolition of the feudal regime in 1806, to be a member of
the high aristocracy of the kingdom meant to be a feudal lord, to be a baron.[1]

In later chapters I shall consider the impact of the aristocracy's feudal position
on its relations with its vassals and with the government. This chapter and the
next one analyze the aristocratic patrimony and its management, with specific
focus on the importance of the ownership of fiefs in determining aristocratic
income and economic behavior. In particular, the present chapter contains a
description of an aristocratic patrimony, the Caracciolo Brienza's, and an
analysis of its various components. I shall examine the acquisition of each
component of the patrimony and the reasons for, and consequences of, this
diversification. As a preliminary step for this it is necessary to define and discuss
the various aspects of what constituted a fief in the kingdom of Naples. I shall

---

[1] By high aristocracy, I here refer to the *Seggio* aristocracy of Naples and to all other noble families
prominent at court and in the capital. As time went by, all these barons acquired titles as well. For
the fusion of the Naples patricians with the provincial barons, see G. D'Agostino, *La capitale
ambigua, Napoli dal 1458 al 1580* (Naples, 1979).

then compare the permanent elements of the patrimony, namely the four family fiefs of Brienza, Pietrafesa, Atena, and Sasso, with all the other possessions of the Caracciolo Brienza, in order to gauge their relative importance to the family's economic and social position. The chapter ends with an overview of the changes in the internal structure of the patrimony over time, to examine how the family responded to the expansion, crisis, and recovery of the economy of the kingdom.

The next chapter will look more particularly at the four fiefs the family owned throughout its history. The richer and more continuous documentation on these four possessions makes it possible to address the issue of the management of aristocratic landed property, and to assess the relative importance of feudal and allodial lands and of feudal rights, the management methods, the investments in production, and the market outlets.

THE FIEFS

Historians of Europe have long debated whether or not the use of the term "feudalism" should be limited to the period from the ninth to the thirteenth centuries. Neapolitan historians, however, following in the footsteps of the Neapolitan eighteenth-century reformers, have always used the terms *feudo* and *feudalità* (indicating the feudatories as a group, the baronage) to describe what Aurelio Lepre has called "the power that shaped the entire society" of the kingdom until 1806. Nonetheless, given the many different meanings and images that the term fief conjures up, a discussion of its meaning in early modern Naples is in order.[2]

The Italian word *feudo* has several meanings, beside that of fief in the medieval context. In Sicily, still in the early decades of this century if not still today, it was used to refer to any piece of land large enough for its owner to be socially above the peasantry. As such, the term did not imply either any particular privileges pertaining to the land's owners, or any peculiar legal status of the land itself. In the kingdom of Naples, on the other hand, it referred to land endowed with special legal characteristics different from those of allodial land, and because of this the term was not used any more after 1806. The transmission and acquisition of a *feudo* took place according to old feudal traditions and usages, complemented by royal laws, and the fiscal status of such property was also different from that of allodial property. No particular privilege, though, pertained to the owners of the land.[3]

---

[2] A. Lepre, *Storia del Mezzogiorno d'Italia* (2 vols.; Naples, 1986), I, p. 47; a general discussion and definition is in M. Aymard, "L'Europe moderne: féodalité ou féodalités?" *Annales ESC* 36 (1981), pp. 426–35.

[3] On Sicily, see literary evidence in Verga's *Mastro-don Gesualdo* (1889), De Roberto's *I vicerè* (1894), Capuana's *Il marchese di Roccaverdina* (1901), and Tomasi di Lampedusa's *Il gattopardo* (1958); materials on feudal society in Sicily are also in A. Italia, *La Sicilia feudale. Saggi* (Rome,

The term *feudo*, however, was also used to describe any village or town in the kingdom, constituted as a community, over which civil and criminal jurisdiction, at least in the first degree, was wielded not by the royal government but by a private individual recipient of a royal investiture for that purpose. Added to jurisdiction could be any number of rights, privileges, and monopolies, as well as ownership of any amount of land included in the territory of the village or town. The transmission and acquisition of these *feudi* and their fiscal status were regulated by the same laws and usages which governed any piece of feudal land; but the owners also enjoyed personal privileges and exemptions, the scope of which was determined by tradition and by the individual royal investitures. In this sense Brienza, Pietrafesa, Atena, and Sasso were the fiefs of the Caracciolo Brienza. In the Spanish period there were over 1,500 enfeoffed *università* (communities) in the kingdom, representing over ninety-five percent of the kingdom's villages and towns, and including about three fourths of the kingdom's entire population.[4]

It is in this latter meaning that fief will be used in this study. To say that Brienza or any other *università* in the kingdom was a fief of a family implies a set of relations that requires some discussion before the role of the fiefs in an aristocratic patrimony can be assessed. Since the Norman conquest of the eleventh century, each fief in the kingdom had evolved into a complex of rights and properties, depending on investitures and sales on the part of the crown. Under the Aragonese kings, most if not all barons in the kingdom were granted first- and second-degree civil and criminal jurisdiction over all the inhabitants of their fiefs, as well as the so-called "four arbitrary letters" that assigned them various jurisdictional powers. Besides the jurisdiction, most fiefs included a castle and a varying amount of land, both in separate cultivated plots (that can be called the tenures), and as feudal domain subject to common use on the part of all residents of the fief. Personal privileges attached to ownership of a fief included the right to levy the traditional feudal *adiutoria*, or contributions paid by the vassals on such occasions as the lord's ransom or the marriage of the lord's aunt, sister, or daughter. But the most profitable and important aspect of ownership of a fief was the many rights attached to the lordship. Davide Winspeare counted hundreds of different feudal rights existing in the kingdom until 1806, but the most common and important ones were only about a dozen. Their effect on the life of the fiefs' population as well as on the barons' income was, however, very strong.[5]

1940). T. Davies, *Famiglie feudali siciliane. Patrimoni redditi investimenti tra '500 e '600* (Caltanissetta–Rome, 1985), is somewhat ambiguous in the use of the term.
[4] See chapter 4. The king could also grant any type of possession in fief, such as palaces or shares of the public debt, thereby subjecting them to feudal inheritance and fiscal laws.
[5] D. Winspeare, *Storia degli abusi feudali* (Naples, 1811); N. Santamaria, *I feudi, il diritto feudale e la loro storia nell'Italia meridionale* (Naples, 1881). The *adiutoria* were still levied in the 1710s for the marriages of Giuseppe II's daughters, and in 1766 for the marriage of Litterio's daughter, ACB

Although discussions of feudal rights can be found in the works of Winspeare and of others, and many feudal rights in the kingdom were similar to those existing in other European states, it is useful briefly to analyze here the most important of those rights. By the Spanish period, *corvées* were no longer required of any man in the kingdom, although contributions to substitute personal labor were not uncommon. Other contributions, such as Christmas gifts or dues on specific animals and products, were levied in some fiefs, but they were relatively rare and of limited economic impact. The more important feudal rights can be divided into four main categories. A first series of rights consisted in the exercise of royal powers other than jurisdiction, especially in the power of enforcing laws and collecting fees from transgressors. A second category was represented by feudal monopolies on particular economic activities. Thirdly, use of the feudal domain on the part of the general population was subject to fees paid to the lord. Lastly, the barons had the right to their vassals' services in specified circumstances.[6]

Among the regalian powers exercised by feudal lords was the right to levy the fees on merchandise or passengers traveling through any pass present in their fiefs. Barons also owned a number of offices which they could rent or manage directly; the holder of each office collected specific fees or was responsible for the enforcement of laws. The *mastrodattia* (actuary office) gave the right to issue all acts for the baronial court and to collect fees on them. The *bagliva*, a very old office, consisted by the Spanish period in the jurisdiction over civil lawsuits, particularly for debts, in which not more than three ducats-worth of money was involved, over cases of non-violent and non-malicious damages worth up to one and a half ducats, and over thefts of agricultural products for a value not higher than four ducats. The *baglivo* kept his own jail, but could only arrest transgressors caught *in flagrante delicto*. The *portolania* gave jurisdiction over the maintenance of streets; the *portolano* levied fines on those who, with garbage or construction materials, defiled or obstructed the public roads, and he granted licenses for constructions, wells, and sewers. The *zecca*, also known as the right of *pesi e misure* (weights and measures), was the right to enforce the use of standard measurements for weights and capacity, and to levy fines on transgressors.[7]

48.2.1–3; earlier examples for other fiefs are in R. Colapietra, *Dal Magnanimo a Masaniello* (2 vols.; Salerno, 1973), II, pp. 385–87.

[6] A discussion of feudal rights is in G. I. Cassandro, *Storia di una terra del Mezzogiorno: Atena Lucana* (Rome, 1946; originally in *Rivista di storia del diritto italiano* 16 (1943)). Very useful for the pages that follow, besides the documents in ACB and the works by Winspeare and Santamaria cited in the previous note, are G. M. Novario, *De vassallorum gravaminibus tractatus* (Naples, 1634), and G. F. Capobianco, *Tractatus de iure et officio baronum erga vasallos burgenses* (Naples, 1614; second edit. 1622). An example of gifts owed to the barons is in ACB 45.1.11: the *università* of Brienza presents the baron with cheese (*caciocavalli*). A survey of baronial rights in Sicily is in Aymard, "L'abolition de la féodalité en Sicile: le sens d'une réforme" *Annuario dell'Istituto Storico Italiano per l'età moderna e contemporanea* 23–24 (1971–72), pp. 67–85.

[7] Besides Cassandro, *Atena*, see ACB 44.1.30 for the *bagliva*; 75.1.14 for the *portolania*; and 48.1.1, fols. 1198v–1200r, for the *zecca*; see ASP notai Potenza 650, fol. 185v, for the fees of the *mastrodatti* in Brienza (*c.* 1650); and ASN Archivio privato Doria d'Angri 249/5 for an example of the *passi*

The monopolies of several economic activities represented another important category of feudal rights. Most barons had the *jus prohibendi*, or monopoly right, for the mills, ovens, and inns of their fiefs. All residents had to use the baronial mill and pay a fee in grain. Residents could not use their ovens for anything but domestic consumption, not could they host travellers in their houses for a fee. All residents also had to use the baronial *valchiera* or *battendiero*, a structure situated on rivers used to wash and prepare cloths. The feudal lord granted hunting and fishing rights in the fiefs. Moreover, he often had the right of *piazza*, consisting of a fee on all merchandise sold or bought by outsiders in his fief. The *catapania*, or right to set prices for basic staples in each village or town, was usually held by the community itself.[8]

Residents of a fief who cultivated part of the feudal domain paid the lord a *terraggio* in kind, usually set at ten percent of the harvest. Parts of the feudal domain were used as pastures, and the owners of all animals grazing there owed the lord a *fida* set by tradition and accords with the community. The feudal lord could in general request the services of his vassals as jailers or porters, but he had to pay them a regular salary. The community had the obligation to guard the feudal castle, and by the Spanish period it acquitted itself of this duty by paying an annual fee to the lord (the *colta*). In many fiefs the community had also to choose each year one or two men to be the administrators of feudal revenues. These two, the *erario* and the *conservatore*, were in charge of the barons' revenues in money and in kind respectively, and they received no salary from the baron. They served one year and drew a budget that the baron had to approve before they could be cleared of any liability. Almost all of these rights produced larger revenues the larger the population of the fief.[9]

Feudal powers in the kingdom of Naples were therefore very extended and varied. Coupled with the strength of feudal civil and criminal jurisdiction, they endowed Neapolitan barons with more unfettered influence and more possibilities for coercion and control at the local level than was the case elsewhere in Western Europe. In Northern Italy feudal powers were much more limited, and even in the Spanish-ruled duchy of Milan the city tribunals placed strict limitations on the exercise of feudal jurisdiction. The judicial powers of the aristocracy were also limited in most of France by the sixteenth century, as were other forms of feudal jurisdiction.[10]

levied by the prince of Angri at Capaccio. (My thanks to Alessandra Bulgarelli Lukacs for this last reference.) On the *bagliva*, see also G. Racioppi, "Gli statuti della bagliva delle antiche comunità del Napoletano" *ASPN* 6 (1881), pp. 347–77 and 508–30; on the *zecca*, see R. Pilati, "La dialettica politica a Napoli durante la visita di Lope de Guzmán" *ASPN* 105 (1987), pp. 145–221, 191–98, and 216–21.

[8] Novario, throughout; ACB 48.1.1, fols. 1002r–1005v, and ASN Creditori dello Stato 275/36, fols. 70r–v, for the *piazza*.

[9] The income of all these rights will be discussed in chapter 3.

[10] In Sicily, feudal powers were very pervasive, see O. Cancila, "Introduzione" to F. di Napoli, principe di Resuttano, *Noi il Padrone* (Palermo, 1982); in Piedmont, feudal powers were limited

Structure of an aristocratic patrimony

Given the power and influence they conferred, it becomes clear why fiefs were at least as profitable and attractive an investment as any other in Spanish Naples. The powers of feudal lords were pervasive and influenced all aspects of the lives of their vassals, giving ample space for the abuses and extortions lamented by eighteenth-century reformers. Compounded with the status in society conferred by fiefs, and especially by the titles that could be obtained on them, these powers explain the strong demand for fiefs in early modern Naples, and why the crown never encountered any problem selling them. There were, however, difficulties associated with the ownership of fiefs that in most instances limited their purchase to the earlier generations of a family. In the second half of the sixteenth century and the first decades of the seventeenth, the prices and revenues of fiefs grew substantially in the kingdom, well above the contemporary inflation, as was also the case in Sicily. The revenues of the Caracciolo Brienza's fiefs, for instance, grew by almost ten times between 1521 and 1625. After about 1625, however, the income from fiefs in the kingdom was unlikely to grow, especially in the absence of any entrepreneurial investments, as the population of the Mezzogiorno began to decrease or at best stabilize, and as the kingdom's agriculture declined. Moreover, it was relatively cumbersome to dispose of fiefs, as of any feudal property, since all transmission of fiefs had to be approved by the king, and the rights of the lawful heir were protected by feudal law even against the will of the individual owner. This meant that, in times of crisis, it was difficult to transform a fief into ready money, and at times creditors would not accept fiefs as guarantees for loans (even if they did, those guarantees would require royal assent to be valid). The lack of flexibility of the fiefs was the main reason for the remarkable diversification of aristocratic patrimonies.[11]

Fiefs were therefore the best way to establish the position of a new family on solid foundations in the sixteenth as well as in the seventeenth century; and, especially if a title had been obtained, the first fiefs purchased by a family remained the core of its patrimony and became identified with each individual

and were most often converted in cash payments, see S. J. Woolf, *Studi sulla nobiltà piemontese nell'epoca dell'assolutismo* (Turin, 1963). On Milan, see U. Petronio, "Giurisdizione feudale e ideologia giuridica nel Ducato di Milano" *QS* 9 (1974), pp. 351–402; on France, see J. Dewald, *The Formation of a Provincial Nobility. The Magistrates of the Parlement of Rouen, 1499–1610* (Princeton, 1980), pp. 162–68; J. L. Goldsmith, *Les Salers et les d'Escorailles, seigneurs de Haute Auvergne, 1500–1789* (Clermont-Ferrand, 1984), chapter 1, part B. See also here chapter 3, footnote 10.

[11] The issue is discussed in Galasso, "Aspetti e problemi della società feudale napoletana attraverso l'inventario dei beni dei principi di Bisignano (1594)" in *Studi in memoria di Federigo Melis* (Naples, 1978), IV, pp. 255–77. On the growth of feudal revenues, see Galasso, *Economia e società nella Calabria del Cinquecento* (Milan, 1975; first edit. Naples, 1967), and recently Visceglia, *Territorio, feudo e potere locale. Terra d'Otranto tra Medioevo ed età moderna* (Naples, 1988), pp. 221–43. The rental value of fiefs in Sicily grew by ten times between 1500 and 1630, while the price of grain grew by only five or six times, see Aymard, "L'abolition," and Aymard, "La transizione dal feudalesimo al capitalismo" in *Storia d'Italia Einaudi. Annali I Dal feudalesimo al capitalismo* (Turin, 1978), pp. 1190–91.

41

family. The example of the Caracciolo Brienza shows that the first two
generations acquired fiefs, and tried to expand their feudal possessions as well as
their power within each fief. After that the family diversified its patrimony and
any fiefs that came into its possession through inheritance were quickly sold, not
only because of economic difficulties but also to ensure stability and balance in
the patrimony.

The Caracciolo Brienza owned their first fief, Salvia, from the 1520s, but we
do not know how much it cost them. In the years between 1557 and 1580, as we
have seen, the family bought the four fiefs it was to keep until its extinction,
Brienza, Pietrafesa, Atena, and Sasso. In 1579, probably because of the
opportunity to buy Sasso that was contiguous to the other three fiefs, Salvia was
sold for 12,000 ducats to the prince of Venosa, whose large feudal *stato*
surrounded it. The very favorable economic situation of those years was
characterized by a quick increase in the value of fiefs. The Caracciolo Brienza
tried to employ their growing revenues to expand their feudal patrimony
geographically and to augment their powers within their fiefs. In these years the
family purchased from the crown several additional rights and jurisdictions in
order to strengthen their new lordship. Marco Antonio I bought the town of
Sala, near Atena, for 14,060 ducats; but by 1579 the town redeemed itself and
returned to the royal domain. The Caracciolo Brienza, however, stretched their
resources too much, in view of the halt to the kingdom's economic growth in the
1590s. In 1592, Giulia Caracciolo made a successful bid to buy the town of
Diano, located near Atena in the same valley, for 82,100 ducats, or almost twice
the price paid in previous years for all four family fiefs together. In 1606,
however, in order to pay the debts incurred by his mother in the purchase of
Diano, Giovan Battista Caracciolo had to sell it for 80,500 ducats. After this the
main branch of the Caracciolo Brienza never bought any other fief, even when
their economic situation improved in the late seventeenth and eighteenth
centuries.[12]

The purchase of fiefs, however, remained the essential step to establish a new
family, even when their value as investments had declined. In fact the only two
fiefs bought by the Caracciolo Brienza in the seventeenth century were
purchased by cadet sons who married and were therefore forming a new branch.
Marino, younger brother of the marquis Giovan Battista, acquired the fief of
Cancellara in 1601 for 30,000 ducats. His marriage proved childless, and four
years after Marino's death, in 1625, his nephew, the marquis Giacomo, sold
Cancellara to Marino's widow for the same price in order to pay Marino's debts
and his own. Also Carlo Caracciolo, second son of the marquis of Sant'Eramo,
after leaving the clergy in order to marry, purchased in 1643 the fief of

[12] For the purchases, see ACB 43.1.1, 75.1.10, and 81.1.1; Diano in 9.15–16; Sala in 9.8 and
89.3.17; and Salvia in 8.6 (ASN Repertori dei Quinternioni 14-III, fols. 82v–83r has the sale
price as 11,000 ducats). The acquisition of feudal rights is discussed in chapter 6.

Montenegro with the *casale* of Montelateglia in the province of Capitanata for 40,000 ducats, and tried to claim the ducal title on Montenegro held by its previous owner. The fief passed to his son and heir Domenico who, as we have seen, became, through his marriage to Cristina Gambacorta in 1658, the seventh marquis of Brienza. The decline in revenues due to depopulation, agricultural crisis, and poor administration made it again impossible to pay the debts incurred for the fief's purchase, and in 1682, after a long lawsuit, Montenegro and Montelateglia were auctioned by the government for 23,000 ducats in order to pay the family's creditors.[13]

In these two instances, the fiefs acquired through inheritance from collateral branches were quickly sold again by the Caracciolo Brienza in order to pay debts. But the family was always less interested in the preservation of scattered isolated fiefs than in keeping the ancestral feudal *stato* on which it had its titles. Feudal property after the sixteenth century became less appealing and profitable for an already established family. When in 1758 Litterio Caracciolo inherited the fiefs of Pentidattilo and Melito in Calabria from his grandmother Teodora Alberti, together with Alberti and Ruffo properties in Messina, he had no urgent need to sell any part of the inheritance. In 1759, however, he sold the two fiefs for 68,000 ducats, while he kept the allodial property.[14]

The four contiguous villages that constituted the Caracciolo Brienza's *stato* were located at the border between the provinces of Principato Citra and Basilicata, in a relatively isolated and poor region, which in the Spanish period was exposed to very little outside influence. The royal road to Calabria that passed by Atena was in very poor condition until the late eighteenth century, and the valley that the road followed – the Vallo di Diano – was not made safe from marshes and floods until the early nineteenth century. The family's feudal *stato* was therefore entirely in what Paolo Macry has called the *campagna*, the poorer internal areas characterized by difficult access and limited change. None of the four communities was closer than forty-six miles to a provincial capital. The Vallo di Diano itself was still mostly given over to pastures, and the neighboring hills were covered with woods. As we shall see in detail, the geographic characteristics of the area stood in the way of the development of large farms and, unlike areas of Puglia or the not very distant plain of the Sele, the Caracciolo Brienza *stato* was mostly fragmented in small plots owned or rented by the local peasantry. The geographic characteristics of the area, and the mostly absenteeist landownership, combined in determining this form of agricultural organization.[15]

[13] For Cancellara, see L. Giustiniani, *Dizionario geografico ragionato del Regno di Napoli* (12 vols.; Naples, 1797–1805), III, pp. 76–77; ASN, notai del '600, 167/4, Giovanni Scalese, 6 June 1625, unnumbered fol. For Montenegro, see ACB 11, especially 11.1.9 and 24. A *casale* was a small village enjoying only limited administrative autonomy and tied to a larger *università*.
[14] ASN Refute dei Quinternioni 226, pp. 528–35.
[15] P. Macry, *Mercato e società nel regno di Napoli; commercio del grano e politica economica nel Settecento* (Naples, 1974), particularly part I; D. Ruocco, *La Campania* (Turin, 1965) and L. Ranieri, *La*

Table 2.1. *Value of the Caracciolo Brienza fiefs in the seventeenth century*
(in ducats)

fief	*1625*	*1640s*	*1676–77*
Brienza	72,749.2.04	95,402.4.17+1/3	61,930.4.09
Pietrafesa	49,291.1.13+1/3	-	35,261.4.11+2/3
Atena	20,313.-.16+2/3	21,352.4.03	-
Sasso	26,625.-.--	21,559.4.03+1/3	25,492.3.06+2/3
totals	168,968.4.14		

Note: Here, and in all subsequent tables, a dash denotes no available data.
Sources: ACB 43.3.7; 77.2.1 bis, 27; 160, unnumbered fol. The high figure for Brienza
in 1646 (ACB 160, unnumbered fol.) is probably exaggerated to favor the marquis.

The value of the four fiefs increased steadily until the 1620s, then declined
somewhat to rise again in the eighteenth century. The total price paid by the
Caracciolo Brienza for their four fiefs was 47,500 ducats. Due to the favorable
economic situation and to the purchase of additional jurisdictions on the part of
the family, the value if its fiefs increased rapidly. In 1584 Brienza, Pietrafesa,
Atena, and Salvia were assessed at 100,000 ducats, capitalizing at four percent
the 4,000 ducats they produced in revenue. In the 1590s and 1600s, Giovan
Battista Caracciolo augmented his allodial holdings in the four fiefs by extensive
purchases of real estate. In 1625 the four fiefs were assessed for a total of ducats
168,968.4.14.[16] After this date, no more significant additions were made to the
sources of revenues each fief comprised.

Assessments in the 1640s show an increase in the value of Brienza, and
relatively stable values for Sasso and Atena. If we assume that Atena was still
worth little over 20,000 ducats in 1676–77, the four fiefs at that date were worth
about 142,700 ducats, which would represent a total loss of about 25,000 ducats
or fifteen percent in fifty years. Table 2.1 summarizes the available data for the

Basilicata (Turin, 1961), vols. XIII and XV of the series *Le regioni d'Italia*; Massafra, "Déséquilibres régionaux et réseaux de transport en Italie méridionale du milieu du XVIIIe siècle à l'Unité
italienne" *Annales ESC* 43 (1988), pp. 1045–80; Giustiniani, *Dizionario, sub vocibus*; a general
work on the area which also discusses accessibility is *Storia del Vallo di Diano*, (3 vols.; Salerno,
1982–85); see also here chapter 4; on roads, or the lack thereof, in the kingdom, see A. Giannetti,
"La strada dalla città al territorio: la riorganizzazione spaziale del Regno di Napoli nel
Cinquecento" in *Storia d'Italia Einaudi. Annali VIII Insediamenti e territorio* (Turin, 1978),
pp. 241–85.
[16] ACB 9.8; 43.3.1. The figures for 1584 and 1625 cannot be compared properly, since the former
includes Salvia instead of Sasso. We know, however, that Salvia was worth about 12,000 ducats in
1580, so that for the other three fiefs there was an increase of about sixty percent in value in about
fifty years.

Table 2.2. *Breakdown of the Caracciolo Brienza patrimony*
(in ducats)

sources of revenues	value		revenues	
	amount	percent	amount	percent
		1584		
fiefs	114,060.-.--	60	4,562,2.01	46
other assets	75,366.3.10	40	5,332.4.18	54
totals	189,426.3.10		9,895.1.19	
		1625		
fiefs	168,968.4.14½	80	6,786.4.13½	73
other assets	42,470.4.--	20	2,590.2.03+2/3	27
totals	211,439.3.14½		9,377.1.17+1/6	
		c. 1680		
fiefs	142,685.2.07+1/3	83	6,432.2.19+1/6	80
other assets	29.984.-.--	17	1,573.2.05½	20
totals	172,669.2.07+1/3		8,006.-.04+2/3	
		1726		
fiefs	157,319.2.10	65	6,294.4.18	65
other assets	85,641.1.12	35	3,399.2.19	35
totals	242,960.4.02		9,694.2.17	

Sources: cited in the relevant footnotes to the text.

seventeenth century. We lack assessments for Brienza and Pietrafesa in the eighteenth century; in 1748 Atena was worth ducats 17,940.-.10+7/12, and Sasso ducats 33,092.4.13+1/48, and in 1776 their value was 27,469 and 45,931 ducats respectively, with an increase of about thirty and eighty percent respectively compared to the last available assessments of the seventeenth century, and of about fifty and thirty-eight percent compared to the 1748 figures. In the 1780s, finally, the revenues of the four fiefs were valued at ducats 10,972.-.18+2/3 which, at the capitalization rate of four percent, would represent a value of 274,304 ducats, or an increase of about ninety percent in little over a century.[17]

[17] ACB 77.2.32, 33; 81.1.17, 18; 161, unnumbered fol. The figure for the 1780s is only an indication of trend, since the document was a private one, not a government-ordered

In the late eighteenth century, the kingdom again experienced a period of inflation, so that the increase in the value and revenues of the fiefs by the 1780s appears probably somewhat greater than it actually was. In the seventeenth and early eighteenth centuries, however, prices rose very little if at all, so that we can compare the available figures. The value and revenues of the four fiefs – the core of the family's patrimony – did not decline too sharply in the seventeenth century, while they rose significantly in the sixteenth and eighteenth centuries. The feudal *stato*, therefore, served relatively well its purpose of providing a foundation for the family's wealth that the family would defend at the cost of its other assets, and that would in its turn guarantee reasonably secure revenues.[18]

OTHER ELEMENTS OF THE ARISTOCRATIC PATRIMONY

It was common for Italian and other European aristocratic families to differentiate their patrimony in order to make it more resilient to economic difficulties. A balanced patrimony would consist of land and other assets so that one part could be used to support the other as circumstances required. Land protected from inflation and its price often increased at a rate higher than that of other goods, though it often yielded revenues at a lower rate than other assets. The latter could include shares of commercial, financial, or manufacturing concerns, but in most instances consisted of credit, urban real estate, and liquid assets. Credit, in particular on the government, offered high and fairly secure yields, especially in the late sixteenth and seventeenth centuries.[19]

The Neapolitan aristocracy in general shied from investments in trade or manufacturing. In the late fifteenth century the aristocratic abstention from commerce was defended by Tristano Caracciolo, in response to Poggio Bracciolini's attack on the laziness of the Neapolitan aristocracy. Machiavelli was to repeat Poggio's criticism. Neapolitan aristocratic theorists as late as the second half of the seventeenth century denied that the aristocracy could engage in trade,

assessment. It should also be considered that the assessments at times used slightly different capitalization rates. This assessment of the changes in the value of the fiefs matches the trend observed for the *stato* of Santa Severina in Calabria, see G. Caridi, *Uno "stato" feudale nel Mezzogiorno spagnolo* (Rome, 1988), pp. 9–13.
[18] On inflation, see R. Romano, *Napoli: dal viceregno al regno, storia economica* (Turin, 1976); L. de Rosa, *Il Mezzogiorno spagnolo tra crescita e decadenza* (Milan, 1987); J. Marino, *Pastorial Economics in the Kingdom of Naples* (Baltimore, 1988), pp. 182–83, on the inflation of the sixteenth century.
[19] Woolf, *Studi*, pp. 35–39, 42–47, 50–53, and 141–45; J. C. Davis, *A Venetian Family and its Fortune 1500–1900: The Donà and the Conservation of their Wealth* (Philadelphia, 1975), chapter 2; P. Malanima, *I Riccardi di Firenze, una famiglia e un patrimonio nella Toscana dei Medici* (Florence, 1977); Aymard, "Amministrazione feudale e trasformazioni strutturali tra '500 e '700" *Archivio Storico per la Sicilia Orientale* 71 (1975), pp. 17–42; R. Forster, *The Nobility of Toulouse in the Eighteenth Century, a Social and Economic Study* (Baltimore, 1960), chapter 5; J.-P. Labatut, *Les ducs et pairs de France au XVIIe siècle, étude sociale* (Paris, 1972), pp. 271–82; V. Reinhardt, *Kardinal Scipione Borghese* (Tübingen, 1984), pp. 236–63; later examples in A. Moroni, "Le ricchezze dei Corsini. Struttura patrimoniale e vicende familiari tra Sette e Ottocento" *Società e storia* 9 (1986), pp. 255–92, and in Macry, *Ottocento. Famiglie, elites e patrimoni a Napoli* (Turin, 1988).

and only in the 1680s did the Spanish government make it clear that the aristocracy could engage in commercial or industrial activities without incurring the stigma of *dérogeance*.[20] Moreover, due to the fact that the foundation of their wealth and status relied on their fiefs, the Neapolitan aristocrats' attitude to land was somewhat different from that of other aristocracies. Though more profitable than feudal land, allodial land, due to its easy marketability, was treated like all other non-feudal assets and readily sold in moments of need in order to preserve the fiefs; in fact the Neapolitan aristocracy seems to have owned relatively little allodial land outside its fiefs. The Caracciolo Brienza, for instance, had no large property in or near Naples, other than what they received through entails, until the later seventeenth century.[21]

As we have seen, the Caracciolo Brienza, after the first two generations, were no longer interested in expanding their feudal patrimony. They invested what they inherited and their profits from the fiefs, not only in raising the value of the fiefs through purchases of additional jurisdictions and allodial property within them, but in various other ways. In general we can divide the elements of the family patrimony other than the fiefs in three main groups. First, real estate in the city of Naples and elsewhere was bought or inherited. Second, several members of the family had credit on individuals and on the government. Lastly, the family also owned luxury items, such as paintings, jewels, or furniture, that could be considered a form of investment. Acquisition and ownership of all of these were constant features of the family's economic history. With the exception of a few entailed properties, however, all of these assets were readily marketable and therefore were easily sold in times of crisis. Moreover, the desire to preserve the family's feudal patrimony intact resulted in the use of these other assets whenever a dowry or a cadet's portion had to be paid.

Allodial real estate

Members of the Caracciolo clan had owned real estate in Naples and the neighboring territory since the tenth century, and ownership of property in the city was one of the early requirements for membership in the *Seggi*. The Neapolitan aristocracy in general had a peculiarly detached attitude towards ownership of palaces in the capital. Gérard Labrot has shown the lack of

[20] T. Caracciolo, *Nobilitatis Neapolitanae Defensio* in L. A. Muratori, ed. *Rerum Italicarum Scriptores*, new edit. by G. Carducci, V. Fiorini, and P. Fedele, vol. XXII, I (Bologna, 1935), pp. 141–48; Machiavelli's criticism in *Discourses*, I, 55; G. B. de Luca, *Il cavaliere e la dama* (Rome, 1675); A. Dominguez Ortiz, *La sociedad española en el siglo XVII*, I (Madrid, 1963); on this issue, see also G. Vitale, "Modelli culturali nobiliari a Napoli tra Quattro e Cinquecento" *ASPN* 105 (1987), pp. 27–103, especially pp. 64–67, 75–83, and 93–103 (on how theorists argued that the aristocracy should closely follow the management of its lands).

[21] Within the fiefs, of course, the aristocracy did own allodial land. To a certain extent, the Piedmontese aristocracy also tried to preserve its ancestral land by selling separated plots, but the reason for this was more economic than legal, see Woolf, *Studi*, pp. 138–41.

personal of familial attachment to a specific palace, evidenced by the frequent moves from one palace to another and by the widespread renting of other families' palaces, as well as by the rarity of any decided personal intervention on the part of individual aristocrats in the architectural structure or the interior decoration of the palaces they occupied. Families were, originally at least, tied to residence in specific areas of the city, and some families became associated with specific palaces – which were at times the object of entails. Neapolitan aristrocrats, however, did not share the frenzied passion of, for instance, the Uzeda to impress their individual decisions on their palaces. Unlike Florentine patricians, they rarely found in the construction, ownership, or arranging of palaces ways of asserting either their individual personality or their sense of lineage. They were also far from the English peers' careful use of urban real estate as a profitable form of investment. This relative detachment may also be explained by the continuing importance of residence in the fiefs.[22]

The example of the Caracciolo Brienza supports Labrot's view, at least for the later period. Ascanio Caracciolo received in 1550 from his uncle Cesare in entail and primogeniture a palace near the church of San Giovanni a Carbonara, in the district of Capuana traditionally associated with the Caracciolo clan. Ascanio spent about 4,000 ducats, probably more than the value of the palace at the time, in repairs before moving in with his family. The palace was not very large and it was probably used as the family's residence for almost a century. In 1644, however, Carlo Caracciolo Sant'Eramo rented it to the Caracciolo college for 300 ducats a year. The palace then passed to the Caracciolo Brienza, and it was never again used by the family itself. In 1690 its value was assessed at 5,000 ducats. Very little work was done on the palace during most of the seventeenth century, and in the eighteenth century several repairs were necessary. In 1710 the rent was at 250 ducats, a decrease of sixteen percent in sixty-five years. Litterio Caracciolo had to pay regularly for repairs and, in 1781, he was able to break the entail and sell the palace for 15,550 ducats, which represented three times the value of the palace a century earlier. The repairs, but especially the increase in population and the high inflation rate of the later eighteenth century, explain the rapid increase in value.[23]

[22] G. Labrot, *Baroni in città. Residenze e comportamenti dell'aristocrazia napoletana, 1530–1734* (Naples, 1979); Labrot, "Un esempio di strategie artistica: il palazzo del nobile napoletano", paper presented at Villa Pignatelli in Naples on 12 January 1978; Labrot and R. Ruotolo, "Pour une étude historique de la commande aristocratique dans le royaume de Naples espagnol" *Revue Historique* 104, no. 264 (1980), pp. 25–48. For Florence, see R. A. Goldthwaite, "The 'Empire of Things': Consumer Demand in Renaissance Italy" in F. W. Kent, and P. Simons, with J. C. Eade, eds. *Patronage, Art and Society in Renaissance Italy* (Canberra–Oxford, 1987), pp. 153–75; on the great expansion of aristocratic building in Genoa, see G. Doria, "Investimenti della nobiltà genovese nell'edilizia di prestigio (1530–1630)" *Studi storici* 27 (1986), pp. 5–55; English examples in L. Stone, *Family and Fortune* (Oxford, 1973). (The Uzeda are the Sicilian aristocratic family of Federico De Roberto's *I Viceré*.) On the palaces of Naples, see also the classic L. Catalani, *I palazzi di Napoli* (Naples, 1845; new edit. 1979).

[23] ACB 5.1.

The first line of the marquis of Brienza, on the other hand, had no ancestral residence in Naples. A large house with garden near the church of Santi Apostoli, only a few blocks from San Giovanni a Carbonara, was inherited by the marquis Giovan Battista from an uncle in the late sixteenth century, but he sold it in 1606 to the neighboring Theatine monastery for 9,000 ducats. Comparison of this sale with the almost simultaneous building of a baronial palace in Atena shows how the Caracciolo Brienza gave priority to residence in their fiefs. Giovan Battista and Giacomo Caracciolo never lived in Naples for any length of time. Their respective wife and mother Diana, however, bought a house in the 1620s, after Giovan Battista's death, again near the church of Santi Apostoli, for 5,000 ducats. She lived there until her death in 1649, while her son Giuseppe, at least at the time of the Masaniello revolt, lived near the viceroyal palace in the neighborhood called Pizzofalcone; this area had experienced a new growth in the late sixteenth century after being included in the new walls built under Viceroy Toledo, and especially after the building nearby of the new viceroyal palace in the early seventeenth century. Giuseppe, a single man, probably rented quarters, and Diana's house was probably rented at her death. The house was valued at 4,500 ducats in 1653, and Giuseppe II sold it in 1701 for 4,300 ducats to the Congregation of the Souls of Purgatory.[24]

In 1658, Giuseppe's sister and heir Faustina, who was prominent in court life and had already lived with her brother in Naples since 1650, bought a large palace with garden in Pizzofalcone from the neighboring Theatine monastery of Santa Maria degli Angeli for 7,500 ducats, roughly the average price for a palace in that area. Although the palace remained in the family until its extinction, Faustina was the only one to use it regularly. As we shall see in a later chapter, the family resided in Naples only at specific moments in its life-cycle, namely when children were of marriageable age. Otherwise the palace was rented out, even in the later eighteenth century when the family alternated every two or three years between residence in Naples and in the fiefs. In most years all three main apartments, as well as the several ground floor spaces, were rented separately. Giuseppe II's mother, Cristina, held the palace in usufruct as a payment for her dowry. She used it personally for a time around 1700 but did not live there during her entire widowhood, retiring in her later years to the convent of Suor Orsola Benincasa. In 1689 the palace was rented for 470 ducats, and in 1717 for 500 ducats. As with the palace at Carbonara, only necessary maintenance expenses were made, including ducats 2,417.1.05 spent in the 1670s for supports and bricklaying. In the mid-eighteenth century, the marquis Litterio paid for extensive repairs. At no time – it seems – did the repairs involve any

24 ACB 5.3; G. Ceci, "Pizzofalcone," *Napoli nobilissima* I (1892), pp. 60–62, 85–89, 105–9, and 129–33; on the development of Pizzofalcone, see also C. de Seta, *Napoli* (Bari, 1981), pp. 145–48. The barons' residence in the fiefs is discussed in chapter 4. The 1653 assessment is in ASN Pandetta Corrente 570, vol. marked 4, fols. 29r–33r; the 1701 sale in *ibid.*, vol. marked 2, fols. 57r–58r.

extensive remodeling or changes. In 1749–53, two of the main apartments were rented for 300 ducats each, and in 1808 the revenues of the entire palace were valued for fiscal purposes at 975 ducats a year.[25]

The Caracciolo Brienza owned other allodial real estate that in general they rented out or, when legally possible, used to pay cadets' portions. At his death in 1536, Cardinal Marino Caracciolo made a long series of bequests including an entail worth 300 ducats a year to his nephew Ascanio. Marino's heir and executors invested most of the estate in land, and by the late sixteenth century, Ascanio's son Giovan Battista owned four plots of land for a total of eighty-eight *tomoli* in Pomigliano d'Arco and S. Anastasia, in the fertile plain to the northeast of Naples. These *masserie* (farms) were entailed to all males descended from Ascanio, and therefore passed to Domenico I who became marquis of Brienza in 1658. The farms seem to have been always rented out on short-term leases (three years), though documentation is scarce. In 1643 two of the farms were rented for thirty *tomoli* of wheat a year.

At the end of the seventeenth and in the first years of the eighteenth century, the tenants and the marquis cooperated in planting poplars in the farms as supports for vines. This was the only significant capital investment in production documented for any property of the Caracciolo Brienza. As we shall see in the next chapter, the agricultural characteristics of its lands, the traditionalism inherent in feudal landownership, and the desire to limit expenses and risks prevented the family from any such investments in its other properties. The fertility of these farms and their proximity to Naples – which ensured an easy market for products and rising prices for the land – explain the investment in the *masserie*. In the 1690s, the rent was between ten and twenty ducats a year for each farm, though in some years the total rent was paid in wheat or in part of the vintage. Between 1688 and 1703 the rent doubled from forty to eighty ducats a year, thanks no doubt also to the new crops and to a well which cost the marquis forty-five ducats. In 1709 the rent was up to 100 ducats. Since the entail was not in primogeniture, beginning in 1681 the revenues were shared between

[25] ACB 5.2; 10.2.4 and throughout (Cristina moved to Suor Orsola in 1706); 23, fol. 28v (the 1689 rent); 23 contains several examples of rents for the ground floor spaces of the palace in the 1680s and 1690s; 14.1.6 on Faustina; the 1670s repairs in Pandetta Corrente, 570, vol. marked 3, fols. 277r–296r. Examples of other rents in Labrot, "Le comportement collectif de l'aristocratie napolitaine du seizième au dix-huitième siècle" *Revue historique* 101, no. 258 (1977), pp. 50–51; the prices of palaces in the area are discussed in Labrot, "Naissance et croissance d'un quartier de Naples: Pizzofalcone 1530–1689" *Urbi* 1 (1979), 47–66 (Faustina was, however, buying soon after the plague); the Theatines of Santa Maria degli Angeli had been in poor financial shape a few years earlier, see M. Campanelli, "Note sul patrimonio dei Teatini in Italia alla vigilia dell'inchiesta innocenziana" in Galasso and Russo, eds. *Per la storia sociale e religiosa del Mezzogiorno d'Italia* (2 vols.; Naples, 1980–82), I, pp. 201–2. The Piedmontese, Sicilian, and French aristocracies also rented their palaces in the capital: see Woolf, *Studi*, p. 145; Forster, *The House of Saulx-Tavanes. Versailles and Burgundy, 1700–1830* (Baltimore, 1971), p. 145; Aymard, "Une famille de l'aristocratie sicilienne aux XVIe et XVIIe siècles: les ducs de Terranova, un bel example d'ascension seigneuriale" *Revue Historique* 96, no. 247 (1972), pp. 29–66, p. 53.

Giuseppe II and his brother Giovan Battista. Though the farms seem to have been managed in common by the brothers, after Giuseppe's death they were administered separately.[26]

Following an attempt to expand their feudal patrimony in the late sixteenth century, the Caracciolo Brienza bought allodial property in towns near their feudal *stato*, which they rented out. The rents remained stable in the seventeenth century and increased considerably after that. When the *università* of Sala in 1579 repurchased its domanial status, it incurred debts that Giovan Battista Caracciolo later acquired. In 1621, Marco Antonio II had a credit of more than 12,000 ducats towards Sala, and a royal tribunal awarded him *tomoli* 1,076.1.1+1/3 of *difese* (enclosed lands) which produced revenues, through rents, of ducats 459.-.17½ a year. In 1625, the rents of the *difese* ascended to ducats 462.2.19+2/3, and other plots of land in Sala worth a total of 2,210 ducats also belonged to the Caracciolo Brienza. In 1623, the marquis Giacomo gave the *difese* in Sala to his brother Giuseppe in payment of the 15,000 ducats their father had bequeathed him. Between 1645 and 1653 Giuseppe rented the *difese* for 480 ducats a year. In 1681, Domenico I left the *difese* to his second son Giovan Battista to cover his portion, and after a long litigation the *difese* were finally awarded to the cadet branch. In 1723–26 the rent was 700 ducats a year (plus one cantaro of "good *caciocavallo*"). The *difese*, and a new palace in Sala, were rented for 1,400 ducats in 1774. Giovan Battista and Marco Antonio II also owned 1,017 *tomoli* of land open to pastures and some vines in Montepeloso, near the family fiefs, which were probably sold in the 1620s.[27]

The Caracciolo Brienza did not own any other real estate in the kingdom of Naples. In 1722, however, through the marriage of Domenico II to Imara Ruffo, they acquired revenues and property in Messina. Besides credit on the city of Messina and liquid assets, Imara's dowry consisted in two palaces with garden and orchard, an apartment, a deteriorating building, and some land planted with olives, vines, and mulberry trees. The dowry also included 1,308 animals (pigs, goats, sheep, cows) for a value of 1,826 ducats. The marriage contract also assessed what the revenues had been in the recent past and their current value. Although probably exaggerated, the figures for the earlier period highlight the dramatic economic decline that hit Messina as a consequence of its failed anti-Spanish revolt in the 1670s, and of the rapid changes in government during and after the War of the Spanish Succession. The net annual revenues of the Ruffo real estate in the past had, in fact, been as high as ducats 2,790.-.10, while

[26] Marino's will in ACB 4.1.2; for the farms, see 6.1.1–9.
[27] For the *difese*, see ACB 89.3.3, 8, 12, 17, 19, and 20; 43.3.1; 163, unnumbered fol. In the years 1625–34, the *università* of Sala also levied a special ten percent tax on its citizens' revenues and assigned its yield to Giacomo Caracciolo, who rented it out for 1,530 ducats in 1628 and 1,800 in 1633 (ACB 89.3.9). In 1573, the family owned a few shops, the value of which was assessed at 1,900 ducats with rents of ducats 114.4.14 a year. The document (ACB 9.8) does not specify the location of these shops.

at the date of the marriage they were assessed at ducats 544.3.08, representing a decline of eighty percent in less than fifty years. The Caracciolo Brienza kept these properties, and in the eighteenth century they entrusted them to an agent residing in Messina. In 1755, the annual revenues from Messina were ducats 686.2.14.[28]

Because of the importance of ownership of fiefs to the identity of Neapolitan aristocratic families, they showed a relatively limited interest in allodial real estate outside of the fiefs. A feudal family was unlikely to buy much land in other families' fiefs, and there were few royal towns in the kingdom. Aristocratic allodial real estate was therefore concentrated in or near Naples; in particular aristocratic palaces were often rented out, in separate apartments or as a whole, whenever the family did not need to reside in the capital. Unless protected by entails, allodial real estate, like all non-feudal assets, was easily and often used to meet extraordinary expenses or to pay debts.

Credit

Loans, to the government and to individuals, represented a second form of non-feudal investment open to the aristocracy. Since most of the documentation is related to lawsuits, it is likely that short-lived investments may be unrecorded, and the largest part of the family archive consists of documents pertaining to the feudal patrimony. This bias in the evidence is particularly strong for the earlier history of the family, since gathering and preservation of documents only began in the late seventeenth century, and for liquid assets, for which only scattered information is available. Moreover, the available information refers most often only to the moment of sale, which was likely to take place in order to pay a debt or divide an inheritance, rather than to the purchase of the revenues or assets. These investments were also more likely to be made by secondary members of the family – mothers, brothers, sisters – rather than by the marquis themselves, and this too is a reason for underrecording in the family archive. With these limitations, it is nonetheless possible to piece together some of the investment activities of the Caracciolo Brienza.

The sixteenth century was a period of economic growth for the kingdom of Naples. As the population grew, agriculture and trade expanded and the fiscal burden was not yet increasing much in real terms. Capital was sought by individuals and institutions alike, and in fact there were many private banks and financiers in Naples until the years around 1600. In general, interest rates in Naples remained high longer than in Northern Italy, because of Naples' integration with the Spanish economy and of the government's poor monetary policies. Interest on loans was around ten percent in the second half of the

---

[28] ACB 3.2.15 for the marriage contract; 18 contains documents referring to the Messina properties; 25, fols. 43r–44v, for the 1755 figure.

sixteenth century, and may at times have been higher. Considering that, as we have seen, fiefs were at this time supposed to yield revenues equal to four to four and a half per cent of their price, it is clear that, while fiefs provided a secure and prestigious investment with important collateral benefits, diversification of investments was desirable and necessary to the aristocracy. In the second half of the sixteenth century, indeed, many investors turned their resources to liquid assets rather than land. The aristocracy invested in shares of the public debt and in government offices, as we shall see in a later chapter, as much as any other social group in the kingdom. It also lent money to towns and villages and to private individuals, both to other aristocrats and to commoners. In Naples, as in other parts of Italy, loans took the form of sales of annuities, guaranteed on real estate, in order to circumvent the canonical ban on interest.[29]

The estate of Marco Antonio I (d. 1573) included several annuities, inherited in large part from his mother, Ippolita Filomarino. Most of these were loans to other aristocrats guaranteed on part of their revenues. Ippolita had invested 37,000 ducats at nine percent on the feudal patrimonies of the dukes of Seminara and Maddaloni and of the marquis of Castellaneta, but these had already been sold by her son's death. 4,000 ducats were represented by a loan guaranteed on the *bagliva* of Marsico Nuovo at nine and a half percent and 11,000 ducats by a loan to the prince of Bisignano at nine percent guaranteed on the silk tax of Calabria. Ducats 4,333.3.10 were invested at nine percent with the royal government in taxes on the family's fiefs of Brienza and Salvia. The duchess of Castrovillari owed 15,000 ducats to the Caracciolo Brienza, but at least for ten years no payment had been received for this loan. Finally, the Caracciolo Brienza owned half of the *mastrodattia* of the city of Taranto, which gave a revenue of 128 ducats a year, capitalized at a six percent rate at 2,133 ducats.[30]

These investments, in addition to the fiefs and the other assets, certainly represented a considerable estate. Already at this date, however, the patrimony was burdened with heavy debts, and most, if not all, of these annuities had to be sold in the following years. Moreover, in this generation the family was quite large and several dowries and portions had to be paid. Giovan Battista Caracciolo's investments seem to have been limited to purchases of allodial land within the fiefs and to the building of the palace in Atena. As we have seen, he had to sell Diano and his house in Naples. In 1608, the government also confiscated and sold the *mastrodattia* of Taranto for 14,000 ducats to pay some of Giovan Battista's debts. Until the later seventeenth century, the marquis themselves rarely owned any annuities, as the feudal part of the patrimony itself

---

[29] De Rosa, *Mezzogiorno*; Galasso, *Economia*, pp. 366–76; C. M. Cipolla, "Note sulla storia del saggio d'interesse" *Economia internazionale* 5 (1957), pp. 255–74. Most of the credits and debts of the Caracciolo Brienza until the early seventeenth century were contracted at an interest of nine or ten percent. For interest rates, see Woolf, *Studi*, pp. 35–39, and 50–53.

[30] ACB 9.8; 74.1.1 and ASN Petizioni Relevi 32, fols. 1r–5v (1572) discuss Ippolita's estate.

was under attack by the family's many creditors. The only asset of this kind documented is the *mastrodattia* of the town of Sala, which in 1625 was valued at 5,000 ducats. It was confiscated with Brienza and Pietrafesa in the 1620s. In 1696 it was eventually redeemed by Giuseppe II, but its value was reduced to 500 ducats. In the eighteenth century, the Caracciolo Brienza rented it out and the rent grew from eighteen ducats in 1747 to forty in 1783 and sixty in 1789 as the town's population increased.[31]

Other members of the family, however, had free use of their money, in particular women and cadet sons. In particular there are records for the economic activities of the widows of the family, who administered their dowries and any other wealth they may have had. The protection the laws offered to dowries probably was the main reason why women tended to invest in loans to individuals and institutions, which not only gave a high yield but were relatively easy to sell or reclaim. Diana Caracciolo, for example, between 1614 and 1647 lent money for ducats 23,260.4.-- to fifteen borrowers at interest rates varying mostly from six and a half to nine percent. Eight of the fifteen loans went to other titled aristocrats, three to the government in exchange for shares of the fiscal revenues, two to untitled women, one to a bank in Naples, and one to the dowry fund of the Caracciolo clan. In the same years, Diana borrowed 4,560 ducats at interest rates between seven and nine percent. Diana's granddaughter, Cristina, also lent money to other aristocrats, though not on such a large scale. Although some of these loans were never entirely repaid, the high interest rates provided Diana with considerable profits. Many of her loans were still open at her death, and it is likely that they were quickly liquidated by her heirs.[32]

The portions of cadet sons were also often paid in annuities. Carlo Caracciolo Sant'Eramo, for instance, owned numerous annuities he had inherited from his mother, Porzia Carafa. As we have seen, in the later seventeenth century his patrimony was joined through his son Domenico I to the marquis of Brienza's. In 1681, Carlo's annuities were assessed at a capital value of ducats 19,187.4.05, though the larger part of this sum was by then impossible to reclaim. The Caracciolo Brienza used these claims to pay some of their own debts, and in particular in the 1710s Giuseppe II assigned portions of these annuities to his daughters as parts of their dowries. A capital of 1,200 ducats on the tax farm of the *zecca* was given to Domenico I's daughter, Faustina, as part of her dowry in 1683. Giuseppe II also inherited his grandfather's credit of ducats 2,997.4.10 on the tax on the silk of Calabria. This credit had a nominal yield of ducats 209.4.05

---

[31] Aristocratic loans to the government will be more closely analyzed in chapter 6. For Sala, see ACB 43.3.1 and 89.1.1–9. The *mastrodattia* of Taranto had yielded an annual rent of 700 ducats around 1600, ASN notai del '600, 508/14, Giuseppe Ragucci, 1681, fols. 42r–53r; ACB 43.2.5; 17.1; 133.2, fols. 120r–21r; 45.7.2.

[32] ACB 22 is Diana's account book; Cristina's is ACB 23. The importance of women's economic position for the family patrimony is discussed in chapter 5. Aristocratic women invested their money in loans also in France, see Forster, *Toulouse*, chapter 5.

a year at seven percent since the original purchase of 1620. By the eighteenth century, however, the yield had considerably decreased, and in 1724 Domenico II sold the credit and all his claims to the Monte Ciarletta for ducats 1,049.1.10, or thirty-five percent of the original value.[33]

Also in the eighteenth century, Teresa Pinto, wife of Giuseppe II, owned a large fortune consisting mainly in annuities. Her large dowry, as we have seen, enabled the Caracciolo Brienza to repurchase their fiefs at the end of the seventeenth century. Over 12,000 ducats of Teresa's dowry (about twenty-five percent) was represented by annuities on several tax-farms (*arrendamenti*). Teresa managed these annuities and lent additional money to the government, the city of Naples, and individual borrowers, usually at an interest of four percent, which was customary in the early eighteenth century. At her death in 1755 her estate passed to the marquis Litterio, who continued to manage her annuities, though he seems to have engaged very rarely in new loans of any sort. In 1770, however, Litterio was the first and only Caracciolo Brienza ever to invest in a commercial and financial company. His were 10,000 of the total 114,200 ducats collected by the company directed by Michele Pignatelli, which was to engage in the sale and purchase of staples and in money exchange. Membership was limited to the aristocracy, and two percent of the profits were to pay for Masses for the Souls of Purgatory. Nothing is known of the company's specific activities, except that they were very short-lived.[34]

Money-lending activities were very common in Naples throughout the early modern period, and they could offer higher yields than real estate. Though loans to individuals might prove risky, loans to the government, especially if guaranteed on tax-farms, were relatively secure and easily marketable. The Neapolitan aristocracy in the late sixteenth and seventeenth centuries was often heavily in debt, and the Caracciolo Brienza were no exception. Though we do not know enough about the aristocracy's creditors, it seems that often they were other aristocrats. Since aristocratic dowries and portions were often paid in annuities and other non-feudal assets, and annuities were a convenient way for aristocratic women and cadets to invest their wealth, it is likely that they may often have been the main creditors of the titled members of their families. The example of the Caracciolo Brienza, and the few other known examples, would support this hypothesis.[35]

---

[33] ACB 16.8c and 8d; 17.4; 11.2.5 (nos. 4 and 7); 3.2.9, 11, and 14 (the marriage contracts of Giuseppe II's daughters); 89.3.17 for Faustina; 6.3.1–10 for the credit on the Calabrian *gabella*.

[34] On Teresa, see 6.2 and 6.4; 8.91, 110, and 111 on Litterio's management of her annuities; on the company, see 16.6.

[35] A. Placanica, *Moneta, prestiti, usure nel Mezzogiorno moderno* (Naples, 1982); Galasso, *Economia*, pp. 366–76; M. A. Visceglia, "Formazione e dissoluzione di un patrimonio aristocratico: la famiglia Muscettola tra XVI e XIX secolo" *MEFRM* 92 (1980), pp. 555–624; in 1590, 135,000 of the 170,000 ducats of Vespasiano Carafa's debts were owed to other titled aristocrats, see Caridi, *Uno stato*, p. 44; there was a similar situation in France, see Forster, *Toulouse*, chapter 5. Usually sources are fragmentary and haphazard on the debts, see footnote 48.

Other assets

The third possible use the aristocracy had for its money was the acquisition of luxury items. Aristocratic collecting of art has for a long time been a subject of research for Neapolitan scholars. In recent years, with the growing attention, also outside of Naples, to Neapolitan painting of the seventeenth and eighteenth centuries, the amount and the quality of this research has increased. Most of the resulting articles have, however, been primarily interested in attributions of paintings or in identifying the passage of paintings from one collection to another. Gérard Labrot, though, has analyzed more closely the cultural significance of collecting for the aristocracy, and has included in his observation artistic objects other than paintings. In his view, the Neapolitan aristocracy's attitude to art matched its behavior towards its palaces. Paintings and other art objects became, in the seventeenth century, things one had to have, and they replaced wall curtains in the decoration of rooms. But very rarely did an aristocratic collection express an individual's personality and taste, and in most cases paintings served a purely decorative function, their value being expressed rather by their size than by their quality. "Paintings" – Labrot has written – "were less a chosen than an imposed object."[36]

Paintings, furniture, and other objects will be here considered, in the sketchy way the documentation allows, primarily as a form of investment, but the example of the Caracciolo Brienza seems fully to confirm Labrot's point of view. The inventories list paintings without mentioning either authors or values, but emphasizing sizes and frames, especially if gilded, and whenever the room distribution is given the impression is of a haphazard gathering rather than a conscious personal choice. Art objects, like any furniture, were given away in dowries, pawned if need be, dispersed in various ways, and often kept in poor condition. Other than Litterio Caracciolo's indulgence in jewelry in the late eighteenth century, no member of the family ever showed personal interest in, or understanding of, art.

The relative absence in Naples of strong individualism or personality in aristocratic patronage of art, the emphasis on ownership of art objects as a familial or even collective endeavor – something the whole aristocracy does primarily because of cultural influences originating in other countries – may perhaps be ascribed also to the different origins and character of the Neapolitan aristocracy compared to Northern Italian, especially Tuscan, patricians; the

---

[36] Labrot and Ruotolo, "Commande," p. 27; see also Labrot's already cited works and his "Images, tableaux et statuaire dans les testaments napolitains" *Revue Historique* 106, no. 268 (1982), pp. 131–66. Labrot rejects Haskell's interpretation and method to look at collecting and collections as expressions of individualism. The journal *Napoli nobilissima* has published since its beginnings many articles based on inventories of palaces. On these issues, see also A. Manikowski, "Aspetti economici del mecenatismo di una famiglia aristocratica fiorentina nel XVII secolo" *Ricerche storiche* 16 (1986), pp. 81–94.

Neapolitan aristocracy's position in society was ensured by long traditions, and its preeminence was less threatened and less in need of legitimation. Their majestic palaces, as Labrot has observed, certainly represented an ideological statement of supremacy, but they did so by pointing to the aristocracy's great wealth and by expressing its power and arrogance rather than its superior culture and sophistication.[37]

Though the inventories rarely assess furniture or art objects, they provide information on their quantity and condition that helps gauge the amount of money the family had available for these expenses.[38] The surviving inventories also allow us to date the passage from curtains to paintings as the main form of room decoration, and to confirm the family's continued attention to their residences in the fiefs. Although the 1584 division of Marco Antonio I's estate mentions furniture and jewels, it provides no detailed information about them. The contemporary inventory of the Loffredo lords of Amendolara also shows much furniture, silver, and other objects but no paintings in the feudal castle. In 1622, the inventory of the estate of Marco Antonio II lists in detail, without assigning values, the very numerous *paramenti di camera* (room ornaments) in several colors of damask and other valuable cloths, and the varied furniture contained in the castle of Brienza. This included over 290 pounds of silver, which, if we assume a value of fifteen ducats per pound (current a century later), were worth 4,350 ducats. Many of these objects are identified as new, testifying to the attention given to the feudal residence and to recent heavy expenses in furnishing it. In contrast to this, the estate in Naples included mostly old pieces of furniture, some linen and clothes, and a few jewels. In 1644, Diana Caracciolo had furniture, linen, and jewels, but no paintings, both in Naples and in Atena. In 1651, a list was drawn of all objects left by the marquis Giacomo in the castle of Brienza, most of which were described as very old, but no value was given. No paintings were listed.[39]

Liquid assets were also often used to meet financial difficulties. Carlo Caracciolo's furniture was sold after his death in 1649 to pay for his funeral and his family's rent. The assessment of Faustina's estate, drawn at her death in 1673, offers the earliest available data about the value of these objects. The

[37] *Ibid.*
[38] No inventory I found for the Caracciolo Brienza until the later years of the eighteenth century ever mentions any books, with the exception of a few administrative papers. Inventories of books were also rare for other families, and indeed infrequent even in upper-middle-class families in the late nineteenth century, see Macry, *Ottocento*, pp. 108–24.
[39] ACB 9.8 for 1584; for the Loffredo inventory see Galasso, "Cultura materiale e vita nobiliare in un inventario calabrese del '500" in Galasso, *L'altra Europa, per un'antropologia storica del Mezzogiorno d'Italia* (Milan, 1982), pp. 284–311. Marco Antonio II's inventory in ASN notai del '600, 839/8, Fulgenzio Gagliardo, fols. 95rff.; an almost identical inventory for the estate of Marco Antonio's father Giovan Battista, drawn in 1620, is in ACB App. 22, unnumbered fol.; it specifies that the goods in Naples were kept in the house of Giovan Battista's mother, Giulia. For Diana, see ACB 12.3.6; for Giacomo, see ASN Pandetta Corrente 570, vol. marked 3, fols. 146r–53r.

furniture in her palace at Pizzofalcone including linen was assessed at a total of 2,332 ducats. Several of these pieces, however, for a value of ducats 1,649.1.10, were pawned. Her silver was valued at ducats 555.3.02. Though she still had many *paramenti*, the palace also contained 214 paintings, which were assessed by the painter Andrea Malinconico at a total value of 613 ducats. A complete list of all her belongings in the palace was drawn but without assigning values. By the following generation the *paramenti*, though still mentioned in the inventories, were almost always in a state of disrepair, while we find paintings also in the residences in the fiefs. We can also see the decline of the Caracciolo Brienza wealth in the scarcity of jewelry and in the poor condition of much of the furniture. In 1681, Domenico I's belongings in the castle of Brienza comprised much furniture, including twenty paintings, but little silver. Some of the furniture was old or broken, and one room's *paramenti* of turquoise damask were pawned for 600 ducats.[40]

In the eighteenth century, the family had more money to spend on furniture and art objects. When in 1722 Domenico II married Imara Ruffo, part of her dowry consisted in these assets. Furniture, mostly *paramenti*, was worth 1,251 ducats, the silver weighed seventy-seven pounds for a value of 1,155 ducats, and Imara also owned eighty-two "paintings by good authors" which, together with other unspecified objects, were valued at 7,800 ducats. Her mother added to the dowry 600 ducats in jewels, twelve chairs worth 250 ducats, and a complete bedroom set in damask worth 960 ducats. Domenico's mother presented the couple with jewels worth ducats 1,065.2.--. Four years later, at Domenico's death, there were several paintings and much furniture in the castle of Brienza. When Imara's mother died in 1758, her grandson inherited the furniture and paintings she kept, both in her apartment in the Caracciolo Brienza palace in Naples, and in her villa in her fief of Melito.[41]

During the long life of the marquis Litterio, the Caracciolo Brienza's economic recovery brought renewed attention to all parts of the patrimony. As we have seen, the two palaces in Naples underwent extensive repairs. Similarly, inventories of the 1770s and 1780s show furniture in good condition and very numerous paintings in the castle of Brienza and in the palaces of Atena and even Pietrafesa. Litterio had a particular taste for jewels, and he bought many from Neapolitan goldsmiths. In 1773 he owned jewels worth ducats 14,087.3.04, gold worth 2,002 ducats, and 496 pounds of silver worth ducats 8,045.1.10. Although

---

[40] For Carlo, see ACB 137.16, fols. 17r–29v; for Faustina, ACB 14.1.11 and ASN Pandetta Corrente 570, vol. marked 2, fols. 410v–23v (vol. marked 3 has slightly different figures for the values of furniture and silver); for Domenico, ASN notai del '600, 398/27, Antonio Crispo, 1682, unnumbered fols. between 91v and 93r; ACB App. 22 unnumbered fol. The Alberti marquis of Pentidattilo had 210 paintings in their feudal palace in 1686, ACB 19.47. The high cost of *paramenti* compared to paintings may help explain the shift in room decoration in the seventeenth century; for a French parallel see Dewald, *Formation*, p. 225.

[41] ACB 3.2.15; 6.4.4–5; 16.8i; 4.1.57.

paramenti had by now almost disappeared from the residences – or at least from the inventories – the paintings were still seen as decorative objects, the value of which was not in their quality but in their function as ornaments, and therefore might decrease with time. In the 1780s, in an assessment of his properties, Litterio set the value of the paintings "of good authors," which had been part of his mother's dowry, at only about 800 ducats, as they were "almost all worn by use."[42]

Whatever the personal pleasure the Caracciolo Brienza took, or failed to take, in the objects with which they surrounded themselves, and whatever the cultural shifts which determined their choices of these objects, paintings and other ornaments seem to have been to them primarily one more form of investment for their revenues. Like annuities, paintings, furniture, and jewels could easily be sold (or pawned); like real estate, if properly managed, they were likely to increase in value. Though they did not produce any regular yield, they, like annuities and real estate, did not require excessive care or management, and they did not in any way violate Neapolitan society's code of what an aristocratic family could properly do with its money. All of these different assets, therefore, were ideal complements to an aristocratic family's fiefs and the example of the Caracciolo Brienza shows how this more "elastic" part of the aristocratic patrimony provided them with a buffer which served to protect their feudal possessions.

EVOLUTION OF THE PATRIMONY

As we have seen, allodial real estate, credit, and other assets were sold or pawned by the Caracciolo Brienza to pay for cadets' portions, daughters' and mothers' dowries, or debts, notwithstanding the larger profits these assets could yield compared to the fiefs. The peculiar legal and social status of feudal property, and the laws and customs regulating the transmission of family patrimony, partially explain this behavior. Part of the explanation lies also in the desire to preserve the integrity of the feudal patrimony, and in the awareness that the alienation of any one part of the old family fiefs would greatly diminish the value of the whole *stato*. It is impossible to assess the value of the Caracciolo Brienza patrimony except in a few instances, but the family's economic vicissitudes can be followed through the changes in the proportion of the patrimony represented by the old family fiefs. This will allow us to gauge the impact of the economic difficulties of the

---

[42] ACB 161 unnumbered fol. (an inventory of the palace in Pietrafesa in 1781 is towards the end of the bundle); 162, unnumbered fol. (the same in ACB 33); 35.2 contains the inventory of the castle of Brienza (pp. 1–29) and the palaces in Atena (pp. 43–51) and Naples (pp. 193–268). ACB 8 has purchases of jewels, silver, and gold. The quote is in a document, ACB 161, unnumbered fol. (this depreciation is certainly exaggerated by the marquis in this document, for he is here trying to decrease the value of the part of his patrimony on which his cadets have rights).

seventeenth century on the patrimony as a whole, before turning, in the next chapter, to the specific revenues from the fiefs.

For real estate, the documents in general report assessments of the revenues of each asset and then posit a capitalization rate in order to arrive at a capital value. For fiefs and feudal property in general this rate was four to four and a half percent in the sixteenth and seventeenth centuries, and around three percent in the eighteenth century. Revenues from allodial real estate, both within and outside the fiefs, were capitalized at a rate of six percent in the sixteenth and seventeenth centuries, and of four percent later. The difference was probably due to the prestige attached to feudal property, as well as to the fiscal exemptions and personal privileges and rights it gave its holders. Annuities on individuals, on the government or on other institutions yielded an interest of nine to ten percent in the sixteenth century, and seven to nine percent in the early seventeenth century, but declined to about four percent in the later seventeenth and eighteenth centuries.[43]

In the difficult years of the seventeenth century, the proportion of both the total value of the Caracciolo Brienza patrimony and of the total revenues represented by the fiefs grew considerably as the family sold most other assets to protect the fiefs. The family's interest in a balanced patrimony, however, remained, and with the eighteenth-century recovery the Caracciolo Brienza again acquired several non-feudal assets and actually sold the two Calabrian fiefs they inherited. This diversification must have appeared as a safe policy even when, as in the eighteenth century, the decline of the interest rates made the yield one could obtain from non-feudal assets more or less equal to that of the fiefs.[44]

The first reliable document we have on the patrimony of the Caracciolo Brienza is the already-cited division of Marco Antonio I's estate, drawn in 1584 but referring to the situation in 1573. Here, as in most later documents, the value of animals, furniture, jewels, and silver is not given, and not all the revenues are calculated, but the picture of the patrimony is fairly clear. The total value of the patrimony was ducats 189,426.3.10, with revenues of ducats 9,895.1.19. Of these, 114,060 ducats were represented by the fiefs, yielding revenues, at four percent, of ducats 4,562.2.01, or sixty and forty-six percent respectively of the totals. Allodial real estate not included in the fiefs was worth 1,900 ducats, and yielded ducats 114.4.14 a year at six percent, which represented one percent both of the total value of the estate and of the total revenues. Annuities on individuals, the government, and some communities represented ducats 73,466.3.10 and yielded ducats 5,218.-.04, or thirty-nine and fifty-three percent respectively of

---

[43] Examples in the sources already cited. Similar differences in the capitalization rate of feudal and allodial property were common in Piedmont, see Woolf, *Studi*, pp. 139–40; rates of return on various investments in the papal states are in Reinhardt, *Kardinal Scipione Borghese*, pp. 236–63.

[44] A similar aiming at differentiation can be observed in other families, see Visceglia, "Formazione," and Aymard, "Une famille."

the totals. Though there were already ducats 81,575.4.02 of debts on the patrimony, equivalent to forty-three percent of the total value, it is clear that the family's wealth was still quite secure, since the value of the fiefs was growing, most annuities were safely guaranteed – which can be seen also by their yielding revenues considerably higher than the fiefs' – and more than a fourth of the debts consisted in Marco Antonio's widow's dowry, which would eventually revert to their children. The high percentage of the total revenues coming from assets other than the fiefs, besides showing the health of the patrimony, may also represent a common feature of the patrimonies of new families. The Muscettola Leporano received more than half of their total revenues from tax-farms, annuities, and allodial real estate in 1649, early on in their history, while in the eighteenth century the fiefs yielded always at least seventy percent of the family's revenues.[45]

Their revenues of about 10,000 ducats a year, as we have seen, placed the Caracciolo Brienza among the fifty wealthiest titled families in the kingdom. Their financial situation, however, worsened considerably at the end of the sixteenth century. Two documents from the 1590s listing the fortunes of the wealthiest barons in the kingdom offer a clear picture of the changes in the economic climate. In 1590, the revenues of the marquis of Brienza were assessed at 10,000 ducats a year, with 30,000 ducats of debts, whereas in 1599, though his revenues were set at 21,000 ducats a year (an obvious exaggeration), the debts had increased even more, so that the marquis disposed of only 4,000 ducats a year in free revenues. Similar situations are recorded for several other barons. Recently, historians have brought renewed attention to the economic difficulties of the 1590s in Europe, and certainly in those years the kingdom of Naples experienced a series of bad harvests, widespread social tension, and the beginnings of a severe financial crisis. The census of 1595 also came probably at the peak of the kingdom's demographic expansion, and after that the population stagnated or declined.[46]

Moreover, the marquis Giovan Battista had six siblings and six children for whom to provide. He lived in his fiefs, not only to save on expenses but also to enact an aggressive policy of expansion of his power and wealth there. In 1596, Giovan Battista also bought a credit worth 13,500 ducats on the town of Sala, which had had to borrow money to repurchase itself from the Caracciolo Brienza

---

[45] ACB 9.8; among the credits are calculated 15,000 ducats owed by the duchess of Castrovillari, but no payment was expected on this old loan. The other annuities were all at nine to nine and a half percent interest, except for 2,133 ducats at six percent. For the Muscettola, see Visceglia, "Formazione," Table 3. See Table 2.2, 1584, for a summary of these data.

[46] ASN Doria d'Angri 65/30; G. Ceci, "I feudatari napoletani alla fine del secolo XVI" *ASPN* 24 (1899), pp. 122–38 (direct comparisons are possible for only about two dozen barons); on the 1590s, see P. Burke, "Southern Italy in the 1590s: Hard Times or Crisis?" in P. Clark, ed. *The European Crisis of the 1590s. Essays in Comparative History* (London, 1985), pp. 177–90; Lepre, *Storia*, I, pp. 224–28; on Italy in general, see R. Romano, *Tra due crisi: l'Italia del Rinascimento* (Turin 1982; first edit. 1971), especially pp. 187–206.

in the royal domain in 1579. He built a baronial palace in Atena and purchased many plots of land in the four fiefs. The Caracciolo Brienza, however, lacked the means to sustain this policy of expansion when the general economic situation was declining. Giovan Battista had to sell Diano in 1606, and at his death in 1620 the patrimony was burdened with large debts.[47]

In 1625, the whole patrimony was assessed by a government agent. Again, no consideration was given to the value of furniture or silver, though, as we have seen, the castle of Brienza contained much silver and many valuable tapestries for room decoration. The total value of the patrimony represented by the four fiefs and the properties and rights in Sala was set at ducats 192,678.4.14½, with revenues, if we calculate allodial property at the usual rate of six percent, of ducats 8,322.4.16+1/6. Since the fief of Cancellara inherited from an uncle had been immediately sold to repay debts, the marquis Giocomo had no other assets. If we calculate, however, the net credit and the house his mother owned, the total value of the family's assets was of ducats 211,439.3.14½, with revenues of ducats 9,377.1.17+1/6. Of these, the four fiefs represented ducats 168,968.4.14½ with revenues of ducats 6,786.4.13½, or eighty and seventy-three percent respectively of the totals; the properties in Sala represented eleven percent of the total value and sixteen percent of the revenues, and Diana's assets nine and eleven percent respectively. Although the lack of an assessment for the silver and furniture diminishes the percentage of the total patrimony represented by non-feudal assets, it is evident that the family's economic situation at this point was less florid than fifty years earlier. The patrimony was worth slightly more, but yielded slightly lower revenues and, moreover, non-feudal assets had shrunk considerably, demonstrating the mounting pressure on the Caracciolo Brienza from their creditors.[48]

This early decline was, however, due only partially to the general economic situation of the kingdom. Family problems, like the large number of children and siblings and the successive deaths of Giovan Battista and Marco Antonio II, which entailed two succession taxes in a two-year period, also played a significant role. The value of the fiefs, in fact, increased or remained the same for at least another twenty years, as we have seen, and the family managed to preserve the

[47] ACB 89.3.17; 43.3.1; Giovan Battista's policies in the fiefs will be analyzed in chapters 3 and 4.
[48] ACB 43.3.1; 22. I have posited a six percent yield for allodial property when none was given in the documents. See Table 2.2, 1625, for a summary of these data. Another assessment was made in 1628, but soon discarded as too biased in favor of the marquis. These assessments remain rather abstract since they fail to consider the by now enormous debts weighing on the patrimony. The scarce documentation and the very complex legal repercussions of each debt (which could, for example, burden a specific source of revenue or a specific individual, thereby providing relatively easy leeway for escape or postponement) make it virtually impossible to come to even an approximate picture of absolute values. It is for these reasons that in this chapter, which attempts to show the general structure and evolution of the aristocratic patrimony, the changes in the proportions of feudal and other assets, rather than the absolute value of the patrimony, have been used as the key to an assessment of the Caracciolo Brienza's economic position.

Table 2.3. *Rent of Brienza and Pietrafesa (1620s to 1680s)*
(in ducats)

year	amount
1624–27	4,275
1643	3,200
1646	3,500
1649	3,150
1652	2,850
1660s	2,250
1673	2,300
1680s	2,450

Sources: ASP notai Potenza 235, fols. 9v–10v; ASN Pandetta Corrente 2026, III, fols. 137r–40v, 291r, 542r–v, 632r–33r, and 806r; *ibid.*, IV, fols. 52r, 231r–v; Pandetta Corrente 570, vol. marked 3, fols. 61r–62v. The rents certainly underestimate the actual revenues, but the trend is clear.

integrity of the patrimony. But in the central decades of the century the revolt, the plague, and a series of poor harvests in the 1660s had severe repercussions for the economy of the kingdom as a whole, and for the fortunes of the Caracciolo Brienza in particular.[49]

Brienza and Pietrafesa, under confiscation to pay the creditors, were rented out by the government and the rents, reported in Table 2.3, clearly indicate the decline in revenues. The 1640s already witnessed a decline of about twenty-five percent in the rent compared to twenty years before. After the revolt, which damaged baronial authority and property, and the 1656 plague, with the decrease in population, the rent declined further by more than a third, and it did not increase again until the 1680s, and then only very slowly. The 1660s and early 1670s represented the most difficult moment for the family's fortunes. When Sasso too was confiscated in 1673 only Atena, the least valuable of the fiefs, remained in the Caracciolo Brienza's full property, and even the joining of the family's patrimony with that of Carlo Caracciolo Sant'Eramo did little to alleviate the situation.[50]

It is possible to reconstruct an approximate picture of the patrimony in the years around 1680. If we assume a value of 20,000 ducats for Atena, with revenues at 1,000 ducats, the four fiefs were then worth a total of ducats 142,685.2.07+1/3, with revenues of ducats 6,432.2.19+1/6. The two palaces

---

[49] Chapter 3 analyzes in detail the decline in revenue in the seventeenth century.

[50] Table 2.3. An analysis of the confiscation and renting of the fiefs is in chapter 6. The central decades of the century were the most difficult period for the kingdom, see de Rosa, *Mezzogiorno*, chapters 1 and 7.

in Naples, the properties at Sala, the *masserie* in Pomigliano, the annuities inherited from Carlo Caracciolo Sant'Eramo, and the liquid assets left by Faustina Caracciolo in 1673, were worth a total of 42,022 ducats, but 12,038 ducats represented by two loans were entirely alienated to cover debts. The revenues of all these assets, evaluating the palaces at five percent and the land at six percent as was common at the time, amounted to ducats 1,573.2.05½. The total value of the patrimony was therefore ducats 172,669.2.07+1/3, with revenues of 8,006.-.04+2/3. This represented a decrease of eighteen and fifteen percent respectively compared to fifty years earlier. The four fiefs represented eighty-three and eighty percent respectively of the totals.[51]

The patrimony in the late 1670s, therefore, had declined in value, notwithstanding the merging of the Caracciolo Brienza wealth with that of the descendants of Carlo Caracciolo Sant'Eramo. Moreover, though the family now owned two palaces in Naples and other allodial real estate, and though for the first time it is possible to include the value of furniture and jewels in the assessment of the patrimony, the percentage of the total value represented by the four fiefs was higher than at any previous time. This shows that the new assets were immediately sold or pawned to protect the feudal part of the patrimony. The state of disrepair of the Caracciolo Brienza's residences at Domenico I's death in 1681 is a further manifestation of the decline in the family's economic position. A sample of the bank records in Naples shows a clear decline in the family's involvement in financial activities between the 1620s and the 1680s.[52]

After 1681, the properties in Sala and one of the *masserie*, together with most of the annuities, went to Giuseppe II's younger brother and were therefore lost to the marquis of Brienza. Both Giuseppe II and his son, however, made very good marriages, and a combination of clever and fortunate family policy with a general recovery of the kingdom's economy beginning in the 1680s allowed the Caracciolo Brienza to restore their patrimony on solid foundations. John Marino has emphasized the strengthening of baronial dominance and wealth that accompanied the post-1685 economic recovery, and the example of the Caracciolo Brienza supports his view. At Domenico II's death in 1726 a list was drawn of the revenues from the fiefs. Although buildings are not listed at all, the recovery is clear, as the total value of the four fiefs, capitalizing their revenues at the usual rate of four percent, was of ducats 157,319.2.10, with revenues of 6,294.4.18. Even larger was the growth of the value of other assets of the patrimony. The two palaces in Naples, the *masseria* in Pomigliano, a remaining

---

[51] Sources cited in Table 2.1 and pp. 46–58. See Table 2.2, *c.* 1680. I am not counting the confiscated fief of Montenegro, which was sold by the royal government in 1682 to pay the debts on it. Faustina's furniture and silver gave, of course, no revenue; in calculating their value, I have deducted the pawned pieces. For the *masserie*, I have assumed a six percent capitalization rate, and for the loans, a six percent interest rate. For the capital on the Calabrian silk tax, I have calculated the actual value, equal to thirty-five percent of the nominal one.

[52] The Appendix on sources discusses the Naples bank records and the sample used in this study.

office in Sala, Teresa Pinto's annuities and tax-farms, the properties in Messina, and all the other assets included in Domenico II's wife's dowry, represented a total value of ducats 85,641.1.12 with revenues of 3,399.2.19. The total value of the patrimony was therefore ducats 242,960.4.02 with revenues of 9,694.2.17, with an increase of forty and twenty-one percent respectively in less than fifty years. The four fiefs represented sixty-five percent of the total value and yielded sixty-five percent of the total revenues.[53]

Though the revenues of the Caracciolo Brienza at this point were still only slightly higher than a century before, the fiefs were now free of debts and the patrimony was more varied and secure. Information on prices and salaries is rare for viceroyal Naples, but it is possible to define approximately what revenues of eight to ten thousand ducats a year meant in terms of living standards of the time. At the end of the sixteenth century, income between ten and twenty ducats a year represented the minimum needed for subsistence, and annual income above forty ducats was relatively comfortable. As we have seen, from about 1620 to about 1760 the kingdom experienced limited long-term inflation. From accounts included in the family archive we know that at the end of the seventeenth century the maids of the marquise of Brienza in Naples were paid twelve to twenty-one ducats a year, while her stableboys (*staffieri*) received three ducats a month and the "gentlemen" (*gentiluomini*) in her pay six to eight ducats each month. It is most likely that all these dependents did not have to pay for their lodging, food, and possibly clothing. In the same years the rent of any of the ground-level spaces, presumably one room each with their own entrance (*bassi*), in the family palace in Pizzofalcone was four ducats a year.[54]

In the mid-eighteenth century, the salaries of the marquis' staff ranged from two and a half ducats a month for a wetnurse, to four or five for a page, to seven or eight for a butler, a secretary, or a coachman; a male kitchen help still received only eight *carlini* per month (little more than nine ducats a year). In the 1730s and 1740s, the daily pay of low-skilled farm labor was twenty *grani*, which, if one counts approximately 250 working days a year, would result in a salary of fifty ducats a year. The same pay went to unskilled labor in Naples; a master carpenter or bricklayer, on the other hand, received thirty-five *grani* each day, or eighty-seven and a half ducats a year. The Caracciolo Brienza's revenues of over 9,000 ducats a year in the early eighteenth century would therefore be equal to almost 200 times the living wages at the time. At the end of the century, when a

---

[53] ACB 16.8i for the fiefs, the palaces (the value of which I have obtained by capitalizing the rents at five percent), the *masseria* (at six percent), and the office in Sala (at five percent). I have calculated the value of wheat at eight *carlini* per *tomolo*, barley at four, and maize at six, as was customary in the early eighteenth century in the region of the four fiefs. For Teresa's assets, see ACB 6.2.1–9, and 3.2.7; for Imara, see ACB 3.2.15 (the real estate and the annuities are here capitalized at a four percent rate in the document itself); for Teresa's jewels, see ACB 6.4.5. See Table 2.2, 1726, for a summary of the data. Marino, *Pastoral Economics*, p. 138.

[54] The data for the late sixteenth century is Braudel's, as presented by Marino, *Pastoral Economics*, p. 174; ACB 23, fols. 21v, 22v, 26v, 32v, 33v, 48v, and 57r–70r.

shepherd sometimes could still expect to make only around thirty ducats a year while the aristocracy's revenues had increased noticeably, the Caracciolo Brienza's position would have been still better.[55]

The renewed health of the family patrimony in the eighteenth century is evident from many sources. From the inventories it is clear that the family had now more numerous and more splendid residences than ever before. The fortunate long life of the marquis Litterio, who was an only child and had only four surviving children, helped avoid some of the expenses that had afflicted earlier generations. In the second half of the eighteenth century Litterio, as we have seen, inherited and sold the two fiefs of Pentidattilo and Melito in Calabria and sold the palace at San Giovanni a Carbonara in Naples. With the money resulting from these sales he paid off the remaining family debts. By the end of the century, the Caracciolo Brienza, for example, were the only members of the dowry fund of the *Monte* Ciarletta who did not owe any money to the *Monte*. In his will of 1806, Litterio proudly declared that no debt weighed on his estate, as he established an entail worth 350,000 ducats in favor of his eldest son Cataldo. The value of the patrimony at that point, just before the French conquest of Naples, was well over 400,000 ducats.[56]

Most studies of aristocratic wealth in the kingdom of Naples have concentrated on the fiefs, at best bringing allodial real estate into consideration. This is in large part due to the reliance on fiscal documents such as the *relevi*, which provide data only on feudal property. Only the use of family papers, as in Visceglia's article on the Muscettola, can enable us to reconstruct a global picture of any one aristocratic patrimony and to follow its evolution over time. The aim of this chapter has been to offer such a picture and to analyze the changes in the internal structure of the patrimony in order to follow, through the changes in the proportion of the patrimony represented by the fiefs, the effects of the economic difficulties of the seventeenth century and of the ensuing recovery.

Once a family had acquired a compact group of fiefs, what was called a feudal *stato*, its goal was to ensure its preservation and integrity, and this could best be achieved by differentiating the family's patrimony. Failure to do so jeopardized the solidity of the patrimony as, for example, happened with the Sanseverino princes of Bisignano.[57] The aristocracy, therefore, purchased allodial real estate outside the fiefs, credit on individuals or on the government, and other assets. These offered high and fairly secure profits, and their relatively easy marketability guaranteed the family a means to pay debts, dower daughters, or settle cadets without endangering or diminishing the feudal patrimony. The possibility a

---

[55] ACB 25, fols. 335rff; Romano, *Napoli*, pp. 161–93; Marino, *Pastoral Economics*, p. 316, n. 3, gives data for the later eighteenth century.

[56] ACB App. 7, 8, 9, and 10 for the *Monte*; App. 22, unnumbered fol., and ACB 9.50 for Litterio's will.

[57] Galasso, "Aspetti."

family had to differentiate its wealth was strictly related not only to the general economic situation of the country, but also to the family's own demographic history, as the example of the Caracciolo Brienza shows, and a family's economic circumstances can best be examined through the changes in the proportion of its patrimony and revenues represented by assets other than the fiefs. The more a family had to rely only upon its feudal property and income, which was certainly prestigious but also subject to legal strictures and relatively difficult to market, the less solid and secure its patrimony was. Their overall skillful policy from this point of view helped the Caracciolo Brienza preserve the basis of their wealth through over two centuries, so that at the end of the eighteenth century they were still among the wealthiest aristocratic families of the kingdom.

3

The management of an aristocratic landed patrimony

Loda i gran campi e il piccolo coltiva
(Praise the large fields and cultivate the small).
N. C. Onorati, *Dell'agricoltura practica* (1813) cited by Marino, *Pastoral Economics*, p. 336

Aristocratic wealth has been the object of attention of many historians of early modern Europe, both in general works and in monographs on the nobility of specific regions or times. These studies, and others which have looked at series of data on tithes or taxes on land, have offered essential information on revenues and agricultural production. However, because they focus on other aspects of the history of the aristocracy, such as consumption or urban life, and because of lack of documentation, these studies have often failed to provide a detailed analysis of the management methods employed by the landowning elite. It is nonetheless possible to draw a few conclusions from the extant literature that are valid for most, if not all, of Western Europe: aristocratic landowners in the sixteenth to eighteenth centuries did not manage directly any significant part of their estates through the employment of wage labor, but preferred to rent the land and all other sources of revenues, either separately or in block. Moreover, whatever the origins of their wealth, they were reluctant to reinvest their revenues in order to improve their land, thereby earning the condemnation of many economic historians, who consider increases in productivity the crucial mark of successful management.[1]

[1] Among the writings on Italian aristocratic patrimonies, see S. J. Woolf, *Studi sulla nobiltà piemontese nell'epoca dell'assolutismo* (Turin, 1963); M. Aymard, "Une famille de l'aristocratie sicilienne aux XVIe et XVIIe siècles: les ducs de Terranova, un bel example d'ascension seigneuriale" *Revue Historique* 96, no. 247 (1972), pp. 29–66; T. Fanfani, *Potere e nobiltà nell'Italia minore tra XVI e XVII secolo, i Taglieschi d'Anghiari* (Milan, 1983); L. Bulferetti, "L'oro, la terra e la società; un'interpretazione del nostro Seicento" *Archivio Storico Lombardo* 80 (1953), pp. 5–66; Bulferetti, "La feudalità e il patriziato nel Piemonte di Carlo Emanuele II (1663–1675)" *Annali della Facoltà di Lettere, Filosofia e Magistero dell'Università di Cagliari* 21 (1953), pp. 367–623; G. Mira, *Vicende economiche di una famiglia italiana dal XIV al XVII secolo* (Milan, 1940); G. Borelli, *Un patriziato della Terraferma veneta tra XVII e XVIII secolo. Ricerche sulla nobiltà veronese* (Milan, 1974); P. Malanima, *I Riccardi di Firenze, una famiglia e un patrimonio nella Toscana dei Medici* (Florence, 1977); R. B. Litchfield, *Emergence of a Bureaucracy: The Florentine Patricians 1530–1790* (Princeton, 1986); R. Sabbatini, *I Guinigi tra '500 e '600* (Lucca, 1979); P. Hurtubise, OMI, *Une famille-témoin, les Salviati* (Vatican City, 1985); G. Pescosolido, *Terra e nobiltà: i Borghese (secoli*

68

Management of the landed patrimony

There were, however, valid social reasons for the aristocracy's absenteeist landownership. What early modern landowners hoped for in their agricultural revenues was not growth, but continuity and predictability, and this was especially true of aristocratic landowners. Stuart Woolf has recently observed that the desire to dispose of large income for conspicuous consumption in order to maintain social status and prestige ought to be recognized as one of the guiding principles of aristocratic economic behavior, together with a concern for the safe transmission of the patrimony and the need to ensure the well-being of cadets and daughters. A high rate of saving was simply not among the aristocracy's economic priorities.[2] These priorities led to the preference for a system of management which could function with minimum expense and offer steady, reliable, and liquid revenues. Moreover, the difficulties aristocratic owners encountered in exercising close control over the running of a land enterprise, and the high cost of labor, particularly in poorer regions such as most of the kingdom of Naples where very little landless rural labor was available, meant that even when landowners did indeed directly manage parts of their land, the result was often lower profits than from renting, if not outright losses. Especially in poor areas, therefore, even resident landowners preferred rents to direct management.[3]

Other explanations for the aristocracy's managerial methods were more

XVIII e XIX) (Rome, 1979); D. Sella, *Crisis and Continuity. The Economy of Spanish Lombardy in the Seventeenth Century* (Cambridge, Mass., 1979); A. De Maddalena, *Dalla città al borgo, avvio di una metamorfosi economica e sociale nella Lombardia spagnola* (Milan, 1982); for non-Italian aristocracies, see R. Forster, *The Nobility of Toulouse in the Eighteenth Century, a Social and Economic Study* (Baltimore, 1960); Forster, *The House of Saulx-Tavanes. Versailles and Burgundy 1700–1830* (Baltimore, 1971); Forster, *Merchants, Landlords, Magistrates. The Depont Family in Eighteenth-Century France* (Baltimore, 1980); J. Dewald, *Pont-St-Pierre 1398–1789, Lordship, Community, and Capitalism in Early Modern France* (Berkeley–Los Angeles, 1987); O. Brunner, *Vita nobiliare e cultura europea* (Bologna, 1972; German edit. 1949); H. Nader, "Noble Income in Sixteenth-Century Castile: The Case of the Marquises of Mondéjar, 1480–1580" *Economic History Review* 30 (1977), pp. 411–28; J. Casey, *The Kingdom of Valencia in the Seventeenth Century* (Cambridge, 1979); N. Salomon, *La campagne de Nouvelle Castile à la fin du XVIe siècle* (Paris, 1964); I. Atienza Hernandez, *Aristocracia, poder y riqueza en la España moderna. La casa de Osuna siglos XV–XIX* (Madrid, 1987); J. Meyer, *Noblesses et pouvoirs dans l'Europe d'Ancien Régime* (Paris, 1973); A. Goodwin, ed. *The European Nobility in the Eighteenth Century* (New York, 1967; first edit. London, 1953); D. Spring, ed. *European Landed Elites in the Nineteenth Century* (Baltimore, 1977). Not all historians blame the aristocracy, or the ennobled *robins* and merchants, for their management techniques, though words like "failure," "inability," and "incapacity" are often used to refer to the lack of investments; F. McArdle, *Altopascio. A Study in Tuscan Rural Society, 1587–1784* (Cambridge, 1978) also searches for capitalist elements in the Medici's management of their estates, but takes into consideration other motivations. A collection of studies on tithes is in E. Le Roy Ladurie and J. Goy, eds. *Les fluctuations du produit de la dîme, conjuncture décimale et domaniale de la fin du Moyen Age au XVIIIe siècle* (Paris–The Hague, 1972).

2 Woolf, preface to T. Davies, *Famiglie feudali siciliane. Patrimoni redditi investimenti tra '500 e '600* (Caltanissetta–Rome, 1985). See also Forster, "Obstacles to Agricultural Growth in Eighteenth-Century France" *American Historical Review* 75 (1970), pp. 1600–15; a rare example of a high rate of saving is in A. Moroni, "Le ricchezze dei Corsini. Struttura patrimoniale e vicende familiari tra Sette e Ottocento" *Società e storia* 9 (1986), pp. 268–69, but only for the later eighteenth century.

3 Examples in G. Pedlow, *The Survival of the Hessian Nobility, 1770–1870* (Princeton, 1988), chapter 5, and J. L. Goldsmith, *Les Salers et les d'Escorailles, seigneurs de Haute Auvergne, 1500–1789*

particular to the kingdom of Naples. The barons in most fiefs collected the surplus production through various forms of rents in kind and sold it. Since prices and production were usually inversely proportional, the value of the landowners' income in grain did not fluctuate too much, especially since they, unlike their vassals, could store the grain and wait for favorable times to sell. This explains why, at least in some areas of the kingdom, the troubled years of the revolt (1647–48), characterized by good harvests and high prices, represented a bonus for the barons. Aristocratic revenues declined when the population declined, as we shall see in detail; but in those periods direct management of land would be even less profitable, given the rising cost of labor and the difficulties in marketing the product. Agrarian relations and the structure of feudal income offered, therefore, to the feudal landlords a maximum of protection from the effects of demographic or economic fluctuations.[4]

The traditionalism that permeated the early modern rural world was probably another reason for the aristocracy's abstention from management innovations. There were objective difficulties in tampering with the statutes, customs, and laws which, in the kingdom of Naples as elsewhere in Europe, protected the communal and feudal domain and guaranteed its use as pasture or its availability to tenant farmers in exchange for rents or shares of the harvest. Presumably the aristocracy shared the belief, expressed by many jurists in Spanish Naples, that the rural community – vassals and lord – was tied by mutual obligations to ensure the maintenance of all its members, what Aurelio Lepre has called the "ethics of survival."[5]

(Clermont-Ferrand, 1984), pp. 230–33; Neapolitan examples in A. Lepre, "I beni dei Muscettola di Leporano nel '600 e '700" in *Studi in memoria di Nino Cortese* (Rome, 1976), pp. 275–307; Lepre, *Terra di Lavoro nell'età moderna* (Naples, 1978), pp. 28, and 45–46; Lepre, *Feudi e masserie, problemi della società meridionale nel '600 e nel '700* (Naples, 1973), p. 147; M. A. Visceglia, "L'azienda signorile in Terra d'Otranto nell'età moderna (secoli XVI–XVIII)" in A. Massafra, ed. *Problemi di storia delle campagne meridionali nell'età moderna e contemporanea* (Bari, 1981), pp. 41–71, and S. Zotta, "Rapporti di produzione e cicli produttivi in regime di autoconsumo e di produzione speculativa. Le vicende agrarie dello 'stato' di Melfi nel lungo periodo (1530–1730)" in *ibid.*, pp. 221–89; Zotta, "Momenti e problemi di una crisi agraria in uno 'stato' feudale napoletano (1585–1615)" *MEFRM* 90 (1978), pp. 715–96; R. Merzario, *Signori e contadini di Calabria, Corigliano Calabro dal XVI al XIX secolo* (Milan, 1975); the essays in P. Villani, ed., *Economia e classi sociali in Puglia nell'età moderna* (Naples, 1974); Aymard, "Une famille."
[4] Particularly Lepre, *Feudi*, pp. 35–37, and 103–19; Lepre, *Terra*, pp. 142–48. On these issues, see the articles in T. H. Aston and C. H. E. Philpin, eds. *The Brenner Debate. Agrarian Class Structure and Economic Development in Preindustrial Europe* (Cambridge, 1987; first edit. 1985), though they make minimal references to Italy and none to Southern Italy.
[5] Lepre, *Storia del Mezzogiorno d'Italia* (2 vols.; Naples, 1986), I, pp. 241–47; see also G. I. Cassandro, *Storia delle terre comuni e degli usi civici nell'Italia meridionale* (Bari, 1943), chapter 7. A similar mentality was at work in Spain, see C. Jago, "The 'Crisis' of the Aristocracy in Seventeenth-Century Castile" *Past and Present* 84 (1979), pp. 60–90; Atienza, *Aristocracia* pp. 291–327; a similar point, in regard to church lands, is in G. Giorgetti, *Contadini e proprietari nell'Italia moderna. Rapporti di produzione e contratti agrari dal secolo XVI a oggi* (Turin, 1974), pp. 85–90.

Although it is impossible to prove that the Neapolitan aristocracy was aware of the extent to which the nature of its feudal power rested on the generalized acceptance of time-honored rules and conventions, and on the assumption that the lords were the public representatives as well as the protectors of their vassals, it is possible that the barons feared that any significant changes in the traditional agricultural relations with their vassals could bring into question the social foundations of the feudal regime. In an economic situation in which innovation was risky and income was needed elsewhere, such social concerns surely contributed to making the risk not worth taking. The analysis of the Caracciolo Brienza's fiefs will show how all these elements help explain the family's management methods. Those methods were successful in the long run, and the abolition of feudalism in the kingdom in 1806 found the Caracciolo Brienza essentially in the same economic and social position they had held two and a half centuries before.

The present chapter will try to throw light on the general economic situation of the kingdom of Naples through the study of a family's choices and circumstances. It will look first at the management methods of the Caracciolo Brienza, and consider the composition of the revenues from the fiefs and its change over time. The relative proportions of revenues from lands and from rights at different moments will be analyzed, as well as their relation to demographic and economic trends. The third and fourth sections of the chapter will study the production of the Caracciolo Brienza fiefs and its markets, and the policy of the marquis in regard to estate maintenance and investments. A final section will relate the evidence of the Caracciolo Brienza's patrimony to the debate on the seventeenth-century "refeudalization."

ADMINISTRATION AND REVENUES OF FEUDAL RIGHTS AND
MONOPOLIES

By the sixteenth century, the Neapolitan baronage lost at least some of its military functions, and its status and power in society came to be based less on personal relations of loyalty with the sovereign than on economic strength. What political power the aristocracy maintained, it held because of its economic power in the kingdom, and this economic power was based primarily upon the fiefs. Often historians assume that the undoubted commercialization and patrimonialization of fiefs in the sixteenth century implied the transformation of feudatories into landowners dedicated primarily to the collection of revenues from real estate; the crown allowed and favored the sale of fiefs, and ownership of a fief began to lose the traditional connotations of a public office held because of a royal grant. Even historians who have noted the resilient power of the feudal aristocracy in the kingdom until the later eighteenth century have tended to see the fief more and more as any other large landed property, attributing limited economic importance to the feudal character of the aristocracy. Although the social prestige and coercive powers over vassals that the aristocracy gained from its ownership of fiefs are recognized by all historians, their precise economic value is all but impossible to assess, and indirect economic benefits of feudal property are at times underestimated.[6] "Feudal income," Maria Antonietta Visceglia has written for Terra d'Otranto, "is essentially landed income."[7]

A study of the Caracciolo Brienza patrimony, however, reveals how the aristocracy reaped large benefits from its feudal character, not only in terms of power and status but also in terms of specific and measurable revenues. However commercialized and patrimonialized the fiefs were, their owners were still feudatories and enjoyed a large and expanding number of feudal rights, several of which were wholly independent of the amount of land the feudatories owned. At least in relatively poor and isolated regions of the kingdom, such as the *stato* of the Caracciolo Brienza, where the developments in agriculture were very limited, the regalian rights and the monopolies held by the barons contributed significantly to their global revenues, representing often more than half the total. As late as the eighteenth century, when revenues from land increased, the growing population of the fiefs led to growing jurisdictional and especially monopoly revenues, and the income from rights unconnected to landownership remained high. In the following pages we shall briefly consider the administrative methods of the Caracciolo Brienza and their relative increase in sophistication in the eighteenth century, and then examine in particular the administration of feudal rights and monopolies and assess their relative importance for baronial revenues as a whole and its evolution over time.

The barons could administer as they preferred all sources of income from the fiefs with the exception of civil and criminal jurisdiction. In some areas of the kingdom it was common in the sixteenth and early seventeenth centuries to rent out the entire fief on short-term leases, particularly when the land was managed

---

[6] The classic version of this assessment is B. Croce, *Storia del regno di Napoli* (Bari, 1931; first edit. 1924), pp. 122–26, and in that original formulation it would today find almost no subscribers. Galasso has pointed to the contradictions in Croce's argument, and to the continuing importance of the aristocracy's position as landowners endowed with many privileges. He too, however, interprets those privileges primarily as sources of power (coercive or not) and influence, rather than actual sources of revenue, see "La feudalità napoletana nel secolo XVI" *Clio* 1 (1965), pp. 535–54; Galasso, *Economia e società nella Calabria del Cinquecento* (Naples, 1967; second edit. Milan, 1975); and Galasso, *Il Mezzogiorno nella storia d'Italia* (Florence, 1984; first edit. 1977), chapter 6 and pp. 182–87. Other historians have varied in their emphasis on, and dating of, the feudatories' transformation in simple landowners, depending mainly on the region of the kingdom, the object of their study; for example, besides the already cited literature, see M. A. Visceglia, *Territorio, feudo e potere locale* (Naples, 1988); Visceglia, "Rendita feudale e agricoltura in Puglia nell'età moderna (XVI–XVIII secolo)" *Società e storia* 9 (1980), pp. 527–60; and M. Benaiteau, "La rendita feudale nel regno di Napoli attraverso i relevi: il Principato Ultra (1550–1806)" *ibid.*, pp. 561–611; for Lazio, see L. Boldini, "Bomarzo, sopravvivenze e trasformazioni di un microcosmo feudale dell'Alto Lazio tra il '700 e l''800" *Studi romani* 34 (1986), pp. 107–18.

[7] "Rendita," p. 537; see also Lepre's cited works.

in large estates with hired landless labor, as in the fertile plains near Naples and in Puglia but also in Calabria. In the hilly region where the Caracciolo Brienza had their *stato*, and where small peasant holdings were common, this type of general rent was only used once, in 1600, when Giovan Battista Caracciolo rented his four fiefs, the town of Diano with its *casali*, and the *mastrodattie* of Taranto and Sala to the Neapolitan Pompilio d'Aragona for seven years for 13,000 ducats a year. The marquis reserved for himself only the castle in Brienza and jurisdiction in Pietrafesa. Nothing is known about the reasons for this rent, but probably it was rescinded before the seven years were completed, since already in 1602 Giovan Battista rented Diano and its *casali* to others.[8]

At all other times the Caracciolo Brienza received the revenues of their four fiefs directly. Management methods remained very simple until the eighteenth century. Throughout the late sixteenth and seventeenth centuries the Caracciolo Brienza, who spent a fair amount of time in their *stato*, confided the collection of their revenues to the *erari* and *conservatori* of each of the four fiefs; these, as we have seen, were appointed by the *università* and received no salary from the marquis, so that the expenses for the administrative staff were almost non-existent. In fact in the *relevi* of the Caracciolo Brienza, very few deductions were made for administrative expenses and these consisted mostly of repairs to the mill or the storage rooms. After the repurchase of the patrimony in the 1680s, increased care was given to the fiefs. In the eighteenth century the family employed a general manager who was responsible for the administration of the entire patrimony, following the "practice of the better part of the Neapolitan barons and noblemen." He received an annual salary of 240 ducats and had under him sub-agents who resided in each of the four fiefs. This trend towards more professional and careful administration was a European phenomenon, although it rarely led to reinvestment of profits in the land.[9]

[8] ACB 45.7.2; examples or discussion of rents are in Lepre, *Terra*, pp. 48–49; Lepre, "Le campagne pugliesi nell'età moderna" in *La Puglia tra medio evo ed età moderna, città e campagna* (Milan, 1981), pp. 273–331; P. Villani, "Signoria rurale, feudalità, capitalismo nelle campagne" *QS* 7 (1972), pp. 5–26; particularly for the late sixteenth century, see Galasso, *Calabria*, pp. 242–47; Galasso, "Aspetti e problemi della società feudale napoletana attraverso l'inventario dei beni dei principi di Bisignano (1594)" in *Studi in memoria di Federigo Melis* (Naples, 1978), IV, pp. 255–77; G. Delille, *Croissance d'une société rurale, Montesarchio et la Vallée Caudine aux XVIIe et XVIIIe siècles* (Naples, 1973), part II; general rents were rare also in Terra di Lavoro, see G. D'Ambrosio, "La feudalità in Terra di Lavoro nella seconda metà del secolo XVII" tesi di laurea, University of Naples, 1984–85, chapter 4. On Diano, see ACB 138.20, fols. 39r–49r.

[9] ACB 48.9 for the agents. The *relevi* were the feudal succession tax. The quote in ACB 77.2.10, from the last years of the seventeenth century. For the general trend to better administration, see Visceglia, "Formazione e dissoluzione di un patrimonio aristocratico: la famiglia Muscettola tra XVI e XIX secolo" *MEFRM* 92 (1980), pp. 555–624; in France, this took the form of the so-called "seigneurial reaction," see Forster's cited works and his "The 'World' between Seigneur and Peasant" *Studies in Eighteenth-Century Culture* 5 (1976), pp. 401–21; the dukes of Osuna had a complex hierarchy of administrators already in the seventeenth century, though its effectiveness is open to doubt, see Atienza, *Aristocracia*, pp. 318–26; in other areas of the kingdom, *erari* had to be paid, and their salaries could be as high as 200 ducats a year already in the late seventeenth century, see D'Ambrosio, "La feudalità," chapter 4.

The many sources of the revenues the family drew from the fiefs can be divided into two general categories: feudal rights and monopolies, and feudal and allodial real estate. We will now consider specifically the administration of feudal rights and monopolies. As we have seen in the previous chapter, feudal rights consisted in regalian powers the exercise of which was granted to the barons. From the point of view of the extension of feudal control over the kingdom, by far the most significant and prominent regalian power given to the barons was that of civil and criminal jurisdiction. Its exercise by the barons was carefully regulated by royal laws. The baron appointed a governor whose court, like those of the governors of royal towns, was the first-degree tribunal for all of the fief's inhabitants. The governor, or captain, who could not by law be a native of the fief, had to be a law graduate, or otherwise had to appoint an assessor who was. The Caracciolo Brienza, like most barons in the kingdom by the late sixteenth century, enjoyed the right of second-degree jurisdiction and also appointed an appeals judge.

Baronial jurisdiction was strictly enforced and protected, and although the royal provincial and central tribunals could reclaim trials from the baronial courts to themselves, in most instances they enforced the observance of all degrees of feudal jurisdiction. The power that jurisdiction gave the barons to influence the life of their vassal communities, and of specific individuals within them, was denounced from time to time by the vassals, by sympathetic jurists, and later by enlightened reformers, and this power was presumably one of the reasons why feudal revenues were capitalized at a lower rate than allodial income throughout the early modern period. It is, however, difficult to evaluate the economic value of jurisdiction, and the many assessments of fiefs generally consider the income from it as only enough to cover the expenses involved in staffing and keeping the court, though there is occasional evidence to the contrary. Baronial civil and criminal jurisdiction was rare outside the kingdom of Naples, and in the few Italian regions where it still existed it was by the early modern period quite limited.[10]

---

[10] *Prammatiche De baronibus* IV, V, VI, VII, VIII, XIX, XXI, XXII, XXIII, XXV, XXVI, and XXVII in L. Giustiniani, ed. *Nuova collezione delle prammatiche del regno di Napoli*; G. F. de Leonardis, *Prattica degli officiali regii e baronali del regno di Napoli* (Naples, 1619; first edit. 1599), part II; F. G. de Angelis, *Tractatus de officialibus baronum* (Naples, 1689); A. Villone, *Privilegi giurisdizionali e dominio feudale: lo stato dei Doria d'Angri nella seconda metà del secolo XVII* (Naples, 1980), pp. 5–14, 27–32, and 41–46; A. Spagnoletti, "Giudici e governatori regi nelle università meridionali (XVIII secolo)" *ASPN* 105 (1987), pp. 415–54 on royal and baronial governors; an eighteenth-century denunciation of the strong feudal power in the provinces is published in F. Cammisa, "Un atto di accusa contro la giurisdizione feudale, redatto a Napoli nel 1764" *ibid.*, pp. 493–520. ACB 48.8, 62.5.1, 76.4.6, and 82.7.6 for examples of appointments of captains in the later eighteenth century; a 1702 example is in ASP, notai Potenza, 1262, pp. 146–47; dispute over an appointment in 1719 is in *ibid.*, 1071, fols. 28r–29r. ACB 45.1.14, 17–19, for examples of the Sacred Council's upholding of the Caracciolo Brienza's second-degree jurisdiction; see also 62.1.1–9 and 82.1.1–3. In 1647, the duke of Parma wrote to his agent in the kingdom about the

All other feudal rights and monopolies were invariably rented out by the Caracciolo Brienza, either separately to various people or in a block to the community (*università*) at perpetual fixed rents. These global rents were not uncommon in the kingdom in the years around 1600, and they can be seen as one other means the aristocracy used to protect itself from the decline in agricultural revenues that began around that time. This form of rent could also be favorable to the *università*, which could decide to lighten the burden of feudal rights on its members in difficult years, while providing the barons with secure revenues which cost nothing to collect. In case the *università* were unable to pay the rent, the lords could then force them to give up lands or rights. The decision to rent all or most of the baronial revenues, especially if at a perpetual rent, was therefore an essential one for the *università*, and divisions arose within them whenever such choices had to be made. We lack documentation on the internal life of the communities, but it is clear that at least in one instance the decision was hotly contested.

In the early 1590s, in fact, the marquis Giovan Battista, in order to guarantee his revenues, and perhaps sensing the impending halt in the kingdom's economy, rented out to the *università* of his four fiefs most of his revenues for a perpetual rent. In 1592, the *università* of Brienza rented all feudal rights (except the *mastrodattia*), the *terraggi*, and the monopoly on ovens for 1,300 ducats, 1,200 *tomoli* of wheat, and 600 *tomoli* of barley a year. The marquis kept the mill, gave up his monopoly on inns, agreed to rebates on many jurisdictional fees, and obtained exemption from local taxes on his allodial lands. The *università* agreed to pay for all repairs to the marquis' mill. The same agreement was entered with the *università* of Pietrafesa in 1593; there the *università* rented the monopoly on the inn as well, and was to pay 500 ducats and 500 *tomoli* of wheat every year. In Atena in 1592 the *università* rented the same rights, the monopoly on ovens, and the *terraggi* for 900 ducats and 600 *tomoli* of wheat a year. A similar agreement was presumably entered with the *università* of Sasso, which in any event was paying 250 ducats a year in 1620 for the rent of the *bagliva*, *portolania*, and other feudal rights.[11]

These rents proved immediately too high. The *università* of Atena denounced the agreement and obtained its annulment within a few years, though it was still paying 174 ducats a year for the rights of *portolania*, *zecca*, and *bagliva* in 1620. The *università* of Brienza and Pietrafesa both proved unable to pay the rents, and

---

considerable losses in jurisdictional income from his Neapolitan fiefs resulting from the revolt, see A. Musi, *La rivolta di Masaniello nella scena politica barocca* (Naples, 1989), p. 188, footnote 16. On other parts of Italy, see also G. Pansini, "Per una storia del feudalesimo nel granducato di Toscana durante il periodo mediceo" *QS* 7 (1972), pp. 131–86; Davies mentions the Sicilian barons' jurisdiction, but never discusses its extent or significance, see *Famiglie*; on France, see Forster, *Saulx-Tavanes*, pp. 98–100; see also chapter 2, footnote 10, above.

11 ACB 45.1.3–4 and 133.2, fols. 104r–15r; 61.2.4; 74.2.3 and 75.1.5; 45.7.2bis.

by the 1620s were heavily in debt to the marquis. Brienza had to levy a tax on flour for eight years to pay its debt, and obtained two successive rebates on the rent, which in 1623 was set at 800 ducats, 500 *tomoli* of wheat, and 200 *tomoli* of barley a year. In a long lawsuit the *università* claimed that the marquis had abused his power so as to elect a local government which would accept the terms of the 1592 agreement. It is hard to ascertain the veracity of this claim, but certainly rival factions must have existed within the community whose animosity towards each other the marquis could exploit to his advantage. In 1627, the *università* of Pietrafesa had to transact its debt of over 1,200 ducats in rent arrears with the marquis. As we shall see in a later chapter, all four *università* fell heavily into debt with the marquis and others in the early years of the seventeenth century. Throughout the kingdom, the *università*'s financial situation worsened significantly in those years.[12]

With the confiscation of Brienza and Pietrafesa and the financial crisis of the Caracciolo Brienza, these agreements seem to have all been rescinded and, as we shall see, baronial revenues declined after the revolt and the plague. In 1677, the *università* of Brienza was not renting any feudal right. As the population increased, beginning in the late seventeenth century, and as the *università* achieved a degree of financial solvency, it again became advisable for them to rent feudal rights at perpetual fixed rents. Though not willing anymore to give up all of their rights as a block, the Caracciolo Brienza still found it convenient to rent out a few rights, in order to maintain administrative expenses at a minimum.

The *università* of Brienza never stopped renting the monopoly on ovens for 220 ducats a year. In 1742 it offered 140 ducats a year for the *bagliva*, and in 1764 it agreed to a perpetual rent of 180 ducats a year for that office. Around 1750, the *università* was paying 450 ducats a year for the ovens, *portolania, colta*, and *zecca*, and by 1785 the *università* was renting the ovens, *bagliva, portolania, colta*, and some houses for a total rent of 675 ducats a year. In 1741, the *università* of Pietrafesa agreed to pay a perpetual rent of 130 ducats a year for the ovens; already since at least 1677 it was paying 194 ducats a year for *bagliva, portolania, zecca*, and *colta*, and the rent was still in effect around 1750. In the mid-eighteenth century and still in 1776, the *università* of Sasso paid a rent of 250 ducats a year for the ovens, *bagliva, portolania, piazza*, and *zecca*. Even the more litigious and autonomous *università* of Atena asked to rent the *portolania* for a perpetual rent of ninety ducats a year in 1746, and the offer was accepted by the marquis in 1765. The interest of the *università* in this form of rents shows how feudal rights were still perceived in the eighteenth century as significant sources of revenues which were likely to increase with time.[13]

---

[12] ACB 75.1.9; 45.1.7–8; 45.7.2bis; 48.1.1 throughout (a very large volume concerning the lawsuit between the marquis and the *università* of Brienza); 61.2.6; ASP, notai Potenza, 232, fols. 25r–33v (the 1623 rebate in Brienza), and 235, fols. 40r–44r (Pietrafesa, 1627). Examples of similar rents abound in the literature already cited.

[13] ACB 45.1.22, 26, and 31; 45.7.18, unnumbered fol. (undated but probably 1750); 61.2.33; 43.3.7; 45.7.21, unnumbered fol.; 81.1.17–18; 75.1.25, 30.

It is indeed clear from the example of the Caracciolo Brienza that feudal rights and monopolies were an essential part of baronial income throughout the early modern period. On several occasions in the sixteenth to eighteenth centuries the revenues the Caracciolo Brienza drew from their fiefs were assessed for various purposes. These assessments are of different reliability and the data they provide are at times contradictory or unclear. Most were drawn for fiscal reasons and included only revenues from feudal rights, monopolies, and lands, leaving out allodial revenues which were subject to a different fiscal regime. These assessments are not always reliable, for the marquis tried to declare lower revenues than they actually enjoyed, and the fiscal officers were not always willing or able to challenge the barons' statement. The *Catasto* documents of the 1740s discuss in detail the allodial revenues, and they occasionally provide assessments of feudal revenues as well. Thanks, however, to the Caracciolo Brienza's indebtedness and litigiousness, we have a few detailed assessments of the global revenues of the four fiefs drawn in the seventeenth and eighteenth centuries by government functionaries to serve in lawsuits between the family and its creditors.[14]

For this family, the revenues from feudal rights independent of ownership of land remained a very important element of the global revenues, and it was only in the later eighteenth century that landed revenues became predominant without, in any event, ever rendering jurisdictional and monopoly revenues wholly insignificant for the barons. The relative backwardness of the region also prevented innovations and limited the possibilities for large expansion of the agricultural production. In a relatively infertile and mountainous land, even the growth of an extensive agriculture very quickly reached its boundaries. Even when, in the late eighteenth century, the income from land grew considerably, the barons could count on one specific feudal right, the monopoly on the mill, to preserve a close link to agricultural production. The revenues from the baronial mills increased markedly in the

---

[14] With the exception of one annuity in one instance, allodial revenue all came from real estate. The documents that constitute the basic sources for the following pages are: ACB 16.8i (*c.* 1720); 43.3.1 (1625); 43.3.7 (1677); 44.1.7 (1655–56); 45.7.10 (1747); 74.1.1 (1572; also in ASN Petizioni dei Relevi 32, fols. 1r–5v); 77.2.1bis (1646); 77.2.27 (1676); 77.2.32 (1748); 77.2.33 (1775); 81.1.17 (1748); 81.1.18 (1776); 160, unnumbered fol. (1646); App. 23, unnumbered fol. (1747); and ASN Relevi 236, fols. 557r–608v, 698r–746r (1623, 1657–58); *ibid.* 254, fols. 112r–14r (1556–60); *ibid.* 266, document no. 2, fols. 1r–14v (1651; also in Petizioni relevi 57, fols. 105v–8v); Petizioni relevi 13, fols. 124r–39r (1521–22); *ibid.* 29, fols. 337r–39r (1570); Significatorie relevi 77, fols. 237v–46v (1680 for 1673; also in Relevi 239, 1r–394r); *ibid.* 81, fols. 117r–19v, 162r–63v (1686 for 1681; also in Relevi 239); *ibid.* 92, fols. 12r–13r (a 1703 correction to the preceding document; Catasto Onciario 5149, fols. 70r–73r and 289r–94v; *ibid.* 5250, unnumbered fol.; *ibid.* 5251, fols. 496r–500r; *ibid.* 5269, unnumbered fol.; Pandetta Corrente 2026, III, fols. 563r–65v (*c.* 1650–53). In these documents, staples are assessed at different prices, depending on the year; in the tables, I have preserved the values given by each document.

later eighteenth century, thereby raising the absolute income from feudal sources.

In general, non-landed revenues proved less flexible than landed ones, and their oscillations in absolute figures were relatively limited. This was due to the fact that several feudal rights and monopolies were rented out for long-term, if not outright perpetual, rents, so that they would be slow to react to a sudden decline or increase in the population or production of the fiefs. Also, one of the major sources of landed revenues, the *terraggi* from the feudal domain, was proportional to the harvest of each year, and was therefore prone to dramatic variations depending on the agricultural situation in each year. Non-landed revenues were in large part tied to the demographic cycle, which tended to oscillate less violently and less rapidly than agricultural production. Even the plague of 1656 does not seem to have hit the Caracciolo Brienza fiefs as hard as it did other, less isolated, parts of the kingdom. Notwithstanding the oscillations of all revenues – and it has to be remembered that the documents are often of dubious reliability as to the absolute figures – their relative proportions did not change significantly over the long period. For instance, though the total revenues from Brienza and Pietrafesa declined from about 6,000 ducats in 1625 to about 4,500 in 1677, a decrease of twenty-five percent, the proportion of these revenues represented by non-landed income changed but little: it was forty-five and thirty-nine percent in the two fiefs in 1625, and forty-three and thirty-seven percent respectively a half-century later.

Table 3.1 presents the data obtained from fourteen documents, spanning the period 1521 to 1776 and referring to a varying number of the fiefs, for a total of thirty-three assessments. Nine more documents provide twenty more assessments, but their doubtful reliability or their proximity in time to other assessments have motivated their exclusion from the table. It should be noted, however, that of the total fifty-three assessments, thirty-three do not include allodial revenues while twenty do.

In only four of the thirty-three assessments that discuss only feudal income did non-landed income – that is, income from feudal rights and monopolies – represent less than fifty percent of the total (and in only one of these four instances it represented less than forty percent of the total). Moreover, all four of these instances took place before 1647. Although it was obviously impossible to increase through purchases the amount of feudal land any fief included – since all feudal land already belonged by definition to the baron – this shows that non-landed feudal income did not fall behind landed feudal income over time. Of the remaining twenty-nine assessments which included only feudal income, six estimated non-landed income at between fifty and fifty-nine percent of the total, twelve placed it at between sixty and sixty-nine percent, five at between seventy and seventy-nine percent, and six at eighty percent or more. Of the four fiefs, it was in Pietrafesa that non-landed income represented the largest share of

Table 3.1. *Revenue in the Caracciolo Brienza fiefs (1521–1776)*
(in ducats)

year		feudal rights		mills		feudal land		allodial land		total
		ducats	percent	ducats	percent	ducats	percent	ducats	percent	
1521–22	B	162	37	18	4	257	59	–		437
	P	78	64	12	10	32	26	–		122
	S	54	50½	6	5½	47	44	–		107
1572	P	321	62	120	23	77	15	–		518
	A	162	62	–		99	38	–		261
1625	B	1,142	32	458	13	1,248	35	722	20	3,570
	P	635	25	360	14	562	23	945	38	2,502
	A	378	50	–		157½	21	221	29	756½
	S	358	37	208	22	324	34	72	7	962
1646	B	1,155	28	412½	10	1,296	31	1,309	31	4,172½
	A	378	44	–		211	25	264	31	853
1648	S	352½	40	132	15	394	45	–		878½
1657–58	B	770	48	195	12	644	40	–		1,609
	P	374	57	175½	27	108½	16	–		658
	A	200	75	–		68	25	–		268
	S	340	43	121	15	326	42	–		787
1676	S	366	37	161	16	359	37	99	10	985
1677	B	823	29	386	14	913	32	707	25	2,829
	P	437	25	213½	12	198	11	917	52	1,765½
1686	B	694	42	288	18	649	40	–		1,631
	P	398	64	189	31	32	5	–		619
	A	90	58	–		65	42	–		155
	S	341	45	162	22	250	33	–		753
1726[a]	B	770	26	528	18	–	1,684	56	–	2,982
	P	514	35	304	21	322½	22	318	22	1,458½
	A	170	21	121	15	–	523½	64	–	814½
	S	361	31	175	15	523	45	109	9	1,168
1747[b]	B	675	29	480	21	824	36	326	14	2,305
	B	696	23	720	23	1,310	43	326	11	3,052
	P	366	21	200	12	321	19	839	48	1,726
1748	A	152	20	–		180	24	431	56	763
	S	309	28	225	20	531	48	47	4	1,112
1776	A	150	13	–		303	27	664	60	1,117
	S	336	21	506	32	641	41	97	6	1,580

[a] In this year there was an income from a mill in Atena. Since, however, the Caracciolo Brienza did not enjoy the feudal monopoly on the mill there, this income must be considered allodial. In Brienza and Atena, feudal and allodial land were counted together, so the figures refer to all landed revenues.
[b] There are three versions of the revenues of Brienza in 1747, differing mostly in the assessment of revenues in grain, both in terms of quantity and of value. I give here the highest and lowest of the three.
Sources: cited in footnote 14. The capital letters stand for the four fiefs (Brienza, Pietrafesa, Atena, and Sasso). The figures read horizontally to obtain the totals. I have rounded figures to the closest half ducat.

feudal revenues; this was due to the fact that in Atena the Caracciolo Brienza enjoyed fewer rights than in the other three fiefs, and that Pietrafesa, as the smallest of those three fiefs in extension though not in population, had the smallest feudal domain.

In only seven of the twenty assessments which included all the revenues of the Caracciolo Brienza did non-landed income represent less than forty percent of the total. Only in the eighteenth century in Atena (the fief where the family had the fewest feudal rights and where, more specifically important, there was no baronial monopoly of the mill) did non-landed income come to represent less than a third of the global revenues. In eight of these assessments, non-landed income amounted to between forty and forty-nine percent of the total, and in the remaining five it was over fifty percent of the total.[15]

It is evident from the data presented in Table 3.1 that the Caracciolo Brienza were not simply privileged landowners. Had they not owned any land – feudal or allodial – their monopolies and rights (the income from the mills did not depend in any way on the amount of land owned by the baron, though it did require ownership of the building) would still have afforded them remarkable revenues. Over the long period there was an undoubted relative decline in the income from feudal rights, but at least until the mid-eighteenth century it continued to represent a fourth or more of the family's income from the fiefs. Moreover, although by the late eighteenth century, as the revenues from the fiefs increased at a pace faster than ever before, the *"baronale potestà"* (baronial power) was seen as declining, in percentage if not in absolute figures, the monopoly on the mill still guaranteed the marquis a secure source of growing revenues. In Sasso, for instance, though income from feudal rights stagnated between 1748 and 1776, income from the mill more than doubled, bringing the share of non-landed income from forty-eight to fifty-three percent of the total revenues. The high revenues from the monopoly on the mill seem to have been a peculiarity of the kingdom of Naples, and especially of its poorer areas; mills are rarely mentioned in the literature on aristocratic estates elsewhere, and in Sicily they seem to have given very low income.[16]

Even after the abolition of the feudal regime, the Napoleonic government of Naples recognized the barons' right to an indemnity for some at least of their abolished feudal powers. In 1812, the government acknowledged that Cataldo

---

[15] Chapter 4 discusses the differences in size, population, and extent of feudal power among the four fiefs.

[16] The quote in ACB 81.1.18, section II; in Terra di Lavoro, for instance, the income from mills represented less than twenty percent of feudal income in the richer areas, but over thirty-three percent in the poorer ones, see D'Ambrosio, "La feudalità." For the mills, see Aymard, "Terranova," table on p. 42; one rare example is the mill in the French village of Lourmarin, which in the eighteenth century still gave twenty-three percent of the local seigneurial revenues, see T. Sheppard, *Lourmarin in the Eighteenth Century* (Baltimore, 1971), pp. 136–39.

Caracciolo had lost an income from feudal rights of 973 ducats a year, equal to a capital value of 19,460 ducats, and he was assigned government bonds to replace that income. In 1824, another sixty ducats a year were assigned to Cataldo to compensate for the lost monopoly on the ovens of Brienza. The importance of feudal rights for aristocratic income was a peculiarity of the kingdom's barons, at least in the poorer provinces: in other West European countries, as well as in most parts of Italy, feudal rights were of much smaller relevance to aristocratic revenues, particularly in the eighteenth century. The Borghese princes in Lazio, for instance, received over eighty percent of their income from their fiefs from land. The nobles of Toulouse received over ninety percent of their revenues from land.[17]

The Caracciolo Brienza's feudal *stato* does not fit the general picture of Southern latifundia. In his studies of Sicily, for instance, Maurice Aymard observes the decline of traditional rights, of non-landed revenues and of tithes, the shrinking of common lands and of small peasant property or farms, the growth of large markets, the domination of village life by local closed oligarchies, none of which took place in the Caracciolo Brienza's fiefs, as we shall see in detail.[18] The Caracciolo Brienza's example demonstrates that, at least in those provinces of the kingdom in which agricultural change was very limited, feudal non-landed income provided by rights and monopolies remained an essential component of baronial revenues. As total revenues declined in the mid-seventeenth century, non-landed income did not decline more than income from landownership and, later, at least until the mid-eighteenth century, it increased with the total revenues. Being a landlord was more than being a landowner and, for the Caracciolo Brienza, feudal income was definitely not essentially landed income.

---

[17] ASN Creditori dello Stato 275/36, fols. 67r–68v, 73r–74v, 80r–81r (my thanks to Dr. de Mattia of the ASN for bringing this document to my attention). The rights were the *portolania*, *zecca*, *bagliva*, and *piazza* of Brienza and Pietrafesa, *portolania* of Atena, and *portolania* and *bagliva* of Sasso. Pescosolido, *Terra*, p. 51 and throughout; Forster, *Toulouse*, chapter 1, p. 38. The opinions of historians of the Italian South vary on this issue with the specific region they study: while Musi, "La spinta baronale e i suoi antagonisti nella crisi del Seicento" in F. Barbagallo, ed. *Storia della Campania* (2 vols.; Naples, 1978), I, pp. 223–44, notes the high jurisdictional revenues of some barons, others have stressed the predominance of landed revenues, see Aymard, "L'abolition de la féodalité en Sicile: le sens d'une réforme" *Annuario dell'Istituto Storico Italiano per l'età moderna e contemporanea* 23–24 (1971–72), pp. 67–85 (which also addresses the problem of the indemnity paid to barons at the abolition of feudal rights); Aymard, "La transizione dal feudalesimo al capitalismo" in *Storia d'Italia Einaudi. Annali I Dal feudalesimo al capitalismo* (Turin, 1978), p. 1191; A. Massafra, "Giurisdizione feudale e rendita fondiaria nel Settecento napoletano: un contributo alla ricerca" *QS* 7 (1972), pp. 187–252; G. Caridi, *Uno "stato" feudale nel Mezzogiorno spagnolo* (Rome, 1988), chapter 2.

[18] See his various works cited earlier in this chapter.

ADMINISTRATION OF REAL ESTATE

The other major source of income from the fiefs was real estate. The fief-holding aristocracy owned land and buildings, both feudal and allodial. Feudal property was for the most part subject to traditional limitations, and its uses were dictated by local statutes and customs. Allodial property could be managed as the owners saw fit. The geographic characteristics of the region and the traditionalism of aristocratic landownership, however, combined in making the Caracciolo Brienza's management of all their property similar throughout most of the early modern period. With one brief exception, the marquis were never directly involved in agricultural production, not even in the form of sharecropping.[19]

In the Caracciolo Brienza fiefs very little land, whether owned by the marquis or by the village residents, was enclosed and managed as autonomous farms or gardens. Many feudal lands were rented out separately in small, unenclosed plots, and the rents were generally set in kind. Large parts of the feudal domain, as was the case for the communal domain, were still open to whoever would cultivate them, and were also subject to grazing rights of all citizens of the fiefs. The vassals enjoyed the so-called *jus serendi* (right to sow) over uncultivated feudal territory, and they could keep the land as long as they did not leave it unworked for over three years. The rent for these lands was the *terraggio*, which in most of the kingdom was proportional to the area of land cultivated; in this way the peasants bore all risks of low production and, since yields were largely irrelevant to the barons, the latter had little incentive for investment or innovation. In the Caracciolo Brienza's *stato*, however, as in other, usually poorer, regions, the *terraggio* was proportional to the harvest; for the Caracciolo Brienza's lands it was almost always ten percent.[20]

The marquis had allodial lands and houses that they generally rented out. All allodial lands paid rents either in kind or in money in the seventeenth century, while in the eighteenth century the marquis very often demanded payment in kind, to avoid the devaluation of money rents. The eighteenth-century emphyteusis contracts almost always required payment in kind.[21] The most common

[19] This policy was common among Western Mediterranean aristocracies, see, for example, Reinhardt, *Kardinal Scipione Borghese*, chapter 6, and Atienza, *Aristocracia*, chapter 5b. Share-cropping was much more common in central Italy (see McArdle, *Altopascio*) than in the South; see Giorgetti, *Contadini*, pp. 72–103, for an analysis of the management of Southern estates.

[20] This latter type of *terraggio* was, in lands of low average yields, obviously more favorable to the peasants, in that it forced the baron to share the losses of any bad harvest; as such it was more consonant to the ethics of survival (Lepre, *Storia*, pp. 172–73; *Feudi*, pp. 54–55); most of the monographs cited above – many of which deal with the richer parts of the kingdom – report *terraggi* of the former type: for example, Zotta, "Momenti," pp. 730–31. Such was the case also in Tuscany (McArdle, *Altopascio*, chapter 3), and in fertile Sicily, Aymard, "Strutture delle aziende e studio della produzione e della produttività agricola in Italia meridionale nell'età moderna: prospettive di ricerca" in Massafra, ed. *Problemi*, pp. 17–24; elsewhere ("La transizione," p. 1188) Aymard claims that Southern *terraggi* were always based on the area cultivated; on *terraggi*, see also Giorgetti, *Contadini*, pp. 90–97.

[21] In 1747, one of the preliminary reports for the *Catasto* noted that the baronial rents were almost all in wheat, see ASN Catasto Onciario 5147, fols. 353v–54r. On emphyteusis, see p. 86 below.

rent in kind was one *tomolo* of wheat for each *tomolo* of land, though rents of half as much were not rare; unlike the feudal *terraggi*, therefore, these rents were based on the area cultivated. Allodial lands, and particularly vines, were, however, the only lands the Caracciolo Brienza at times managed directly. The characteristics of the region, though, did not favor the formation of large units of management.

In other areas of the kingdom, particularly in Puglia, Terra di Lavoro, and the plain of the Sele, large parts of the barons' reserves and of their allodial lands were managed directly by the owners, or by large-scale tenant farmers, in the form of *masserie*, large farms producing mainly wheat and employing a numerous staff of both permanent and seasonal workers, many of whom were landless or came from poorer provinces. The production of these farms in general was aimed at the large market for wheat the city of Naples had become by the mid-sixteenth century. The large revenues of these farms, and the aristocracy's policy of increasing its allodial holdings through purchases, particularly in the late sixteenth and early seventeenth centuries as the market for wheat expanded with the population of Naples, are probably the main reasons why many historians consider the feudal lords by this time mostly as landowners.[22]

The Caracciolo Brienza followed this policy only for a few years. When the marquis Giovan Battista rented to his vassal *università* all feudal revenues in the fiefs in 1592–93, he kept various plots of land for his own *masserie*, but we know nothing about these enterprises at this point. In March 1593, Giovan Battista's agent contracted with two brokers to hire fifty men for the coming harvest on "the cultivated field of wheat and barley of the marquis." But the only example of a relatively stable large-scale enterprise came about twenty years later.[23] Beginning in the last decade of the sixteenth century, and especially in the years 1607–11, Giovan Battista, who was residing regularly in his fiefs and who began in 1606 the construction of a palace in Atena, enacted a policy of extensive purchases of land in all four of his fiefs. He also frequently exchanged plots with local owners with the aim of concentrating and rationalizing his allodial holdings. Probably the expense involved in these purchases contributed to the financial debacle of the family beginning in the third decade of the century. Giovan Battista also carried on an active policy of commercial grain production, and on a few occasions, as we shall see later, he sold large quantities of wheat to the city of Naples. Besides the purchase of land, this attempt at large-scale production involved the adoption of the production methods of the *masseria*.

In 1611, Giovan Battista contracted five *società di campo* (companies for cultivation) with several residents of Brienza and Pietrafesa. In three of these contracts the marquis provided about 600 *tomoli* of land, in the other two only

[22] To the literature already cited, add Galasso, *Il Mezzogiorno*, pp. 360–405, on Puglia.
[23] ACB 133.2, fols. 9r–14r; in the agreements cited in footnote 11, there is mention of Giovan Battista's *masserie* in Brienza and Pietrafesa; since the term could refer also to a livestock breeding enterprise, we cannot assume that these were farms.

300 *tomoli*. He also provided each of the five groups of partners with oxen, half the necessary seed for the first year, use of half of the buildings present on the farms, and some additional land to use as pasture. The land was to be divided in three equal parts, the first of which was to produce wheat, the second was to be used as pasture for seven tenths and to produce barley for the remaining three tenths, and the third was to lie fallow and receive the preparation necessary for a new year of wheat production. The marquis would pay for half the expense of the harvest, while the *massari* would pay for all the tools and for transportation of the harvest to the baronial storage rooms, and would replace at their expense any animal that were to die. One fifth of the entire harvest would go to the marquis. Then the seed for the following year would be subtracted from the remaining four fifths, and what was left after that would be divided in two parts, one going to the marquis and one to the *massari*. The contracts were made for nine years.[24]

Though there are occasional other references in later years to land managed by the marquis directly, these five farms are the only well documented example of involvement of the Caracciolo Brienza in large-scale production, and the fact that they were established soon after Giovan Battista's extensive purchase of land points to a conscious new policy on the part of the marquis. The financial problems of the family, the relative poverty of the region, and also the changing economic climate for the kingdom in general, caused this policy to be very short-lived. Giovan Battista's successors made very few additional purchases of land, and no other contract for a *masseria* exists among the family papers. In the 1625 assessment all baronial lands appear rented out. In general, from then on, the only plots of land that were managed directly by the baronial administration were a few vineyards intended to provide for the consumption of the baronial household, as was true in fiefs of other families. The only exception is a *masseria* kept by the family in the early eighteenth century but discontinued later because "it brought more expenses than profits since the wheat and barley sold for low prices and often were not sold at all but rather rotted in the storage rooms."[25]

We know nothing of the success or failure of the 1611 *masserie*, though the fact that the experiment was not repeated seems to indicate that the Caracciolo Brienza did not consider it an advisable form of management. In other regions of the kingdom these *masserie* could be quite successful. A contemporary example

[24] ACB 46.2.10bis, 11, 12, 12bis (9 is a copy of 12), and 63.1.9 (this last one is reproduced in R. Villari, *La rivolta antispagnola a Napoli, le origini (1585–1647)* (Bari, 1967), Appendix); a discussion of *società di campo* is in Giorgetti, *Contadini*, pp. 72–79. In 1624, the marquis Giacomo rented a large *masseria* of 2,500 *tomoli* to the *abate* Manilio Palmieri for a total over four years of 2,800 *tomoli* of wheat; Palmieri then sublet it to many local farmers. Giacomo was not at all involved in the production in this case. Palmieri in 1625 also rented from Giacomo the tithes the *università* of Sala had assigned to the marquis, ASP, notai Potenza, 235, fols. 1r–2r, 4r, and 8v–9r.
[25] ACB 161, unnumbered fol., a mention of this *masseria*, without the actual contract. Examples of *masserie* for wine or oil are in Lepre, "Le campagne"; Visceglia, "L'azienda," pp. 60–61; Massafra, "Giurisdizione."

taken from a fiscal source refers to an uninhabited piece of feudal land in the plain near Foggia in Capitanata, farmed by the Cavaniglia marquis of San Marco in 1609. The farm occupied over 2,000 *tomoli* of land cultivated primarily with wheat, and to a much smaller extent with barley and other products. The fiscal document, probably exaggerating the expenses, reports gross revenues of ducats 11,881.3.05, and expenses of ducats 11,264.2.15, with a net profit of ducats 617.-.10, or only about five percent. The document, however, assesses the seed at the prices current in November, while assessing the yield at the prices current at the harvest, which were only about half of the former. Since there is no reason to suppose that the owner did not wait until the months of high prices to dispose of his production, it is necessary to calculate the value of the harvest at the same high price as that of the seed. The revenues, this way, ascend to ducats 23,445.3.10, with a net profit of over one hundred percent. It has to be considered, however, that the yield for the wheat in this instance was of 1:8.25, while in the land of the Caracciolo Brienza, from the few available data, we can conclude that yields probably rarely rose over 1:4–5. Given the cost of labor, large-scale farms could be profitable only with high yields, such as were common in a few regions of the kingdom, in the Lombard plains, and especially in Sicily.[26]

The attempt, therefore, to innovate the management of the Caracciolo Brienza's allodial lands remained an isolated one. As we shall see in a later chapter, the four *università* strenuously defended their rights over the feudal domain, so that the marquis seem never to have tried to innovate the system of old rents and *terraggi* existing on their feudal lands. The mentality of preservation of traditional agricultural methods, social situations, and economic relations that Lepre has shown applied to the feudal landowners of the plains of

---

[26] ASN Petizioni dei relevi 41–I, fols. 113v–21v; the marquis of San Marco was the husband of Giovan Battista Caracciolo's sister. In the same year, 1609, a smaller *masseria* the Cavaniglia owned in San Marco (in the province of Principato Ultra) gave a profit of about eighty percent, with a yield for the wheat of slightly over 1:6 (*ibid.*). On these issues, see Galasso, "Strutture sociali e produttive, assetti colturali e mercato dal secolo XVI all'Unità" in Massafra, ed. *Problemi*, pp. 159–72, particularly pp. 162–63; yields in different areas of the kingdom are discussed in Lepre, *Feudi*, pp. 53–54, 86, 96, 120–22, 126–27, and 138–42; Lepre, *Il Mezzogiorno dal feudalesimo al capitalismo* (Naples, 1979), pp. 126–37, and 185, and Lepre, "Azienda feudale e azienda agraria nel Mezzogiorno continentale tra Cinquecento e Ottocento" in Massafra, ed. *Problemi*, pp. 27–40; G. De Rosa and A. Cestaro, *Territorio e società nella storia del Mezzogiorno* (Naples, 1973), pp. 337–80; Marino, *Pastoral Economics in the Kingdom of Naples* (Baltimore, 1988), pp. 60–61 and notes. Average yields for the kingdom were between 1:4 and 1:6, but the inner mountainous provinces often had lower ones. In general they only began to increase in the late eighteenth and nineteenth centuries. The rotation system was based on the traditional three-year cycle in most of the kingdom (Caridi, *Uno stato*, considers the three-year cycle typical for Calabria, while D'Ambrosio, "La feudalità," finds frequent examples of two-year cycles in Terra di Lavoro). The yields in the kingdom were similar to those in other parts of Italy. Yields of 1:5–6 were frequent in inner Tuscany (Fanfani, *Potere*, pp. 221–25), and in Lazio (Pescosolido, *Terra*, pp. 63–66; R. Ago "Braccianti, contadini e grandi proprietari in un villaggio laziale nel

Puglia, was even stronger in the less fertile and more fragmented lands of the Caracciolo Brienza.[27]

Even in the eighteenth century, when more attention was given by the now solvent Caracciolo Brienza to the administration of their repurchased fiefs, no direct management was involved. The marquis Litterio had recourse instead to a very old type of contract, which had only occasionally been used in his fiefs in the previous century, that of emphyteusis, that had in the distant past served to cultivate previously unused land. Now small plots of land were rented to residents of the four fiefs in exchange for a fixed perpetual rent, which in most instances was paid in kind and therefore protected the marquis from devaluation of his revenues. The tenant was responsible for the proper upkeep of the land, and was by contract obligated to improve the land, most often by planting vines or fruit trees. Failure to meet these obligations, or to pay the rent for more than three years, would result in the reversion of the land to the marquis. Usually the plot could be sold or bequeathed by the tenant with the approval of the marquis who charged a fee at each change of hands, but occasionally the contract was subject to renewals when the rent could be increased. In Atena, some of these contracts took the form of investitures of subfeudal land, particularly in the last decade of the eighteenth century. Emphyteuses, used more and more frequently from the 1740s, guaranteed the marquis, who often resided in the fiefs and whose administration could by now count on a regular salaried staff and at least rudimentary book-keeping, the easy collection of secure revenues and allowed him to increase the value of his lands – over which, at least until the early decades of the nineteenth century, he kept close control – at practically no cost. Emphyteuses were enacted in several other areas of the kingdom and of Spain in the eighteenth century.[28]

The revenues from real estate, as Table 3.1 shows, oscillated in ways similar to the variations of non-landed income. The *terraggi* from the feudal domain were proportional to the harvest, while the rents for most allodial lands were proportional to the cultivated area so that baronial revenues from land followed closely the agricultural and demographic cycles. In a region of poor agriculture

primo '700" *QS* 16 (1981), pp. 60–91; Villani, "Ricerche sulla proprietà e sul regime fondiario nel Lazio" *Annuario dell'Istituto Storico Italiano per l'età moderna e contemporanea* 12 (1960), pp. 97–263; R. de Felice, *Aspetti e momenti della vita economica di Roma e del Lazio nei secoli XVIII e XIX* (Rome, 1965), pp. 53–55); McArdle finds yields of 1:6–8 in Altopascio, and reports that yields of 1:5 were considered quite low, *Altopascio*, pp. 94–95, and 104. The Lombard plains had higher and increasing yields and better rotation systems (Sella, *Crisis*, pp. 26–29). Sicily had average yields of up to 1:8–10 from Cicero's times to the twentieth century, see Aymard, "Rendements et productivité agricole dans l'Italie moderne" *Annales ESC* 28 (1973), pp. 475–98; Aymard, "En Sicile, dîmes et comptabilité agricole" in Le Roy Ladurie–Goy, eds. *Dîme*; O. Cancila, *Baroni e popolo nella Sicilia del grano* (Palermo, 1983), part I, chapter 6.
[27] Lepre, *Storia*, I, pp. 241–47.
[28] Contracts of emphyteusis in ACB 46.2, 47, 63.3, 76.3, and 82.4, (many documents from 46.2 and 76.3 are missing; summaries can be found in vols. 69 and 90 respectively); vols. 119, 121, 124, 127, and 130, compiled in the early years of the nineteenth century, record the rents and

and almost no innovation, it was only in the later eighteenth century that landed revenues grew considerably, not only in absolute figures – because of population growth – but also in comparison with the other components of baronial income. With the short-lived exception of the *masserie*, there was also no substantial difference in the ways allodial and feudal property were managed.

This analysis of baronial revenues shows that the Caracciolo Brienza, similarly to many another aristocratic family in the kingdom, did not as a rule try to innovate in the way in which any of the revenues of their fiefs were administered. With a few short-lived exceptions, over two centuries renting out feudal and monopoly rights and feudal and allodial lands was the common practice. Besides its undoubted advantages of very limited cost and compliance with a tradition-oriented mentality, this method of management suited the geographic characteristics of the four fiefs and the financial vicissitudes of the family. For non-landed income, the amount of revenues in each year depended on the expectations of profit that prospective tenants had in making their offers for the rent to the baronial administrators. Those expectations were based on the fiefs' population and general economic situation, and of course on the profits made by previous tenants. To a certain extent these elements influenced also the revenues from land. But the types of production, the possibilities for commercialization of the products, the varying yields of each year, and the strong traditional patterns of land management, also played a central role in determining the Caracciolo Brienza's landed revenues.

PRODUCTION AND MARKETS

In the preceding section we discussed the Caracciolo Brienza's revenues from their fiefs in terms of their monetary value and the relative importance of their sources. But a significant part of baronial revenues was actually levied in kind, particularly landed revenues and the rent of the mill. As in most of the kingdom, the baronial administration was the largest collector of grains in the fiefs, and therefore the main source of grains for the market. We shall analyze the family's revenues in grains and their evolution over time, then briefly consider other crops, and discuss the possibilities for commercialization of the baronial revenues in kind.

emphyteuses in the four fiefs; 76.1, the subfiefs in Atena. Examples of emphyteusis are in Visceglia, *Territorio*, pp. 240–41; Visceglia, "Formazione," p. 597; Visceglia, "L'azienda"; M. Benaiteau, "Les dépendances féodales des di Tocco en Calabre Citérieure: 1788–1810" in acts of the Sixth Congresso Storico Calabrese *La Calabria dalle riforme alla restaurazione* (2 vols.; Catanzaro, 1981), II, pp. 15–26; Delille, *Croissance*, pp. 239–43; Villani, ed. *Economia e classi sociali nella Puglia moderna* (Naples, 1974), p. 10 and pp. 123–34; Hurtubise, *Une famille*, chapter 11; J. M. Torras i Ribé, *Evolució social i econòmica d'una família catalana de l'antic règim* (Barcelona, 1976), pp. 117–20; a discussion of emphyteusis, as a contract typical of poorer areas, is in Giorgetti, *Contadini*, pp. 94–103. The Caracciolo Brienza did not, therefore, display the activist management that has been observed for other areas of the kingdom in the early eighteenth century, see D'Ambrosio, "La feudalità."

The region was by and large not favorable to any form of agricultural production other than the traditional combination of grain with livestock breeding, and the baronial lands in particular were devoted to grain cultivation. The fragmentation of the rents for the Caracciolo Brienza's lands makes it very difficult to gather precise information about the production and yields of the land, also because the accounts of the *conservatori* are in general not available before the later eighteenth century. The assessments discussed above, however, provide useful data at least on the *terraggi*. The data on other rents are less useful for comparisons since the cultivated plots were often different in different years, and frequently, even if a plot of the same name appears in more than one year, the cultivated area is different. The *terraggi*, on the other hand, referred always to the same land, namely the open feudal domain, and can therefore give an approximate picture of the oscillations and of the types of production in the four fiefs. The *terraggi* refer only to grain production because, since the land on which they were levied was subject to grazing rights, no other cultivation would be possible. A variation in the size of the *terraggi* – which represented ten percent of the production of these lands – could be determined by a change both in the land's yield and in the area of the domain cultivated in any given year. Either way, the *terraggi* offer a reasonably accurate picture of the variations in the grain production of the fiefs. Similar information can be obtained from the revenues of the mills, where the local residents paid a fee in kind equal to a fixed share of the grain they milled.

Tables 3.2 and 3.3 present the available data. Though some of the fluctuations must be attributed to the different characteristics of the documents, the basic trend is clear. Production increased considerably in the sixteenth century, and more outside the feudal domain (as shown by the revenues from the mill) than on it, which was certainly due to the large increase in population in this period. After the 1620s there was a decline, first gradual and then quite rapid, especially in the 1650s and 1660s. Though the figures for 1680 and 1686 probably underestimate the Caracciolo Brienza's income, the recovery seems to have been fairly slow until the last decade of the seventeenth century. By the 1720s, production increased to a level higher than that of a century before, and the increase continued into the later eighteenth century, this time affecting – as the demand for land grew considerably – also the feudal domain, though still at a lower rate than the land outside of it.

The Caracciolo Brienza *stato* seems, therefore, to have had a slightly different chronology of economic difficulties from that of other, more prosperous and less isolated regions of the kingdom. Until about 1620, the four fiefs do not seem to have experienced the fairly severe economic crisis that touched parts of Puglia, though the 1590s marked a halt in the preceding growth. Perhaps also because of the financial difficulties of the family, however, in the 1620s the four fiefs witnessed a sharper, earlier, and quicker decline in agricultural production than

Management of the landed patrimony

Table 3.2. *Revenue in kind from the feudal terraggi* (1521–1776)
(in *tomoli*)

year	Brienza wheat	Brienza barley	Braide	Pietrafesa wheat	Pietrafesa barley	Sasso wheat	Sasso barley	rye
1521–22	1,219	140½	–	104½	12	–	–	–
1570	–	–	–	–	–	215	82	–
1592–93	1,200	600	–	500	–	–	–	–
1623	1,000	300	500	500	–	175	30	2½
1625	500	200	600+200	500	–	150	–	–
1646	500	200	500	–	–	–	–	–
c.1650	200	100	–	250	100	100	–	–
1651	140	127	400	–	–	–	–	–
1657	400	200	300	100	50	210	80	30
1677	952	331	–	–	43	–	–	–
1680	378½	–	350	–	–	106	37	–
1686	382	200	266½	–	–	110	40	48
1726	800	400	–	400	–	348	116	58
1747	1,000/700	500/350	150	150	–	270	–	–
1748	–	–	–	–	–	262½	81½	45
1762	866½	433	–	183	–	334	110	–
1776	–	–	–	–	–	309	121½	67½

Sources: these are the same as for Table 3.1, plus, for the 1590s, the agreements cited in footnote 11, and for 1762, the accounts in ACB vols. 57, 66, and 87. The documents that provide these figures are of different origins: the assessments of 1625, 1646–48, 1676–77, 1748, and 1776 were drawn up by government functionaries and are probably the most reliable; many of the other figures are derived from fiscal documents that probably underestimate the family's revenues. The Braide was a feudal territory that the Caracciolo Brienza rented out regularly throughout the years for a rent in wheat. Its rent was not included in the general agreement of 1592. In 1625, its rent was 600 *tomoli* of wheat and 200 of barley. In 1677, its rent was included in the general *terraggi*. The figure for Pietrafesa in 1726 includes wheat, barley, and oats. In Sasso in 1762, the 334 *tomoli* of wheat also include rye. In 1776, the 309 *tomoli* of wheat include 132½ *tomoli* of *mischio*, a mixture of wheat and rye. L. Granata, *Economia rustica per lo regno di Napoli* (2 vols.; Naples, 1830), II, part IV, observed that rye was particularly common in the mountainous regions of the kingdom; see also A. Placanica, *Uomini, strutture, economia in Calabria nei secoli XVI–XVIII* (Reggio Calabria, 1974), p. 46. Differences in prices in the various years are not taken into account in this or the following table. In Atena, the *terraggi* were included in the 1592 agreement for 600 *tomoli* of wheat. After that, however, the feudal lands in Atena were rented out in separate plots, and there are almost no data on *terraggi*. I have rounded figures to the closest half *tomolo*.

89

Table 3.3. *Revenue in wheat from the feudal mills (1521–1776)*
(in *tomoli*)

year	Brienza	Pietrafesa	Sasso
1521–22	225	144½	75
1570	–	300 (1572)	121½
1625	572½	450	260
1648	500 (1646)	–	165
c.1650	220	200	150
1651	300	250	–
1657	300	270	186
1676–77	551	305	200½
1680	356	270	180
1686	360	270	180
1726	660	380	132 + 116 rye
1747	600/900	250	250
1748	–	–	322
1762	1,020	450	445½
1776	–	–	349 + 196 *mischio*

Sources: these are the same as for Table 3.2; the mill in Atena was not a feudal monopoly.

provinces like Terra di Lavoro, Principato Ultra, or the plains of Principato Citra, where production was supported by the needs of the neighboring and expanding capital. Later, however, their relative isolation and the ensuing smaller losses in the 1656 plague helped bring about an earlier and possibly faster recovery in the economy of the Caracciolo Brienza's fiefs, which began in the 1680s and by the 1720s had more or less compensated for the losses of the previous century. The huge losses of the city of Naples in the plague also brought about a decline in its demand for grain that hit particularly the wealthier provinces that provided that grain rather than other provinces.[29]

If we can glean a relatively clear picture of grain production in the Caracciolo Brienza's *stato*, it is much more difficult to assess any other production, though it is evident that grains were by far the most important product. As mentioned above, the baronial administration often managed directly a vineyard, probably intended for household consumption. In general, the seventeenth-century assessments mention few vines and even fewer olive trees, and none of the four

[29] For the decline in the rent for Brienza and Pietrafesa, see chapter 2, Table 2.3. Zotta, "Momenti"; Benaiteau, "La rendita"; Lepre, *Feudi* and *Terra di Lavoro*; Villone, *Privilegi*; Visceglia, "Durata e rinnovamento delle famiglie feudali in Terra d'Otranto tra Medioevo ed età moderna" paper presented at the department of history in the University of Naples on 11 June 1986; L. Masella, "Mercato fondiario e prezzi della terra nella Puglia barese tra XVII e XVIII secolo" *MEFRM* 88 (1976), pp. 261–96; Lepre, "Rendite di monasteri nel Napoletano e crisi economica del '600" *QS* 5 (1970), pp. 844–65; for Sicily, see Aymard, "Strutture."

fiefs had an olive press, which constituted an important feudal monopoly in other provinces of the kingdom such as Puglia. In the eighteenth century a few more vines were planted in the fiefs, and the *Catasto* of the 1740s reports a fair number of vines in the four fiefs. Still at that time, however, from two thirds to three fourths of the taxed land in the villages was "naked arable land" (*seminativo nudo*), with the exception of Sasso, the fief with the least fertile and cultivated land, where the percentage was fifty-one percent. These figures are higher than in other parts of the kingdom, and therefore reinforce the view of the Caracciolo Brienza's *stato* as a region of relatively backward agriculture.[30]

Of the cultivated land in Sasso, which as a whole represented only thirty percent of the territory of this fief mainly dedicated to pasture, forty-two percent was "tree-covered arable land" (*seminativo arborato*, grain fields with trees – fruit, olives, vines) and "enclosures" (*chiuse*, fenced or hedged fields that may in part include trees). In Atena nine percent, or 251½ *tomoli*, of the taxed land consisted of vineyards, and seven and a half percent of *seminativo arborato*. Atena, less mountainous than the other three fiefs, also had more olive trees. In the much larger taxed territories of Brienza and Pietrafesa, *seminativo arborato* represented thirteen and twelve percent respectively, and there was no land clearly marked as vineyards. Most often, to judge from the lists of plots of lands included in the family papers, *seminativo arborato* referred to either fruit trees (especially pear and apple trees) or oaks.

These figures refer to taxed land belonging to the whole population of the fiefs. The baron at the time of the *Catasto* owned no vines in Sasso, only two percent of the vineyards in Atena, and only three and a half and five percent of the vines existing in Brienza and Pietrafesa respectively, showing the limited role wine production played in the baronial economy. The *Catasto* considered only allodial land, but we know from the assessments that at the most one or two small plots of feudal land were vineyards, and the feudal domain was always only available for grain production.[31]

The baronial administration therefore received relatively large revenues in kind that consisted mostly of wheat, though other grains like barley or rye and

[30] Delille, *Croissance*, pp. 179–84, notes that tree-covered arable land (*seminativo arborato*) was considerably more profitable; see the comments of L. Granata, *Economia rustica per lo regno di Napoli* (2 vols.; Naples, 1830), II, part IV; E. Sereni, *Storia del paesaggio agrario italiano* (Bari, 1982; first edit. 1961), pp. 227–29 and 266–69, describes the advanced areas of Southern agriculture, with their abundance of trees; many fiefs in Calabria, for instance, had numerous mulberry trees.

[31] The percentages here reported, as well as most of the information in these pages, are derived from Villari, *Mezzogiorno e contadini nell'età moderna* (Bari, 1961; new edit. 1977), particularly the tables on pp. 76, 82, 98, and 108. These tables concern the land taxed in the *Catasto*, and they include pastures for Brienza and Atena and woods in Pietrafesa. The total area about which data are available was 1,488 *tomoli* in Sasso, 2,808½ in Atena, 6,933½ in Pietrafesa, and 11,116 in Brienza. This did not include feudal land and the commons.

small quantities of wine or oil were also part of the income of the Caracciolo Brienza's *conservatori*, particularly in the eighteenth century. Around 1726, for instance, the baronial storage rooms in the four fiefs contained a total of 12,080¼ *tomoli* of wheat, 1,494 *tomoli* of barley, 172 *tomoli* of rye, 1½ *tomoli* of broad beans, 600 *some* of wine, and several barrels of oil. This was far from the forty or fifty thousand *tomoli* of wheat produced annually by the *masserie* of the Jesuits in Puglia, but it represented nonetheless a large enough amount to market. The *conservatori* were responsible for the use of these products and they stored them, delivered them to the barons' household for consumption, and, most often, sold them. Throughout the kingdom, as in Sicily, feudal lords collected much of their revenues in kind and served as the link between their vassals and outside markets for agricultural production. Though the Caracciolo Brienza rarely played a significant role in long-distance grain trade, they were heavily involved in the commercialization of grain at the local level.[32]

It is not until the 1750s that we have records of the *conservatori*'s administration. In the years 1756–63, for instance, they were selling an average of about 2,500 *tomoli* of wheat a year in Brienza, 1,300 *tomoli* in Pietrafesa, 800 *tomoli* in Atena, and 500 *tomoli* in Sasso. A summary look at these records indicates that at that time most of the sales took place in the fiefs themselves, in relatively small quantities and to local residents. In fact in the 1730s, the annual fair of Brienza was reinstituted and served mainly the needs of the village's residents and of the inhabitants of the neighboring region. We know that grain production in Sasso was insufficient to meet the needs of the village's population, and in Pietrafesa and Atena many people needed to buy at least some of the grain their families consumed. A fair was established in Atena in 1767. It is therefore most likely that a large part of the baronial reserves in kind was sold to the population of the fiefs and of the neighboring villages, thereby emphasizing the central role of the Caracciolo Brienza in their communities and no doubt strengthening their local power. This is confirmed by the observation on the part of the 1775 appraiser of Atena that the wheat produced in that fief was to be evaluated at a low price because of the difficulties the marquis encountered in selling it, since the neighboring villages usually produced enough wheat to meet their needs. The

---

[32] ACB 16.8i. All cited works refer to the role of the barons in the commercialization of agricultural production, though local markets are almost never analyzed; see especially Lepre, *Feudi*, tables on pp. 138–42, on the production of the Jesuits' *masserie*, and pp. 23–24, and 149 (an example of local markets in Abruzzo); Lepre, *Storia*, I, pp. 73–74, and 109–113, and "Le campagne"; for Sicily, see Aymard, "Une famille"; E. Pontieri, *Il tramonto del baronaggio siciliano* (Florence, 1943), pp. 53–56; M. Verga, "Un esempio di colonizzazione interna nella Sicilia del XVIII secolo" in M. Mirri, ed. *Ricerche di storia moderna* (2 vols.; Pisa, 1979), II, pp. 261–95. No maize production appears for the Caracciolo Brienza's fiefs, even in the eighteenth century; in Northern Italy, maize production was by that time quite important, see McArdle, *Altopascio*, chapter 4.

relatively poor quality of the barons' grain reserves may also be part of the reason for this.[33]

In the eighteenth century, the fiefs constituted a primary market for the revenues in kind of the baronial administration. There are indications, however, that the situation might have been different one or two centuries before. The Caracciolo Brienza's fiefs were certainly in a relatively isolated region of the kingdom, and the impervious roads or paths that led to them, and particularly to Sasso, were frequently the object of disparaging remarks well into the eighteenth century on the part of government appraisers and especially of elderly or less than sedulous bishops. The *stato* had nonetheless a compact internal organization and, though few *vaticali* (traveling carriers) were seen in Sasso, Atena, down in the valley, represented a relatively easy outlet for men and goods that could from there reach by land either Salerno or any of the small harbors on the coast of the Cilento. In fact, even when in the mid-eighteenth century the sale of the baron's wheat seems to have been limited to the neighboring villages, the marquis Litterio pointed out that it was important that Atena and Sasso be owned by the same baron, since Atena served as an outlet for goods produced in the other fief.[34]

In the previous centuries the family had at times sold its wheat outside of the region. In the sixteenth and early seventeenth century, the rapid growth of the population of the city of Naples created an enormous problem for the Spanish government, which had to ensure the provision of bread for the city's populace. The system of the *Annona* (grain dole) organized then remained a central economic structure of the kingdom until the end of the old regime. Much of the needed grain in normal years came from the fertile plains of Puglia, but the largest part came by land from the three provinces closest to the capital, the two Principati and Terra di Lavoro. At least on some occasions, however, the Caracciolo Brienza succeeded, probably through the help of high-placed relatives, in selling the products of their own distant fiefs to the city government of Naples.[35]

---

[33] ACB 32 contains the accounts of the *erari* and *conservatori* for the years 1756–63; vols. 57, 66, 79, and 87 are the accounts from 1763 to the end of the 1770s. Information on the fair of Brienza in ACB 45.6.1–4, quoted also by Villari, *Mezzogiorno*, p. 70. The fair in Atena in ACB 76.4.9–10. For the needs of the local population in the mid-eighteenth century, see Villari, *Mezzogiorno*. For 1776, see ACB 77.2.33, section II. The poor quality of the baron's wheat is blamed by the Caracciolo Brienza's *erario* in 1747 for the failure to sell it to outside merchants, see ASN Catasto Onciario 5149, fols. 170r–71r. For examples of sales of grain on the local market by the Doria of Melfi, see R. Colapietra, *Dal Magnanimo a Masaniello* (2 vols.; Salerno, 1973), II, p. 431.

[34] ACB 77.2.25.

[35] P. Macry, *Mercato e società nel regno di Napoli; commercio del grano e politica economica nel Settecento* (Naples, 1974); Marino, *Pastoral Economics*, chapter 7. The fief of Eboli, in the plain of the Sele, produced grain, oil, and cheese that were sold in Naples, see Villani, ed. "Eboli nel 1640" *Rassegna storica salernitana* (1953), pp. 196–207. A good discussion of the trade situation is in P. Chorley, *Oil, Silk and the Enlightenment. Economic Problems in Eighteenth-Century Naples* (Naples, 1965).

In 1600, the marquis Giovan Battista sold 20,000 *tomoli* of wheat to the city of Naples at a price of thirteen *carlini* each, for a total of 26,000 ducats. In 1616 he sold another 16,000 *tomoli* at a price of eleven *carlini*, or 17,600 ducats total, that were to be brought to Naples by boat from the Cilento port of Libonati. In 1620, at Giovan Battista's death, among his properties in Naples were counted 8,000 *tomoli* of wheat sold in the city at different prices. In the same year, the new marquis Marco Antonio II paid for the transportation by boat of 4,398 *tomoli* of wheat in three separate instalments from the port of Oliva to the capital. For the contract of 1616 we know that the prince Caracciolo Avellino, Giovan Battista's cousin, was the mediator and guarantor in his position as *Grassiero*, the viceroy's deputy in the city government's dealings with the *Annona*, and we can suspect a similar intervention on the other occasions.[36]

There is no evidence of any other envoys to the capital in later years, and as we have seen in the mid-seventeenth century, the amount of grain available to the Caracciolo Brienza declined somewhat, as did the city of Naples' need for grain, particularly after the 1656 plague. Indeed, the scale of these envoys is such that they probably involved the Caracciolo Brienza's revenues in kind for several years. In the later seventeenth century, however, there was still some market for the family's products outside of its fiefs. In 1674, though he complained that he "could sooner receive news from Spain than from Sasso," the prince of Macchia – then administrator of that fief – mentioned shipments of wheat to Salerno, and his agent in the fief paid for the transportation of wheat and cheese from Sasso to Salerno. Both also mentioned the shipment of a limited quantity of raw silk to the same city.[37]

It seems, therefore, that the geographic isolation of the Caracciolo Brienza's *stato* could be overcome when favorable circumstances – the increasing production in the fiefs until the 1620s, the growing needs of the population of Naples, and the close family ties with the *Grassiero* – allowed it, and that large profits were available on these occasions. After the recession in the kingdom's economy, however, the sales of the baronial revenues in kind remained limited to the fiefs themselves and to the immediate region. Even when in the eighteenth century production increased again, the parallel growth and social

---

[36] ACB App. 22 unnumbered fol., the inventory at Giovan Battista's death; ASN Assensi Feudali 3, unnumbered fol., act of 9 November 1616; ASBN, Popolo, Giornale Banco 27, p. 66, 2 September 1600; ASBN, AGP, Giornale Cassa 76, unnumbered fol., 4 July and 4 August 1620, and Giornale Banco 77, unnumbered fol., 4 July 1620. No other examples of such sales appeared in my sample of the documents in ASBN.

[37] ASN Pandetta Corrente 570, vol. marked 2, fols. 426v–35r and 448r–97v (a series of letters of the prince to his agent; the quote is on fol. 458r); there is never, with the exception of some linen produced in Pietrafesa, any mention of any other textiles among the baronial production in the four fiefs. The fact that the prince of Macchia was in litigation with his sister, the marquise of Brienza, may help explain why he tried to sell the products of Sasso outside the surrounding region.

differentiation in the local population, and the decreased needs of the city of Naples, led the family to continue the now established policy of using the local markets. With presumably high transportation costs, and relatively low chances of profit, there were few incentives for the long-distance commercialization of the agricultural production of the fiefs. This policy may have also been encouraged by the innate conservatism of the baronial administration, intent on preserving things as they were, and especially in the eighteenth century – when slow and gradual changes were taking place also at the local level – particularly weary of potentially dangerous innovations and of any initiative of uncertain consequences.[38]

INVESTMENTS

The same conservatism of the baronial administration was evident in the Caracciolo Brienza's investment policy. While a few initiatives were taken in the decades around 1600, after the 1620s the family withdrew from any attempt to increase or differentiate the production of its lands. In a relatively unfortunate region, this policy did not prove harmful to the baronial revenues and favored fairly peaceful relations with the vassals.

As we have seen, the Caracciolo Brienza's revenues declined somewhat and then grew again in the course of the seventeenth century, so that in the early eighteenth century they were about equal to what they had been in the late sixteenth, also in real terms. Their further growth in the later eighteenth century was not due to any intervention of the marquis, or to any significant changes in the management techniques, but to the general expansion of the kingdom's economy and population. Though his patrimony had more solid bases, in most respects the marquis of Brienza in the 1780s was still making his money in the way his ancestors had two centuries before. In assessing this continuity one ought to consider that, again, in most respects the latter marquis' economic and social position within the kingdom differed but little from that of his forebears.

Ultimately, therefore, unlike barons in more prosperous regions, the family did not need to alter its economic relations with its vassals and the traditional administration of its landed wealth. The few attempts we can document to innovate and to reinvest profits in the fiefs took place in the late sixteenth and early seventeenth centuries, when the aristocracy was involved in a general move to protect and enlarge its grip on its lands. These attempts were discontinued with the family's financial troubles and the general economic difficulties of the kingdom in the central decades of the seventeenth century, and were never resumed to the same degree, perhaps also out of a concern to preserve good relations with the vassals after the revolt of 1647–48. We have seen that the five

---

[38] Besides the cited literature, see the contrasting arguments of the marquis of Brienza and his creditors on the proper management methods for baronial property in Sasso, ASN Pandetta Corrente 2026, II, fols. 117r–22r and 169r–78r (May 1748).

masserie of 1611 remained an isolated instance of direct involvement in grain production on the part of the Caracciolo Brienza. Long-distance commercialization of revenues in kind also appears to have been tried only in the first two generations of the family's feudal rule. Other practices that can be considered as investments were the ownership of livestock and the extension of land holdings.

All four of the Caracciolo Brienza fiefs, but especially Pietrafesa and Sasso, included large pastures and woods where livestock grazed, particularly sheep, goats, and pigs. The fiefs were not involved in the system of transhumant breeding typical of the northeastern provinces of the kingdom, and the animals were kept in the local territory the whole year. Livestock was, obviously but unfortunately, allodial, non-landed property, and therefore it is almost never mentioned in the fiscal documents or in the appraisals of the fiefs, making it difficult to assess the family's involvement in livestock breeding. The marquis collected revenues from the *fida* levied on their vassals' livestock, but we have scant and random information on their own animals. In general, large livestock like cattle and horses could be managed by the barons directly – the enterprise was also referred to as a *masseria* – while pigs, sheep and goats were usually farmed out to local peasants for a rent or under agreements to share the profits. Almost nothing is known about the products of these endeavors and about their outlets.[39]

The marquis Giovan Battista owned livestock, and in the general lease of his fiefs in 1600 he reserved the right to keep up to 4,000 animals grazing on the land; two years later the rent for Diano granted the marquis pasture rights for his two *masserie* of cows, mares, and buffaloes. Giovan Battista left his animals to his widow Diana, who was active in "the businesses of grain and livestock." Their son, Giacomo, faced with a diminished patrimony and many creditors, sold half of his livestock in 1623 including buffaloes, cows, and 500 sheep. He inherited his uncle Marino's livestock – consisting of at least 100 cows, 60 sows, 20 mares, and 1,500 sheep – at Marino's widow's death, but probably these two were sold by mid-century.[40]

Livestock required very little labor and was therefore an easy investment for the baronial administration. We know nothing of the profitability for the family of these limited enterprises, but of all the marquis' properties in the fiefs they were obviously the easiest to sell in times of need. In 1673–74 in Brienza and Pietrafesa, the Caracciolo Brienza owned only 35 mares, a few mules for the stables, and 146 pigs. In 1672 in Sasso, the baron's agent listed 1,044 sheep and goats, but most had already been sold. In 1674, the prince of Macchia kept a *masseria* of buffaloes in Sasso and marketed the resulting cheese in Salerno. By

---

[39] Woolf, *Studi*, p. 123, laments the same problems with the evidence on livestock for the Piedmontese aristocracy. On the legal situations of private and public pastures, see P. Rendella, *Tractatus de pascuis, defensis, forestis et aquis . . .* (Trani, 1630).
[40] ACB 45.7.2; 138.20; 4.1.14; ASN Pandetta Corrente 570, vol. marked 3, fols. 168v–72v, 332r (the quote about Diana); ASP notai Potenza 235, fols. 2v–3v.

the 1680s in Brienza and Pietrafesa, the marquis only owned twenty-four pigs and sows, fifteen calves, a few stable mules, and twenty oxen to use in the fields. The livestock in Sasso was also sold in these years. In 1720, Imara Ruffo's dowry included 71 pigs and sows worth 171 ducats, 1,308 sheep and goats worth 1,205 ducats, and 18 mares and colts worth 450 ducats, all in her mother's Calabrian fiefs. No other mention is made of this livestock, and by the late eighteenth century the marquis Litterio, discussing his mother's dowry, did not refer to it at all.

The *Catasto* documents of the 1740s identified several households as "shepherds" – though most of these owned some land too – and showed several animals in the four fiefs. Although the baron owned all of the 1,100 *tomoli* of pasture in Brienza, 606 *tomoli* of woods in Pietrafesa, and 340 of the 350 *tomoli* of pasture in Atena, however, his livestock included only thirty cows and oxen in Brienza, and twenty-three horses and seventy-five buffaloes in Atena, without any in either Pietrafesa or Sasso, the two fiefs more devoted to livestock breeding. The family therefore kept few animals after the mid-seventeenth century, mostly the less valuable and more easily manageable sheep and goats, and by the eighteenth century withdrew even from this modest entrepreneurial activity. In 1761–62, Litterio sold a few colts in Salerno and Gravina (in Puglia) and expressed his pride in the quality of his horses, but this seems to have remained an isolated instance.[41]

This contrasts with the situation in other regions of the kingdom that were better suited to livestock breeding. Besides the government-regulated transhumance of Abruzzo and Capitanata, in fact, the marshes and plains of the Sele basin and of Terra di Lavoro offered the opportunity of good profits with relatively little expense, particularly for buffalo breeding for which they were, and are, renowned. The Caracciolo Brienza in any event never invested much in their livestock, and even some of their neighboring barons proved more active in this field. In the seventeenth century, for instance, the Doria princes of Melfi kept almost 10,000 ovines, 1,400 pigs, 500 cattle, and over 250 buffaloes in their fiefs between Basilicata and Puglia.[42]

[41] ASN Pandetta Corrente 570, vol. marked 2, fols. 380v–81v, 408r–9r, 426v–35r, 487r–89v; vol. marked 12, fols. 61r–66r; ACB 3.2.15; 161, unnumbered fol.; 140.40, fols. 16r, 19r, and 35r–39v; Villari, *Mezzogiorno*, throughout and tables. Two lists of books included in ACB refer to accounts kept for a *masseria* of cows and one of mares, but these books do not exist anymore in the archive; they seem to date from the last third of the eighteenth century, see ACB 109, fols. 72r–74r, and 69 under the heading "Scanzia 13." On the labor required for livestock breeding, see Massafra, "Giurisdizione," pp. 244–47. Livestock breeding became more common in the Vallo di Diano (which includes Atena) in the nineteenth century, see G. Aliberti, *Potere e società locale nel Mezzogiorno dell'Ottocento* (Bari, 1987), chapter 4.

[42] Zotta, "Rapporti," pp. 267 and 277–78; Colapietra, *Dal Magnanimo*, II, pp. 480–86. Villani, "Vicende della proprietà fondiaria in un comune latifondistico del Mezzogiorno" *Annuario dell'Istituto Storico Italiano per l'età moderna e contemporanea*, 12 (1960), pp. 17–96; Villani, "Eboli"; Lepre, *Feudi*, App. I; M. L. Storchi, "Un'azienda agricola della piana del Sele tra il 1842 ed il 1855" in Massafra, ed. *Problemi*, pp. 117–39. A buffalo needed more than twice as much land as an ox, see Musi, "Il Principato Citeriore nella crisi agraria del XVII secolo" in *ibid.*, p. 182. The Calabrian *stato* studied by Caridi (*Uno "stato"*) was marked by a combination of livestock breeding and grain production.

Another form of investment to increase the revenues of the fiefs was the purchase of additional rights and lands. The Caracciolo Brienza bought several feudal rights from the crown in the early years of their feudal rule. The marquis Giovan Battista engaged in a policy of relatively extensive purchase of land that can be related to his attempt to establish a few farms in the fiefs and to the marketing of his grain reserves in Naples. Between 1584 and 1599, and then again between 1603 and 1607, he bought numerous plots of land in his fiefs, usually bordering on land he already owned. He also exchanged several plots in order to consolidate his fragmented holdings. Most of the plots he purchased were used for grain production, with or without fruit trees, but a few included buildings or vines. In general, Giovan Battista bought the land directly, but in a few instances the property passed to him because of a credit. Other means could be used too: in 1607 a resident of Pietrafesa donated a vine and eleven *tomoli* of land worth 100 ducats to Giovan Battista "out of affection," though the fact that the donor was involved in a lawsuit to be decided by the baronial court may have contributed to that worthy feeling. In 1586, the marquis appropriated thirty-seven *tomoli* of land in Pietrafesa, worth 150 ducats, as a transaction fee for a case of uxoricide.[43]

Table 3.4 presents the total value and extension of Giovan Battista's purchases, without considering the exchanges. These purchases did not involve too large an amount of money (ducats 9,654.1.12), since the Caracciolo Brienza had at this time annual revenues of about nine or ten thousand ducats, though, coming as they did at a time when the patrimony was burdened with increasing debts, they certainly represented a further strain on Giovan Battista's wealth and may be seen as an attempt to counter the financial crisis towards which the family was headed with a more active presence in the fiefs. The purchases, in any event, succeeded in enlarging considerably the family's lands; in 1625 the appraiser assessed at least 4,800 *tomoli* of allodial land, of which the land bought by Giovan Battista represented more – probably much more – than twenty percent.

Again, it was Giovan Battista's son Giacomo who had to withdraw from his father's policy. In the years after 1625 the marquis sold several of the plots his father had bought. Throughout the rest of the century, the family only on one occasion purchased real estate in the fiefs – a house for ten ducats in Pietrafesa in 1663 – though it received a few donations and exacted real estate from a couple of debtors. Only in the eighteenth century, and particularly from about 1755 on, did the Caracciolo Brienza again buy land in the fiefs and still on a much smaller scale than before; the marquis Litterio also sold a few plots. For large-scale purchases we have to wait for the dissolution of ecclesiastic property in 1798, when Cataldo Caracciolo bought land in Atena that had belonged to chapels and charitable institutions for a value of 6,438 ducats.[44]

---

[43] ACB 63.2.15 and 26 (I have not counted these two acquisitions in Table 3.4).
[44] Giacomo's sales in ASP notai Potenza 232 and 235; for the other information, see ACB 46.1.55–67; 63.2.34–38; 76.2.17–29; 82.2.20–21; and 82.3.1–2; ASP notai Potenza 235, fols. 36v–37r (sales may be underrepresented in ACB and the notai Potenza documents in ASP are not

Table 3.4. *Giovan Battista's purchases in the fiefs (1584–1611)*

fief	ducats	tomoli	buildings	vines
Brienza	2,217.-.02	200+	9	13
Pietrafesa	4,694	610+	3	8
Atena	2,276	103+	3	5
Sasso	215.2.10	9+	–	7
Satriano	251.4.-	60½	–	–
totals	9,654.1.12	1,072½+	15	33

Sources: ACB 46.1.4 (an unnumbered list of notarial acts, several of which duplicate the acts in the following bundles); 46.1.5–53; 133.2; 63.1.1–8; 63.2.1–33; 76.2.1–16; 82.2.2–19; ASP notai Potenza 46, fols. 164r–67v (some of the acts in ACB are duplicated in the registers of local notaries in ASP). Only one sale of land by Giovan Battista is documented, that of a garden for thirteen ducats in 1604, ACB 47.2.1. Satriano was an uninhabited fief bordering Pietrafesa in which the Caracciolo Brienza – and many Pietrafesani – owned several plots of arable land. Though the prices paid are always reported, the extension of the plots is not, so the figure for the latter is certainly, and probably considerably, underestimated.

The relative poverty of the region and the inherent traditionalism of aristocratic landownership combined, therefore, to minimize the Caracciolo Brienza's interventions to change the economy of their fiefs. In a primitive agriculture in which investments and innovations were risky, the marquis preferred to preserve their revenues as they were, and the attempts to expand their landed properties, add new sources of revenues, enter a larger commercial network, or become directly involved in agricultural production, were overall remarkably short-lived, if not altogether unsuccessful. An increase in productivity was very unlikely, and would have required substantive changes in the structure of property, such as eliminating the communal use of the feudal domain. This could have had unpredictable consequences on the lords' relationship with the communities, and the family pursued instead a policy of stability and continuity. Its revenues were in large part dependent on the size of the fiefs' population, and thereby almost always protected from sudden or extreme declines. Even the losses of the plague were relatively smaller and shorter-lived than elsewhere.

It is not surprising, therefore, that, with the partial exception of the *masserie*, the few more entrepreneurial activities of the Caracciolo Brienza were designed

complete, so it is possible that the family sold more than I can properly document). In 1680, the marquis obtained a vine in a transaction for a murder case, but it was soon donated to a local chapel, *ibid.*, 648, fols. 21v–22v. In 1800, Cataldo also took advantage of the dissolution of the property of the Carthusian monastery of San Lorenzo in nearby Padula to buy more than 200 *tomoli* of land there for 14,940 ducats (ACB 90, under 89.4.1–7).

to increase their revenues by increasing the number of their sources rather than the productivity of any existing source. Only in the later eighteenth century did the numerous contracts of emphyteusis demonstrate an interest on the marquis' part in improving the productivity of his land, and, significantly, this was achieved through recourse to a very old form of contract, that moreover placed all the burdens and the risks of the innovation solidly on the shoulders of the tenant farmer. Again, the population growth of the later eighteenth century made it possible for the marquis to enforce these contracts, as competition for land among the local peasants increased. As shown in the previous chapter, the only documented investment of the Caracciolo Brienza in increasing the productivity of their land took place outside of the fiefs, in their allodial *masseria* in the fertile plain near Naples.

Even the attention given by the marquis Litterio to a careful administration, his organization of an archive, and the regular use by his agents of account books, signaled no new conception of the primary goals of the feudal administration. No better and more accurate surveys of revenues and lands, such as the *terriers* commissioned by the French aristocracy in the eighteenth century, were produced for the Caracciolo Brienza. The account books – like those of the princes Borghese in Rome and of many other aristocratic landowners across Europe – were simple lists of income and expenses, all counted together without any distinction or accounting sophistication.[45]

This policy of continuity suited the widespread mentality of respect for past ways that was particularly strong in the region of the Caracciolo Brienza's fiefs. Jurists like Novario had always defended time-honored customs and traditions in the relations between lords and vassals; the communities' right to use the feudal domain and the old institutions of village self-governance survived until the end of the old regime, at least in some regions of the kingdom. The commons of Atena were still distributed periodically among the villagers in the 1780s as they had been two or three centuries before, and when in 1792 the government allowed all *università* to parcel and assign permanently the commons, Atena chose to continue its practice of short-term leases. It took the French government to transform the traditional open village assemblies into oligarchic councils. The aristocracy itself needed most of its revenues to maintain the standard of conspicuous living that set it apart in society, and was not ready to jeopardize its traditional ties with its vassals. When it had excess profits, as we

---

[45] See the many account books in ACB. A list of these books drawn in 1780 includes a "librone grandissimo per la scrittura doppia," a definition that seems to imply a certain awe towards the mysteries of double-entry book-keeping. The *librone*, if it was indeed ever used, is now lost, ACB 109, fols. 72r–74r. Neapolitan aristocratic book-keeping never reached the sophistication of the Medici estates in Tuscany, see McArdle, *Altopascio*, pp. 11–15; for instance, Merzario, *Signori*, pp. 91–95, remarks on the inadequacy of the Saluzzo's book-keeping. More modern book-keeping began to be used by Neapolitan landowners only in the late nineteenth century, see Macry, *Ottocento* (Turin, 1988), part II. The Borghese only adopted double-entry book-keeping

have seen in the previous chapter, it invested them in diversifying its patrimony through the acquisition of new fiefs, or through the purchase of annuities of various kinds and other assets, rather than in a possibly dangerous and unprofitable attempt to change the management or the agriculture of its lands.[46]

This form of management also kept administrative expenses to a bare minimum. Until the eighteenth century, all assessments of the Caracciolo Brienza's revenues mention very few expenses, namely a few repairs to the mills or inns – that the marquis tried on occasion to shift upon the communities – and the salaries of the governors and of the few policemen who enforced the baron's justice, usually covered by the fees of the baronial court. Only in the mid-eighteenth century, as the marquis Litterio set up a staff of agents and administrators beside the traditional *erari* and *conservatori*, did management expenses rise somewhat. Still in the 1770s and 1780s, the management expenses for the four fiefs amounted to, at most, thirteen percent of the revenues, and only less than ten percent of them – or about 1.3 percent of the total revenues – consisted in expenses in the direct management of land, namely vines. This was in line with most other aristocratic families in the kingdom, as well as in Sicily or in other European countries. The preservation, not the increase, of income was the goal of the feudal administration, not only for the Caracciolo Brienza but also in other regions of the kingdom and of Italy. Guido Pescosolido, discussing the vast lands of the Borghese princes in Lazio, has commented on the "immobilistic purposes" of aristocratic land management, the aim of which was the "unchanged permanence of unitary landed capital."[47]

Limited and cautious investments were expected of barons, as the documen-

---

in the 1840s (Pescosolido, *Terra*, pp. 129–30). The backwardness of book-keeping as a mark of the impossibility of any real planning or investments is noted for France by Forster, *Saulx-Tavanes*, pp. 62–63, and "Obstacles," (also Dewald, *The Formation*, pp. 193–95), and by Brunner, *Vita nobiliare*, pp. 285–90, for the Austrian lands. Although Aymard has claimed that double-entry book-keeping was used by Sicilian aristocrats in the sixteenth and seventeenth centuries ("En Sicile," "L'abolition," p. 71, and "La transizione," p. 1140), neither his work on the Terranova nor Davies' book offer any evidence of this, and Verga, "Rapporti di produzione e gestione dei feudi nella Sicilia centro-occidentale" in Massafra, ed. *Problemi*, pp. 73–89, remarks on the low level of sophistication of aristocratic book-keeping in Sicily. The English aristocracy profited handsomely from improvements in surveying and book-keeping, see L. Stone, *Family and Fortune* (Oxford, 1973).

[46] G. M. Novario, *De vassallorum gravaminibus tractatus* (Naples, 1634), discussed also by Lepre, *Storia*, I, pp. 241–47; for Atena, see Villari, *Mezzogiorno*, pp. 83–92. The internal organization of the villages is discussed in chapter 4. The persistence in Naples of "feudal" attitudes towards management is emphasized by Macry in his study of late-nineteenth century landowning families, *Ottocento*, part II.

[47] For the years 1773–83, see ACB 161, unnumbered fol., for the marquis Litterio's calculation of his cadets' rights on his estate – which, moreover, probably emphasizes expenses and underestimates revenue (taxes are not included here in the expenses, and they represented probably another five percent of the revenue). Massafra, "Giurisdizione"; A. Guarneri, "Alcune notizie sovra la gestione di una casa baronale" *Archivio Storico Siciliano* 17 (1892), pp. 117–50, tables on pp. 124–50. The dukes of Saulx-Tavanes reinvested only four percent of their revenue, as

tation relating to one of the many lawsuits in which the Caracciolo Brienza were entangled shows. In 1748, creditors of the marquis Litterio accused him of culpable neglect in the management of Sasso that resulted in low revenues. Whatever the truthfulness of either side's statements, it is to be noted that the actual suggestions made to increase the revenues did not foresee any active involvement of the marquis in agricultural production, or any infusion of capital into the fief. The creditors, in fact, believed that the *terraggi* would yield more if levied by baronial agents rather than farmed out; furthermore, the marquis could use his reserves in kind more profitably if he lent seed to the vassals "as do the barons of the neighboring villages," or kept the grain until the prices grew most. These policies might, perhaps, have raised the income, but only by way of usurary pressure or price speculation that involved almost no risk and especially no reinvestment of any of the revenues.[48]

"REFEUDALIZATION" AND THE ECONOMIC DIFFICULTIES OF THE SEVENTEENTH CENTURY

The first marquis of Brienza, Marco Antonio Caracciolo, and his mother, Ippolita Filomarino, purchased additional jurisdictions and fiscal credit on the four fiefs in the 1560s and 1570s. This policy can be ascribed to a desire to strengthen the family's new lordship, and, as other examples show, was common among new barons in any period.[49] This desire for a stronger new lordship might have been present also in Giovan Battista Caracciolo's attempts to innovate in the management of his fiefs. But his activities are better understood as an aspect of the general policy of the Neapolitan aristocracy to expand its grip on its fiefs in the decades around 1600, a trend often referred to as "refeudalization." The extent to which this process was caused by economic decline in the kingdom beginning in the 1590s and, a few years later, by a decline of feudal revenues in

opposed to a much higher proportion for the English aristocracy (Forster, *Saulx-Tavanes*, pp. 90–91); the nobles of Toulouse spent about five percent of their revenue in administration (Forster, *Toulouse*, p. 38); similar low rates of reinvestment were common for the Medici lands, see McArdle, *Altopascio*, chapter 3. Pescosolido, *Terra*, pp. 175, 128, and throughout: he shows that the Borghese began an active policy to increase their landed income only in the 1840s; Lepre, *Storia*, I, pp. 72–78; Lepre, *Feudi*, pp. 18, and 26–27. Merzario, *Signori*, chapters 3 and 4, shows that the Saluzzo only began to reinvest in their lands in the eighteenth century, as they established large *masserie*, favored by high yields; a similar example from Puglia is in A. Sinisi, "Una famiglia mercantile napoletana del XVIII secolo" *Economia e storia*, second series, 3 (1982), pp. 139–203. Different practices were possible in the Lombard plains, see E. Roveda, "Una grande possessione lodigiana dei Trivulzio tra '500 e '700" in Mirri, ed. *Ricerche di storia moderna*, II, pp. 25–139.

[48] ASN Pandetta Corrente, II, especially fols. 117r–22r and 169r–78r (the quote is on fol. 175v). Similar arguments were advanced in the dispute over the decreased revenues of Montenegro, see later in this chapter. The practice of lending grain to local peasants was used also by the Doria in the difficult years of the seventeenth century (Zotta, "Momenti," pp. 778–79 and 793, and "Rapporti," pp. 281–82), but the lack of account books and of administrative correspondence makes it impossible to ascertain whether the Caracciolo Brienza ever enacted this policy in their fiefs.

[49] For instance Villone, *Privilegi*, pp. 8–14, and Visceglia, "Formazione." Chapters 5 and 6 discuss the changes in the relations between the crown and the baronage and the purchases of rights and annuities.

general, and the question of whether it signaled an increase in the pressure placed by the aristocracy on the population of the kingdom and a change in how that pressure was perceived, are issues that have been the subject of debate among historians of the Mezzogiorno for the last twenty-five years or so.

Rosario Villari first proposed the term "refeudalization" to refer to this increased pressure in the five or six decades preceding the 1647 revolt. "Refeudalization" and the related decline in the monarchy's ability to control the aristocracy and to assert itself as the arbitrator of social conflict within the kingdom – what Villari termed the "crisis of the state" – were crucial to his interpretation of the revolt as a class conflict, pitting the peasantry and part of the middle classes against the feudal aristocracy and speculating international financiers. Although he acknowledged the inherent weakness of the lower and middle classes in the kingdom at the time, Villari saw the revolt as a failed last opportunity for the Mezzogiorno to solve the problem of its historical "delay" and to start on a new "modern" course.[50]

This interpretation was vigorously contested from a Crocean point of view by Giuseppe Galasso, who denied that the revolt could possibly have had the results Villari proposed. Galasso saw the revolt as a mostly backward-looking rural phenomenon with no real chance of success and no serious political, economic, or social program; its success, Galasso claimed, would have had even direr consequences for the kingdom than its defeat. He denied the crisis of the state and saw in Villari's argument a resurgence of the tendency to blame Spain for all of the kingdom's evils. In particular, Galasso attacked Villari's term "refeudalization" as implying a previous – and to Galasso unproven and unprovable – "defeudalization" in the sixteenth century. He denied that the sixteenth-century expansion in the kingdom's economy had created new classes in society large or strong enough to be the basis for a "modern" economic development. In his most recent discussion of these issues, Galasso has again denied the alternative "modern" character of the revolt, while accepting some elements of a class analysis, though with such complex qualifications as to be of little actual help.[51]

The debate has now lost its polemical power – heavily shaped by Italian politics of the 1960s – and both authors have backed away from their most extreme positions. These two positions, articulated over twenty-five years ago

[50] The influence of the historiographical debates of the 1950s and 1960s – particularly of Porshnev's work on rural revolts in France and of Hobsbawm's on the seventeenth-century crisis – is obvious, as is that of Gramsci's ideas. See Villari, *Rivolta, Mezzogiorno*, "Baronaggio e finanze a Napoli alla vigilia della rivoluzione del 1647–48" *Studi storici* 3 (1962), pp. 259–305, "Note sulla rifeudalizzazione del regno di Napoli alla vigilia della rivoluzione di Masaniello" *ibid.* 4 (1963), pp. 637–68, 6 (1965), pp. 295–328, 8 (1967), pp. 37–112, and "La feudalità e lo stato napoletano nel secolo XVII" *Clio* 1 (1965), pp. 555–75; Villari has returned to these ideas most recently in his *Elogio della dissimulazione. La lotta politica nel Seicento* (Bari, 1987).

[51] This is, of course, a simplification of both arguments. Galasso, *Economia, Il Mezzogiorno*, "La feudalità napoletana nel secolo XVI" *Clio* 1 (1965), pp. 535–54, and most recently his preface to Musi, *La rivolta* (in which he coyly does not refer to Villari by name). A new interpretation of the revolt as a struggle of the *togati* (Naples' robe leadership) against pro-aristocratic policies of the

and based respectively on the ideas of Gramsci and Croce, remain, however, the basic interpretations of the political and social history of Spanish Naples. It is in any case undoubted that baronial pressure on the vassal population increased in the kingdom in the fifty years before the revolt. Several studies have demonstrated this, and Galasso himself writes of a "renewed and strengthened baronage" involved in a "great reactionary attack," and of a "strengthening and widening of feudal authority." In many instances historians have related this increase to the transformation of feudal lords into landowners, and have seen the pressure particularly in the purchase of land and in its more exploitative management through aggressive use of feudal powers and privileges, giving limited consideration to feudal rights as sources of revenues in their own right.[52]

Giovan Battista Caracciolo's activities fit in very well with the picture of "refeudalization." His purchases of land, his contracts with the *università* (whether or not they were obtained with undue force), his attempt to innovate in the management of his land through the *masserie*, his intervention in the large-scale long-distance grain trade, his purchases of livestock, are all expressions of an active presence in the fiefs, with the purpose of increasing and differentiating baronial revenues. The financial troubles of the family, due no doubt also to Giovan Battista's expensive new management, meant an early end for the Caracciolo Brienza's "refeudalization." By the 1620s the patrimony was divided, and all of Giovan Battista's policies had been discontinued; after that the family would never again try to change the way in which its fiefs were administered.

The example of the Caracciolo Brienza fiefs, however, also offers a different perspective on the effects of "refeudalization" and of the economic difficulties of the mid-seventeenth century on feudal revenues. Giovan Battista's policies notwithstanding, the family's revenues from land did not rise very significantly, and the composition of the total revenues changed little until the revolt and especially the plague of 1656 reduced all types of feudal income. In the ensuing recovery, until well into the eighteenth century, feudal rights again played a large part as the population grew once more. Neither the attempted "refeudalization" nor the crisis changed the Caracciolo Brienza into mere landowners.[53]

Spanish government in the years preceding the revolt, which threatened the power achieved by the *togati*, has recently been offered by legal historians, in particular P. L. Rovito, "La rivoluzione costituzionale di Napoli (1647–1648)" *RSI* 98 (1986), pp. 367–462; Rovito has seen the same "civil" notables behind the provincial revolts, "Strutture cetuali, riformismo ed eversione nelle rivolte apulo-lucane di metà Seicento" *ASPN* 106 (1988), pp. 241–308.

[52] Galasso, "La feudalità," p. 554 – also in *Il Mezzogiorno*, p. 161 – and *Economia*, pp. 272–73. The increase in feudal pressure is discussed by Visceglia, Benaiteau, and Zotta in their cited articles. A survey of Neapolitan agriculture in the Spanish period is in F. Caracciolo, *Il regno di Napoli nei secoli XVI e XVII* (Rome, 1966), chapter 5.

[53] Several historians have studied the effects of the seventeenth-century economic difficulties on feudal income in the kingdom; besides the literature already cited, see G. Labrot, "Trend économique et mécénat dans le royaume de Naples, 1530–1730" in acts of the Seventeenth Settimana di Studio dell'Istituto Internazionale di Storia Economica "Francesco Datini" di Prato *Gli aspetti economici del mecenatismo in Europa (secoli XIV–XVIII)* (Prato, 1985); Visceglia, "Sistema

We have seen earlier in this chapter that an isolated region of traditional agriculture, such as that of the Caracciolo Brienza's fiefs, experienced less extreme fluctuations in production and population than other regions, and that therefore baronial revenues in such regions underwent less sharp a decline, although the financial and legal vicissitudes of the family limit the amount of detailed information available on the specific revenues in those years. How dramatic that decline could be is shown by the example of the fief of Montenegro with its *casale* of Montelateglia, located in the plain of Capitanata. This province produced wheat, oil, and wine, and served as pasture fields for the herds managed by the *Dogana delle pecore* of Foggia, a government office established in the mid-fifteenth century to administer the complex system of transhumance between the provinces of Abruzzo and Capitanata.

During the sixteenth century, the expansion in the kingdom's agriculture and the growing herds of the Dogana increased the value of Montenegro, and its barons drew considerable revenues from the pass fees they levied on the region's traveling livestock. Montenegro was sold for 8,000 ducats in 1561 but in 1597, together with Montelateglia and with a few additional feudal rights, it was worth 48,010 ducats, with revenues of ducats 3,269.4.13. Revenues were, however, already declining when in 1643 Carlo Caracciolo Sant'Eramo bought the fief for 40,000 ducats.[54]

In the mid-1640s, the revenues were down to 1,300 ducats a year. The 1647–48 revolt and the plague caused a further decrease, and, more importantly, the irrevocable decline or disappearance of some sources of income. Montenegro lost possibly up to two thirds of its inhabitants in the central decades of the century, and depopulation led to decline in the revenues from rights and lands. The violence of the revolt, and possibly neglect by the Caracciolo, destroyed the baronial mill and inn, while a series of bad years for olives damaged another major source of income. The results are clear from Table 3.5.[55] In 1679, the government assessed the revenues of Montenegro at

feudale e mercato internazionale: la periferizzazione del paese" *Prospettive Settanta* 7 (1985), pp. 69–88; R. Moscati, *Una famiglia "borghese" del Mezzogiorno* (Naples, 1964); Masella, "Mercato"; Musi, "Il Principato," "La spinta," and *La rivolta*, pp. 105–6; M. R. Pelizzari, "Per una storia dell'agricoltura irpina nell'età moderna" in Massafra, ed. *Problemi*, pp. 189–200; Benaiteau, "L'agricoltura nella provincia di Principato Ultra nell'età moderna (secoli XVII e XVIII)" in *ibid.*, pp. 201–19; G. Laporta, "Agricoltura e pastorizia nel feudo di Monteserico nei secoli XVI e XVII" in *ibid.*, pp. 291–308; for general comments on the economic crisis in the kingdom, see Marino, *Pastoral Economics*, pp. 191–92. See McArdle, *Altopascio*, for a reassessment and chronology of the crisis in Tuscany.

54 On the Dogana, see Marino, "I meccanismi della crisi nella Dogana di Foggia nel XVII secolo" in Massafra, ed. *Problemi*, pp. 309–20, and *Pastoral Economics*. For Montenegro, see ASN Refute Quinternioni 204, fols. 79r–93v; Registri Quinternioni 18, fols. 32v–37v; Cedolari Nuovi 33, fols. 186v–88r, 283v–87v, 453r–60r; Taxis Adohae 121, fols. 101r–5v; Certificatorie relevi 150, fols. 396r–411v; Petizioni relevi 49–I fols. 130v–136v; Significatorie relevi 35–I, fols. 46r–52v; 44, fols. 13v–18r.

55 For the population figures, see L. Giustiniani, *Dizionario geografico ragionato del regno di Napoli* (12 vols.; Naples, 1797–1805), VI, pp. 110–11 (a decline of one third in the fiscal assessments), and ACB 11.1.30, unnumbered fol.; ACB 11.1, especially 9, 11, 17, 24, 30 (a large unnumbered bundle), and 11.2.3 and 5 (nos. 4 and 14).

Table 3.5. *Revenue of Montenegro and Montelateglia (1646–1666)*
(in ducats)

1646–47	1,200	1656–57	843
1647–48	700	1657–58	700
1648–49	120	1658–59[a]	950
1649–50	1,070	1659–60	–
1650–51	1,080	1660–61	–
1651–52	1,150	1661–62	800
1652–53	1,050	1662–63	780
1653–54	1,065	1663–64	870
1654–55	906	1664–65	750
1655–56	958	1665–66	740

[a] In 1658–59, Domenico Caracciolo leased Montenegro to a Giovanni Angeletti for 950 ducats a year for three years, but in those years the government confiscated all revenues to pay the owners' debts.

Sources: ACB 136.15 and 137.16 (the disputes between the Caracciolo and the Greco, former owners of Montenegro, on the causes of the decline in revenues), and the sources cited in footnote 54.

ducats 755.-.16, and in 1682 the fief was sold for 19,810 ducats, a decrease of over fifty percent in its value in less than forty years, reflecting not only the decrease in revenues but also the loss of the potential for recovery and growth in the fief. To give only two examples of the decline of specific revenues, the mill, which yielded 135 ducats in 1597 and 1616 and 144 ducats in 1646, was destroyed in 1648 and never rebuilt. The rent of the *mastrodattia* was 250 ducats in 1597, 260 in 1616, 220 in 1633, and still 160 in 1646, but only seventy-seven ducats in 1661 and fifteen in 1664.

Though in other areas of the kingdom feudal income actually increased as a result of the high prices of grain the revolt brought about, the demographic stagnation of the early seventeenth century and the heavy losses of 1656 did considerable damage to feudal income of all types, and, with variations due to the scope of the demographic loss, in all provinces. The demographic losses also made it impossible for the Neapolitan aristocracy to follow the model of the Sicilian aristocracy, which launched a vast program of internal colonization to reverse the decline of its agricultural revenues in the seventeenth century.[56]

The analysis of the management of the Caracciolo Brienza's fiefs, and of the composition and use of their revenues, supports a view of Neapolitan aristocratic landowning as mainly directed to the preservation of existing conditions and of

[56] Davies, *Famiglie*; Davies, "Village-Building in Sicily: An Aristocratic Remedy for the Crisis of the 1590s" in P. Clark, ed. *The European Crisis of the 1590s. Essays in Comparative History* (London, 1985), pp. 191–208; Davies, "La colonizzazione feudale della Sicilia nella prima età moderna" in *Storia d'Italia Einaudi. Annali* VIII *Insediamento e territorio* (Turin, 1978), pp. 415–72; Aymard,

time-honored relations with the peasantry, rather than to innovation or increase in revenues. Particularly in a region of low agricultural yields, fragmented but solid peasant land holdings, and limited involvement in long-distance trade, the reinvestment of revenues in the land to increase its production – or, even more difficult, its productivity – was a risky enterprise, the effects of which on baronial revenues were not sure, while its consequences for the stability of feudal rule on the vassal communities might be dangerous indeed, as the revolt of 1647–48 would show. Feudal administration therefore favored continuity of the old ways. Even the innovations that were made by the marquis Giovan Battista were short-lived and did not attempt to change the agricultural methods or the relations between the landowning baron and the vassals; their aim was rather to diversify the sources of income and augment the capital value of the fiefs by adding new revenues, not by improving the existing ones. Giovan Battista expanded his landed properties but, with the brief exception of a few farms, he administered them as he had administered all of his land before and as his successors would after him.

This managerial continuity did not prove harmful. The internal composition of the revenues, tied as they were mostly to the size of the fiefs' population, survived the mid-seventeenth century troubles without much change, and only in the later eighteenth century, as revenues generally increased, did one element of them, feudal non-landed income, lag behind. Their role as feudatories was essential to the Caracciolo Brienza; their income was not limited to landed income, and feudal rights and monopolies independent of any ownership of land remained a significant part of the family's revenues well into the eighteenth century. Being a baron brought prestige and power but also obvious and direct economic advantages, and the barons had little interest in changing the system. Even when in the later eighteenth century the expansion of the kingdom's economy and population led to an automatic increase in revenues, the only innovation on the part of the Caracciolo Brienza was the widespread use of emphyteusis, a risk-free contract to increase productivity without investing any capital. By 1806, after 250 years in which the family had kept management and maintenance costs to a minimum, the Caracciolo Brienza's feudal patrimony was worth more than ever before, was free of debts, and produced revenues that allowed its owners to occupy more or less the same social position within the kingdom's elite that their elders had enjoyed since the mid-sixteenth century.[57]

"Amministrazione." On the economic crisis in Italy, see Romano, *L'Italia tra due crisi*, pp. 187–206; D. Carpanetto and G. Recuperati, *Italy in the Age of Reason, 1685–1789* (New York, 1987), pp. 38–44; the effects on the Spanish aristocracy lasted longer, see Atienza, *Aristocracia*, chapter 3, especially pp. 130–31; also on the issue of refeudalization in Spain, see B. Yun Casalilla, *Sobre la transición al capitalismo en Castilla. Economía y sociedad en Tierra de Campos (1500–1830)* (León, 1987).

[57] A survey of the refeudalization debates and of the economic crisis of the seventeenth century is in G. White, "La feudalità meridionale tra crisi economica e ripresa politica" *Studi storici Luigi Simeoni*. 35 (1986), pp. 29-55.

4

The feudal lord and his vassals: between traditional paternalism and change

Beatrice: Rustic people, indiscreet people! It does not befit you to decide the rights of those who are destined to be your masters.

(Goldoni, *Il feudatario*, III, xi)

The preceding chapters have discussed the patrimony of the Caracciolo Brienza and have shown the considerable importance that feudal lands and rights had for the barons' income throughout the viceroyal period. The traditionalism and continuity that marked the barons' management of their revenues from the fiefs also characterized other aspects of the relationship between the lord and his vassals. Feudal power affected the communities beyond its strictly economic consequences, and the presence of the lord was not only a burden for the communities but could represent an advantage, due to the paternalism that at times informed feudal rule. The location, population, and economic and social characteristics of the communities, their local traditions of feudal rule, and the ease with which external powers like the church or the central state could intervene between lords and vassals, determined the strength and traits of feudal power. The four communities which constituted the feudal *stato* of the Caracciolo Brienza differed greatly in the degree and form of their subjection to their lord, and their study allows us, therefore, to discuss the varying conditions of feudal rule in the kingdom of Naples.

Very little scholarly attention has been focused on this issue. More than a century ago Davide Winspeare, Nicola Santamaria, Nunzio Federico Faraglia, and others devoted highflown pages to the plight of the Southern communities under the barons. Although their works contain plenty of useful information, they obviously had a political agenda, showing feudal relations in the darkest light, and often assuming their readers to be familiar with the workings of feudal institutions. In this century, legal historians have worked on the communities and published several statutes. In particular, Giovanni Italo Cassandro has published the statutes of Atena Lucana with an introductory essay on that community. Yet, apart from legal studies, almost no work on the feudal aristocracy has analyzed the community of the fief.[1]

[1] D. Winspeare, *Storia degli abusi feudali* (Naples, 1811); N. Santamaria, *I feudi, il diritto feudale e la loro storia nell'Italia meridionale* (Naples, 1881); N. F. Faraglia, *Il comune nell'Italia meridionale*

The feudal lord and his vassals

In a series of articles written over thirty years ago, Rosario Villari studied the fiefs of the Caracciolo Brienza. Two of these articles deal with the ascent of a rural bourgeoisie in the South in the later years of the eighteenth century, traced through the *Catasto* records of the 1740s and the documents relating to the abolition of feudalism after 1806. The third article looks at antifeudal movements in the South, from the revolt of Masaniello in 1647 to the Jacobin republic of 1799 using the example of the Caracciolo Brienza fiefs. Villari's articles will be frequently used in this chapter, but his interest is in the eighteenth century, and his chief concern is to find the roots of the rural bourgeoisie of the nineteenth century and the beginnings of its class consciousness and opposition to the baronial regime.[2]

This chapter will describe and analyze the character of the relations between the feudal lord and his vassal communities from the sixteenth to the eighteenth century, focusing in particular on the non-economic aspects of those relations. The fact that the barons held regalian rights, and were to a large extent the mediators between their vassals and the outside world, created a web of relations in which both parties abided by time-honored conventions and local traditions. It is not possible, within a study of an aristocratic family, to investigate thoroughly the social structure of the communities, and from this point of view Villari's analysis of the cadastral data will provide useful background information. The emphasis here will be on the presence and position of the feudal lords in the communities and on the challenges they had to face. A description of the communities and their basic institutions will lead to an examination of the local effects of the lord's presence and of the role of the church and the clergy. I will then study the growth of a local notability with its consequences for the community and the lord, and the areas and manifestations of tension between the lord and his vassals.

THE *UNIVERSITÀ*

In the kingdom of Naples several legal terms were used to define a conglomeration of people, depending mainly on its size. A city (*città*) was larger than a village

(1100–1806) (Naples, 1883); N. Alianelli, *Delle consuetudini e degli statuti municipali nelle province napoletane* (Naples, 1873); M. Palumbo, *I comuni meridionali prima e dopo le leggi eversive della feudalità* (2 vols.; Montecorvino Rovella-Cerignola, 1910–1916; reprint Bologna, 1979); G. I. Cassandro, *Storia di una terra del Mezzogiorno: Atena Lucana* (Rome, 1946; originally in *Rivista di storia del diritto italiano* 16 (1943)); R. Moscati, "Le Università meridionali nel viceregno spagnolo" *Clio* 3 (1967), pp. 25–40; G. Muto, "Strutture e funzioni finanziarie delle 'università' del Mezzogiorno tra '500 e '600" *Quaderni sardi di storia* 1 (1980), pp. 101–22; Muto, "Lo 'stile antiquo': consuetudini e prassi amministrativa a Napoli nella prima età moderna" *MEFRM* 100 (1988), pp. 317–30; A. Musi, "Amministrazione, potere locale e società in una provincia del Mezzogiorno moderno: il Principato Citra nel secolo XVII" *Quaderni sardi di storia* 4 (1984), pp. 81–118. These texts are the basis for the general description of the *università* in this chapter. The statutes of Atena, dating from 1475, are in ACB 133.1, those of Brienza (1543) in 45.7.1.
2 The articles, originally published in the early 1950s, were united in R. Villari, *Mezzogiorno e contadini nell'età moderna* (Bari, 1977; first edition 1961).

The continuity of feudal power

(*terra*), which in turn was larger than a hamlet (*casale*). Whereas most hamlets were not autonomous and depended on a neighboring city or village for their administration, all *città* and *terre* constituted *università*.[3] This term was used in the expression "the *università* of the city or village of X," and denoted all the citizens of that center who had a right to participate in its administration according to the statutes. Not all residents were citizens, and local statutes regulated the conditions for conferring citizen rights on newcomers. The Napoleonic government replaced the term *università* with commune (*comune*).

By the Spanish period, most larger *università*, particularly in wealthier regions, were developing an oligarchic administration with a restricted council.[4] The phenomenon was, however, not as widespread as many historians have assumed from looking at the larger cities. In many smaller villages and poorer areas the old medieval local parliament remained open to all male heads of households and elected the community's administrators, who supervised the levying of local taxes, the *università*'s budget, and whatever administrative jurisdiction the *università* might have. These local institutions were the same whether the *università* was in the royal domain or in the hands of a baron as a fief, and the term used to describe the residents in relation to their lord – be he the king or a baron – was always vassals (*vassalli*). Titled and untitled lords were all called barons (*baroni*).

The predominance of latifundia in the Southern agriculture meant that almost all the population of the kingdom lived in villages or cities, and even today the Southern countryside has few of the scattered houses and farms which grace the Northern Italian, especially Tuscan, landscape. The kingdom's territory was divided among all the *università*, and some of them had control over a fairly large area, including private and feudal lands, commons, forests, and pastures. In most cases, the borders of the old *università* are the same as those of the modern communes. Occasionally uninhabited pieces of land constituted the so-called rustic fiefs (*feudi rustici*), the lords of which had agricultural rights but no jurisdictional powers, since the peasants working these lands were residents of other *università*. These fiefs paid lower feudal taxes.

The large majority of the *università* were feudal. Around 1531 there were

---

[3] Juridically there was no middle term between a *città* and a *terra*, and *città* was used for Naples as well as for towns of less than 5,000 people. A discussion of the *università* is in A. Lepre, *Terra di Lavoro nell'età moderna* (Naples, 1978), pp. 97–123.

[4] For instance, in Puglia, most *università* had oligarchic councils, or councils divided into orders, by the early sixteenth century, see A. Spagnoletti, "Le aggregazioni alla nobiltà nelle università di Terra di Bari nel XVIII secolo" *Società e storia* 3 (1980), pp. 35–59; Spagnoletti, *"L'incostanza delle umane cose": il patriziato di Terra di Bari tra egemonia e crisi (XVI-XVIII secolo)* (Bari, 1981); for Calabria, see G. Galasso, *Economia e società nella Calabria del Cinquecento* (Naples, 1967; second edit. Milan, 1975), pp. 293–324. The same phenomenon has been observed for Sicily, see O. Cancila, *Baroni e popolo nella Sicilia del grano* (Palermo, 1983), pp. 193–95. Musi, *La rivolta di Masaniello nella scena politica barocca* (Naples, 1989), chapter 5, notes that most cases of conflict during the revolt took place in *università* with separate orders of citizens.

fifty-five royal cities out of 1,563 centers. During the Spanish period, new *università* were created and their total number grew to about 2,000. Only about fifty to sixty of these, the largest, fortified, or strategically located ones, were royal. In 1786, according to Bianchini who wrote in 1835, 384 *università* were royal, including those which were held by the king in fief as heir to the Farnese family. This meant that slightly over one million people out of a total population of about 4.8 million lived in royal *università*. Other sources report 1,365,000 people in royal *università*, as opposed to 3.3 million in feudal ones at the end of the eighteenth century. This predominance of feudal centers distinguished the kingdom from all other Italian states. The concentration of feudal power differed considerably in the various provinces. Of the two provinces in which the Caracciolo Brienza had their fiefs, Principato Citra was, with Terra di Bari, the province with the kingdom's lowest degree of concentration of feudal power, whereas in Basilicata only about twelve percent of the population lived in royal *università*.[5]

Since the Aragonese period, most barons had enjoyed first- and second-degree civil and criminal jurisdiction. Some barons had obtained third-degree jurisdiction as well. Vassals could always appeal from baronial justice to the royal courts, but this meant that they might have to go through three trials before reaching the provincial courts or, with one more appeal, the tribunals in Naples. All the residents of a feudal *università* were subject to baronial justice, even if they had no economic relations with the baron. The barons were considered as public officials to whom the king had delegated the administration of justice. In fact, being free from baronial justice, as a vassal only to the king, was almost a precondition for nobility, and generally only royal cities could have a closed noble order of citizens. This system remained in function until the beginning of the nineteenth century.[6]

We shall now look at the Caracciolo Brienza *stato* and discuss the location, economy, and internal organization of the four villages, and their financial

[5] G. Coniglio, *Il regno di Napoli al tempo di Carlo V. Amministrazione e vita economico-sociale* (Naples, 1951), p. 61; Moscati, "Le Università," p. 30, for the Spanish period; L. Bianchini, *Per la storia delle finanze del regno di Napoli* (Naples, 1859; first edit. 1835), pp. 294–95; the other figures are in A. Massafra, "Un problème ouvert à la recherche: la 'crise' du baronnage napolitain à la fin du XVIIIe siècle" in *L'abolition de la féodalité dans le monde occidental*, Actes du colloque international (Toulouse, November 1968), I, pp. 245–62. Massafra gives 2,300 feudal *università* out of a total of 3,000 in the 1780s, without referring to Bianchini. All these figures tend to exclude Naples; in 1586, 69 out of 1,973 *università* were royal, see A. von Reumont, *The Carafas of Maddaloni. Naples under Spanish Dominion* (London, 1854; German edit. 1850), pp. 82–83. Other data are in D. Musto, ms. preface to *Inventario 103 (Conti delle Università)* in ASN; P. Villani, *Mezzogiorno tra riforme e rivoluzione* (Bari, 1973; first edit. 1962), pp. 188–99; Villani, "La feudalità dalle riforme all'eversione" *Clio* 1 (1965), pp. 599–622; at the end of the sixteenth century, there were only four royal *università* in Basilicata, see G. Intorcia, "Problemi del governo provinciale: l'Udienza di Basilicata nel Seicento" *ASPN* 102 (1984), pp. 139–55. In Lombardy in 1761, there were 565 domanial centers and 650 feudal ones, see S. J. Woolf, *Studi sulla nobiltà piemontese nell'epoca dell'assolutismo* (Turin, 1963), p. 165, footnote 1.

[6] The descriptions of the kingdom cited in chapter 1 discuss at length the noble orders of royal cities.

situation in the early modern period. Over the centuries, feudal *stati* developed close internal ties and in many ways functioned as territorial units. The four *università* enfeoffed to the Caracciolo Brienza were contiguous, but they lay in different provinces: Atena and Brienza in Principato Citra, Pietrafesa and Sasso in Basilicata.[7] The total area of the four communes today is 186.6 square kilometers. Their total population oscillated in the early modern period between 12,000 and 15,000, following the demographic pattern of the kingdom in general: growth in the sixteenth century, then decline to the lowest point in the 1650s, then new growth, particularly strong in the mid-eighteenth century. In the last two centuries, like most of the rural South, the four communes have lost population due to emigration, and in 1951 their total population stood at 11,548.

The feudal *stato* was divided among three dioceses: Pietrafesa was in the bishopric of Campagna-Satriano, Brienza and Sasso in that of Marsico Nuovo, and Atena in that of Capaccio.[8] All four *università* lay at the border of their respective provinces most distant from the provincial capitals, Salerno and Matera respectively. Morever, two of the bishoprics were very small and poor, and the see of the third, Capaccio, was quite far from Atena. This distance from the centers of rival powers certainly represented an advantage for the lord's position.[9]

The four *università* differed in their economic situation as well as in their past feudal history. Brienza and Pietrafesa are located on top of two hills rising halfway between the plain of the Vallo di Diano and the Lucan Apennines, at an altitude of 713 and 630 meters respectively. Their large territories, crossed by two streams, produced mostly grain, oil, and wine. Some land was given to pastures, and a large area was covered by woods, especially in Brienza which had by far the largest territory of the four, constituting more than two fifths of the

[7] In 1811, Brienza was assigned to Basilicata; in 1886, Pietrafesa changed its name to Satriano di Lucania. For a study of another feudal *stato* as a unit, see P. Ebner, *Storia di un feudo del Mezzogiorno. La baronia di Novi* (Rome, 1973).

[8] This information is in L. Giustiniani, *Dizionario geografico ragionato del regno di Napoli* (12 vols.; Naples, 1797–1805), *sub vocibus*, and in the descriptions of the kingdom cited in ch. I. A. De Matteis, *L'Aquila e il contado. Demografia e fiscalità (sec. XV-XVIII)* (Naples, 1973) surveys demographic data for the kingdom. The recent information is in *Dizionario Enciclopedico Italiano*. Brienza, Pietrafesa, and Sasso (total population, in 1951, 8,960) were, in 1971, down to 7,448, see G. De Rosa and F. Malgeri, eds. *Società e religione in Basilicata* (2 vols.; n.p., 1978) I, pp. 368–77; Atena (2,588 inhabitants in 1951) was recently down to 1,908, see Ebner, *Chiesa, baroni e popolo nel Cilento* (2 vols.; Rome, 1982), I, pp. 533–42 (which presumably uses the 1981 census).

[9] For the bishoprics, see ASV Sacra Congregazione del Concilio, *Relationes ad limina*, vols. 177 (Campagna-Satriano), 185 (Capaccio), and 491 (Marsico Nuovo); see also G. Colangelo, "La diocesi di Marsico dal concilio di Trento al 1656" in De Rosa–Malgeri, eds. *Società*, II, pp. 163–98. Intorcia, "Problemi," p. 141, cites an episode involving the marquis of Brienza as an example of the baronial powers that resulted from the distance of centers of royal authority; see Musi, "Amministrazione," on the provincial administrative structure. See the map in this chapter. A very different situation occurred, for instance, in the fief of Santa Severina in Calabria which, though not much larger than Brienza, was an archiepiscopal see, had an oligarchic council and two separate orders of citizens, and a fairly lively trade life, see G. Caridi, *Uno "stato" feudale nel Mezzogiorno spagnolo* (Rome, 1988), especially chapter 3.

entire state. Sasso is located further up towards the mountains at an altitude of 940 meters. Its fairly large territory (one fourth of the whole state) was mostly given to pasture with little agriculture. Its population, the smallest of the four, lived in almost complete isolation, and the eighteenth-century government functionaries who travelled there to appraise the fief were appalled at the savagery of the inhabitants; Sasso, then as today, must have been very similar to the village described by Carlo Levi. As we have seen in the preceding chapter, Pietrafesa, the smallest of these three fiefs in extension, had the smallest feudal domain. The large pastures and woods of Brienza and Sasso were mostly part of the feudal domain, and in Sasso the Caracciolo Brienza's allodial income was never more than ten percent of their total income.

Although Atena itself is on a hill at an altitude of 642 meters, its territory, the smallest of the four, was mostly in the plain of the Vallo di Diano, the long valley that separates the Lucan Apennines and the mountains of the Cilento. The marshes and swamps of the plain, the absence of large pastures or woods, and the frequent floods of the river Tanagro, damaged the economy of Atena, which relied mainly on grain and wine. Atena was, however, just off the royal road to Calabria. The marquis owned an inn on the royal road, and, as we have seen, Atena functioned as the commercial outlet for the four *università*.[10]

In its relations to the baron, however, Atena had a considerable advantage over the other three *università*. Whereas Brienza, Pietrafesa, and Sasso had been enfeoffed with full jurisdiction since the fifteenth century, and there is evidence that Brienza at least had been feudal soon after the Norman conquest, Atena, because of its important location and of its past as a Roman district capital, had remained much longer in the royal domain. In fact, it was only in the mid-sixteenth century that Atena became definitely a fief. This meant not only that the barons had a shorter tradition of rule over Atena and that they owned little feudal land there, but also that the *università* itself had been able to buy from the royal court feudal jurisdictions and rights which it managed on its own. Morever, Atena was the only one of the four *università* to include a few subfiefs (*suffeudi*), parcels of feudal land given to local notables with an investiture by the baron, so that the *università* had an obvious and self-conscious elite, wealthier and more prestigious than the other inhabitants. With the exception of a few professionals, the society of all four *università* was otherwise quite undifferentiated, with only a few part-time artisans, and this situation continued well into the eighteenth century. As a visible symbol of its limited degree of subordination, Atena did not have a baronial castle, and only in the early seventeenth century

---

[10] For these descriptions, see chapter 3, the bishops' reports, the assessments (*apprezzi*) in ACB 43.3.1 and 7, 77.2.1bis, 77.2.27, 77.2.32–33, 81.1.17–18, 160, unnumbered fol., and Villari, *Mezzogiorno*. Still today the arrival of a car with a Naples license seems to constitute the event of the month in Sasso.

did the Caracciolo dispose of a palace in the town. As we shall see, this situation would be reflected in the events of 1647–48.[11]

The Caracciolo Brienza's *stato* was in a relatively poor area of the kingdom. Hilly or mountainous for the most part, it was rather isolated from long-distance commerce. Land tenures were fragmented, and most residents were small farmers who typically owned or rented a bit of land and a few animals, and found sustenance in the common lands and pastures and perhaps in small-scale artisanal activities. Already in the early seventeenth but especially in the eighteenth century, men from the four villages emigrated seasonally to the plains of Puglia to work in the harvest, and they continued to do so in the following century. Local trade was probably fairly active, at least in grain, though the marquis controlled most of it. Only in the eighteenth century did a small local landowning elite develop. Manufacturing, particularly textiles and a few smiths, served only the local communities and remained limited until at least the early nineteenth century. Silk was produced in Sasso, and we have seen that some was sold in Salerno in 1674. In 1754–55, about thirty-five Sassesi worked part-time in the production of silk, though by the early nineteenth century this manufacture had almost disappeared.[12]

The four *università* all maintained their old representative institutions. The parliaments met regularly and were open to all citizens, and sizeable meetings are documented to the end of the old regime in all four communities. The parliament elected a mayor (*sindaco*) and four aldermen (*eletti*) who ran the *università* from September to August. Records of parliament meetings and other documents show that the administrators were no more likely than the other citizens to be able to sign their name. The marquis had in theory no right to influence the election in any way, and, although there are records of very strong

---

[11] On the situation under the Normans, see E. Jamison, ed. *Catalogus baronum* (Rome, 1972), p. 102, with E. Cuozzo's *Commentario* (Rome, 1984), pp. 157–58. On Atena, see M. Lacava, *Istoria di Atena Lucana* (Naples, 1893); Cassandro, *Atena*, pp. 138–40; Ebner, *Chiesa*, II, pp. 533–42; L. Mandelli, *La Lucania sconosciuta*, 2 vols., BNN ms. X-D-1/2 (mid-seventeenth century), II, pp. 275–77. Neapolitan jurists debated for centuries whether subfeudatories were noble or not, see A. Pezzana, "Note sui suffeudi nell'Italia meridionale nel secolo XVIII" *Rivista araldica* 67 (1969), pp. 37–48. Atena was among the richest communes in the Vallo di Diano at the beginning of the nineteenth century, see M. Coppola, "Distribuzione del reddito e squilibri socio-economici nel Vallo di Diano durante il Decennio francese" *Rassegna storica salernitana* new series, 3 (1986), pp. 91–102. C. de Frede, *Rivolte antifeudali nel Mezzogiorno* (Naples, 1984; first edit. 1977), notes that antibaronial tumults occurred almost always in recently enfeoffed *università*.

[12] Villari, *Mezzogiorno*, pp. 68–110; T. Pedio, "Condizioni economiche generali e stato dell'artigianato e delle manifatture in Basilicata attraverso la statistica murattiana del regno di Napoli" *ASCL* 32 (1963), pp. 235–73, and 33 (1964), pp. 5–53; in these fiefs there is nothing like the extent of putting-out textile production of central Italy or of other areas of the kingdom, see for instance Caridi, *Uno "stato"*, p. 133, and F. McArdle, *Altopascio. A Study in Tuscan Rural Society, 1587–1784* (Cambridge, 1978), pp. 81–82. For the migrations, see also ASN Dipendenze Sommaria, II serie, 227/58, unnumbered fols., for the 1710s and 1750s, and G. Aliberti, *Potere e società locale nel Mezzogiorno dell'Ottocento* (Bari, 1987), p. 130. For Sasso, see ASN Pandetta Corrente 570, vol. marked 2, fols. 448r–97v; ACB 82.7.2.

protests when such interference did occur, the loudness of the protests seems to show that most elections did indeed reflect the will of the majority of the citizens. The barons often supported one faction of the population, thereby influencing the *università*'s internal life, but this intervention is harder to trace in the records. The *sindaco* and *eletti* dealt with both the baron and the royal government as representatives of the *università*. They signed the contracts and agreements with the baron, or the protests against him and the appeals to royal justice. They farmed out the *università*'s revenues and drew up the *università*'s budget; after they had served their term the accounts of their administration were subject to judgment (*sindacato*) before they were officially cleared of all liabilities.[13]

Since the reign of Alfonso of Aragon (d. 1458), the *università* had been responsible for the yearly payments to the royal government, calculated on the basis of their population. By the late sixteenth century these payments amounted ordinarily to about five ducats per household. The number of households of each *università* was determined through censuses which ought to have been held every fifteen years. Censuses were held in 1532, 1545, 1561, and 1595, when the population of the kingdom was at its peak for the Spanish period. After that the General Parliament of the kingdom preferred to avoid new censuses, fearing a further growth of the population and therefore of the fiscal burden. With the 1620s, when the demographic trend was reversed, the government granted case-by-case reductions but opposed a new census until 1648. The last census of the Spanish period, in 1669, recorded the damage inflicted by the plague of 1656.

The censuses did not, therefore, reflect the actual number of households present in each *università*, and did not include exempt households, like those in which a cleric was the official property owner. The Spanish government assigned most of the payments owed by the *università*, the so-called *fiscali*, to its own creditors, known as *fiscalari*. In many cases the barons themselves had bought the *fiscali* owed by their own fiefs, in order to strengthen their power on their vassals. There is no evidence, however, that the Caracciolo Brienza owned *fiscali* on their, or others', fiefs after the sixteenth century. In fact, in 1576 Ippolita Filomarino had ducats 270.2.07 on the *fiscali* of Brienza, and her son Marco Antonio Caracciolo gave 150 ducats on the *fiscali* of Brienza to the monastery he founded there. In 1604, 160 ducats on Brienza were assigned to

---

[13] Examples of parliament records survive in ACB, particularly vols. 43–50, 61–63, 73–77, and 81–82. On the organization of the *università*, see the *prammatiche De administratione universitatum* in L. Giustiniani, ed. *Nuova collezione delle prammatiche del regno di Napoli* (15 vols.; Naples, 1803–8); L. Cervellino, *Direttione overo guida dell'Università* ... (Naples, 1686); R. Pecori, *Del privato governo delle università* (2 vols.; Naples, 1770–73). Cassandro, *Atena*, pp. 158–60, and 193–94. Villari mentions a series of parliament records in the communal archive of Atena. The presence of local communal institutions contributed to lessen the villages' dependence on the barons, see the opposite example of Altopascio in McArdle, *Altopascio*, especially chapter 8.

the dowager marquise Giulia Caracciolo, but after that date there is no more mention of any *fiscali* held by the Caracciolo Brienza.[14]

The government requested a certain amount of taxes from each *università* based on its population. Each *università* then decided on its own how to raise the money it owed the royal government for the *fiscali*, and its baron for the feudal payments. In many cases, in fact, the *università* as a community rented feudal rights from its baron and then administered and collected them as it saw fit. Francesco Caracciolo has argued that during the Spanish period the *università* passed from a system of direct taxes (*apprezzo*, *catasto*) to a system of indirect taxes (*gabelle*), as the result of the growing strength of a local notability which wanted to shift the fiscal burden to the poorer members of the community. The applicability of his interpretation to the entire kingdom has been questioned, though Caracciolo's studies remain the only ones in recent years on this issue.[15]

In the late years of the sixteenth century, several *università* came to agreements with their barons to rent all feudal rights for a perpetual rent. This happened in Brienza, Pietrafesa, and Atena in the early 1590s. When the population declined and the economic situation worsened, these fixed rents constituted an additional heavy burden for the communities, and by the 1620s most *università* in the kingdom were heavily in debt and could not pay all of their taxes, feudal dues, and interest on loans. A similar pattern of transactions with the lords followed by heavy indebtedness – due to damages inflicted by war – took place for the Piedmontese communities. The petitions addressed to the Collateral Council in Naples by the four *università* of the Caracciolo Brienza, as well as by other *università* in the later years of the sixteenth and early years of the seventeenth centuries, show the constant need for credit in this period. The *università* asked for royal permits to contract loans, levy indirect taxes, or alienate revenues and property. In 1627–28 Carlo Tapia, then dean of the Collateral Council and one of the major jurists in seventeenth-century Naples, ordered all the *università* of

---

[14] ASN Fiscali e adoe 29.4, fol. 51r, for Ippolita; ACB 49.1.16 unnumbered fol. (an act relating to a later lawsuit) for Marco Antonio; ACB 48.1.1, fols. 2003r–v (accounts of Brienza for 1603–4), for Giulia. An account of provincial taxation in G. Muto, "Una struttura periferica del governo dell'economia nel Mezzogiorno spagnolo: i percettori provinciali" *Società e storia* 6 (1983), pp. 1–36.

[15] F. Caracciolo, "Fisco e contribuenti in Calabria nel secolo XVI" *Nuova rivista storica* 47 (1963), pp. 504–38; Caracciolo, "Finanze e gravami cittadini in Calabria e nel regno di Napoli al tempo di Filippo II" *ibid.* 66 (1982), pp. 37–58; Caracciolo, *Sud, debiti e gabelle. Gravami, potere e società nel Mezzogiorno in età moderna* (Naples, 1983). See the review of Caracciolo's work by A. Bulgarelli Lukacs in *Nuova rivista storica* 69 (1985), pp. 170–77, Caracciolo's shrill response in *ibid.*, pp. 668–72, and R. Mantelli's comment (against Caracciolo) in *ibid.* 70 (1986), pp. 659–70; P. L. Rovito, "Strutture cetuali, riformismo ed eversione nelle rivolte apulo-lucane di metà Seicento" *ASPN* 106 (1988), pp. 247–48, recently seems in agreement with Caracciolo's interpretation of this matter.

Table 4.1   *Budgets of the università in 1627*
(in ducats)

	Brienza	Sasso	Atena
fiscal households	150	151(?)	100
Income:			
indirect taxes	750	420	none reported
direct taxes	2,800	97	924.3.17½
feudal rights	381	165	none reported
terraggi	480	none reported	none reported
università properties	none reported	120	none reported
totals	4,411	802	924.3.17½
Expenses:			
fiscali	1,656.2.11½	654	584.3.17½
debts	671.4./	265	none reported
to the marquis	800	250	174
ordinary	1,317	65	200
extraordinary	500	none reported	none reported
totals	4,945.1.11½	1,234	958.3.17½
annual deficit	534.1.11½	432	34
Overdues:			
overdue *fiscali*	13,050	1,450	none reported
overdue debts	c.3,000	1,000	10,300
other overdues	224	none reported	none reported
totals	16,274	2,450	10,300

Sources: ACB 45.7.4 (Brienza), 82.6.2–3 (Sasso), and 74.2.9 (Atena, for which only a shortened version is available). I have corrected minor arithmetical mistakes of the sources. Pietrafesa's budget is not in ACB. According to *Storia del Vallo di Diano*, III.1, p. 72, Atena had a debt of 20,000 ducats in 1597 and 30,000 ducats in 1638. Tapia's papers in ASN were among those destroyed by the Nazi fire in 1943. Faraglia (*Il comune*, App., pp. 357–97) published the 1627 budgets of eight *università*.

the kingdom to submit their budgets to the royal government, which was to analyze and reform them in order to force saving and achieve solvency.[16]

The original budgets and the corrections suggested by Tapia for three of the

[16] The rents are discussed in chapter 3; the petitions are in ASN Collaterale Provvisioni (cited below, footnote 69). A new *gabella* was instituted in Brienza in 1606, ACB 48.6.1. All the seventeenth-century *prammatiche De administratione universitatum* address the problems of local finances, numbers X to XX in Giustiniani, *Nuova collezione*. On Tapia, see V. I. Comparato, *Uffici e società a Napoli (1600–1647)* (Florence, 1974), chapter 9; Muto, *Le finanze pubbliche napoletane*

four *università* of the Caracciolo Brienza have survived. The revenues came from
direct and indirect taxes, from *università* property, and from feudal rights and
dues the *università* had rented from the marquis. These consisted of jurisdictions
and monopolies which gave a return in species, and of the *terraggi* in kind. The
expenses were fiscal payments, interest payments on loans (mostly at seven
percent by the 1620s), rent owed to the marquis for feudal rights, and regular
expenses, including salaries to officers, repairs to public buildings, and expenses
for the levying of taxes. Extraordinary expenses were generally those incurred in
lawsuits. Table 4.1 shows a breakdown of the budgets of the three *università* in
1627.

The salaries which were part of the regular expenses covered only the
administrative life of the *università* and its legal expenses. The only welfare Sasso
could pay for, for instance, was eighteen ducats a year to keep a doctor. Brienza
spent twelve ducats a year in alms to a chapel, ten for a barber who also engaged
in bloodletting, and four ducats to upkeep the town clock, which the 1625
government assessment did not fail to remark upon and commend. Sasso could
not afford such a luxury.

The middle decades of the seventeenth century were indeed very difficult for
the *università*. In 1627 the regular *fiscali* alone represented between three eighths
and three fourths of the total revenues, and the debt arrears were already
between three and ten times larger than the revenues. Moreover, all three
università had an annual deficit, as high as over half the revenues in the case of
Sasso. The situation probably did not improve until after the revolt. Though the
plague reduced the taxpaying population, fiscal pressure decreased considerably
in the later seventeenth century, and by the end of the century population and
production were again on the increase. In the eighteenth century, the *università*
achieved financial solvency. In 1728, for instance, Pietrafesa and Sasso owed no
tax arrears and their income matched their expenses.[17]

This brief look at communal institutions and finances constitutes a background for discussing the presence of the baron in his fiefs. It is difficult to assess
the relative poverty of these communities, though the eighteenth-century
appraisers of Sasso were struck by the misery of the residents and a 1748 lawsuit
concerning that *università* stressed its poverty.[18] The four *università* were

tra riforme e restaurazione (1520–1634) (Naples, 1980), pp. 115–18; Muto, "Strutture"; Rovito,
Respublica dei togati (Naples, 1981), chapter 2. On Piedmont, see Woolf, *Studi*, pp. 39–42, 71–75,
and 164–70.

[17] For the general economic history of the period, recently L. de Rosa, *Il Mezzogiorno spagnolo tra
crescita e decadenza* (Milan, 1987); M. A. Visceglia, *Territorio, feudo e potere locale* (Naples, 1988),
pp. 267–78; for the eighteenth century, see ASN Tesorieri e Percettori, Basilicata fascio 1688
(my thanks to Alessandra Bulgarelli Lukacs for this reference), and Bulgarelli Lukacs, "Le
'Universitates' meridionali all'inizio del regno di Carlo di Borbone, la struttura amministrativa"
Clio 17 (1981), pp. 5–25, and Bulgarelli Lukacs, "Le 'universitates' meridionali all'inizio del
regno di Carlo di Borbone" *ibid.* 18 (1982), pp. 208–26.

[18] ASN Pandetta Corrente 2026, II, fols. 117r–22r.

probably fairly typical of the internal regions of the kingdom not integrated to any significant degree in larger commercial or productive networks. Aside from the óccasional travellers who stopped in Atena, very few outsiders ever entered the state of the marquis of Brienza, other than the provincial fiscal officers, who were certainly not welcome visitors. In contrast to this, the baron was often present and very visible in his lands, not only as a despotic economic master but also, at least at times, as a source of justice, help, and contact with the outside world.

THE LORD'S PRESENCE IN THE FIEFS

Historians of all Western European countries have long observed that in the sixteenth and seventeenth centuries the old aristocracy moved to provincial and state capitals, as the growth of the bureaucratic state made it advisable to be near the centers of patronage and the tribunals. Historians of the kingdom of Naples generally agree that with the viceroyalty of don Petro de Toledo (1532–53), the high aristocracy began to live in the capital and at court. The viceroyal court could not offer as many opportunities for service and education to aristocratic scions as the courts of other Italian states like Piedmont; economic and social historians, however, have emphasized the importance for the aristocracy of solid connections at court and in the tribunals, and commented on the expenses that life in Naples entailed and the consequent aristocratic indebtedness. Gérard Labrot has studied the importance of the "barons in the city" for the building and decoration of palaces in Spanish Naples. Although Labrot has also alerted historians to aristocratic building in the fiefs, his suggestions have not been pursued.[19]

The Caracciolo as a clan always had an urban character. As we have seen, they owned property in Naples since the tenth century, and settled in the district of Capuana, where they represented one third of the aristocratic *Seggio*. All the members of the clan were citizens of Naples and members of the *Seggi*. In this sense it is difficult to speak, for the Caracciolo as for other old Neapolitan aristocratic clans, of a process of urbanization in the sixteenth century. Members of the Caracciolo clan had obtained fiefs in the fourteenth and fifteenth century, but many members of the clan still lived in the capital, where some played an

---

[19] G. Labrot, *Baroni in città. Residenze e comportamenti dell'aristocrazia napoletana 1530–1734* (Naples, 1979); Labrot, "Trend économique et mécénat dans le royaume de Naples 1530–1750" paper presented at the seventeenth Settimana di Studio dell'Istituto Internazionale di Storia Economica "Francesco Datini" di Prato, *Gli aspetti economici del mecenatismo in Europa (secoli XIV-XVIII)* (1985), also in *MEFRM* 98 (1986), pp. 329–81; Labrot has also pointed to aristocratic residence in the fiefs in "Le comportement collectif de l'aristocratie napolitaine du seizième au dix-huitième siècle" *Revue historique* 101, no. 258 (1977), pp. 45–71, and in Labrot and R. Ruotolo, "Pour une étude historique de la commande aristocratique dans le royaume de Naples espagnol" *ibid.* 104, no. 264 (1980), pp. 25–48. The Piedmontese aristocracy moved to Turin in the late seventeenth and early eighteenth centuries, see Woolf, *Studi*, pp. 61–66, 90–97, and 126–29.

important political role. With the consolidation of large feudal states in the fifteenth and sixteenth centuries, however, the barons spent a considerable amount of time in their fiefs, reinforcing their local rule, and constituting, at times, strong regional power bases. In the Spanish period the feudal aristocracy had to be present both in the capital and in its fiefs, and palace-building in Naples was paralleled by the attention given to feudal residences and to relations with the vassals. There is evidence that the paternalistic rhetoric that often accompanied contemporary descriptions of the feudal regime found some echoes in reality, in the behavior of the lords towards their vassals.

Giuseppe Galasso has repeatedly spoken of a definitive urbanization of the aristocracy in the sixteenth century, but to do so he has had to minimize the evidence he himself provided. The Loffredo barons of Amendolara still lived in their feudal castle in 1582, and in 1594 several of the twenty-nine feudal residences of the Sanseverino princes of Bisignano were still ready to accommodate the prince's visits. Although in the mid-seventeenth century some of the most indebted families let their palaces and castles in the fiefs decay, they never completely abandoned them. An aristocratic family typically divided its time between the capital and the fiefs. The Caracciolo Brienza never moved to Naples permanently, and in fact in the eighteenth century they spent more time in the fiefs than before. Even when the aristocracy lived in Naples there is evidence that it did not neglect either its feudal residences or its close paternalistic relations with its vassals.[20]

The Sant'Eramo branch of the Caracciolo Brienza owned a palace near San Giovanni a Carbonara in Naples since the mid-sixteenth century, which had been entailed to them by Cardinal Marino Caracciolo. The first branch of the marquis of Brienza, on the other hand, did not own any regular lodgings in Naples until 1658. In fact, they seem to have rarely resided in the capital, and a late sixteenth-century document mentions that Giovan Battista Caracciolo, marquis of Brienza, "does not like the way the world is, resides always in his state and gives vent to his fierceness [*terribilità*] by hunting." Giovan Battista's weak economic position probably confirmed his desire to live away from the expensive capital, and the same document shows that in most cases residence in the fiefs was due to a desire to save or to express discontent. Luigi Carafa, prince of Stigliano, and Ferrante Carafa, duke of Nocera, had both retired to their *stati* in 1590 in order to be able to meet their debts.[21]

20 G. Galasso, "Aspetti e problemi della società feudale napoletana attraverso l'inventario dei beni dei principi di Bisignano (1594)" in *Studi in memoria di Federigo Melis* (Naples, 1978), IV, pp. 255–77; Galasso, "Cultura materiale e vita nobiliare in un inventario calabrese del '500" in Galasso, *L'altra Europa, per un'antropologia storica del Mezzogiorno d'Italia* (Milan, 1982), pp. 284–311; the need for the aristocracy to be in Naples to deal with the royal administration is affirmed also in R. Pilati, "La dialettica politica a Napoli durante la visita di Lope de Guzmán" *ASPN* 105 (1987), pp. 173–75.
21 G. Ceci, "I feudatari napoletani alla fine del secolo XVI" *ASPN* 24 (1899), pp. 122–38; ASN Archivio Doria Angri 65/30 for 1590.

A few important family acts, such as the division of Marco Antonio I's estate in 1584 or the inventory at Marco Antonio II's death in 1621, were drawn in Naples, but it is not clear where the family was lodging at the time; they probably rented their living quarters while in town. It seems from these instances that inheritances and minorities brought the family to Naples, possibly because of the legal proceedings which accompanied those moments. Similarly, sojourns in Naples coincided with periods in family life when there were marriageable children. While in the capital, the Neapolitan aristocracy indulged in much the same court and social life and shared in the same urban culture and lifestyle as its Northern Italian counterparts.[22]

The marquis Giovan Battista certainly spent most of his adulthood in his fiefs where, as we have seen, he bought extensive tracts of land and intervened actively in the local economy. He also began construction, around 1612, of the family palace in Atena, the only one of the fiefs which did not have a feudal castle. His son, Giacomo, also spent long periods in the fiefs, and in 1639 Giacomo's daughter, Diana, was confirmed in Brienza, while his brother, Giuseppe, was active in Naples in the 1630s. Both brothers were in Naples at the time of the revolt of Masaniello. Giuseppe, when in Naples, lived in the area of Pizzofalcone, a hill opposite the new royal palace occupied by a fort and several aristocratic palaces.[23]

It was there in 1658 that Giuseppe's sister, Faustina, bought the palace adjacent to the Theatine monastery of Santa Maria degli Angeli. Giuseppe had worried in his will that Faustina would neglect the fiefs "since she is a woman and will easily want to live in Naples." Faustina's desire to move to Naples, where she was quite active at court, was criticized also by her son, Pietro Gambacorta, who accused her of having needlessly spent money in the capital, while her husband had always lived in his fief of Celenza. But after her death, the Caracciolo Brienza returned to spend long periods of time in the fiefs, and we have seen from the inventories that the feudal residences were never totally neglected. Between 1689 and 1698, seven children of Giuseppe II, marquis of Brienza, were baptized in Brienza. Even when the family returned to Naples in the early eighteenth century – mainly to marry off Giuseppe's daughters – one or

---

22 ACB 9.8 (1584) and ASN notai del '600, Fulgenzio Gagliardo, 839/8, fols. 95rff. (in this case the act is drawn in a house near the church of San Tommaso Apostolo by the Vicaria, which does not belong to the family). In 1620, when his sister Vittoria entered a nunnery, Marco Antonio II gave as his address in Naples the office of his notary, ASN notai del '600, G. A. Cassetta, 848/9, fols. 161v–63v. In the same year, the family paid 120 ducats for the rent of a house with small garden in the Chiaia neighborhood, ASBN, AGP, Giornale Cassa 76, unnumbered fol., 8 August 1620. For evidence of court and social life in seventeenth-century Naples, one needs only to read the city chronicles of A. Bulifon, D. Confuorto, and I. Fuidoro.

23 ACB 43.3.1, fols. 10v–11r on the new palace in Atena. F. Capecelatro, *Diario 1647–1650* (3 vols.; Naples, 1850–54), and Capecelatro, *Degli annali della città di Napoli 1631–1640* (Naples, 1849), from the indexes for the presence of the two brothers in Naples and Giuseppe's lodging (Giuseppe was a personal friend of Capecelatro's and is often mentioned). ACB 134.3, unnumbered fol., for the confirmation in Brienza.

the other member of the family resided in the fiefs, especially the cadet sons, like Giovan Battista in the first and Gennaro in the third decade of the century. After the death of Giuseppe II in 1720, the family went back to spend at least half of its time in the fiefs.[24]

When they resided in the fiefs, the Caracciolo Brienza had several options for their lodging. Brienza, Pietrafesa, and Sasso had old feudal castles belonging to the ruler of the fiefs. In 1625 in Sasso, "on a raised height of a rocky mountain stays the castle of the village, not any more fit for habitation because it is mostly in ruins, but when it was still in good shape it was sufficient to defend and protect the inhabitants whenever enemies should cause trouble," but the marquis, when he was in Sasso for his hunting expeditions, used a house he owned, with stable, cellar, courtyard, and eight rooms. In Pietrafesa in 1625, the castle was "in the highest peak and height of the village," with stables, a courtyard, storage spaces, two apartments, "the jail for the criminals, and other conveniences." But the marquis rarely stayed in Pietrafesa, and by 1677 the castle needed repairs. It was by that time used mainly as a storage and administration space.[25]

The physically prominent position of the castle, and the fact that it was at once the baron's residence, the economic center of the feudal domain, the judicial center of the village, and the jail, made it the most visible symbol of feudal rule. These characteristics were heightened in Brienza where the castle, located on top of a hill, with its high circular tower even in ruins as it is today, commands the observer's attention and dominates the houses of the now abandoned old village. An old medieval building, in the seventeenth century it consisted of strong tall walls, which made it fit for "defense in times of storms or of enemies' movements," with a narrow entrance to a vast courtyard. From the courtyard there was access to stables, cellars, rooms with water cisterns, lodgings for the guardian, kitchens, pantries, the rooms for the baronial tribunal, and to the tower, which served as a jail. Upstairs were two large apartments and several smaller living quarters, a chapel "in which a daily Mass is celebrated, for the ease and devotion of the lord of this village and of his whole court," and numerous servants' rooms and storage spaces. "And from all parts of this castle, he [the lord] enjoys the happiest view of the countryside, dominating from it his entire village."[26]

---

[24] ACB 5.2.1–2, 12.2.3, 77.2.7, 17.6, and 17.9. ASP notai Potenza 1353 and 1354, especially fols. 20v–22r, for Giovan Battista. The baptisms are in ACB 3.1.8 a–g. Giuseppe's will is in ASN Pandetta Corrente 570, IV, fols. 5r–16r (12r). On Faustina's life at court, see the negative comments of I. Fuidoro, *Giornali di Napoli dal MDCLX al MDCLXXX* (3 vols.; Naples, 1934–39), III, p. 97; "Frammento d'un diario inedito napoletano" *ASPN* 13 (1888), pp. 788–820, and 14 (1889), pp. 34–68, and 265–352, especially p. 300. On Pizzofalcone, see Ceci, "Pizzofalcone" *Napoli nobilissima* I (1892), pp. 60–62, 85–89, 105–9, and 129–33; Labrot, "Naissance et croissance d'un quartier de Naples: Pizzofalcone, 1530–1689" *Urbi* I (1979), pp. 47–66.

[25] The assessments of 1625 and 1677 are in ACB 43.3.1 (fols. 17v and 14r–v) and 43.3.7. The house in Sasso is described in the 1622 inventory in ASN notai del '600, 839/8, already cited.

[26] ACB 43.3.1, fols. 2r–v.

The feudal lord and his vassals

The inhabitants of the four *università* felt the presence of the imposing castles, and the tower jail in Brienza was the object of fear and resentment. The baron often kept prisoners in the dark and damp basement of the tower, and he did not allow them visitors. On occasion delinquents were moved from the other three *università* to the tower in Brienza, which was considered safer and a heavier punishment. These and other abuses related to conditions in the jail often appear in protests from the *università* to the royal government. In fact, a seventeenth-century treatise on barons' abuses discusses twenty possible cases of baronial excesses relating to the managing of feudal prisons.[27]

The baron, as we have seen, had several representatives in the fiefs. The captain could not be a vassal of the baron, and these positions as feudal judges were the preserve of a middling group of provincial lawyers about whom very little is known. Giovan Battista Basile, the author of the *Pentamerone*, was the most famous of them in the seventeenth century. The captain disposed of a small staff, consisting in general of a chancellor, a scribe (*mastrodatti*), a jailer, and one or two guards, who were the only people in the villages permitted by law to carry certain weapons. As we saw, the salaries for these baronial dependents came out of the fines and fees of justice. The baron also had a staff of dependents responsible for the economic management of the fief. The Caracciolo Brienza at times appointed a general agent who resided in Brienza, though the position became a regular one only in the mid-eighteenth century, when the general agent had subordinates in Atena, Pietrafesa, and Sasso, and supervised the management of the entire patrimony. With a salary of 240 ducats a year, he was then by far the best paid of the barons' dependents, and had to control the actions of the guardians of the castles and of the *erari* and *conservatori* of each fief. The position of the *erari* and *conservatori*, as simultaneously members of the *università* and agents of the marquis, might have been an awkward one, but in general they seem to have acquitted themselves of their responsibilities without too many difficulties.[28]

It is hard to say how the Caracciolo Brienza occupied the time they spent in

---

[27] G. M. Novario, *De vassallorum gravaminibus tractatus* (Naples, 1634; I have used the 1774 edition). The protests of the Caracciolo Brienza vassals against the abuses are discussed on pp. 143–53 below. On jails, see the *prammatica* XIX *De baronibus et eorum officio* (1559) in Giustiniani, *Nuova collezione*.

[28] On captains, see the *prammatiche De baronibus*, especially numbers IV, V, VI, XXI, and XXIII in Giustiniani, *Nuova collezione*. On baronial guards, see Winspeare, *Storia*, note 99, pp. 111–12 of the notes. The fees the captain levied in Brienza are reported in ASP notai Potenza, 650, fol. 185v (*c.* 1650); appointment letters are in ACB 16.10, 48.8 and 9, 62.5.1. Giovan Battista's will in 1620 mentions a general agent (ASN notai del'500, Giovan Simone della Monica, prot. 40, fascicolo 156); an agent is in Brienza in 1635 (ASN notai del '600, Pietro Antonio dell'Aversano, 912/13, fols. 278r–79v); a general agent was in the fiefs in 1658 (ASN Relevi 236, fol. 699r). Accounts for *erari* and *conservatori* survive in ACB, but most date from the 1750s onwards. There is evidence in ACB of only one case of embezzlement on the part of an agent in the fiefs, when Cesare Ganga was tried for fabricating accounts in 1735, ACB 17.8. Chapter 3 discusses administrative expenses.

their *stato*. Apart from a few references to hunting there is no evidence as to the life of the baronial family in its fiefs before the eighteenth century. In the 1720s, Domenico II lived with his wife in her mother's fiefs in Calabria, while his brother, Gennaro, resided in the family fiefs where he acted so injudiciously that the communities convinced the royal courts to prohibit him from entering the fiefs again. When Marquis Litterio came of age in the 1740s, the whole family resided in the fiefs, and the general agent often stayed in Naples. The priest's list of families for the new *catasto* of Brienza in 1747 ends with the "family of the castle," including the young Litterio with his wife, his paternal grandmother, and his, by now tamed, uncle Gennaro.[29]

From the mid-eighteenth century on, the family spent a few years in Naples and a few in Brienza, alternating regularly between the two residences. While the Caracciolo were in Brienza, the entire palace in Naples was rented out and they kept a smaller staff of servants than in Naples. The records of births and deaths of Litterio's many children show that the family was in Brienza in April and September 1746, July 1749, May 1750, April and December 1753, and in Atena in May 1768 and 1769. In the early 1760s, following the death of his first wife, Litterio travelled outside the kingdom. In the later third of the eighteenth century the family began to spend a few weeks in the fall in Vietri, as a *villeggiatura* (vacation), a term never used for the long periods spent in Brienza. From the account books kept in this period we know that the family was in Brienza or Atena for a total of about eight years between July 1774 and January 1794.[30]

There was no possibility of social interaction for the baronial family in Brienza, and the fiefs of other aristocrats were not nearby. This explains why residence in the capital was necessary when marriages had to be arranged. The family's *stato* was isolated and did not include any center large enough to host any significant provincial nobility, such as to provide the Caracciolo Brienza with noble clients to patronize. Nothing like the small but culturally active court assembled by their cousins, the princes of Avellino, would have been conceivable in Brienza or Atena, even if the Caracciolo Brienza had shown much interest in such projects. Networks of patronage and clientage between the high aristocracy and the provincial elite have not been investigated by historians of the kingdom of Naples. There is, however, no evidence of any involvement of the Caracciolo Brienza in such networks, and in any case the family never spent any time in the provincial capitals.[31]

[29] On Gennaro's problems in the fiefs, see ACB 17.6 and 9, 10.1, and ASN Collaterale, Consulte originali VII, 14. The list is in ASN Catasto Onciario 5149, fol. 245v.
[30] ACB 28, 36 (with the births and deaths), 37, and 38. The trip to and from the fiefs for the whole family could take up to two weeks.
[31] B. Croce, *Uomini e cose della vecchia Italia* (2 vols.; Bari, 1956; first edit. 1926), I, pp. 144–83, for the court in Avellino in the seventeenth century. These issues have been recently investigated for the French aristocracy, see S. Kettering, *Patrons, Brokers and Clients in Seventeenth-Century France*

The marquis Litterio, however, seems to have enjoyed his stays in the villages, and, particularly after the death of his first wife, he spent a lot of time in his fiefs with his children. He was very reluctant to leave them even for a few days, and he sought to entertain them as best he could. In 1762 he wrote to his agent in Naples wishing him "a happy Carnival, which for me means mad head-aches with these children of mine, who today have really blown my head off, and we are still in the first day"; he therefore asked his agent to send several masks from Naples, including two of Pulcinella. Though its social life was less active, the atmosphere in Litterio's family when it resided in Brienza must have closely resembled that of the gentry families described by Jane Austen.[32]

In his marriage contract with his second wife, Litterio enjoined her to live "in the state of the lord marquis, where he intends to remain, and where he wants the children who may come from this marriage to be raised, and not in the city of Naples." By 1781, the Caracciolo Brienza had added a palace in Pietrafesa to their residences in Brienza and Atena, and all three buildings were fully equipped to host the family. Life could be hard for aristocratic youths in Brienza, however, and in 1768, one year after his second marriage, Litterio wrote to his agent in Naples asking him to find a violin teacher for his fifteen-year-old son who

stays here and is bored stiff, and were he not of adorable character he would fight with his father because of this. Music, fencing, riding, shooting with his pistol barely hold him from further arguing with me, as he does with others, saying he does not want to remain here, where he is most desperate.

We lack evidence for previous times, but by the eighteenth century there was obviously no lack of affection and concern within Neapolitan aristocratic families.[33]

In the eighteenth century, therefore, the aristocracy was spending probably even less of its time in the capital than before. The Saluzzo resided almost continuously in their Calabrian duchy of Corigliano. The Caracciolo princes of

(Oxford, 1986), and K. Neuschel, *Word of Honor. Interpreting Noble Culture in Sixteenth-Century France* (Ithaca, 1989).

[32] ACB 140.40, fols. 28v–29r and throughout. See also G. W. Pedlow, *The Survival of the Hessian Nobility, 1770–1870* (Princeton, 1988), pp. 138–43.

[33] ACB 3.2.28 the contract; the letter in 140.40, fols. 68v–69r. The inventories for the residences are in ACB 35.2 (Brienza and Atena), and 161, unnumbered fol. (Pietrafesa). G. Paternoster, *Ritratto di paese, Brienza 1872* (Venosa, 1984) mentions a theater in the castle in the eighteenth century, but I have not found any other evidence of this. The young prince was not the only member of the baronial household to seek pleasurable distractions, and on at least two occasions in the 1760s, Litterio had to intervene to break up illicit sexual liaisons among his dependents (clerical or otherwise), further evidence of his paternalistic approach to his household and fiefs, ACB 140.40, fols. 55v–56r, and 69r. There is, of course, a large bibliography on the rise of the affectionate family in the early modern period; for an introduction, see L. Stone, "Family History in the 1980s: Past Achievements and Future Trends" *Journal of Interdisciplinary History* 12 (1981), pp. 51–87.

Plate 3 View of the feudal castle and old village of Brienza.

Avellino and the Francone also spent time in their fiefs, and devoted their care to their feudal residences in the eighteenth century. Litterio Caracciolo's increased attention to the administration of his fiefs, and his careful observance of traditions in their management, the economic reasons for which we have seen in the preceding chapter, point also to his interest in maintaining and strengthening close relations with the vassals. Ideally, the relations were of a paternalistic nature and the lord was the protector of the communities. This ideal was reflected in reality to a certain extent, and after the events of 1647–48 the barons tried to stress these traditional aspects of the relationship.[34]

[34] R. Merzario, *Signori e contadini di Calabria. Corigliano Calabro dal XVI al XIX secolo* (Milan, 1975); A. Caracciolo di Torchiarolo, "Alcune notizie sulla famiglia Francone e l'arredamento di una casa patrizia napoletana al principio del secolo XVIII" *Studi in onore di Riccardo Filangieri* (3 vols.; Naples, 1959), III, pp. 29–50; Caracciolo di Torchiarolo, "I Caracciolo di Avellino e un inventario del XVII secolo," offprint from *Samnium* 35 (1962); Ebner, *Storia*, chapter 6.

Plate 4 Tower of the feudal castle of Brienza.

Several wills of the Caracciolo Brienza contain bequests of money or property in favor of the decendant's vassals. In most instances, this took the form of a bequest to the village church to pay for Masses for the deceased, but other forms of charity were also frequent, especially dowries. For instance, in the 1580s, Giulia Caracciolo had established a fund to dower orphan girls in Atena. Porzia Carafa in 1618 left thirty ducats a year for the dowry of a girl in her marquisate of Sant'Eramo. In 1621, Marino Caracciolo, lord of Cancellara, enjoined his widow to continue the distributions of bread to poor women of the village that he had started. In his will of 1640, Carlo Gambacorta, marquis of Celenza and prince of Macchia, left seventy-five ducats a year to Celenza and 140 to Macchia in perpetuity, to be used for the dowries of village girls. Giacomo Caracciolo, marquis of Brienza, in his will of 1638 (later revoked) granted a six-month amnesty to his vassals. A similar general amnesty had been granted by Giacomo's

Plate 5 Tower of the feudal castle of Sasso.

father, Giovan Battista, in his will of 1620, enjoining his heir to redress any grievances his vassals might have had. Giovan Battista also left thirty-six ducats to dower two women in Brienza or Sasso. In 1652, Bernabò Caracciolo, duke of Sicignano, left all of his private and liquid assets to a chapel in the village parish. Faustina Caracciolo, in her will of 1665, left 400 ducats for dowry funds in Macchia and Celenza, and in the will of 1673 she added ten *maritaggi* of twenty-four ducats each in the Caracciolo fiefs. In 1650, Andreana Pignatelli, marquise of Sant'Eramo, absolved her *università* from the money it owed her. In 1686, Francesco Gambacorta made several bequests to the churches of his fiefs. In the eighteenth century, Litterio's two grandmothers, his mother, and his uncle Gennaro, all founded chaplaincies in their villages.[35]

These bequests and other provisions to benefit one's vassals bore an element of *noblesse oblige*, and the French early modern aristocracy behaved similarly. The fact that the Neapolitan aristocracy, though, was also spending quite a bit of its time in the fiefs must have made the impact of these bequests greater. In particular, providing for dowries, though certainly designed in part to represent

[35] Giulia's donation is in ASP notai Potenza, 45, fols. 209r–10v; the wills are in ACB 137.16, fols. 17r–29v (1618); 4.1.14, 17, 20, 29, 31, 37, 45, 52b, 55, and 56a; Giovan Battista's is in ASN notai del '500, G. S. della Monica, already cited; ASN Pandetta Comune 513 (1686), fols. 2r–8v.

one more form of patronage, also responded to a widespread and vital concern of early modern Neapolitans to ensure the safe marriage of as many women as possible. The baronial household, in Naples and in the fiefs, also offered employment opportunities to the vassals. The fact, moreover, that the barons sold most of the grain that entered the local market certainly contributed to making them the dominant figures in the lives of their vassals.[36]

In the eighteenth century, Litterio Caracciolo emphasized his protective role *vis-à-vis* the communities. In his will, he asked his heir to be a good lord to the vassals, and in his life he frequently intervened in community life in Brienza. In 1762, on the occasion of a contagious fever in Brienza, Litterio "was forced to act truly as a father in order to help the public ... [he] summoned several doctors and surgeons from afar at [his] expense." In 1774, he donated fifty ducats a year to the parish priest from the revenues of his chapels. In 1775, the *università* appealed to him to contribute to the restoration of the parish church. On other occasions he helped support a grain fund for the peasants, donated jewels and silver to the local churches, and accepted to offer some of his own pastures temporarily to the *università*. In 1788, as we shall see, he founded a school for the village children. These policies also served to diffuse the potential challenge to baronial rule posed by the rise of families of local notables.[37]

Besides these interventions in the life of their communities, the Caracciolo Brienza had a strong sense of their position as rulers of their state, and did not miss chances to express it publicly. Still in the eighteenth century, the *università* of Brienza presented the marquis with gifts at Christmas and Easter. The ascension to the title was marked by a ceremony known as the "taking of possession" (*presa di possesso*) during which the new marquis or his representative performed a series of acts symbolizing the various powers of the new ruler, such as opening and closing the doors of the jail, sitting at the judge's bench in the baronial court, visiting all parts of the castle, looking at administrative and economic accounts, visiting the mill and the baronial inn and oven, picking

---

[36] E. Teall, "The Seigneur of Renaissance France: Advocate or Oppressor?" *Journal of Modern History* 37 (1965), pp. 131–50; J.-P. Labatut, *Les ducs et pairs de France au XVIIe siècle* (Paris, 1972), pp. 311–20; similar patterns can be seen in the behavior of the dukes of Osuna (who resided in Madrid) towards the populations of their estates, see I. Atienza Hernandez, *Aristocracia, poder y riqueza en la España moderna* (Madrid, 1987), chapter 3; paternalism did not, on the other hand, pervade the relationship of the magistrates of Rouen with their peasants, see Dewald, *The Formation of a Provincial Nobility* (Princeton, 1980), pp. 179–83. For the importance of dowries, see chapter 5, below. On villagers in the baronial household, see ASN Pandetta Corrente 570, vol. marked 3, fols. 517r–v. Paternalism has continued to mark the relationship between European aristocrats and their dependent peasant populations well into this century, see, for instance, the fascinating example presented by the memoirs of Countess Marion Dönhoff, discussed in G. Craig, "Witness" *The New York Review of Books*, 6 December, 1990, pp. 2–7.

[37] Litterio's will in ACB App. 22, unnumbered fol. His interventions in community life in ACB 140.40, fol. 51r; 49.1.30, 32; 50.5; 134.3, unnumbered fol.; 161, unnumbered fol.; and App. 22, unnumbered fol. (the Monte Pio in Brienza, 1788). Similar policies, with similar purposes, were followed by other families, of the old and new feudal aristocracy, see A. Sinisi, "Una famiglia mercantile napoletana del XVIII secolo" *Economia e storia* second series, 3 (1982), pp. 139–203.

leaves and moving soil in baronial lands, and taking the keys to the village's gates. The procedure was duly notarized. The vassals, for their part, publicly swore allegiance and paid homage.[38]

The main expression of the barons' position took place in religious life. In 1562, Marco Antonio I built a monastery for the Franciscan friars in Brienza, and the family had patronage over some chapels in the new building. On the occasion of family events, the whole village took part in ceremonies which, if not as solemn as Litterio's own baptism in the cathedral of Messina, performed by the archbishop with two Sicilian princes as godparents, must have strengthened the sense of awe and the traditional tie that bound the vassals to their lords. The marquis Domenico died in Brienza in 1681, and the last rites were performed by his Theatine brother. Domenico's son, Giuseppe, had been born in Brienza in 1660, and the bishop of Marsico had come to baptize him in the presence of the whole clergy and people of the village. The bishops of Marsico travelled to Brienza – not an easy task, if one is to believe their own *Relationes ad limina* – also for the confirmation of Diana, daughter of marquis Giacomo in 1639, and again, when the infant's health allowed a delay, for the baptisms of some of Giuseppe's children in the 1690s and of Litterio's own in the 1740s and 1750s. In 1746, Litterio's first son, Domenico, heir apparent to the title, was baptized by the local midwife because of his frail health, but then rebaptized by the bishop of Marsico in a pompous ceremony in the main church of Brienza, while the bishop of Capaccio and the duke of neighboring Polla acted as god-fathers.[39]

Throughout the old regime, therefore, the feudal aristocracy maintained and stressed its position as ruler and protector of its vassals. Particularly after the revolt of 1647–48, the Caracciolo Brienza presented themselves to their vassals, at least in part, as benevolent and beneficiary masters, committed to local welfare, in the same years in which their management of their revenues abided more strictly than before by local conventions and traditions. Their lifestyle, which in Naples followed the fashions of a court aristocracy, in the fiefs closely resembled that of the rural knights of Austria or Germany. Especially in a relatively isolated and poor region, the aristocracy succeeded in keeping its relations with the vassals remarkably quiet. As we shall see later, there is little evidence in the kingdom of Naples of the presence of troublemaking lawyers

---

[38] Gifts, for example, in ACB 45.1.11; the *presa di possesso* in, for example, 43.3.4–5, 21, 37–38; 75.2.8; 81.1.11; ASN notai del '600, Nicola Evangelista, 205/24, fols. 61r–62v (1645). The ceremony is parodied, as a Neapolitan phenomenon, in Carlo Goldoni's *Il feudatario* (1752), III, xv.

[39] ACB 134.3 for Diana, and 3.1 for the baptisms; for the monastery, see N. Barbone Puglise, "Due tavole di Silvestro Buono a Brienza" *Napoli nobilissima* new series, 24 (1985), pp. 93–99, and the sources she quotes on the Franciscans; A. Grelle Iusco, ed. *Arte in Basilicata, rinvenimenti e restauri* (Matera, 1981), is the catalogue of an exhibition which included works in the churches of Brienza and Pietrafesa.

and of the increasing tension that characterized the relations of the French aristocracy with its peasants in the later eighteenth century.[40]

While the church and its representatives could serve to assert the position of the feudal lord through public rituals, they constituted also a rival claim to that of the barons' to both the allegiance and the wealth of the vassals. Particularly in an economy characterized by small peasant landholdings, the possibility the church had to lend money in times of difficulty gave it a powerful means to develop a wide patronage network that could compete with that of the marquis. The clergy was often in conflict with the *università*, but more often it contrasted with the marquis both in jurisdiction and in economic relations with the villagers. The patronage that the marquis exerted over ecclesiastic benefices and their income created further friction. The poverty and distance of the bishoprics, however, and the peculiar organization of the Southern church, made the local clergy quite autonomous and often placed it at odds as much with its hierarchical superiors as with the marquis themselves, so that the latter never lost their preeminent role in the fiefs. The marquis could actually often enlist the support of the local clergy who, like all elements of village society, distrusted any intervention of outside authorities. Only in the later eighteenth century did the government enact a vigorous policy towards the church, but at that point the marquis was able to take advantage of the prevalent anticlerical climate.

As we have seen, the four *università* of the Caracciolo Brienza state were included in three different dioceses, two of them very poor and small, Marsico Nuovo and Campagna-Satriano, and one quite large but centered in a distant city, Capaccio. The clergy of the four *università* was therefore very autonomous, also because it was organized, as most of the clergy in the rural South, around the *ricettizia* church. In this system, each parish had some lands and revenues which were shared among the participant clergy (*porzionari*). Each priest had a portion of the lands, which he cultivated with his family, and all the priests shared the liturgical obligations and the revenues of the tithes. The *arciprete* (head priest) simply enjoyed a larger share than the other priests. In this situation, the bishops and the local clergy were often fighting over the former's share of the tithe and, with the arrival of post-Tridentine bishops in a few Southern dioceses, over the degree of control exercised by the bishops over the spiritual fitness and moral

---

[40] Could one speak, for the post-1647 period, of a "refeudalization with a human face"? O. Brunner, *Vita nobiliare e cultura europea* (Bologna, 1972; German edit. 1949); R. Forster, "The 'World' between Seigneur and Peasant" *Studies in Eighteenth-Century Culture* 5 (1976), pp. 401–21; and pp. 143–53 below.

behavior of the local clergy. Complaints about the poor quality of the local clergy abound in the *Relationes ad limina.*[41]

Though there is debate as to how widespread the *ricettizia* system was in the kingdom, it is clear that its main consequence consisted in the close ties between the local priests and their flock, since the priests came from the local peasantry and were involved in the same agricultural production as their fellow-villagers. The parishes of the four *università* of the Caracciolo Brienza were all organized as *ricettizie*, and they had no shortage of clergy. Brienza had a friary that hosted twelve Franciscans and often acted as the center of the village's religious life, more than the two parish churches. There were a total of five churches in Brienza in 1625, seven in 1659 (plus six outside of the village), and sixteen in 1714. The two parish churches were managed by one *arciprete*, who could count on the help of a number of priests and deacons that grew from twelve in 1594 to fifty-four in 1659 and then declined to forty-five by 1714. Roughly the same number of clerics served Pietrafesa's churches: one parish in 1625 to which were added nine other churches or chapels by 1742. Atena had two parishes and one other church in 1625, and two parishes and nine other churches or chapels in 1748, served by at least thirty clerics. The parish church of Sasso had eight priests and eighteen deacons in 1625, and in 1659 this village of 800 people had thirteen churches or chapels served by thirty-one clerics. In 1714 it had nine churches with twenty-two clerics.[42]

This clergy came from the villages themselves and shared its flock's dislike for outside powers. Prominent among these outsiders were the bishops, whose visits were the occasion for tension and clashes with the local population described in the episcopal reports. Even discounting the topical character of much of the language of the *Relationes*, the doctrinal and moral conditions of the clergy and faithful of the four villages seem fully to justify the Jesuit dictum that the internal areas of the kingdom represented *las Indias de por aca* (the Indies of this side). The natural characteristics of the dioceses made frequent visitations difficult, and preserved the isolation of the communities. Marsico Nuovo and Satriano lacked a diocesan seminary for a long time, and the quality of the clergy matched that of its flock.

[41] G. De Rosa, "Per una storia della parrocchia nel Mezzogiorno" and "Pertinenze ecclesiastiche e santità nella storia sociale e religiosa della Basilicata dal XVIII al XIX secolo" in De Rosa, *Chiesa e religione popolare nel Mezzogiorno* (Bari, 1978), pp. 21–46 and 47–101 (the latter also in De Rosa and F. Malgeri, eds. *Società*, I, (1978), pp. 15–73); the *Relationes* are in ASV 491, 177, and 185. Ebner, *Storia*, pp. 165–74, on the *ricettizia*; *ibid.*, pp. 271–336, on the bishops of Capaccio; on the latter, who were all aristocratic, see also De Rosa, *Vescovi, popolo e magia nel Sud* (Naples, 1971), chapter 2.

[42] The 1625 assessment (ACB 43.3.1) reports only the churches, not the rural chapels. The 1677 assessment for Brienza (ACB 43.3.7) counts ninety-five clerics. The assessment for Atena in 1748 is in ACB 77.2.32; ASV *Relationes* vols. cited above; the *Relationes* for Capaccio are very uninformative, because of the size of the diocese, which in 1630 included 147 towns and 85,160 people. I am counting deacons, subdeacons, and simple *chierici* as clergy. The archiepiscopal town of Santa Severina was blessed in 1687 with seventy-three clerics, which represented eight percent of its total population, see Caridi, *Uno "stato"*, pp. 138–39.

In 1598, the bishop of Marsico wrote that "the people of this city and diocese have so grown in savagery that often they dare act violently against the clergy, both regular and secular." In 1659, writing about Brienza, the bishop remarked that "the clergy is especially ignorant, in fact, they are preserved by their poverty, so that they do not study; the people are given to avenging themselves of their enemies." In Sasso in the same year the clergy is ignorant, but the people, for once, "obedient and devout." In 1685, "the people of the whole diocese have little devotion." In the eighteenth century, more enlightened bishops were shocked by the violence and wildness of the people. In 1736, the people of the diocese were "agrarian men, of vile birth, with evil minds, mischievous, of daring spirit, deceitful, feigning in all things, overtaken with hatred like dogs [*odio perfusi caniniano*]," and still in 1795 the bishop found in them "every type of corruption." This echoes the impressions of the appraiser of 1748 who remarked that in Sasso "the mores of these vassals are rather rough and very prone to fights, and previously they were even worse, since now they are slightly more tame and human because they deal with a few outsiders." In 1776, still the inhabitants were "of very robust complection and of rather ferocious character."

The situation in the other two dioceses was no better. In 1682, the bishop of Capaccio remarked that "the people of this diocese are savage and fierce, very ready to take arms, so that even in the smallest villages there are frequent homicides ... ignorance about the foundations of the faith is overabundant." The bishops of Satriano were more concerned with the economic conditions of their diocese, and they remarked in 1592 and 1619 on the extreme poverty of the people and of the local clergy. In the 1660s, the bishop of Satriano was the reformist Giovanni Caramuele, but by the eighteenth century the reactions of the bishops to the behavior of their people were again very negative. In 1742, the bishop noted that the people of Pietrafesa were "quarrelsome and ... because of their rusticity and crass ignorance they have become proverbial, so that if one wants to call someone an imbecile one will call him a Pietrafesan."[43]

The local clergy was not very rich. The *Relationes* report that each priest's annual share of the ecclesiastic patrimony was between ten and twenty-five ducats, depending on the date and the village. Besides the alms for Masses, the church received a tithe of one tenth or a rent on all the cultivated territory in Brienza. In Sasso the tithe was set at one twenty-fifth of the product. Tithes were levied also in Atena but the amount is not known; in Pietrafesa tithes were personal and not based on lands. The size of the bishop's share is not always known; but, for instance, the bishopric of Marsico Nuovo, which included Brienza, Sasso, and five other villages, had revenues of only 600 ducats in 1594 and 500 in 1675. The church, however, owned an increasing amount of lands that grew particularly in the late seventeenth and eighteenth centuries. For instance, in 1700 the church had rights over 160 plots of land in Brienza, and by

[43] *Relationes*, cited above. ACB 81.1.17–18 for the assessments of Sasso.

Table 4.2   *Church properties in the fiefs (1740s)*

owners	Brienza land (tomoli)	vines	animals	
			cattle	sheep
ecclesiastical institutions (1)	643.2./	–	–	–
pious foundations (2)	685.1.2	44,600	–	–
clergy (3)	471.5.1	145,450	7	21
outsider clergy (4)	112.2./	–	–	–
total in village (5)	11,116.6.2	1,267,404	606	5,723

owners	Pietrafesa land (tomoli)	animals			
		cattle	sheep	pigs	horses
(1)	150.7.2	–	–	–	–
(2)	315.3./	–	–	–	–
(3)	1,023.5.1	7	344	2	19
(4)	43.2.1	–	–	–	–
(5)	8,832.2.2	191	3,774	152	144

owners	Atena land (tomoli)	vines (tomoli)	animals			
			cattle	sheep	pigs	horses
(1)	560	–	–	–	–	–
(2)	534./.2	3.1	18	142	–	29
(3)	124.3.2½	24.6.1½	45	204	30	16
(4)	120.6./	–	–	–	–	–
(5)	2,810.1.1	251.6.1½	174	2,829	539	205

owners	Sasso land (tomoli)	vines	animals	
			cattle	sheep
(1)	246.6./	1,160	–	–
(2)	67.2	4,800	34	621
(3)	174.2./	34,320	74	865
(5)	1,488.5.2	661,502	298	7,377

Sources: Villari, *Mezzogiorno*, pp. 73, 79, 95, 99, and 106–7. Outsider clergy means ecclesiastical institutions located outside of the villages. Vines in Brienza and Sasso are given in number of plants, and in Atena in *tomoli* (included in the *tomoli* of land in general). For the animals in Atena and Sasso, (1) and (4) are not mentioned, but there are "other categories." In Sasso, the lands given for ecclesiastical institutions include those belonging to outsider clergy.

1733 it owned 918 plots.[44] Table 4.2 shows the amount of land and animals owned by the church and the clergy in the four villages according to the cadastral data of the 1740s.

Particularly in the eighteenth century, chapels were the religious institution that most increased its wealth. Villari has observed that the small peasant farmers who represented the majority of the population of the fiefs constantly needed credit, not to increase investments but to support consumption and subsistence, and he has stressed the chapels' role in meeting this need. If this situation strengthened the position of the church in the villages, it also caused a struggle between the church and the marquis. The wealth accumulated by the chapels, and especially the patronage networks their loans formed, made them the object of controversies between the marquis, the bishops, and the *università*.[45]

Chapels were founded and patronized by the marquis, the *università*, or private individuals, and had therefore an ambiguous jurisdictional status that provided ground for conflict between lay patrons, bishops, and communities. The oldest and wealthiest chapel in Brienza was the one of the confraternity of the Virgin of the Rosary, founded in 1574 by Giulia Caracciolo, widow of Marco Antonio I. The confraternity was attached to a chapel in the monastery of Brienza, and its administrator was a layman appointed by the marquis. The confraternity received large donations from villagers, particularly in 1643, 1672, and 1721, and by 1719 there were enough revenues to endow two benefices, the larger of which – with revenues of ducats 378.3.02 a year – went to Nicola and then to Gennaro Caracciolo, brothers of Domenico II. Specific revenues of the chapel were assigned to the benefices. The confraternity acquired real estate, animals, and credits. In the 1690s, its annual revenues from lands oscillated around 200 ducats a year in money, plus several hundred *tomoli* of wheat and barley. In 1750, there were 131 people in Brienza and Sasso paying rents or emphyteuses to the Rosary for a total of ducats 121.1.05¼. The chapel also owned around 400 sheep and goats and a few dozen cattle.

Most importantly for the local economy, the chapel gave out loans to residents of Brienza and of the neighboring villages. These loans could be as small as four ducats and yielded an interest, in the early eighteenth century, of eight percent. In the 1740s, there were sixty-five small debtors for a total annual revenue from the loans of ducats 59.1.01. The loans were usually guaranteed on real estate. In

---

[44] *Relationes.* ACB 48.6.19, unnumbered fol., report on the boundaries of Atena and Brienza (1730), for the tithe. On church lands, see ACB 135.7, fols. 115r–28r, and ASP Corporazioni religiose 173. The bishopric of Capaccio, on the other hand, had revenues of 2,900 ducats in 1590, though these too declined in the seventeenth century. The bishop of Marsico received one third of the tithes levied in Sasso (Villari, *Mezzogiorno*, p. 109); on Pietrafesa, see ACB 62.4.3: each landowning peasant paid half a *tomolo* of wheat a year, each laborer one eighth of a *tomolo*. On the poverty of the bishop of Marsico, see P. Villani *et al.*, eds. *Nunziature di Napoli* (3 vols.; Rome, 1962–70), II, p. 278 (no. 255, 1583).

[45] Villari, *Mezzogiorno*, pp. 20–27, and 74–75. Heavy peasant indebtedness was common in early modern agriculture, see, for instance, McArdle, *Altopascio*, chapter 5.

the eighteenth century, the chapel also gave loans to wealthier villagers for large sums, as much as 400 ducats in 1702, for example. Even the *università* occasionally borrowed from the chapel: in 1643, for example, it took a loan of forty-two ducats. In the later eighteenth century, the marquis himself took out loans, and in 1772 Litterio owed ducats $622.2.13+\frac{3}{4}$ to three chapels, with an annual interest of ducats $21.3.18+\frac{2}{3}$. All religious institutions in the fiefs were active in money-lending, and, for example, the clergy of Sasso in the mid-eighteenth century had given out loans for a capital of 4,281 ducats. The records of the notaries of the fiefs in the eighteenth century consist in large part of loans from various ecclesiastical institutions to the villagers.[46]

The Caracciolo Brienza had patronage over at least four other chapels in Brienza, all founded around 1700. The endowment of chapels was a form of devotion particularly favored by women. The chapel of the Conception was founded by Cristina Gambacorta, that of Sant'Antonio da Padova by Teresa Pinto, while only that of Santa Rosa was founded by Giuseppe II himself. That of the Virgin of the Carmine was active by the 1740s, but there is no information on its foundation. None of these was as successful as the Rosary, but their revenues could reach four or five hundred ducats a year. By the early eighteenth century, as we shall see, there were several chapels in the patronage of local families in Brienza and in the other villages. In 1736, there were sixteen benefices, chapels, and confraternities in Brienza, and nine in Sasso; Pietrafesa had seventeen in 1690.[47]

Besides the loans to the local peasantry, the church also rivaled the marquis and the *università* itself in providing welfare and education to the villagers, and the bishops took notice of all welfare institutions in their reports. The diocese of Satriano had no Monte di Pietà, but the bishop's report for 1684 mentioned a grain fund in Pietrafesa. In 1742, there were two grain funds in Pietrafesa, lending grain to the peasants at a fee of one twelfth of the loan, recently reduced from the previous fee of one eighth. Already in 1584 and in 1632 there was a hospital in Pietrafesa managed by the *università*, which the 1742 report described as a "house open to vagabonds." A hospital for the poor, the vagrants, and the sick existed in Brienza but not in Sasso in 1633, and in 1736 it was still being maintained with fifteen ducats a year by the *università*. It seems to have ceased to operate by 1779. A similar hospital existed in Atena in the eighteenth century. Atena had a Monte di Pietà since at least 1577. The monastery in Brienza accepted young clerics and provided them with education; throughout the seventeenth and early eighteenth centuries there were three to six students in the monastery. In 1788 the marquis diverted 241 ducats a year from the revenues of his chapel of the Rosary for the establishment of a school in Brienza. The teachers were chosen by the marquis to teach catechism, writing, reading,

---

[46] ACB 49. Villari, *Mezzogiorno*, pp. 20–21. On Sasso, see also ASP Corporazioni religiose 155 (1732). ASP notai Potenza (see Appendix on sources).
[47] ACB 49.1.29; 50.1–4; ASV *Relationes*.

arithmetic, and elementary grammar, and prizes went to the best pupils, while 100 ducats were to go every year as dowries to four village girls who had diligently attended catechism. Another thirty ducats a year were earmarked for the purchase of medicines for the village poor.[48]

The relative autonomy of the local clergy from its bishops caused the former to give more importance to its economic situation in the villages than to problems of ecclesiastical jurisdiction. In fact, the conflicts between the marquis and the church were fought on two fronts. Property disputes opposed the marquis to the local clergy, while conflicts arising from jurisdictional problems put them in opposition to the bishops. All three bishops of the Caracciolo fiefs remarked on the obstacles and dangers posed to ecclesiastical jurisdiction by feudal power. Already in 1606, the bishop of Capaccio remarked on the difficulties he encountered in visiting his diocese due to "the differing [feudal] jurisdictions." In 1630, the dioceses included fiefs of eighty-four barons, and there were still sixty-eight different barons with jurisdiction in the diocese in 1682. The bishop of Marsico wrote in 1687 that there were six barons in his small diocese, "so that the heaviest care to pain the bishops is in maintaining peace with these barons, without jeopardizing ecclesiastical immunity, freedom, and jurisdiction." The joint diocese of Campagna-Satriano was divided in two separate parts, so that it was difficult for the bishop to check lay usurpations of ecclesiastical lands and institutions in the old diocese of Satriano. The fights between bishops and barons arose especially over civil and criminal jurisdiction over clerics, appointments to benefices, and the levying of tithes. The barons were unsympathetic to any outside interference in their states.[49]

The Caracciolo Brienza had relatively little to do with the bishops until the eighteenth century, with the exception of an episode of violence that took place in 1598, when two brothers of marquis Giovan Battista attacked and jailed the *arciprete* of Brienza, who had protested about the killing of a subdeacon by baronial dependents. On that occasion, the bishop of Marsico excommunicated the two brothers, only to have the archbishop of Salerno lift the excommunication soon afterwards, in a forceful example of the degree of violence feudal power could still produce with impunity.[50]

---

[48] ASV *Relationes*. ACB 49.1.32; for Atena 77.2.32–33; ASP notai Potenza, 42, fols. 325r–30v (1584). In both organization and intent, this village school fits Ariès' description of the *petites écoles*, P. Ariès, *L'enfant et la vie familiale sous l'Ancien Régime* (Paris, 1960), part II, chapter 7. The founding of hospices for vagrants and the sick was also a general European phenomenon in the seventeenth century.

[49] ASV *Relationes*. On Satriano, see also G. Cestaro, "Il feudo ecclesiastico di Castellano e Perolla" in De Rosa–Malgeri, eds. *Società*, II, pp. 121–35. On bishops and barons, see C. Russo, "Poteri istituzionali e poteri di fatto nelle campagne meridionali in età moderna: chiesa e comunità" *ASPN* 104 (1986), pp. 159–76; the potential disadvantages of fiefs which were also episcopal sees are exemplified by the frequent conflicts between the Doria princes and the bishops of their town of Melfi, see R. Colapietra, *Dal Magnanimo a Masaniello* (2 vols.; Salerno, 1973), II, pp. 338–40, and 465–67.

[50] ASV *Relationes*, 491, fol. 187v.

After this episode, the marquis and the bishops had apparently no more struggles until the early eighteenth century, when the increasing wealth of the chapel of the Rosary made it the focus of a long jurisdictional dispute. When, in 1719, the two benefices of the chapel were established, following an agreement between the marquis and Bishop Donato Anzani of Marsico, the marquis claimed the right of appointment. The benefices carried very limited religious obligations, and the first appointees were Nicola Caracciolo and the bishop's two nephews, Donato and G. A. Anzani. In 1734 the new bishop, Alessandro Puoti, claimed patronage over the two benefices, then in the hands of G. A. Anzani and Gennaro Caracciolo. Puoti cited Gennaro's dissolute life to support his attempt to assign the revenues of the benefices to the seminary in Marsico. Though the lawsuit was first discussed in Rome, the Caracciolo could, under the new Bourbon government, appeal to royal jurisdiction with good results. In 1737, a royal tribunal ordered the arrest of two brothers of the confraternity who had upheld the bishop's appointment of a new administrator. The lawsuit ended with the recognition of the marquis' patronage, while the marquis agreed on his part to support one student from Brienza in the Marsico seminary. After the 1740s we have no more evidence of conflicts between the marquis and the bishops.[51]

Disputes with the local clergy, on the other hand, focused on property. In the early eighteenth century, the clergy of Brienza began a lawsuit with the marquis over tithes and lands. The clergy claimed that the marquis had usurped over 200 *tomoli* of ecclesiastical land, and that the marquis' lands were not paying their full tithes. The lawsuit reached the Sacred Royal Council in Naples, which in the 1750s ruled in favor of the marquis, granting to the clergy of Brienza only thirty *tomoli* of wheat a year in additional tithes. The same years saw the resolution of a dispute over lands claimed by the clergy of Pietrafesa, to which the marquis agreed to pay 400 ducats in exchange for the withdrawal of all claims.[52]

After 1734, the royal government's attitude towards the church changed. In the early years of the reign, Charles of Bourbon's government acted to limit ecclesiastical immunity and jurisdiction, and a concordat was signed in 1741. In the second half of the century, the government directly attacked the church's patrimony in the kingdom. By doing so it responded to proposals by the intellectual elite of the kingdom, and favored wealthy landowners, noble and non-noble, without addressing the more serious problem of the feudal organization of the kingdom. Ecclesiastical wealth, as we have seen, played an essential role in permitting the survival of small peasant landowning, and the expropriation of ecclesiastical property in the last decades of the eighteenth century

---

[51] ACB 49.1, and 134.2–3; G. A. Anzani became bishop of Campagna-Satriano in 1736, where he remained for over thirty years. Villari, *Mezzogiorno*, pp. 141–44, has a rather idealistic view of the litigation around the chapel, and makes a hero of the new administrator, Antonio Casella. Though certainly the barons were capable of violence, Villari tends to take each word of the antibaronial litigants as absolute truth.

[52] ACB 50.6, 140.45, and 62.4.

destroyed a number of charitable institutions. Moreover, these expropriated properties were bought, not only by the barons themselves, but by the local notables, who thus strengthened their economic position *vis-à-vis* the poorer peasants.[53]

The peculiar organization of the rural clergy in the Mezzogiorno, therefore, while strengthening the ties between the village faithful and their shepherds, also weakened the power of the church to represent an alternative force to that of the barons. The church could rival the baron for the allegiance of the villagers, particularly in its welfare and money-lending activities; but the Caracciolo Brienza succeeded, through their patronage of chapels and their own direct involvement in welfare initiatives, in remaining the predominant source of patronage in the fiefs. The marquis and the local clergy occasionally quarrelled over property; but the fact that the clergy was composed of vassals of the marquis and that its own interests lay in resisting the attempts of the bishops to assert their control over the local clergy's spiritual qualities, membership, and sources of revenues, insured that the church would not offer a unified challenge to the marquis' authority. The influence of the bishops over the clergy or the population of the villages was very limited, and their few contrasts with the barons over jurisdictional matters ended in the defeat of any attempt to limit baronial power.[54]

GROWTH AND CHARACTERISTICS OF A LOCAL NOTABILITY

By the time ecclesiastical properties were expropriated at the end of the eighteenth century, there was, in the four fiefs, a group of notables able to buy them. Although the development of a local notability in the late eighteenth century is not the focus of the present work, the increasing social differentiation within the communities is important in understanding the relations between the communities and their lord. Villari has seen the development of an agrarian bourgeoisie in the eighteenth century as a fracture in the antifeudal front of the previous century which weakened the *università*'s institutions, and indeed there was less conflict between the communities and the marquis in the eighteenth century than before. The social compactness of the population of the *università*, however, cannot be the only explanation of the conflicts of the seventeenth century. The marquis faced the most obstinate resistance to their power from the *università* of Atena, where social differences were stronger than in the other fiefs. In fact in other fiefs, like the Doria's, the high degree of social stratification

---

[53] The most extensive work on the Bourbon reign remains M. Schipa, *Il regno di Napoli al tempo di Carlo di Borbone* (Naples, 1904). Also Villari, *Mezzogiorno*, pp. 20–27, 100–3. The family purchased land in Atena and Padula, ACB 76.2.28 (quoted also in Villari, *Mezzogiorno*, p. 101, footnote 58); 165, unnumbered fol.; 90, under 89.4.1–7.

[54] This situation was similar to that in Calabria, see Galasso, *Economia*, pp. 325–38.

was seen as the cause for the turbulent relations between the *università* and the barons. The degree of social differentiation interplayed with the conditions of the feudal relations between the lord and each fief.[55]

Lack of documents does not permit us to establish whether the wealthy farmers that Galasso has identified as the ascending elite of many Calabrian centers in the sixteenth century until their disappearance in the difficulties of the 1580s and 1590s existed also in the Caracciolo Brienza fiefs.[56] By the early seventeenth century there were few notables in the Caracciolo fiefs, found mainly in the legal professions. Slowly this elite grew in numbers and wealth and began to imitate some of the exterior signs of status that the marquis themselves displayed, such as ecclesiastical patronage and prestigious residences. In some instances, the marquis had a central role in the development of this local elite, through their political patronage and through the various profitable positions available in the baronial administration. By the late eighteenth century there was a clear difference in wealth between these families and the mass of their fellow villagers, so that the French government's institution of restricted village councils found a group ready to take advantage of it. Until the end of the old regime, however, the increasing economic power of these notables was not paralleled by an increase in their political power in the communities. The isolation and poverty of the region, the persisting power of the baron to influence communal life, and the strong traditionalism of village life, all contributed to the preservation of the established political system.

Before turning to a description of the growth of the local elite, it is useful to consider the demographic development of the four *università*. Table 4.3 provides the available data on the population of the fiefs. It is remarkable that Atena was the village with the slowest rate of growth. This was probably because of its unhealthy location amidst swamps and marshes. The assessments always comment on the salubrious air of Brienza, Pietrafesa, and Sasso, while making disparaging remarks about Atena. Although good population figures for the later seventeenth century are lacking for Atena, it is very probable that the plague hit Atena more severely than the other three more mountainous and isolated communities, and a report of the bishop of Capaccio after the plague confirms the heavy losses among Atena's clergy. The four fiefs followed the general trends of the demographic history of the kingdom: considerable growth in the sixteenth century, then stagnation and decline in the seventeenth, growth in the early eighteenth, and a relative slump in the 1760s and again at the end of the century.

[55] A. Villone, *Privilegi giurisdizionali e dominio feudale: lo stato dei Doria d'Angri nella seconda metà del secolo XVII* (Naples, 1980), pp. 15–27; Villani, ed., "Eboli nel 1640" *Rassegna storica salernitana* (1953), pp. 196–207. McArdle, *Altopascio*, pp. 178–81, discusses the rise of a rural bourgeoisie in Tuscany.
[56] Galasso, *Economia*, chapters 5 and 6.

The feudal lord and his vassals

Table 4.3 *Population of the fiefs (1532–1811)*

year	Brienza houses	Brienza people	Pietrafesa houses	Pietrafesa people	Atena houses	Atena people	Sasso houses	Sasso people
1532	168	–	81	–	181	–	59	–
1545	199	–	118	–	211	–	65	–
1561	243	–	150	–	277	–	104	–
1595	391	–	194	–	285	–	151	–
1632	–	–	180	1,242	–	–	–	–
1646	–	–	–	–	–	900	–	–
1659	309	1,400	–	–	–	–	188	807
1675	320	1,600	–	1,000	–	–	200	900
1685	–	1,722	–	–	–	–	–	1,250
1690	–	–	–	1,200	–	–	–	–
1714	538	2,798	–	–	–	–	205	1,112
1721	–	–	–	1,660	–	–	–	–
1732	–	–	–	–	317	–	–	–
1736	–	3,439	–	–	–	–	–	1,560
1748	836	3,435	365	1,606	400	1,614	242	1,651
1766	835	4,226	–	–	–	–	377	1,643
1794	–	4,300	–	2,210	–	2,348	–	2,267
1811	1005	4,169	–	–	–	2,300	–	–

Sources: The sixteenth-century data are from the censuses as reported in Giustiniani, *Dizionario*. The 1648 and 1669 censuses are not reliable, since by then the number of fiscal households was considerably different from the actual numbers. Those censuses give 305 and 206 households respectively for Brienza, 194 and 118 for Pietrafesa, 113 and 67 for Atena, and 100 and 99 for Sasso. Most of the other data are from the *Relationes*, which are also not entirely reliable. The figure for Atena in 1646 is from the assessment in ACB 77.2.1bis, and refers to communicant faithful, to which one should probably add some 300 children. The figure for Atena in 1732 is in ACB 74.2.11 (a list of households); it contrasts with the figure of 221 in *Storia del Vallo di Diano*, II, pp. 62–63 (see also *ibid.*, III.1, p. 68). The 1748 and 1794 figures are from Villari, *Mezzogiorno*, p. 61, footnote 1; for 1748, the assessment of Atena in ACB 77.2.32 gives 338 households and 1,748 inhabitants. See also Cassandro, *Atena*, pp. 146–48, and De Rosa–Malgeri, *Società*, I, pp. 368–77. The figures for Brienza in 1811 are in ASP Intendenza di Basilicata, 578/237, fols. 18r–v; for Atena in 1811, in Coppola, "Distribuzione."

As a further proof of their isolation, the losses in the plague seem to have been rather limited.[57]

---

[57] On the effect of the plague in Atena and in the Vallo di Diano in general, see F. Volpe, *Il Cilento nel secolo XVII* (Naples, 1981), chapter 5, and pp. 221–42 (the bishop's report); *Storia del Vallo di Diano* (3 vols.; Salerno, 1982–85), III.1, pp. 25–91. The plague hit other areas much more severely, see G. Delille, *Croissance d'une société rurale: Montesarchio et la Vallée Caudine aux XVIIe et*

Atena was the last of the four *università* to be enfeoffed, as we have seen, and it alone had a traditional elite, the subfeudatories. Although the feudal dues they paid were largely symbolic, it was still necessary for them to obtain the marquis' consent whenever their land passed to a new holder through inheritance or sale. As late as 1800, the marquis could obtain the reintegration of subfeudal land alienated without his consent. There were about a dozen subfiefs in Atena, and a few were held by the same family since before the Caracciolo's rule over the village, constituting a visible and conscious elite with a traditional presence in the community. When Atena was in the royal domain, a few local families had therefore paid the *relevio* to the royal government.[58]

In the seventeenth century, however, several of the subfeudatories resided outside of Atena, and Atena's parliament was never divided in two orders. The only identifiable elite in this period in the four fiefs was represented by a few professionals. The assessments and the bishops' *Relationes* allow us to follow the slow increase in the degree of social differentiation within the communities. The 1625 appraiser noted that in Brienza "they are all peasants [*gente rustiche*] ... the civil people [*persone civili*] in this village are only two law graduates [*dottori*] and a notary"; there was no doctor and few artisans. Atena had a few artisans, "a pharmacist and a doctor, two law graduates [*dottori di legge*], and there are a few subfeudatories, and other civil people," and the houses were "of agreeable appearance." On the other hand, in Pietrafesa they were "all peasants," and the same was true of Sasso, where, however, there were more animals and pastures. In general the assessments and *Relationes* stress the poverty of the local peasantry. As we have seen, many villagers migrated seasonally to Puglia throughout the seventeenth and eighteenth centuries.[59]

In 1646 in Brienza there were still only two lawyers and a notary, but also "artisans of all types," and "a doctor salaried by the *università*." The 1677 appraiser noted in Brienza "very few civil people, among whom two lawyers, a doctor, and three notaries; there is in this village the comfort of a pharmacy for the citizens and for the comfort of the inhabitants of the neighboring villages; moreover there ... [is] a midwife." There were also numerous craftsmen. "A few of the women are better off, and they dress in a civil way, in the Neapolitan style, but in general they dress like peasants." The same appraiser wrote that in Pietrafesa "there are no civil people, other than a notary and a few others who live with their poor revenues ... very few, who are more comfortable, wear finer

XVIIIe siècles (Naples, 1973), part III. On the demographic history of the kingdom, see Lepre, *Storia del Mezzogiorno d'Italia* (2 vols.; Naples, 1986), I, pp. 221–28, and 298–312; Villani, *Mezzogiorno*, pp. 27–103.

[58] ACB 76.1, especially 46. ASN Relevi 226, fols. 312rff. (Pessolano family, 1554) and 229, fols. 846rff. (Labro family, 1561).

[59] ACB 43.3.1bis, pp. 3–5, 64–5, 89, and 109; see pp. 108–18 above.

clothes." In 1676, Sasso still had no professional group at all, though the appraiser lauded the village's peaceful life and good climate.[60]

With the economic recovery and the demographic expansion of the early eighteenth century there was a marked increase in the degree of social differentiation of village society. In 1748 in Atena there were eight families living nobly (*nobili viventi*): "the civil people, who have a decent appearance [*compariscono mediocremente*] wear in some cases also floss silk [*tela di ragno*]." There were eight lawyers and law students (*professi in legge*), four doctors, a surgeon, a notary, two pharmacists, and several artisans. The richest citizen owned 300 sheep, ten goats, twelve oxen, fifteen cows, 160 pigs, and 200 asses. Even in Sasso there were now a few changes. Ten women were described as "civil," and "though the gentlemen and gentlewomen [*gentiluomini e gentildonne*] daily wear the same cloths [as the others], sometimes they wear floss silk." A few manage, through their trades, "to support themselves in their civil lifestyle [*nel di lor civil vivere*]"; there were, in fact, three lawyers, a doctor, a surgeon–barber, a notary, and a contract-drawer (*giudice a contratti*). The wealthiest citizen owned 450 sheep and goats, three oxen, and ten cows. Lawyers, doctors, surgeons, notaries, and contract-drawers, since they did not practice a "vile art," were considered as *nobili viventi* and enjoyed fiscal exemptions in the 1740s *Catasto*.[61]

In 1776 these numbers had increased. Atena had now three notaries or contract-drawers, and twenty-two residents were identified as wealthy farmers (*massari di campo*). Sasso had three lawyers, three doctors, four notaries, and three contract-drawers. Seven people, including the *arciprete*, were mentioned as the wealthiest in the village. The surviving registers, even when due allowance is made for the loss of earlier documents, show a steep rise in the number of notaries active in the region, an obvious sign of increased economic activity and of the existence of local notables. In the 1740s there were six notaries in Brienza. The growth of the local market for grains in the eighteenth century, as we have seen in the preceding chapter, also points to a broader social differentiation in the villages.[62]

By the 1740s, this small elite of professionals and wealthy farmers disposed of a considerable amount of the local wealth, which was to increase further in the second half of the eighteenth century. Table 4.4 shows their share of the village wealth as reported in the cadastral data. It appears from these data that particularly in Atena, the *massari* were still quite weak, whereas the professionals

---

[60] ACB 160 (a large bundle of unnumbered documents; the 1646 assessment was one of the top ones when I saw it), fol. 2v; 43.3.7, fols. 2r, 3v, and 12r–v; 77.2.27, unnumbered fol.

[61] ASN Catasto Onciario 5149, fols. 259r–v (1747) on the exemptions.

[62] ACB 77.2.32–33, 81.1.17–18; ASP notai Potenza, throughout and the inventory. ASN Catasto Onciario 5146, fols. 104r–v. *Massari* in the eighteenth century designated wealthier farmers (no longer renters of other people's lands) producing for the market, see Villari, *Mezzogiorno*, pp. 69–71. Most of the villagers were, however, still very poor in the early nineteenth century, see Pedio, "Condizioni."

Table 4.4   *Elite wealth in the fiefs (1740s)*

	number of families	land (tomoli)	vines	oxen	sheep	pigs	horses
					animals		
massari				Brienza			
massari	80	1,808.1.2	180,590	509	1,269	105	–
benestanti	17	904.2.1	48,400	30	734	22	–
total in village	836	11,116.6.2	1,267,404	606	5,723	535	–
			Pietrafesa				
massari	40	1,224.1.2	–	125	942	79	41
benestanti	6	2,416	–	42	1,155	47	20
total in village	365	8,832.2.2	–	191	3,774	152	144
			Atena				
massari	23	58./.2½	15.5./	46	282	184	27
benestanti	12	255.5.1	16.1./	35	672	81	32
total in village	400	2,810.1.1	251.6.1½	174	2,829	322	539
			Sasso				
massari	31	232.4./	112,622	125	2,980	103	5
benestanti	9	56.1.1	33,400	4	220	16	–
total in village	242	1,488.5.2	661,502	298	7,377	167	14

Sources: Same as in Table 4.2. In the *benestanti* (wealthy) are included professionals. Again, the vines are given in number of plants for Brienza and Sasso, in surface (in *tomoli*) for Atena. In Atena the *massari*, besides the animals they owned, rented fifty-two oxen, thirty-one sheep, and ten horses.

were weakest, in wealth if not in numbers, in Sasso and strongest in Atena, a pattern that confirms the more "aristocratic" outlook of Atena's society.

Since the seventeenth century, these local notables strove to make their status visible in the community, and the appraisers clearly viewed lifestyle and clothes as signs of status. The main expressions of their wealth, however, were the same as those of the marquis, namely ecclesiastical patronage and luxurious residences. The 1776 assessment noticed in Atena buildings "of more than one storey, in the style of city buildings, though not too well built or planned," and next to the baronial palace it mentioned the palace of the De Benedictis family as a building worthy of admiration. In Sasso the appraiser saw seven remarkable houses, belonging to two doctors, two lawyers, two ecclesiastics, and a man worthy of the title of *magnifico*. Today, walking through the main street leading from the older center of Brienza to the newer part of the village, one can see several dignified, small, eighteenth-century *palazzi*, the façades and doors of which bespeak the pride and gentility of their builders.

The *Relatio* of 1594 already mentioned chapels of lay patronage in Brienza and Sasso, though without giving the names of the patrons. Chapels and benefices appear in all the seventeenth-century *Relationes* for Brienza and Sasso. In 1736, there were nine chapels under the patronage of seven families in Brienza, and two in Sasso. Pietrafesa had a few chapels in the seventeenth century, and in 1690 there were fifteen benefices of lay patronage. The new parish church consecrated in 1739 was built thanks to the liberality of a local notable. Chapels of lay patronage are mentioned in the 1748 and 1776 assessments for Atena and Sasso. In 1627, among the creditors of the *università* of Brienza, were two Monti di Pietà founded by local notables. In 1714 in Brienza there were two dowry funds (*Monti*) to benefit the founders' families, and indeed at least two such *Monti* already existed in Brienza in 1668. These were common ways to assert status, and, for instance, in nearby Melfi the notables had already established a convent for their daughters in the late sixteenth century. In larger towns, the founding of charitable institutions also strengthened the paternalistic ties between the ruling notables and the local population.[63]

Although by the later eighteenth century this local elite had a clear economic predominance in the communities, reflected in its ownership of lands and animals, this was not matched by an equivalent political supremacy. Despite the presence of several professionals, the mayors and aldermen of Brienza were often chosen from among illiterate citizens as late as the 1770s, and participation in the parliament of the *università* was very large to the end of the old regime. The formation of the *Catasto* in the 1740s was the occasion for contrasts, not only between the barons and the administrators of the *università*, but also between the latter and the wealthier citizens, who did not think their interests well served by the village government. In Atena, the commons were the object of the wealthier citizens' covetousness, but the parliament of the *università*, as we have seen, resisted every attempt to divide the common lands in parcels and to distribute them to the population in full property, even when, in 1792, the royal government authorized such a division in all the *università* of the kingdom, because the citizens feared that the parcels would soon be bought by the wealthier among them. It was only when the Napoleonic government abolished the old parliaments and instituted new councils in 1806, membership of which was restricted in small villages to citizens with annual revenues of at least twenty-four ducats, that the local notables achieved a political power in the communes corresponding to their economic and social position. This survival of a traditional, egalitarian organization was rather rare in early modern Europe.[64]

[63] Assessments and *Relationes*. ACB 50.1.1 for 1668. On the *Monti* see chapter 5. On the two Monti di Pietà see ASN Collaterale Provvisioni 158, fols. 83r–v. For Melfi, see S. Zotta, "Momenti e problemi di una crisi agraria in uno 'stato' feudale napoletano (1585–1615)" *MEFRM* 90 (1978), p. 772; examples also in Caridi, *Uno "stato"*, pp. 104, and 139; on larger towns, see Spagnoletti, "Forme di autocoscienza e vita nobiliare: il caso della Puglia barese" *Società e storia* 6 (1983), pp. 49–76.

[64] The mayors' signatures (or crosses) are in ACB 48.1.14, 61.2.47, and 74.1.20–21 (receipts for the marquis' *bonatenenza*). Villari, *Mezzogiorno*, pp. 42, 63ff., and 83–92; on Atena after the reforms, see *Storia del Vallo*, III.1, pp. 200–03, 256–57, and 266. On the *decurioni* (the new council

The economic and demographic expansion of the kingdom in the eighteenth century, therefore, made possible the continued growth of a local notability that had begun to appear in the late sixteenth and early seventeenth centuries. At first these notables were professionals, though later the economic developments allowed a few farmers to join the ranks of the local elite. Though this elite came to constitute probably more than ten percent of the population of the villages, it did not acquire a privileged political position within the communities. The strong traditionalism of the region, and also probably the Caracciolo Brienza's policy of paternalism and close ties with the vassals, helped preserve the villages' old institutions until the early nineteenth century. Though the local elite acquired the symbols of gentility the marquis themselves employed, it never achieved the monopoly on local government exercised by the closed patriciates of larger centers and other regions.[65]

LITIGATION AND CONFLICT BETWEEN THE *UNIVERSITÀ* AND THE BARONS

The traditionalism and paternalism of feudal rule did not prevent tension or outright conflict between the *università* and their barons. There are few studies of conflict at the local level, even for the revolt of 1647–48, and Villari's works of the 1950s and 1960s remain the most complete analysis of the topic. From a Marxist perspective, as we have seen, he has spoken of a "crisis of the state" in the early seventeenth century that left the vassals almost defenseless in the face of an aggressive aristocratic "refeudalization." After the 1647 revolt, and especially in the eighteenth century, he detected – basing his conclusions on a study of the Caracciolo Brienza fiefs – a fragmentation of the antifeudal front in the countryside, with the separation of a middle class from the peasantry: the interests of the two groups were at odds with each other, since the former aspired to expand its private properties, while the latter defended the traditional, communal organization of agriculture.[66]

members), see also Faraglia, *Il comune*, chapter 4; on local notables in the nineteenth century in this area, see Aliberti, *Potere*, chapters 1 and 3. See the example of the French village of Lourmarin, which, though smaller than the Caracciolo Brienza's fiefs, was administered by an oligarchic council, T. Sheppard, *Lourmarin in the Eighteenth Century* (Baltimore, 1971), chapter 3.
65 Spagnoletti, "Le aggregazioni"; Galasso, *Economia*, pp. 293–324. Both authors actually analyze fairly large centers, several of which were in the royal domain, though they claim to speak of all *università*. There are almost no studies of provincial notables, besides R. Moscati, *Una famiglia "borghese" del Mezzogiorno* (Naples, 1964). Brienza did produce one famous notable: Mario Pagano, one of the most prominent intellectuals of the Neapolitan Enlightenment, executed in 1799 after the failure of the Jacobin Republic, together with Admiral Francesco Caracciolo, second cousin of the marquis of Brienza, was born in an old family of Brienza, patrons of a chapel in the village.
66 Villari, *La rivolta antispagnola a Napoli. Le origini (1585–1647)* (Bari, 1967); Villari, *Mezzogiorno*, pp. 111–55; Villari has returned to these themes in *Elogio della dissimulazione* (Bari, 1987), chapter 3; see also Rovito, "Strutture"; de Frede, *Rivolte*, on episodes of conflict in the sixteenth century.

The feudal lord and his vassals

To a large extent, Villari's conclusions are accepted here. As we have seen, at least between 1590 and 1620, the Caracciolo Brienza tried to reinforce their grip on their fiefs, whereas, particularly after the 1647 revolt, the family's relations with the *università* were much more peaceful. It does not seem, however, that the role of the state changed as much as Villari thinks, and in fact the royal government intervened in favor of the *università* more frequently before the revolt than after – though with what results is open to doubt. Moreover, the differences in the tradition and extent of feudal power on each fief must also be taken into account to explain the conflicts between the barons and the communities. As for the period after the revolt, to explain the decrease in the level of conflict and the shift to more economic conflicts, one should look also at the actions of the barons; the Caracciolo Brienza were able to maintain their power over their fiefs and to prevent any recurrence of the events of 1647–48, and they deserve perhaps a fairer hearing than Villari has given them.

There is very little information on the *università* before the end of the sixteenth century. Atena and Brienza received their statutes in 1475 and 1543 respectively, and these regulated both the relations of the villages with the lord and their internal life until the end of the feudal regime. There is no evidence for any statutes in Pietrafesa and Sasso where, as we have seen in the preceding chapter, feudal power, as reflected in the number and revenues of feudal rights, was stronger than in the two other fiefs. As neighboring Sala had done in 1579, Atena, where the marquis enjoyed few feudal rights and monopolies, tried to repurchase its domanial status in 1585, though the attempt failed due to the growing indebtedness of the *università*. Several *università* of the kingdom tried to enter the royal domain between 1560 and 1590, when the kingdom's economy was expanding and the *università* had more money available. Neither Atena nor any of the other three fiefs ever again tried to enter the royal domain.[67]

Conflicts in the sixteenth and early seventeenth century concerned mainly the enforcement of feudal rights. Especially in the first half of the seventeenth century, the general difficulties in the economy of the kingdom made the burden of feudal rights and monopolies heavier. The increasing fiscal pressure of the government on a population which was stable or declining after the 1590s certainly contributed to the intensified tension at the local level. The indebtedness of the *università* was a useful tool in the hands of the barons, since often the feudal lords managed to be the creditors of their own communities. Heavy expenses in long lawsuits in the Naples tribunals compounded the economic difficulties of the *università*, and corruption in the appointment and the payment of the *università*'s legal agents in the capital was ground for a series of laws issued by the royal government in the sixteenth and early seventeenth centuries. The

[67] ACB 89.3.17 for Sala; ASP notai Potenza 44, fols. 106r–9v for Atena; Galasso, *Economia*, pp. 293–324. In other regions, the statutes were granted later, even in the late seventeenth century, see Lepre, *Feudi*, pp. 43–45.

147

late sixteenth and early seventeenth centuries also witnessed a recrudescence of banditry in the kingdom, and collusion was frequent between barons and bandits. Giovan Battista, marquis of Brienza, was accused of using bandits for private vendettas by one of his vassals in Atena.[68]

The fact that the Caracciolo Brienza had only recently acquired their fiefs was also probably a reason for tension with the communities. The *università* fought with their new lords, and by the 1590s, as we have seen, Brienza, Atena, and Pietrafesa entered agreements with the Caracciolo Brienza for a perpetual rent of most feudal rights, monopolies, and *terraggi*. The *università* could now themselves regulate the enforcement of feudal rights. In 1594, the bishop of Marsico noted that Brienza "was almost consumed because of the fights with its lord." The agreements imposed, however, a heavy financial burden on the *università*, and within a decade, as the economic and demographic situation of the kingdom worsened, all three *università* were heavily in debt and appealed to the royal government to obtain licenses to impose new taxes. They claimed that the yield of the feudal rights was decreasing and that the agreements had been entered by communal governments controlled by the marquis. In the case of Brienza, the royal courts agreed with the former allegation and lowered the rent. The marquis Giacomo then transacted with Brienza and Pietrafesa for their debts with him. Atena, too, obtained the annulment of the agreements. Sasso did not have such struggles with the marquis in this period. The large extent of feudal power in this smallest and most isolated of the communities, and the lack of any local notability, probably explain this lack of conflict.[69]

In the 1620s, the marquis Giacomo withdrew, as we have seen, from his father's initiatives aimed at increasing the family's revenues from the fiefs. Giacomo's agreements with Brienza and Pietrafesa also eased his relations with his vassals. His brother, Giuseppe, on the other hand, tried to strengthen his power in Atena.

Since the early 1590s, the *università* of Atena had contracted a debt of 10,000 ducats with the marquis' uncle, Fabrizio Caracciolo, bishop of Tropea, at an interest of eight percent. In 1597, the *università* borrowed 10,300 ducats from Costanza Gesualdo, duchess of Gravina, in order to pay back the previous debt, at an interest of 7.75 percent. This loan was guaranteed by the domanial lands of

---

[68] *Prammatiche De administratione universitatum* in Giustiniani, *Nuova collezione*, particularly I, IV, and V; for Giovan Battista, see de Frede, *Rivolte*, p. 18, footnote 22; on bandits, see most recently Musi, *La rivolta*, pp. 190–200.

[69] The bishop's report is in ASV *Relationes* 491, fols. 323v. The appeals to the government are in ASN Collaterale Provvisioni 18, fols. 95r–97r and 339r–v (1592); 25, fols. 27r–v, 32r, 34r, 297r–98v, and 301r–v (1597), for Atena; for Brienza, *ibid.*, 42 I, fols. 205r–v (1607); 61, fols. 284r–91v (1614); 66, fols. 367r–73v (1615); 78, fols. 19r–v, and 307r–13v (1616); for Pietrafesa *ibid.*, 19, fols. 75r–78v (1593). In the same years, Sala also appealed to the government to be allowed to levy new taxes to face its debts, see *ibid.*, 12, fols. 303r–12v (1585); 19, fols. 2r–6r (1593); 23, fols. 214r–15r (1596); 24, fols. 204r–v (1597); 42, II, fols. 15r–19r, and 92r–93r (1607); 68, fols. 69r–81r (1615).

the *università*. The *università* was unable to meet its payments, and in 1641 – after a long lawsuit – the royal courts assigned part of the lands to the duchess, over the heated opposition not only of the *università* but of its lord as well, who feared the presence in his fief of another aristocratic landowner. When in 1645 Giuseppe Caracciolo, prince of Atena, bought the duchess' credit, the possibility for conflict between the *università* and its lord increased significantly. Atena had always been the least docile of the four fiefs, and in the early days of the 1647 revolt it presented to the viceroy a strong antifeudal appeal that ended by asking for permission to "resist *armata manu*" the lord's injustices.[70]

This long-standing tension was reflected in the local events in 1647–48. The Caracciolo Brienza state was on the borderline of a vast rebel area in Basilicata, and, in fact, a notary from Atena was among the local leaders of the armed revolt. The marquis of Brienza and his brother, the prince of Atena, were active among the aristocracy supporting the viceroy in Naples. In the late spring and summer of 1648, Giuseppe Caracciolo led 400 armed men in the state and repressed the local revolt. According to the *università*, Giuseppe took advantage of the situation to step up the policy of aggression he had practiced before and to stifle all local opposition. In May 1648, eight promient citizens of Atena agreed to guarantee with their property the repayment to the marquis of ducats 2,127.3.08 and 242 *tomoli* of wheat he had lost in the disorders. But that proved not to be enough for Giuseppe, and in 1657 his actions prompted the *università* of Atena to send an appeal to the viceroy with forty grievances against the prince. This document skillfully presented the prince in the light most likely to impress the royal government in favor of the *università*, and, although it has no explicit author, its language points to a relatively educated local leadership.

The document opens with a denunciation of abuses and violence committed by Giuseppe before 1647, and names specific victims, including nine ecclesiastics, three lawyers, and a notary, guilty of supporting the *università* in one way or another. Giuseppe was further accused of threatening the honor of local women, of ordering the murder of the *arciprete* of nearby Sala, and of refusing to comply with the bishop's jurisdiction. In May 1648, Giuseppe came to Atena, promised peace to his vassals, attended the celebration of a *Te Deum*, but then, with the arrival of his 400 men, "one witnessed an unimagined slaughter; every home was in ruins, since besides food and drink they had to pay enormous sums of money

---

[70] For the loan, see ASN Collaterale Provvisioni 25, already cited; ACB 77.1, especially 2, ASN *Bollettino delle sentenze della Commissione Feudale* vol. 30, pp. 62–93, and ASN notai del '600, Francesco Antonio de Monte, 802/52 (1645), fols. 366r–72v. Cassandro, *Atena*, pp. 178–80; Villari, *Mezzogiorno*, pp. 166–67. For the 1647 appeal, see ACB 75.7.4. The *università*'s debts were used by the marquis also in the other fiefs as instruments of pressure, see ACB 45.1.6 for Brienza. In 1591, Pietrafesa borrowed 1,000 ducats from the marquis' wife, Diana, at eight percent, see ACB 46.1.4 (unnumbered long list of notarial acts), and in 1621 Sasso levied a new tax to pay 400 ducats it owed to Fabrizio Caracciolo, ASN Collaterale Provvisioni 108, fols. 327r–31v. In the seventeenth century, the Caracciolo Brienza also used the *università*'s debt to obtain lands in the town of Sala, ACB 89.3.

for everything, so that many fled away from these burdens and ruin, also to protect the honor of women." One witness testified that Giuseppe, on being begged for clemency, replied: "Let these rebel dogs lose their life and honor." This went on for eighteen days, during which "many ecclesiastics and people of religion were ill-treated and beaten," and resulted in damages for more than 10,000 ducats. In the following three years, Giuseppe usurped rights pertaining to the *università*, confiscated domanial and private lands and animals, claiming both the losses incurred during the revolt and the Gravina loan, and incaracer-ated, in the dreary tower of Brienza, leading citizens of Atena.[71]

This document, and the witnesses' supporting statements, which all stress the gratuitous violence and the insults to the clergy, do not give an entirely reliable picture of what happened in Atena in 1647–48. According to the document, that reports the new oath of allegiance sworn to Giuseppe, the *"università* never wavered from that allegiance," and the witnesses ascribe all blame to one or two "troublemakers" (*capipopolo*) from neighboring communities, which Villari's own reconstruction shows to be an untruthful description of the events. We know, in fact, that Giuseppe's palace in Atena was pillaged by local rebels. The petition and testimonials document the extreme conflict which could surface in a moment of crisis, and the political weapons and relative strength the two sides could muster. They also point to the existence of a conscious local elite, whose presence is evident in the form of the document and in the events themselves, first as victims of baronial abuses and later as guarantors for the community.[72]

The revolt extended throughout the Caracciolo Brienza state, but in the other fiefs it remained a much less violent and extreme confrontation than in Atena. As early as August 1647, the *università* of Brienza asked the government for an amnesty blaming "a few malicious men" as well as "its extreme poverty" for any excesses which may have been committed. In 1650, the *università* then agreed with the marquis Giacomo to repay the damage the latter had suffered during the revolt. In May 1648, the *università* of Sasso also agreed to pay ducats 1,643.–.16+⅓ to Giuseppe Caracciolo for the income he had failed to receive

---

[71] On the Caracciolo during the revolt, see Capecelatro's *Diario*, I, pp. 23–24, 169, 175, and 223–35; II, pp. 348–50, 360, and 477–79; III, 11–13, 210, 236, 270 (on the repression in the fiefs), and 446; and ACB 1.3. The 1651 document in ACB 135.1, fols. 459r–65r, with depositions of sixteen witnesses, fols. 465v–99r (the phrase on the rebels is on fol. 466r; the eight citizens are named on fol. 467r). Giuseppe had threatened the honor of local elite women by forcing them to "dance with the men of the village and with his [Giuseppe's] servants and himself until late at night, which was a great scandal for the citizens" (fol. 481v). On the revolt in the area, see Cassandro, *Atena*, pp. 200–03, Villari, *Mezzogiorno*, pp. 111–23, and Rovito, "Strutture," pp. 280–300. The marquis of Sant'Eramo, cousin of the Caracciolo Brienza, was among the barons who participated in the ill-fated royalist attack on Altamura in Puglia in March 1648, see *ibid.*, pp. 297–98.
[72] Rovito, "Strutture," p. 251, gives other examples of these accusations of dishonoring women and injuring clerics; his article in general stresses the role of local notables in the leadership of the revolt in the provinces. The role of village notaries and lawyers in drafting "revolutionary" documents has been stressed, for the French Revolution, by Forster, "The 'World'."

because of the turmoil. In his will, Giuseppe later praised the *università* of Sasso "always most faithful to its masters."[73]

In the later seventeenth and eighteenth century the conflicts were fewer and shorter, usually ending in compromises. The government's fiscal pressure decreased after 1648, and the kingdom's economic situation began to improve by the end of the seventeenth century. In the eighteenth century the Caracciolo Brienza themselves had restored their finances; the presence in the fiefs and the improved management of marquis Litterio also contributed to this change in the characteristics of litigation. By the eighteenth century the *università* had also, in general, regained their solvency. Conflict remained, and, for instance, the *università* of Sasso, then confiscated by the government, rented itself from 1694 to 1699 to avoid the Caracciolo Brienza's rule. But the level of conflict was definitely lower, and the decades after the revolt certainly did not witness the increase in baronial pressure that took place in other regions, such as Abruzzo.[74]

More importantly, the focus of the litigations shifted to the status of specific pieces of land, especially parts of the feudal or communal domains, or woods and pastures, while jurisdictional disputes became less central. Although the income from feudal rights and monopolies did not decline significantly until the later eighteenth century, the better economic and demographic situation of the *università* made those rights less burdensome. Again in the eighteenth century, some feudal rights were the object of agreements between the *università* and the marquis which set the procedures for their management and regulated the income the marquis drew from them, thereby limiting the opportunity for conflict. In a situation of expansion, these perpetual rents were now to the *università*'s advantage. The demographic growth of the communities, on the other hand, caused growing pressure on land, so that the uses of feudal and communal domains became the focus of heated controversies. This shift in focus meant that conflicts became much more specific, and, in fact, one rarely finds in the eighteenth century the long lists of several dozen grievances against the marquis presented by the *università* to the royal government in the previous period.[75]

It is possible to examine closely this change in the emphasis of litigation. In the late sixteenth and early seventeenth centuries, casuistry on feudal rights reached unprecedented levels of sophistication. Feudal rights were so numerous and

[73] For Brienza, see ASN Collaterale Partium 419, fols. 97r–100r (my thanks to Vincenzo Telesca for this reference), and ACB 46.1.4, unnumbered fol.; for Sasso, 81.4.2; Giuseppe's will is in ASN Pandetta Corrente 570, IV, fols. 5r–16r (11r); Brienza's grievances against the baron, contained in Collaterale Partium 419, are also mentioned by Rovito, "Strutture," p. 250.

[74] Besides the *Catasto* records and the documents cited in footnote 17, a few eighteenth-century budgets survive for Atena and Brienza in ASN Conti delle *Università* 344, 348, and 479–82 (fol. numbers are rather confusing in these documents, but the accounts of each *università* are clearly marked under its name). For Sasso, see ASN Collaterale Provvisioni 289, fols. 167r–v (1697), and ASP notai Potenza, 1353 and 1354; also *ibid.*, 1070 and 1071, for Pietrafesa.

[75] Examples of these rents in the eighteenth century are in ACB 45.1.13, 26; 75.1.30.

Table 4.5a   *Breakdown of Novario's* On Vassals' Grievances *(1634)*

type of grievance	no. of cases	percent
criminal and civil jurisdiction, prisons, penalties, procedures, treatment of the defendants (1)	203	27.8
abuses of power (new or more) (2)	111	15.2
services claimed by baron (3)	91	12.5
interference in economic relationships among vassals or abuses in economic relationships between vassals and lord (4)	85	11.6
abuses of baronial administrators (5)	63	8.6
interferences in the *università*'s economic, administrative, or jurisdictional life (6)	56	7.7
quality of relationship in general (7)	51	7.0
monopolies, rights, tolls (8)	48	6.6
pressures and violence (9)	13	1.8
interference in vassals' religious life (10)	9	1.2
totals	730	100.0

Sources: Novario, *De vassallorum gravaminibus tractatus* (Naples, 1634; I have used the 1774 edition). The table is my own and, of course, many grievances are hard to place in any one area, but the general trend is, I believe, reliable. On baronial abuses, see also the *prammatiche De baronibus et eorum officio* (On barons and their office) in Giustiniani, *Nuova collezione*, especially those of 1536. An enumeration of feudal dues and exactions of all kinds is in Santamaria, *I feudi*, pp. 312–53. Winspeare offers a very long list of feudal rights and monopolies, *Storia*, note 154, pp. 151–213 of the notes. Another long list of baronial powers is in M. Miceli, "La giurisdizione civile e criminale nel regno di Napoli" *Rivista araldica* 66 (1968), pp. 62–66 and 87–96.

diverse that their enactment could create very tangled legal situations. Each fief had different conditions, and the king could grant any type of right, but the actual procedures for the exercise of each right were a matter of interpretation and of local tradition and precedent. In 1634, Giovanni Maria Novario, a provincial judicial functionary, published his *On Vassals' Grievances* which discussed 730 cases in which the vassals could seek satisfaction against their lords. Although Novario's cases are not a discussion of abuses in any one specific fief, his treatise can be used to determine the general areas of tension between lords and vassals. Table 4.5a attempts a breakdown of Novario's bewilderingly diverse materials.

The information contained in this table confirms Villari's thesis of strong pressure on the part of the barons to expand their powers, and demonstrates how crucial the jurisdictional prerogatives of the barons were, at least in the perceptions and consciousness of contemporaries. The lords were primarily the

Table 4.5b   *Breakdown of grievances of the Caracciolo Brienza vassals*

type	up to 1650		1693–1738	
	number	percent	number	percent
(1)	30	18.3	8	8
(2)	18	11.0	18	18
(3)	23	14.0	23	23
(4)	7	4.3	15	15
(5)	11	6.7	4	4
(6)	43	26.2	17	17
(7)	2	1.2	1	1
(8)	24	14.6	4	4
(9)	5	3.1	6	6
(10)	1	0.6	3	3
other	–	–	1	1
totals	164	100.0	100	100

Sources: For the earlier period, ACB 48.1.1, fols. 897r–900v (six grievances, Brienza, end of the sixteenth century); *ibid.*, fols. 935r–941v (twelve grievances, Brienza, same time); 75.7.2 (twenty-seven grievances, Atena, 1603, and twelve grievances, Atena, 1584); 75.7.4 (forty-three grievances, Atena, 1647); 75.7.7 (fourteen grievances, Atena, 1589, and thirty-eight others, Atena, same year); ASN Collaterale Patrium 419, fols. 97r–100r (sixteen grievances – but four refer to relationships between the *università* and the government and have not been used here, Brienza, 1647); for the later period, ACB 61.2.22 (sixty-one and then eleven grievances, Pietrafesa, 1729); 81.4.10 (eleven grievances, Sasso, 1738); 136.11, fols. 6r–11r (seventeen grievances, Sasso, 1693). I have not used the grievances listed in ACB 75.7.8 (Atena, 1728) and 75.7.19 and 135.3–4 (Atena, 1731–32), which refer specifically to two lawsuits over the toll on cattle and over the *università*'s domain. Again, the classification is my own, and, with these specific cases, the attribution of a grievance to one or the other category requires even more arbitrary judgment than in Novario's more general cases. On Atena's grievances, see Cassandro, *Atena*, pp. 195–200.

administrators of justice. In fact, feudal rights of a more economic character feature less significantly (6.6 percent), than almost any other area of conflict.

We can compare this information with a similar breakdown of the grievances presented by the Caracciolo Brienza vassals up to the first half of the seventeenth century and then in the eighteenth century (see Table 4.5b). The grievances of any particular *università* will obviously show a concentration on specific issues and a lack of the more abstract cases found in Novario's treatise. Moreover, Novario devoted considerable attention to the relationship between the baron and his vassals taken as individuals, whereas the grievances presented by the *università* were more concerned with problems of the community. When these limitations are kept present, a comparison of the data for the earlier period with those in Novario's book shows strong similarities. The major difference is in the area of interference with the life of the *università* (6), but sixteen of the forty-three cases in this area in Table 4.5b refer to one particular problem concerning the marquis' usurpation of lands the *università* claimed as its own. It is also not surprising to find more attention to this area of conflict in documents emanating from the *università* itself. Similarly, the low number of grievances dealing in general with the quality of the relationship (7) in Table 4.5b is to be expected, since the *università* were obviously less interested than Novario in defining an ideal situation. The low number of grievances dealing with the economic relations of the baron with his vassals (4), and, conversely, the high number of grievances dealing with the baronial monopolies (8) in Table 4.5b, can be explained by the *università*'s concern with collective issues rather than with individual problems. If one adds together the data for these two areas of conflict, the percentage for conflict in the economic sphere in general is practically the same in Novario as in the *università*'s documents (about eighteen percent).

The smaller sample for the later period shows the sharp decline in the importance of jurisdiction as an area of conflict. There are a few more cases of baronial violence (9). The large number of grievances relating to services (3) in Table 4.5b is misleading, because eight of the twenty-three cases are due to a lawsuit that concentrated on procedural details of the obligations of the *erari* and *conservatori*. In this sample, because the *università* of Pietrafesa presented among its grievances a series of complaints made by individual citizens against the marquis, the number of individual economic grievances is again higher than the number of grievances referring to baronial monopolies.

In the eighteenth century, therefore, conflicts arose from more specific issues, mainly relating to common lands and woods. Though there is evidence for several lawsuits on these problems, relations between the barons and the *università* were quite peaceful. On occasion, the marquis was able to enlist one *università* against another, and, around 1730, the *università* of Brienza and Atena entered a lawsuit on their borders. As the royal functionary in charge of the judgment was quick to observe, the marquis, whose rights over the lands and people of Brienza were more extensive than those over Atena, stood to profit from any enlargement of the borders of Brienza. In the 1740s, as Villari has shown, some tension arose over the evaluation of the marquis' properties since the marquis claimed that much of his land was feudal to avoid the *Catasto*, which only applied to allodial property. After the *Catasto*, the *università* finally managed to have the marquis pay the due *bonatenenza*, or local tax, on his allodial holdings. Still in the later eighteenth century, Atena proved the least docile of the four fiefs.[76]

[76] On the borders dispute, see ACB 48.6, especially 8 and 12; Cassandro, *Atena*, pp. 184–87. For the *Catasto*, see Villari, *Mezzogiorno*, and ASN Catasto Onciario vols. 5146–60 (Brienza), 5267–70

Stuart Woolf has observed similar developments in the relations between the Piedmontese aristocracy and its communities, from the agreements of the late sixteenth century to the heavy debts and high level of tension of the seventeenth. With the reign of Vittorio Amedeo II (1684–1730), however, the Piedmontese government intervened directly in the life of the communities: feudal powers were abolished, agreements rescinded, and disputes decided in favor of the villages; as a result, aristocratic management of the fiefs lost most of its traditional characteristics and, in particular, all manifestations of the paternalism that had existed before, even during the litigations.[77]

In the kingdom of Naples, on the contrary, in the early eighteenth century, the royal courts consistently defended feudal rights whenever challenged by the *università*, though in the 1740s they ordered the marquis to abide by the *Catasto* and pay his *bonatenenza*. It was only at the end of the century that the government and public opinion shifted their perception of the relationship between lords and vassals to positions hostile to the feudatories. The language itself changed, and in 1776 the appraiser of Atena remarked that "the *università* of Atena is very respectable for the zeal with which it has always defended its rights against its own princes."[78] But only in the years after 1806 did a new wave of conflict arise from the abolition of the feudal regime in the kingdom. Now the communes were governed by a local oligarchy that was willing to use its new power to increase its wealth at the expense of the marquis and of the poorer citizens. The marquis strove this time to present most of his property as allodial and not feudal, but the *Commissione Feudale* was less accommodating than previous courts, and the Caracciolo Brienza lost not only all of their judicial, administrative, and economic prerogatives, but also a considerable part of their patrimony as a result of defeudalization. The loss in annual income was estimated at a total of fifteen to twenty thousand ducats. The Caracciolo remained for a while the single largest landowners in their state, and were involved in several lawsuits with other local landowners.[79] But by the time an earthquake made the castle of

---

(Sasso), 4216–23 (Atena), and 5249–51 (Pietrafesa). Persistent hostility between Litterio and Atena appears in his letters of the 1760s, see ACB 140.40, fols. 16v–17r, 43r, and 45v–46r. On a specific source of conflict, namely the abuses of baronial officials, see Visceglia, *Territorio*, pp. 272–74, and Visceglia, "Comunità, signori feudali e *officiales* in Terra d'Otranto fra XVI e XVII secolo" *ASPN* 104 (1986), pp. 259–85.

77 Woolf, *Studi*, pp. 39–42, 71–75, 97–102, 119–22, and 164–70.

78 ACB 77.2.33; see also Villani, *Mezzogiorno*, pp. 155–212. This constituted a clear change from the time (150 years earlier) when the viceroy ordered the arrest of the procurator of Brienza in Naples for his troublesome behavior, see F. Palermo, ed. "Narrazione tratta dai giornali del governo di Don Pietro Girone duca d'Ossuna viceré di Napoli, scritti da Francesco Zazzera" *ASI* 9 (1846), p. 479.

79 Villari, *Mezzogiorno*, pp. 157–82. Data on the nineteenth century situation are in ACB vols. 143 to 166. For the defeudalization, see also ASN Creditori dello Stato 275/36, and the series Ministero dell'Interno II inventario and Affari demaniali Winspeare (see the inventories for the volume and page numbers referring to the four communities) in ASN; see also the printed *Bollettino delle sentenze della Commissione Feudale*, its *Supplemento* (with indexes), the *Bollettino delle ordinanze dei*

Brienza uninhabitable in the 1850s, the family and the communities had parted ways almost completely. By the early twentieth century the Barracco, heirs to Giulia Caracciolo Brienza, had sold most of their lands in the old feudal "state."

In the first eighty years or so of their feudal rule, the Caracciolo Brienza were often in conflict with their vassal communities, particularly over the extent and exercise of feudal powers. Conflicts were especially harsh with Atena, the *università* where feudal powers were weakest and feudal rule most recent. Their heavy debts considerably weakened the *università* at this time. The violence of the tensions found expression in the revolt of 1647–48, and in the repression subsequently wrought by Giuseppe Caracciolo. By the late seventeenth century, the financial situation of both the baronial family and the *università* was sounder than before and, as the population of the villages grew and the economic situation of the kingdom improved, conflicts between the *università* and the marquis became more specific, on a smaller scale, and focused rather on property than on feudal powers.

But a more striking change took place after the revolt in the relations between the marquis and their vassals. The family had always resided in the fiefs, at least for part of its time, and the barons had always been thought of as the protectors of the population over which they ruled. But in the later seventeenth and eighteenth centuries, the paternalistic and traditional aspects of the feudal relationship were emphasized. The family regularly spent long times in the fiefs, and increased attention was given to the upkeep of feudal residences. The marquis intervened frequently in the life of the communities, and their presence and role there were marked by various ceremonies. Through the chapels they patronized, through their bequests, and, in the case particularly of the marquis Litterio, through the institutions they established, the Caracciolo Brienza presented themselves as interested in, and committed to, the welfare of their vassals, and successfully met the challenges to their preeminence posed by the church and the local notability. In an isolated region where change was limited, the marquis' emphasis on traditional paternalism – which paralleled the traditionalism of their management of the patrimony – probably played a key role in preserving a relatively peaceful relationship with the *università*, and even in insuring the continuation of the existing communal institutions until the end of the old regime.

To a certain extent, Litterio Caracciolo perceived himself, to judge from some of his actions and words, as the fatherly judge and small prince of his vassals, who preferred residing amongst them to the life of the capital, committed to their welfare, to traditional values – witness his establishment of a catechism school – and to the continuation of the old ways. He strove to appear, and must in part have appeared, to his vassals as their native, traditional, and perhaps natural,

commissari ripartitori dei demani 3, pp. 181–226, and R. Trifone, *Feudi e demani. L'eversione della feudalità nell'Italia meridionale* (Milan, 1909), on which see Villani, *Mezzogiorno*, pp. 202–03.

representative and ruler, in contrast to the distant and greedy state power. I do not intend to suggest in these pages a rehabilitation of the feudal regime, but simply an additional perspective to serve as a counterweight to some of the antifeudal extremes traditional in Neapolitan historiography. The system had its logic, and did not survive as long as it did on sheer brute force. In this picture the royal government had little to do, and in fact it was only at the very end of the old regime that the state really tried to interfere in the feudal organization of the kingdom; only the Napoleonic government eliminated the bases on which Litterio Caracciolo's world had worked.[80]

[80] Antifeudal rhetoric is strongest in the works of Marxist historians (Villari, Villani, Lepre). For a stronger expression of nostalgia for a world we have lost, see Merzario, *Signori*; also critical of antifeudal historiography is the rather limited study of C. Trasselli, *Lo stato di Gerace e Terranova nel Cinquecento* (Vibo Valentia, 1978). On the local power and abuses of the barons, see also P. L. Rovito, "Funzioni pubbliche e capitalismo signorile nel feudo napoletano del '600" *Bollettino del Centro di Studi Vichiani* 16 (1986), pp. 95–156. Rovito sees a Spanish policy to transform the barons into royal officers with a regulated, delegated jurisdiction; this, however, still resulted in the consolidation of the traditional local control on the part of the barons.

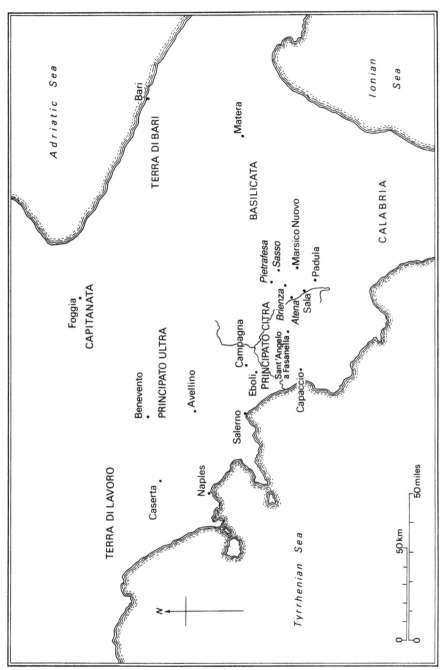

Map 2 The central part of the kingdom of Naples. Names in capitals refer to provinces, the others to towns. Names in italics refer to the four fiefs of the family

5

Aristocratic strategies for the preservation of family wealth

My daughter! O my ducats! O my daughter!
Merchant of Venice, II, viii, 15

In its feudal *stati*, the Neapolitan aristocracy was secure. With a minimum of expense and care, the stability of feudal revenues and of feudal rule over the *università* could be maintained. Even after the mid-seventeenth century difficulties, the feudal aristocracy preserved most of its powers and income and kept them well into the eighteenth century. In the fiefs, the aristocracy met with limited challenges to its position, and in most cases the vassals shared the aristocracy's tendency to follow the ways and traditions of the past. It was in the capital that the old feudal aristocracy had to face more forceful challenges to its status, due to the consolidation of Spanish rule on the kingdom. The last two chapters of this study will examine how the aristocracy responded to these challenges in its defense of family wealth and prestige, and in its relations with the state.

The main aim of an aristocratic family was the preservation of its wealth and status. Each of these two was needed to support and legitimate the other. Genealogists and others who wrote about the aristocracy in Spanish Naples saw an explicit link between social prestige and economic power. As in all of Western Europe at the time, with the growth of bureaucratic states and of complex systems of state finances, numerous new families acquired wealth and ascended in society. In the kingdom of Naples, these new families included not only financiers, magistrates, and lawyers, but also international merchants and bankers, especially Genoese, who began to reside permanently in the kingdom. The old feudal aristocracy could not arrest this process, but it needed to defend its own prominent position within the kingdom's elite, and it achieved this goal by adapting to new circumstances and enacting remarkable innovations in its family policy. The limitation of marriage to one son in each generation, the establishment of entails and dowry funds, and the shrewd use of litigations, enabled the Caracciolo Brienza, like many other families of the old feudal aristocracy, to protect their wealth and balance the rival claims of clan, families, and individual members, without jeopardizing their privileged and prestigious status at the pinnacle of the kingdom's society.[1]

In recent years, a few historians who have studied the economic situation of the Neapolitan feudal aristocracy have analyzed family policy, mainly in connection with the preservation and transmission of the patrimony. Gérard Delille in particular has studied the aristocratic family in the context of the demographic history of the kingdom of Naples. Maria Antonietta Visceglia has written on aristocratic marriage and inheritance, and has touched on the same issues in an article on the economic situation of the aristocracy.[2] These studies are based on wills and marriage contracts, drawn from various aristocratic archives in Naples and elsewhere, and, on the data available for a dozen or so families, they indicate a trend towards more rigidity and formalization in family policy. With the partial exception of Visceglia's article on the Muscettola, they do not reconstruct in detail specific decisions and strategies. In this chapter I shall look more closely at the behavior of one aristocratic family and speculate on its motivations; I shall try to relate that behavior to the family's economic and genealogical history, and to offer a comprehensive analysis of all aspects of family policy and of their connections to each other. After a general look at the changes in the aristocratic family in the sixteenth and seventeenth centuries, I shall examine specific aspects of marriage policy and the lot of children. I shall then analyze the forms of familial and clan aid available to the Neapolitan aristocracy, and discuss the importance and significance of litigation within the family, considering particularly the role of women in preserving and enlarging the patrimony.

CLAN AND FAMILY: CHANGES IN THE SIXTEENTH CENTURY

Historians of late medieval and early modern Northern Italian patriciates, especially those of Florence and Venice, have devoted many pages to the issue of the relation between the individual family, with its vertical descendance, and the

---

[1] For the ascent of magistrates and lawyers, see A. Cernigliaro, *Sovranità e feudo nel regno di Napoli, 1505–1557*, (2 vols.; Naples, 1983); P. L. Rovito, *Respublica dei togati* (Naples, 1981); V. I. Comparato, *Uffici e società a Napoli (1600–1647)* (Florence, 1974). On the Genoese, see large, if undigested, amounts of information in R. Colapietra, *Dal Magnanimo a Masaniello, II I Genovesi a Napoli durante il viceregno spagnolo* (Salerno, 1973); also A. Calabria, "Finanzieri genovesi nel regno di Napoli nel Cinquecento" *RSI* 101 (1989), 578–613, and G. Felloni, *Gli investimenti finanziari genovesi in Europa* (Milan, 1971), pp. 300–13. To face the ascent in the sixteenth century of new families, sumptuary laws were passed in the kingdom, as elsewhere in Italy, see G. Vitale, "Modelli culturali nobiliari a Napoli tra Quattro e Cinquecento" *ASPN* 105 (1987), pp. 27–104; R. Pilati, "La dialettica politica a Napoli durante la vistia di Lope de Guzmán" *ibid.*, p. 152, footnote 19; D. Owen Hughes, "Sumptuary Laws and Social Relations in Renaissance Italy" in J. Bossy, ed. *Disputes and Settlements. Law and Human Relations in the West* (Cambridge, 1983), pp. 69–99. The relations of the aristocracy with the government will be discussed in the next chapter. For aristocratic theory of the time, see the genealogical literature cited in chapter 1, especially Ammirato and Aldimari, and G. B. de Luca, *Il cavaliere e la dama* (Rome, 1675).

[2] G. Delille most recently in *Famille et propriété dans le royaume de Naples (XVe–XIXe siècles)* (Rome, 1985); M. A. Visceglia, "Corpo e sepoltura nei testamenti della nobiltà napoletana (secoli XVI–XVIII)" *QS* 17 (1982), pp. 583–614; Visceglia, "Linee per uno studio unitario dei testamenti

large horizontal clan which included many families sharing a common name and common ancestors. Although there have been major disagreements on the chronology and modality of the process, there is a fundamental consensus that by the mid-sixteenth century, families had little sense of belonging to a larger clan. Little in their specific policies shows that membership of a clan played any significant role for aristocratic families. The situation is more complex in states like Genoa or Piedmont, where peculiar institutions, like the Genoese *Alberghi* or the survivial of feudal jurisdictions held in common, led to a larger role for clans than in Florence. It is the contention of this study that the old Neapolitan aristocracy – steeped in its military and feudal traditions – remained conscious of its clan membership and conducted its policy, at least in some areas, in ways which were influenced by the general interests and traditions of a kinship group larger than the family itself, and this well into the eighteenth century. Common traditions and ancestors were claimed as their own by all the families in each clan, and genealogical treatises typically mention, among each family's glories, distinguished members of the clan even if they belong to families quite distant from the one whose virtues they are extolling.[3]

The Caracciolo, like the Carafa, the Capece, and a few other feudal families of the highest aristocracy of the kingdom, constituted a very large clan, subdivided into many families. These families, more than forty for the Caracciolo in the sixteenth century, recognized common ancestors, belonged to the same *Seggio*, traditionally lived in the same district of Naples, often held common patronage of chapels or other ecclesiastic institutions, subscribed to, and benefited from,

e dei contratti matrimoniali dell'aristocrazia feudale napoletana tra fine Quattrocento e Settecento" *MEFRM* 95 (1983), pp. 393–470; Visceglia, "Formazione e dissoluzione di un patrimonio aristocratico: la famiglia Muscettola tra XVI e XIX secolo" *MEFRM* 92 (1980), pp. 555–624; Visceglia has recently gathered her essays in *Il bisogno di eternità* (Naples, 1988).

[3] On Florence, see R. A. Goldthwaite, *Private Wealth in Renaissance Florence. A Study of Four Families* (Princeton, 1968); Goldthwaite, "Organizzazione economica e struttura famigliare" in acts of the Third Convegno di studi sulla storia dei ceti dirigenti in Toscana *I ceti dirigenti nella Toscana tardo comunale* (Florence, 1980); F. W. Kent, *Household and Lineage in Renaissance Florence. The Family Life of the Capponi, Ginori, and Rucellai* (Princeton, 1977); Roberto Bizzocchi, "La dissoluzione di un clan familiare: i Buondelmonti di Firenze nei secoli XVI e XVII" *ASI* 140 (1982), pp. 3–45. In his articles on the Venetian aristocracy, Stanley Chojnacky sees clan ties weakening after the fifteenth century, "Patrician Women in Early Renaissance Venice" *Studies in the Renaissance* 21 (1974), pp. 176–203; Chojnacky, "Dowries and Kinsmen in Early Renaissance Venice" *Journal of Interdisciplinary History* 5 (1975), pp. 571–600; Chojnacky "Kinship Ties and Young Patricians in Fifteenth-Century Venice" *Renaissance Quarterly* 38 (1985), pp. 240–70; see also A. F. Cowan, *The Urban Patriciate. Lübeck and Venice, 1580–1700* (Köln, 1986), chapter 5. On Genoa, see E. Grendi, "Profilo storico degli Alberghi genovesi" *MEFRM* 87 (1975), pp. 241–302; on Piedmont, see S. J. Woolf, *Studi sulla nobiltà piemontese nell'epoca dell'assolutismo* (Turin, 1963). Silvia Marchisio, "Ideologia e problemi dell'economia familiare nelle lettere della nobiltà piemontese (XVII–XVIII secolo)" *Bollettino storico–bibliografico subalpino* (1985), pp. 67–130, mentions the existence of general meetings of clans in Piedmont and Genoa (pp. 72–73), but her only evidence seems to be an 1811 letter (I thank Anna Maria Rao for directing me to Marchisio's article). On Italian families in general, see N. Tamassia, *La famiglia italiana nei secoli XV e XVI* (Rome, 1971; first edit. 1910); M. Barbagli, *Sotto lo stesso tetto* (Bologna, 1984); on clans, with no reference to Southern Italy, see J. Heers, *Le clan familial au Moyen Age* (Paris, 1974).

common funds for the support of members of the clan, and often developed additional ties through intermarriage. To be a Caracciolo had a meaning well beyond the household or close family; it implied membership in a social, economic, and, to some extent, political unit with traditions, customs, and even an ideology all its own. The greatness of the clan was the greatness of all its constituent families. The memoir written for Giuseppe Caracciolo in the 1650s remarked with emphasis that Giuseppe's quarters were all Caracciolo, since his mother and two grandmothers all belonged to the clan.[4] Although – as Visceglia points out – the Caracciolo did not choose to be all buried in one church, and some "subclans" are detectable among them,[5] they all identified with the larger clan and drew their first allies from it. By clan and family I am here making a distinction which was quite obvious at the time, although the sources rarely mention it explicitly. The act of foundation in 1585 of a common dowry fund among various families makes the connection between the two realities clear: in case a replacement of extinct families with new members was called for, preference should be given to "noblemen of the same clans to which the extinct families [belonged]."[6]

Until the mid-sixteenth century, the aristocracy acted to establish new families within the clans, but after the 1550s this attitude was reversed; due primarily to political changes, the aristocracy diverted its efforts from the exercise of political power to the preservation and expansion of its economic and social status. Many of the families which were part of the Neapolitan aristocratic clans were established and acquired lands and titles between the late fourteenth and the mid-sixteenth centuries. This was a troubled period of wars between claimants to the throne and of weak monarchical rule. Before the consolidation of Spanish rule under Viceroy don Pedro de Toledo (1532–53), the aristocracy therefore wielded a direct political power, particularly through the Parliament of the kingdom and the *Seggi* of Naples. Since only fief holders (titled or untitled) could participate in Parliament, it was in the interest of an aristocratic clan to endow as many of its members as possible with feudal lordships. The kingdom's population was slowly increasing, and so were the value of fiefs and the availability of money. At the same time the monarchy was willing to sell fiefs and jurisdictions, especially under the late Angevins, Alfonso the Magnanimous (d. 1458), and later under Ferdinand of Aragon and Charles V.

The establishment of numerous families also constituted a form of insurance

---

[4] ACB 1.3; the genealogical literature on the Neapolitan aristocracy is cited in chapter 1.
[5] On the other hand, the Carafa (the dead ones, at any rate) were present in San Domenico with all their families, "Corpo," pp. 598–99.
[6] ASN, Archivio del Monte dei Giunti, busta I categoria I, 12, "Carte del Monte delle ventinove famiglie"; this is a printed nineteenth-century account of the fund, which contains (pp. 25–40) a copy of the foundation act of 25 November 1585. The quotation in on p. 36: "cavalieri dell'istesse casate delle famiglie, che si estinguessero." A close definition of the two terms is offered in chapter 1.

Aristocratic family strategies

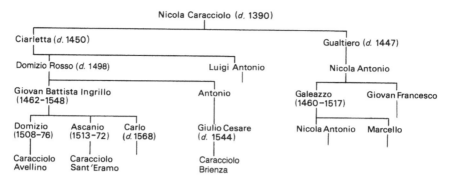

Figure 4 The descendants of Nicola Caracciolo (d. 1390). A vertical line under a name indicates issue. Carlo's descendance became extinct after two generations.

for the aristocracy. In the conspiracies of 1465 and 1487, and during the French invasion of 1528, many aristocratic clans split between the rival sides, and often the lands confiscated from a rebel family were sold or assigned to its cousins of the same clan after the revolts.[7] All these factors led to a policy of division of inheritances, whenever possible, and of marriages of most sons and daughters of the aristocracy – also because of the need for alliances between families and between clans – since a clan's numerical strength played a key role in determining its possibilities for political maneuvering and power.[8]

The genealogy of the Caracciolo Brienza family illustrates this policy of clan fragmentation. During the fifteenth century, four families were created from the descendants of Nicola Caracciolo (d. 1390). In one of these, at least two of the sons of Domizio Caracciolo Rosso (d. 1498) – Giovan Battista Ingrillo and Antonio – married daughters of feudal lords and acquired fiefs in the early years of the sixteenth century, and in the following generation three of Giovan Battista's sons, Domizio, Ascanio, and Carlo, did likewise. Within two generations, therefore, four separate families – three of which later received titles on Avellino, Brienza, and Sant'Eramo – were established among the descendants of one individual. After the mid-sixteenth century, no more new families were created among the descendants of Domizio Caracciolo Rosso until the end of the seventeenth century, and the same is true of the descendants of Domizio's cousins.[9]

[7] Examples in G. Incarnato, "L'evoluzione del possesso feudale in Abruzzo Ultra, 1500–1670" *ASPN* 96 (1971), pp. 219–87, and N. Cortese, *Feudi e feudatari napoletani della prima metà del Cinquecento da documenti dell'AGS* (Naples, 1931; first appeared in *ASPN* 54–56 (1929–31)).

[8] Visceglia, "Linee"; general works on the history of the period are A. Lepre, *Storia del Mezzogiorno d'Italia* (2 vols.; Naples, 1986), and A. Ryder, *The Kingdom of Naples under Alfonso the Magnanimous. The Making of a Modern State* (Oxford, 1976).

[9] Genealogical sources are cited in chapter, 1, especially ASN, Archivio Serra di Gerace, ms. 73; see Figure 4.

163

The continuity of feudal power

After the 1550s, in fact, when the kingdom went through a period of economic expansion and inflation, this trend towards clan fragmentation was reversed. The last major political attempt of the old barons directly to challenge monarchical rule, that of the Sanseverino prince of Salerno, was punished with exile and the loss of lands. The firm grip of Spain on the kingdom reduced the space for direct aristocratic political power in the kingdom, and the Parliament devoted itself more to maintaining and enforcing the social and economic privileges of the aristocracy, by shifting the fiscal burden onto other groups, than to representing possibly independent political positions. The crown had accepted and allowed, partially in response to requests from the aristocracy itself, a degree of commercialization of the fiefs, and there was indeed a high rate of turnover of fiefs, especially in the areas near Naples. The financial needs of the crown, and the increasingly subordinate and peripheral position of Naples in the Italian economy, had brought wealthy Genoese and Iberian financiers to Naples who were themselves able to take advantage of the crown's readiness to sell lands and jurisdictions. By the end of the century, the aristocracy, although its revenues and the value of its fiefs grew at a rate possibly higher than inflation, entered a period of economic instability and indebtedness. The causes of this have traditionally been assigned to the expenses incurred in military service to the king of Spain, and in the luxurious lifestyle necessitated by the aristocracy's move to the capital, with its competitive court life and palace-building. Aristocratic indebtedness preoccupied contemporaries and led to the demise of a few huge old patrimonies, such as that of the Sanseverino of Bisignano, and to a generalized need for economy and recovery.[10]

The aristocracy's response to these developments consisted in closing ranks and adopting more rigid and formalized succession strategies, designed to preserve the patrimony, prestige, and purity of the families. Entails, limits to children's marriages, and legal bounds on dotal money, were all enacted or emphasized in these years. The Caracciolo Brienza also began – or continued – to spend much of their time in the fiefs, to save on expenses to be sure, but also to strengthen their position there by purchasing lands and reinforcing baronial rights. In the last quarter of the sixteenth century, the Caracciolo clan also established several dowry funds to help prevent the need for their daughters to marry beneath their status.[11]

Many aristocratic families in the sixteenth and seventeenth centuries

[10] R. Villari, *La rivolta antispagnola a Napoli. Le origini (1585–1647)* (Bari, 1967); G. Galasso, *Economia e società nella Calabria del Cinquecento* (Naples, 1967; reprint Milan, 1975); G. Labrot, *Baroni in città. Residenze e comportamenti dell'aristocrazia napoletana, 1530–1734* (Naples, 1979); G. Ceci, "I feudatari napoletani alla fine del secolo XVI" *ASPN* 24 (1899), pp. 122–38. On the decline, see "Ruina di case napoletane del suo tempo scritta da don Ferrante della Marra duca della Guardia (1641)" *ASPN* 25 (1900), pp. 355–86; on the high turnover of fiefs near Naples, see G. D.Ambrosio, "La feudalità in Terra di Lavoro nella seconda metà del secolo XVII" tesi di laurea, University of Naples, 1984–85, chapter 2.
[11] See pp. 178–85 below; Visceglia, "Linee' and "Formazione."

attempted to preserve their patrimonies through entails, following a common European pattern. Spain had allowed entails since 1505, and in most Italian states they began to be established in the mid-sixteenth century. Entails tended to reinforce the ties between the aristocracy and the monarchy, and in Spain in particular the aristocracy's frequent need to break the rules of its own entails forced it to depend on royal favor. Visceglia has observed that the Neapolitan aristocracy first imposed entails, beginning in the late sixteenth century, on those elements of the patrimony – such as palaces – most closely related to the family's prestige and image. Later entails were established on entire estates. Although the succession of fiefs was regulated by feudal law, in 1655 Philip IV made it possible, in practice, for the aristocracy to establish entails on the fiefs. Most entails excluded women unless married in the family or in the clan. Whereas some of the wealthiest families established large entails early in the viceroyal times, newer or less wealthy families adopted this policy, and primogeniture, later, even as late as the eighteenth century.[12]

The Caracciolo Brienza had an entailed palace at San Giovanni a Carbonara near their *Seggio*, and some entailed lands near Naples from the heritage of cardinal Marino Caracciolo (d. 1538). Atena and Sasso were left by Giuseppe Caracciolo, fifth marquis of Brienza, to his sister, Faustina, in 1656, but entailed to their cousin Domenico. In 1755, Teresa Pinto Caracciolo left an entail for the value of 10,000 ducats to her descendants on her personal property. No general entail was established on the entire Brienza patrimony until 1806, when Litterio Caracciolo imposed an entail for the value of 350,000 ducats in favor of his oldest son Cataldo, but this was probably an attempt to save the patrimony from division under the new French laws.[13]

These strategies of formalization were quite successful, and after the seventeenth century the social and economic preeminence of the old aristocracy was largely untouched. Its numbers, in a situation in which only one son in each generation married, had shrunk, and the establishment of entails had protected several aristocratic patrimonies from dispersion. By the eighteenth century, however, the aristocracy felt the need to free itself from some of the restrictions it had previously imposed on its wealth. In this, too, the Neapolitan aristocracy

---

[12] Visceglia, *Territorio, feudo e potere locale* (Naples, 1988), p. 223; A. Sinisi, "Una famiglia mercantile napoletana del XVIII secolo" *Economia e storia* second series, 3 (1982), pp. 139–203; the 1655 law is in L. Giustiniani, ed. *Nuova collezione delle prammatiche del regno di Napoli* (15 vols.; Naples, 1803–8), IV, *De feudis, prammatica* XXXV, pp. 352–55; also in Tuscany, by the late seventeenth century, only about fifteen percent of the real estate of the Riccardi was free from entails, see P. Malanima, "Patrimonio, reddito, investimenti, spese di una famiglia dell'aristocrazia fiorentina nel '700" in Mirri, ed. *Ricerche di storia moderna*, II (Pisa, 1979), p. 233; on entails among the European aristocracies, see the survey by J. P. Cooper, "Patterns of Inheritance and Settlement by Great Landowners from the Fifteenth to the Eighteenth Century" in J. Goody, *et al.*, eds. *Family and Inheritance* (Cambridge, 1976), pp. 192–327; on Spain, see I. Atienza Hernandez, *Aristocracia, poder y riqueza en la España moderna* (Madrid, 1987), p. 99.

[13] Visceglia, "Linee" and "Formazione"; Litterio's entail is in ACB App. 22, unnumbered fol. Other strategies enacted in these years are discussed later in this chapter.

acted like other Italian aristocracies. Many entails were broken with royal licenses. Parts of the revenues were placed in earmarked reinvestment funds, the *moltiplichi*, which eventually created additional revenue free from the obligations of the entails. The Caracciolo Brienza, for instance, sold their palace at San Giovanni a Carbonara for 15,550 ducats in 1781, after receiving a royal license to break the entail. Sale of the same property had been forbidden in 1671.[14]

The enactment of these policies was gradual, and its precise chronology varied with the specific patrimonial and demographic situation of each family. Entails and the limitation of sons' marriages in each generation were only two of the strategies the aristocracy employed to protect its status in society. The elements in the family structure whose lot underwent the most decisive changes were cadet sons and daughters.

FAMILY POLICY: MARRIAGES, DOWRIES, CHANGING LOT OF DAUGHTERS AND CADET SONS

The essential goal of aristocratic family policy was the preservation of the patrimony. Children, especially cadet children, should be prevented from dispersing the family wealth, and yet at the same time they ought to be supported in a lifestyle that would not cause the family to lose status. This could be achieved through several means, such as limitation of births, delay or limitation of marriages, and careful choice of marriage partners. Any combination of these policies was used by the aristocracy all over Europe.[15] The next two sections of this chapter will analyze these marriage policies and their consequences for the aristocracy. In particular, I shall study the lot of cadet sons and daughters and the alliances entered by the eldest sons and heirs.

Cadet sons

After 1530, only five cadet cons of the Caracciolo Brienza family married out of twenty who reached adulthood. From 1530 to 1700, only two such marriages occurred. Marino Caracciolo (1567–1621), brother of Giovan Battista, second

14 Visceglia, "Linee"; the sale of the palace is in ACB 5.1.25; the previous attempt in 141.65. Woolf, *Studi*, pp. 129–35, and 150–53, on entails and the problems they caused in the eighteenth century.
15 Studies that address this issue include J. C. Davis, *A Venetian Family and its Fortune, 1500–1900: The Donà and the Conservation of their wealth* (Philadelphia, 1975); Woolf, *Studi*; R. Forster, *The Nobility of Toulouse in the Eighteenth Century, a Social and Economic Study* (Baltimore, 1960); Forster, *The House of Saulx-Tavanes. Versailles and Burgundy, 1700–1830* (Baltimore, 1971); Forster, *Merchants, Landlords, Magistrates. The Depont Family in Eighteenth-Century France* (Baltimore, 1980); J. Boutier, "Les 'Notizie diverse' de Niccolò Gondi (1652–1720). A propos de la mémoire et des stratégies familiales d'un noble florentin" *MEFRM* 98 (1986), pp. 1097–151; Cooper, "Patterns"; T. H. Hollingsworth, *The Demography of the British Peerage*, supplement to *Population Studies* 18 (1964–65); L. Stone, "Inheritance Strategies among the English Landed Elite, 1540–1880" in G. Delille and F. Rizzi, eds. *Le modèle familial européen*

Table 5.1 *Frequency of marriage of adult daughters and cadet sons of the Caracciolo Brienza (1500–1800)*

	Daughters			Cadet sons		
	total	married	unmarried	total	married	unmarried
up to 1620	20	19	1	11	1	10
1620–60	8	3	5	4	1	3
after 1660	7	7	none	5	3	2
totals	35	29	6	20	5	15

marquis of Brienza, and an infantry captain, married the widow Ippolita Pappacoda della Noia late in life, and thereby became lord of Cancellara in Basilicata. Although he had two illegitimate sons, his marriage was childless. Carlo Caracciolo (1591–1648), second son of the marquis of Sant'Eramo and father of Domenico, seventh marquis of Brienza, was destined to an ecclesiastic career, and only married Cornelia Caracciolo Celenza, twice a widow, in 1639, after his elder brother Marino's marriage had failed to produce a son.[16]

In the eighteenth century, two more cadets married, both against their family's wishes – and one, indeed, apparently against his own wishes as well. In 1711, Giovan Battista Caracciolo (1671–1736), second son of Domenico, seventh marquis of Brienza, married Candida, daughter of Bartolomeo Grassi, baron of Pianura, whose brother he had supposedly killed in a duel, so that the marriage served to reconcile him with the bereaved family. The marriage gave rise to the branch of the Brienza family extant today. In 1724, Nicola Caracciolo (1694–1728) left the ecclesiastical benefice which his brother Domenico, ninth marquis of Brienza, had bestowed on him in order to marry Teodora Alberti, marquise of Pentidattilo and duchess of Melito, who was his own brother's mother-in-law. Teodora, fifty when she married Nicola – her third husband – survived him by thirty years, after, not unexpectedly, failing to beget any children by him. In the last generation of the Brienza family, Antonio, younger brother of the last marquis of Brienza, married at the age of almost fifty,

(Rome, 1986), pp. 267–90; S. Marshall, *The Dutch Gentry* (New York, 1987); R. B. Litchfield, "Demographic Characteristics of Florentine Patrician Families" *Journal of Economic History* 29 (1969), pp. 191–205; D. Zanetti, *La demografia del patriziato milanese* (Pavia, 1972); C. Lévy and L. Henry, "Ducs et pairs sous l'Ancien Régime" *Population* 15 (1960), pp. 807–30.

[16] Carlo's marriage can hardly be considered a severe loss for the Neapolitan church, if one is to trust contemporary reports of his unseemly behavior, "Aggiunta alli Diurnali di Scipione Guerra" *ASPN* 36 (1911), pp. 368–71, 536, and 562.

when his elder brother had only one daughter living, and died childless shortly thereafter.[17]

The active discouragement of cadets' marriages by the Brienza family was not unusual. Similar attitudes can be found within the Caracciolo Avellino, the Gambacorta, or the Ruffo families, all related to the Caracciolo Brienza. This preceded the formal establishment of entails and the enforcement of primogeniture. This tendency to limit marriage to one son in each generation was blamed in the later eighteenth century for the extinction of many aristocratic families.[18] The phenomenon, is of course, not confined to Naples. There was a similar high frequency of extinctions in the Venetian aristocracy, due to the same practice of allowing only one son per generation to marry. Similar patterns have been observed for the Piedmontese and Sienese aristocracy, and such behavior seems to have been the rule for the Sicilian aristocracy, the Lombard provincial nobility, and any number of aristocrats across continental Europe. In general, older, more established families lasted longer than families of more recent noble status, and this was certainly the case in Naples.[19]

The occupations to which unmarried cadet sons of the Neapolitan aristocracy devoted their lives changed with time. In the sixteenth and early seventeenth centuries, the inclusion of Naples in the Spanish empire opened up numerous opportunities for military service. The Caracciolo clan produced many generals, captains, *maestres de campo*, and admirals, who fought in Africa, Northern Italy, Flanders, Germany, and Spain. Whereas many titled lords themselves played prominent roles in the Spanish armies, many more cadets often occupied the lower officer ranks. At least two of the brothers of Giulo Cesare Caracciolo, baron of Salvia and father of the first marquis of Brienza, were captains in Flanders, as was Giulio Cesare's grandson, Marino, as well as one of Marino's own sons before entering the clergy. In 1546, the will of Giovan Antonio Caracciolo, count of Oppido, established a fund to benefit noblemen of the

---

[17] A. Caracciolo di Torchiarolo, *Una famiglia italianissima: i Caracciolo di Napoli* (Naples, 1939), pp. 159–60; ACB 15.10, unnumbered fol., for the Grassi marriage (the Grassi had been barons of Pianura since around 1675, see D'Ambrosio, "La feudalità," p. 80); the marriage contract between Teodora and Nicola (ACB 3.1.18) refers to him as "*conjunx inops* (the penniless spouse)"; the family's opposition to this marriage is in ACB 12.4, especially 7; Antonio's marriage is in ACB 161, unnumbered fol.

[18] For example, in the new provisions of the *Monte delle ventinove famiglie* or of the *Monte Ciarletta*, cited later in this chapter.

[19] Davis, *The Decline of the Venetian Aristocracy as a Ruling Class* (Baltimore, 1962); Woolf, *Studi*, pp. 58–61, and 158–59; Marchisio, "Ideologia," pp. 78–81; G. R. F. Baker, "Nobiltà in declino: il caso di Siena sotto i Medici e gli Asburgo-Lorena" *RSI* 84 (1972), pp. 584–616; M. Aymard, "Une famille de l'aristocratie sicilienne aux XVI et XVII siècles: les ducs de Terranova, un bel example d'ascension seigneuriale" *Revue historique* 96, no. 247 (1972), pp. 29–66; G. Mira, *Vicende economiche di una famiglia italiana dal XIV al XVII secolo* (Milan 1940), especially chapter 1; Cooper, "Patterns"; a remarkable example is in D. J. Sturdy, *The D'Aligres de la Rivière* (Woodbridge, 1986), throughout, and pp. 228–30.

Aristocratic family strategies

Caracciolo clan, "the needier ones, aged forty years or more, so that they may live comfortably and not exert themselves anymore in arms."[20]

But by the mid-seventeenth century, the Spanish army attracted fewer and fewer aristocratic scions, probably because of the decline of Spain's military activity and effectiveness. The relative domestication of the aristocracy, through life in the capital and at court, must also have contributed to this development. More lasting was the possibility of employment offered by the church. In the sixteenth and early seventeenth centuries, the Caracciolo Brienza enjoyed an informal family right over some ecclesiastical preferments, which passed from uncle to nephew, such as the bishopric of Catania in Sicily and the abbey of Sant'Angelo a Fasanella. The latter, an abbey defined as "episcopal" (*mitrata*) by Giustiniani, was near the Caracciolo fiefs, and passed to five Brienza cadets over four generations until the early seventeenth century. The bishopric of Tropea in Calabria and the archbishoprics of Trani and Bari in Puglia, together with some smaller abbeys, were bestowed on other Brienza children in this period, and at least one cadet – Giulio Cesare, brother of the second marquis of Brienza – became a knight of Malta in 1579, a position which entailed the crucial vow of chastity. Carlo Caracciolo Sant'Eramo had himself been titular of an abbey before his marriage. Marino, brother of Domenico, seventh marquis of Brienza, became a Theatine.[21]

In the early eighteenth century, the Caracciolo Brienza, blessed for a couple of generations with few surviving sons, had patronage over an ecclesiastical benefice in their own fiefs. Following an agreement in 1719 with the bishop of Marsico Nuovo, the marquis and the bishop awarded the two benefices of the chapel of the Rosary in the church of Brienza, which provided by then a hefty annual income of ducats 378.3.02 and 244.-.07 respectively, with few obligations for the incumbents. The first recipients were Nicola Caracciolo, brother of the marquis, and the brothers Donato and Giovan Angelo Anzani, two of the bishop's nephews. On Nicola's marriage in 1724, the benefice served to secure a position for his younger brother, Gennaro (1697–1770), who also received a chaplaincy in a church in Atena. Gennaro, who was a turbulent character in the style of the literary ecclesiastic uncle don Blasco Uzeda, created frequent problems for his nephew, the marquis of Brienza.[22]

[20] Quoted in Visceglia, "Linee," p. 411.
[21] Giustiniani, *Dizionario geografico ragionato del regno di Napoli*; Giulio Cesare's knighthood in ACB 9.9 and in 17.3, fols. 80r–81r; documents on Marino in ACB 12.1. See the parallel example of Catalonia in J. M. Torras i Ribé, *Evolució social i econòmica d'una família catalana de l'antic règim* (Barcelona, 1976), pp. 55–56; on the decline of the military vocation of the French aristocracy, see E. Schalk, *From Valor to Pedigree. Ideas of Nobility in France in the Sixteenth and Seventeenth Centuries* (Princeton, 1986).
[22] ACB 49, especially 49.1.11; a different estimate in ACB 49.3.1–2 gives ducats 401.2.17 and 262.4.07 for the two benefices; the chaplaincy in ACB 76.4.4. Don Blasco is a character in Federico De Roberto's *I Viceré* (1894), a marvelous recreation of the decline and survival of a Sicilian aristocratic family in the nineteenth century. On Gennaro, see especially ACB 10.1., the

In the late seventeenth and early eighteenth centuries, an ecclesiastical career was often the only occupation open to aristocratic cadets. Several families established partial entails to support their sons in the clergy, and in 1737, Guglielmo Ruffo, prince of Scilla, earmarked part of his estate for a special fund "so that the cadet sons may comfortably fulfill the goal which is set for them, that is to enter the ecclesiastical state."[23] In the last generation of the Caracciolo Brienza, the marquis Litterio simply enjoined his two cadet sons to live as bachelors unless their brother reached the age of fifty-five without a surviving son. The injunction was obeyed. Not all cadets were happy with their lot, and the Brienza cadets in the eighteenth century were cause for embarrassment or expense for their family. There is no evidence that the Neapolitan aristocracy practiced any form of birth limitation. Indeed, the two wives of Litterio Caracciolo Brienza begat a total of twelve children. But certainly it was becoming difficult to deal with more than one or two cadet sons. It is perhaps legitimate to detect a hint of annoyance in the decision of the prince Caracciolo Santo Buono in the 1780s, having used up most of the traditional family names, to call his seventh and eighth sons Settimio and Ottavio.[24]

Cadet sons proved, therefore, to be the most dangerous element of the family for the aristocratic patrimony. The Neapolitan aristocracy was able to deal effectively with daughters and to turn even the claims of widows into potential advantages, as we shall soon see, but for cadets it never found a perfect solution. They were discouraged from marrying, and indeed seem to have done so only either in direct opposition to their family's will, or in circumstances in which the very biological survival of the family was at stake. The army and the church represented in Naples, as elsewhere, the usual lot of cadets, and there was a marked shift from the former to the latter after the mid-seventeenth century. Lombard law had almost disappeared from the kingdom, so that, unlike Piedmont where the fragmentation of inheritance was not rare, Neapolitan feudal law limited the amount of the feudal patrimony to which cadets were entitled to a small annuity added to their legal share of allodial assets; the life of cadets, therefore, was not an easy one. Overall, however, the Caracciolo Brienza,

trials in ACB 17.6 and 17.9, and ASN, Consulte originali del Collaterale VII, 14, fols. 351r–432v; Gennaro did indeed keep a concubine, but "without any complaints from his relatives," ACB 17.9i, fol. 134v.

[23] Quoted in Visceglia, "Linee," pp. 427–28. J. L. Goldsmith, *Les Salers et les d'Escorailles* (Clermont-Ferrand, 1984), p. 216, shows the opposite pattern, as cadet sons of the lower French aristocracy shifted from the church to the armies in the mid-seventeenth century.

[24] ACB 9.50 (Litterio's donation to his first son in 1806). The Santo Buono case is in ASN Museo 99B92, *Libro d'oro* (1807). The same choice of church or army faced the Piedmontese cadets, see Marchisio, "Ideologia," pp. 78–81, and Woolf, *Studi*, pp. 61–66, and 158–59. For examples of accepted celibacy in the nineteenth century see A. Moroni, "Le ricchezze dei Corsini. Struttura patrimoniale e vicende familiari tra Sette e Ottocento" *Società e storia* 9 (1986), pp. 255–92.

like many other families, succeeded in avoiding both any significant diminution of their patrimony, and the extinction of the family.[25]

Eldest sons and their marriages

We shall now look at the family members who were not barred from marriage, namely the eldest sons and the daughters. An examination of the marriage alliances of the Caracciolo Brienza will serve to illustrate the various factors which determined the size of dowries and the choice of spouses. Dowries grew generally throughout the early modern period; and the antiquity and traditions of the Caracciolo Brienza, their position in the *Seggi* of Naples, their previous alliances, and the actual cash value of the dowries they paid and received, play an important role in explaining the motivations and conditions of their marriage policy.

The eldest sons of the Caracciolo Brienza brought in much more in dowries than the family paid out until the later eighteenth century. The choice of their spouse was obviously the most important decision of each generation's policy. Until 1792, no man married before the death of his father. This was partly due to the relatively young age at death of most men of the family, but it was also an attempt to save on expenses, by having only one household live on the family income at any given time. Even in the lone instance of Cataldo Caracciolo's marriage in 1792, when his parents were both still alive, the new couple lived in the same palace with its elders. This was a common practice of the Neapolitan aristocracy.[26]

The amount of the dowries of Ippolita Filomarino, mother of the first marquis of Brienza, and of her son's two wives (Diana and Giulia Caracciolo), are not known, but Ippolita was able to buy three of the family's fiefs herself and to bequeath them to her son, and in 1580, Giulia Caracciolo bought Sasso for her own son. In 1590, Giovan Battista, second marquis of Brienza, married Diana Caracciolo Sicignano, who brought a dowry of 33,000 ducats, which proved essential, as will be seen below, to save the Brienza patrimony at her indebted husband's death. Their son Giacomo, heavily in debt and deprived of access to his family patrimony by royal courts, was the only marquis of Brienza to receive a

---

[25] Woolf, *Studi*, pp. 20–30; the legal aspects are discussed more closely in chapter 6. On cadets, see also Forster, *Toulouse*, pp. 126–31, and Forster, *Saulx-Tavanes*, pp. 132–35; in England, the strict settlement often excluded cadets from most of the family wealth, although by the eighteenth century one finds examples of more generosity towards cadets, see L. Stone, *Family and Fortune* (Oxford, 1973), G. E. Mingay, *The Gentry* (London, 1976), chapter 5, and G. Montroni, "Aristocrazia fondiaria e modelli di trasferimento della ricchezza in Inghilterra tra XVII e XIX secolo: lo 'Strict Settlement'" *Studi storici* 30 (1989), pp. 595–98.

[26] Marco Antonio II (d. 1621) and his nephew Giovan Battista (d. 1651), for instance, died at the age of twenty-eight and twenty-seven respectively without having married, probably because their fathers were either still alive, or had died shortly beforehand; see Delille, *Famille*, especially pp. 230–50. In France, the early age at marriage forced many Parisian aristocratic families in the eighteenth century to support two, or even three, households on one income, see Forster, *Saulx-Tavanes*, p. 50. Lévy and Henry, "Ducs et pairs."

small dowry – only about 5,000 ducats were acually paid – from his wife Maria Gesualdo, who belonged to a poor family of an old clan. Carlo Caracciolo Sant'Eramo, a relatively old cadet when he married, received 19,000 ducats as the dowry of his wife Cornelia. In 1658, Domenico, seventh marquis of Brienza, received a dowry of 46,000 ducats from his wife Cristina, which served to reinforce his claims on the whole Brienza patrimony.[27]

The marriage of the eighth marquis of Brienza to the daughter of an ennobled financier in 1688, illustrates how the amount and mode of payment of dowries were closely linked to the partners' needs and expectations in the alliance. It also illuminates the mechanism of the alliance of sword and finance. The indebted Giuseppe Caracciolo, who was trying to repurchase his alienated ancestral fiefs of Brienza and Pietrafesa, married Teresa, daughter of Emanuele Pinto, of a Portuguese family of financiers and bureaucrats which had become very wealthy in the kingdom of Naples in the later seventeenth century. Teresa's father held the *Scrivania di Razione*, one of the top financial offices of the kingdom and one of the highest venal ones, responsible for authorizing all government payments. He had become a member of the royal council, a knight of Calatrava, and, as recently as 1681, prince of Ischitella. He had married Geronima Capece Bozzuto, of the powerful Capece clan of the *Seggio* of Capuana. The arrogance of the family and its recent ascent into the aristocracy were noted with criticism by the chronicler Confuorto.[28]

Teresa received a dowry of 50,000 ducats. This was a very considerable sum, since at the time her groom's entire patrimony was worth about 200,000 ducats. But the main advantage of Teresa's dowry was its solidity. Most aristocratic dowries, in Naples as elsewhere, consisted in claims and annuities, often of difficult, always of slow and painful, exaction.[29] Teresa's dowry, however, came in hard cash. 30,000 ducats consisted of a deposit of 26,000 ducats in a bank

[27] Diana's and Cristina's dowries will be discussed later in this chapter. Cornelia's dowry is in ACB 11.1.20. Maria Gesualdo was the daughter of the lord of Santo Stefano, second son of the lord of Ruvo and Pescopagano, all lands near Brienza. Her nominal dowry was 30,000 ducats, but most of it was never paid. Maria and Giacomo's daughter was to marry her cousin on her mother's side, but he died before the marriage took place, see C. de Lellis, *Discorsi delle famiglie nobili del regno di Napoli* (3 vols.; Naples, 1654–71; reprint Bologna, 1968), II, p. 24.

[28] D. Confuorto, *Giornali di Napoli dal MDCLXXIX al MDCIC* (2 vols.; Naples, 1930), see the index. The Pinto title is in ASN Museo 99B136, 137, 138, and in AGS Secretarías provinciales Nápoles 250, fols. 240vff., 6 April, 1681. Another chronicler, I. Fuidoro, *Giornali di Napoli dal MDCLX al MDCLXXX* (3 vols.; Naples, 1934–39), refers to "don Emanuel Flettespint [Freitas Pinto], rich Portuguese" (III, p. 252), and mentions his purchase of the hereditary Scrivania office for three generations for 46,000 ducats in 1675 (III, p. 267); on the Pinto, see also V. Pacelli, "La collezione di Francesco Emanuele Pinto, principe di Ischitella" *Storia dell'arte* 11 (1979), nos. 36–37, pp. 165–204; on the Scrivania's revenues, see R. Mantelli, *Il pubblico impiego nell'economia del regno di Napoli* (Naples, 1986), pp. 389, 416, and 435.

[29] See Forster, *Toulouse*, chapter 6, on the mode of payment of aristocratic dowries; Woolf, *Studi*, pp. 31–35, 53–56, 102–8, and 153–58. For instance, when in 1628 the marquis del Vasto married Geronima Doria, daughter of the prince of Melfi, one of the most important aristocratic marriages in the century, less than twenty-five percent of the 98,000 ducats dowry was in cash, see Colapietra, *Dal Magnanimo* II, pp. 444–45.

account, 2,000 ducats worth of jewels, and a cash gift of 2,000 ducats at the wedding. 12,542 ducats were in capital on tax-farms with guaranteed yields, 3,000 ducats were a cash gift from Teresa's father, and the remaining 4,458 ducats Teresa's father pledged to pay within four months of the wedding. This money was to be earmarked for the purchase of Giuseppe's alienated fiefs, accomplished in 1690, and only for that purpose could it be freed from the usual limitations imposed on dotal money.

In return for this welcome infusion of capital, Giuseppe provided the Pinto family with the social credentials necessary to enter Neapolitan high society. After the wedding, for example, Teresa's brother and nephew began calling themselves Caracciolo Pinto Capece Bozzuto, and the nephew was later admitted to the *Seggio* of Porto. The marriage, in 1718, of Teresa's daughter, Giulia, with her cousin, Francesco Emanuele Pinto, did not serve, therefore, the purpose of returning a dowry – far from it – but rather reinforced the Pintos' claim to membership in the high aristocracy of the kingdom.[30] In 1695, Teresa's brother, Luigi Pinto, prince of Ischitella, married another Caracciolo woman and was made a knight of Saint James, in a ceremony at which the prince of Cellamare and Marino Carafa acted as patrons. The alliance of new wealth – however much ennobled – and old name did not meet with general approval, and was in fact relatively rare in Naples. Confuorto criticized the marriage of Giuseppe and Teresa and considered that the dowry – which he thought was of 30,000 ducats – was "a small dowry for such a marriage, but so great is the poverty of this nobility that it is no surprise that they should do it." Confuorto and other chroniclers mentioned similar alliances and hinted at disapproval within the aristocratic families. It was the marriages of aristocratic men with women of apparently lower birth that met with most criticism, while this rarely happened when aristocratic women married below their rank. An important exception is the notorious and politically charged instance in 1640 when the aristocracy almost staged an urban revolt in order to prevent the marriage of Anna Acquaviva, sister of the count of Conversano, to the upstart financier Bartolomeo d'Aquino, but in this case the motivations went far beyond the rejection of *mésalliance*.[31]

---

30 The contract in ACB 3.2.7. For the later membership of the Pinto in the *Seggio* of Porto, see ACB 3.2.8. (a genealogy of the family), and ASN Museo 99B92, the *Libro d'oro* (1807). The earliest book on the Neapolitan aristocracy to mention the Pinto is Aldimari (1691), though they are not yet in the *Seggi* at that date. All occasions were used to mark social ascent. Teresa's own godparents in 1668 had been the prince Caracciolo Santo Buono, and the princess d'Avalos Ottajano, ACB 3.1.7.

31 Confuorto, *Giornali*, II, pp. 153 and 175 for Luigi, and I, p. 213 for his comment on Teresa's marriage. In 1693, the duke of Fragnito of the Montalto family married a woman of another branch of the Pinto "with a rich dowry," and Confuorto mentions the approval of the duke's mother and the "great revulsion" of the duke's sister and of her husband, the prince Filomarino della Rocca (II, p. 51). Fuidoro (*Giornali*, I, p. 304) mentions the marriage in 1665 of the duke of Celenza – another Caracciolo – to the daughter of the prince of Misciagna, Benedetto d'Angelo, "who had been born a *popolare* [commoner]," with a "large" dowry of 70,000 ducats: "the whole

In 1722, Giuseppe and Teresa's heir, Domenico, ninth marquis of Brienza, married Imara, daughter of Francesco Ruffo Bagnara, of an untitled family of the Ruffo clan, one of the oldest and wealthiest of the Sicilian aristocracy, with claims to a Roman republican origin. Imara was the only child of the heiress Teodora Alberti, marquise of Pentidattilo and duchess of Melito, and brought a dowry valued at 50,000 ducats, consisting in properties in Messina and Calabria, and annuities and claims belonging to her late father. The actual value of the dowry was open to doubt. Property in Messina had lost value after the revolt of the 1670s, and the end of the Spanish Habsburgs had led to repeated dynastic changes both in Sicily and in Naples, so that the services of Imara's father had not always been to the winning side. Imara's claim on her mother's possessions, however, made marrying her a very profitable enterprise. Her second marriage to a cousin, Paolo Ruffo, prince of Castelcicala, was childless, so that when she and her mother died in the 1750s, her only son, Litterio Caracciolo, tenth marquis of Brienza, inherited the whole Alberti patrimony.

Nothing is known about the intermediaries who arranged this or other aristocratic marriages, but again the Caracciolo Brienza could offer a prominent position in the aristocracy of the capital. The Ruffo had never been related to the Caracciolo Brienza, and their status was above improvement, but until the early eighteenth century they had been based mainly in Sicily and had only recently become members of the *Seggio* of Porto in Naples. With the Alberti fiefs in Calabria, consideration of the decline of Messina, and of the separation between 1707 and 1734 of Sicily from Naples, probably urged Imara Ruffo to look for an eligible marriage among the high Neapolitan aristocracy.[32]

Litterio, tenth marquis of Brienza, married twice, both times with non-Neapolitan women. His first wife, in 1745, was Lavinia Bonelli (d. 1759), daughter of the duke of Selci. She belonged to the Roman aristocracy and

Caracciolo clan [*casa*] disapproved; but the duke said 'Who of my clan [*casata*] or family [*famiglia*] will pay the debts of my house?' and so he was forced to this marriage." For d'Aquino, see F. Capecelatro, *Degli annali della città di Napoli 1631–1640* (Naples, 1849), pp. 200–9, and A. Musi, *Finanze e politica nella Napoli del '600: Bartolomeo d'Aquino* (Naples, 1976). *Mésalliances* were much more common among the eighteenth-century aristocracy in Paris, see G. Chaussinand-Nogaret, *The French Nobility in the Eighteenth Century, from Feudalism to Enlightenment* (Cambridge, 1985; French edit. 1976), pp. 117–29, whereas J. Cannon, *Aristocratic Century. The Peerage of Eighteenth-Century England* (Cambridge, 1987; I edit. 1984), chapter 3, sees them as still rather limited.

32 The contract is in ACB 3.2.15. ACB 3.2.15bis has the contract between Imara and Paolo, and 17 and 19 consist in genealogies of the Ruffo and Alberti families (the latter included Leon Battista di Lorenzo "*scrittore celebre*"). Paolo entered into a long lawsuit with the Caracciolo Brienza, but his lawful claim was only to one tenth of Imara's dowry, see ACB 139.22, 28–I, and 28–II. Imara's will is in ACB 4.1.52bis. All the books on the nobility mention the Ruffo, but only in 1691 Aldimari reports their very recent entry in the *Seggio* of Porto (*Memorie*, pp. 136–39). Capecelatro, *Origine della città e delle famiglie nobili di Napoli* (Naples, 1769; written in the 1630s; reprint Cosenza, 1989), repeatedly mentions the greatness of the Ruffo (pp. 47, and 86) and lists them among the greatest families who, because of their "foreign" origins, are not yet members of any *Seggio* (p. 169).

Aristocratic family strategies

brought a dowry of 20,000 Roman *scudi* (c. 24,000 ducats) which had to be returned when all of her children died without heirs. In 1767, Litterio married the widow Sofia Ruffo, a noble woman from Fermo in the Marches, unrelated to the Sicilian Ruffo, whom Litterio probably met during his tour of Italy in 1766. Remarkably, this marriage seems to be the only one among those studied here and those analyzed by Visceglia contracted for explicitly personal, sentimental, reasons. Sofia indeed had a dowry from her first marriage, but since it was much below "what was customary among the magnates" of Naples, Litterio, "believing her spiritual qualities [in Italian *doti*, which is the same word as dowry] to conform to his temperament [*genio*]" married her "without any dowry or trousseau, being contented with the qualities [*doti*] of her spirit, which he prefers to any rich patrimonial dowry [*dote*]." In 1792, Litterio and Sofia's first son, Cataldo, married Teresa, daughter of Luigi Serra, duke of Cassano, of a Genoese family which had acquired fiefs in the kingdom in the seventeenth century. The Serra lived in a palace neighboring the Caracciolo Brienza's, and had long before entered the *Seggi* of Naples. Teresa's dowry was 60,000 ducats, but it was not paid in full.[33]

The eldest sons of the Caracciolo Brienza all married in the highest and oldest aristocracy of the kingdom. The only, partial, exception to the rule – the Pinto were after all very quickly collecting all the marks of nobility – can be explained by the specific financial situation of the family at that point, and brought in by far the largest and most secure dowry ever to come the Caracciolo Brienza's way. Also with their daughters, the Caracciolo Brienza, like all other aristocratic families, could not afford to lapse in their choice of marriage partners.

Daughters

The Neapolitan aristocracy was perhaps unique in only partially limiting the number of daughters who were allowed to marry. Whereas cadet sons were actively discouraged from marrying, and had to enter military or ecclesiastic careers to support themselves, most daughters did marry without having to accept a significant diminution in their social standing. Among the many descendants of Domizio Caracciolo Rosso (d. 1498) up to the early seventeenth century, it is possible to identify the lot of at least twenty women, only one of whom entered a nunnery. Although it is, of course, more likely that a daughter who became a nun should escape the attention of genealogists than that they should overlook a woman who helped form a prestigious alliance, this difference between the lot of daughters and cadets is striking. Even in the seventeenth century, the Caracciolo families placed only a few of their daughters in convents.

[33] Contracts in ACB 3.2.20–23, 28 (quoted also in Visceglia, "Linee," p. 470, footnote 175), and 44–48; on the Serra, see G. Labrot, "Naissance et croissance d'un quartier de Naples: Pizzofalcone, 1530–1689" *Urbi* I (1979), p. 56.

175

The clan devised ways, as will be seen later, to provide large dowries without placing excessive strain on the family finances. This enabled daughters to marry men of suitable status, and prevented enforced and insincere religious vocations.[34]

The religious life remained the destiny of several aristocratic daughters, especially if their families went through economic hard times. In 1632, for example, the will of Carlo Caracciolo Celenza mentions seven women of the clan in convents, and in 1710 there were at least twelve Carafa nuns in the convents of Naples. In 1642, Naples had at least thirty-seven enclosed female convents. In 1772, the Caracciolo had no fewer than thirty-three women of the clan in sixteen convents. Aristocratic nuns tended to be more numerous in a few most prestigious convents, especially in Donnaregina and San Gregorio, a Benedictine convent which was the richest in Naples and where all the nuns were of aristocratic birth. But this was not a generalized policy, and whenever possible families tried to avoid it, out of concern for the dangers of imposing the religious life on unwilling women. Only during the worst period for the family finances – the years 1620 to 1660 – did the Caracciolo Brienza place their daughters in convents. Two of the three daughters of both Giovan Battista, marquis of Brienza, and Carlo Caracciolo Sant'Eramo became nuns. In both instances, it seems, the eldest daughter was the one allowed to marry. No other woman in the family entered a convent after this generation.[35]

The relative success of the policy of allowing most daughters to marry while limiting cadet sons' access to marriage, poses an obvious arithmetical question which it is difficult to answer through the study of one family. Possible solutions, however, include the different rates of remarriage between men and women: widowers almost always remarried, widows rarely did. More importantly, at least in the case of the high aristocracy of the kingdom, it seems that men almost always married women from the highest families, while their sisters often married members of junior families (in terms of antiquity or wealth). Giacomo

---

[34] See Table I. The Piedmontese aristocracy seems to have been less fastidious. Faced with his brother's twelve daughters, archbishop Gontery suggested, one wonders how facetiously, to build a convent large enough to house them all, see Marchisio, "Ideologia," p. 75. Looking particularly at Northern Italian patriciates, D. Owen Hughes concludes that between one half and three fourths of aristocratic women entered a convent, "Representing the Family: Portraits and Purpose in Early Modern Italy" *Journal of Interdisciplinary History* 17 (1986), p. 29.

[35] Carlo Caracciolo Celenza's will is in ACB 4.1.17; the twelve Carafa nuns appear in ASBN, Banco della Pietà, Pandetta II for 1710; for the 1772 figure, see ACB 7.6.6., the budget of the *Monte Cassa Grande*. The church and cloister of San Gregorio are still today among the most beautiful in Naples; on San Gregorio's wealth and the number of convents, see C. Russo, *I monasteri femminili di clausura a Napoli nel secolo XVII* (Naples, n.d.); on Donnaregina, see Villani, *et al.*, eds. *Nunziature di Napoli* (3 vols.; Rome, 1962–70), III, pp. 168–71. The nuns of the family, apart from the genealogies, are mentioned in some of the wills, see ACB 4.1.17, 22, 22 bis, 27, 37, and 45. One daughter of Faustina, Anna Gambacorta, was in a convent in Celenza at her mother's death in 1673. On post-Tridentine convents and their social function, see A. D. Wright, *The Counter-Reformation* (New York, 1982), pp. 47–49.

Aristocratic family strategies

Caracciolo, fourth marquis of Brienza, was the only marquis of his family to marry a woman from a poorer and untitled family within a great clan, and that marriage came at the nadir of the family's fortunes. Women also seem to have played a crucial role in the relations between the various strata of the kingdom's elite. Although, according to aristocratic theory of the time, a woman had the status of her husband, a woman from an old feudal family might marry a man from an ascending robe or finance family – provided the latter had had the decency to acquire lands and preferably a title as well – before that woman's titled brother would marry into the newer family. As we have seen, the chroniclers seem to criticize more harshly this latter type of union.[36]

In their daughters' marriages, the Caracciolo families were able to compensate for an, at-times, precarious economic situation with the prestige attached to an old and powerful name, and with their prominent position within the aristocracy of the *Seggi*. The Caracciolo's institutional position as one third of the *Seggio* of Capuana, in its turn one sixth of the city government of Naples, placed them in a particularly favored position when making marriage alliances. "The strength of Capuana," Galasso has written, "means especially, if not essentially, the strength of the Caracciolo." Visceglia has quoted the example of a family (the Muscettola) supporting its application for admission to the *Seggio* of Montagna with the fact that its wives had come from the Sanfelice and Seripando families, of old *Seggio* stock, and the statutes of some *Seggi* required or favored applicants for aggregation to have contracted marriages with the families already in the *Seggio*. Similar rationales were probably behind some of the Caracciolo Brienza's alliances. Marriage to a Caracciolo Brienza was advantageous to many smaller or newer families, since it allied them with one of the most prestigious clans in Naples and provided access to the patronage network that was the *Seggio* of Capuana.[37]

In arranging their daughters' marriages, the Caracciolo fathers had to set the size of dowries and to decide whether to look for a husband within the clan itself or outside of it. In general, the dowries given and received by the Caracciolo Brienza were high compared to the value of their patrimony, although they never approached the sums Visceglia considers very high.[38] The dowries given by the

[36] See footnote 31; for aristocratic theory of the time on women's status, see G. B. de Luca, *Il cavaliere*, especially chapter 27 (the book draws its examples mainly from the Neapolitan aristocracy).

[37] Galasso, "Ideologia e sociologia del patronato di San Tommaso d'Aquino su Napoli (1605)" in Galasso and C. Russo, eds. *Per la storia sociale e religiosa del Mezzogiorno d'Italia* (2 vols.; Naples, 1980–82), II, p. 223. Visceglia, "Formazione," pp. 565–67. Another example of social ascent through marriage with *Seggio* families, first in the provinces, then in Naples, is the Orefice family, see Pilati, "La dialettica," pp. 180–81, footnote 123. For the statutes of Nido on the question of marriage, see G. Vitale, "La nobiltà di Seggio a Napoli nel basso Medioevo: aspetti della dinamica interna" *ASPN* 106 (1988), pp. 151–69, which also emphasizes the strength of clan solidarity in the internal power dynamic of the *Seggi*. The *Seggi* of Capuana and Nido were considered to be one third of the city, the other three *Seggi* and the Popolo representing the other two thirds.

[38] Visceglia, "Linee," pp. 434–59.

family amounted in general, in the seventeenth century, to about fifteen to thirty percent of the total value of the fiefs, or to the revenues of four to eight years, which is, for instance, more than the nobles of Toulouse, Piedmont, or Verona could afford to give their daughters. Though dowries grew in Naples as across Western Europe, especially with the predominance of primogeniture, their rate of growth was never as high as, for instance, in Stuart England, which witnessed an increase six times higher than the rate of inflation. During the seventeenth century in particular, Neapolitan aristocratic dowries grew moderately, as did inflation. Until the early eighteenth century, the dowries the Caracciolo Brienza received were on average larger than those they gave, which again shows that even a relatively new and modest family of the Caracciolo clan could attract important alliances. The Caracciolo Brienza's alliances show no regular pattern, such as the tendency to marry primarily into three specific other families that Visceglia identified in some of the examples she analyzed.[39]

The degree of intermarriage within the Caracciolo clan was high until the early seventeenth century when there were more Caracciolo families and more children had access to marriage. After 1650, I have found only one instance of a marriage between two members of the clan – indeed two very distant ones – and excessive endogamy was perceived, in the eighteenth century, as harmful to the family's health.[40] Before 1650, several of the descendants of Domizio Caracciolo Rosso – himself married to a Caracciolo – married within the clan. At least twelve such marriages can be identified, not counting Domizio's own. The first and the second marquis of Brienza both married women from the clan (the father married two of them, of the Vico and Avellino families), as did Ascanio Caracciolo in 1540 and Carlo Caracciolo Sant'Eramo, who married Cornelia Caracciolo Celenza, widow of two other Caracciolo. These marriages strengthened clan solidarity and could be used to support one family in difficult moments with a large dowry. As has already been seen, Giuseppe Caracciolo in 1655 underlined the prestige of having all his four quarters from the clan.

Remarriages were also frequent. Men would invariably remarry, if their wives died early, which was not rare, in particular in childbirth. In three centuries, only one member of the family here studied died a widower, Giovan Battista Caracciolo, marquis of Sant'Eramo (d. 1631), who had been married for forty-four years to Porzia Carafa (d. 1618). Women remarried less frequently, but it was less expensive for a family to find a second husband for a widowed

[39] Forster, *Toulouse*, chapter 6, particularly p. 132; Visceglia, "Linee" and "Formazione"; Woolf, *Studi*, pp. 153–58; G. Borelli, "Nozze e doti in una famiglia nobiliare durante la prima metà del XVIII secolo" *Economia e storia* 8 (1971), pp. 321–42; on the origins of dowries and their growth, see Owen Hughes, "From Brideprice to Dowry in Mediterranean Europe" in M. A. Kaplan, ed. *Women and History*, X, *The Marriage Bargain* (1985), pp. 13–54; on aristocratic dowries in Europe, see Cooper, "Patterns"; on England, see Stone, "Marriage among the English Nobility in the Sixteenth and Seventeenth Centuries" *Comparative Studies in Society and History* 3 (1960), 182–206.
[40] Visceglia, "Linee," pp. 434–41. See the genealogical sources cited in chapter 1.

daughter than to marry a yet unmarried one, because the original dowry could be reused without any additional expense. The Caracciolo Brienza offer three examples of widows remarrying once or twice.[41] Visceglia observes a pattern of marriages between crossed cousins in successive generations, and links it to an attempt to avoid real transfers of dowry money: the same money would simply be returned to the first family after one generation. I have found no evidence of this pattern, and the only instance of two marriages of cousins in two successive generations in the Caracciolo Brienza – with the Pinto – responded to different goals and needs, as we have seen.[42]

No daughter of the Caracciolo Brienza family ever entered a *mésalliance*, although sometimes a spouse with a resounding name belonged to a poorer family of a prestigious clan. In fact, the prestige of some clans allowed for marriages with families that, in terms of actual wealth, might have been considered of lower status in other countries. In the first generations of the Caracciolo Brienza, the daughters all married members of old aristocratic families, such as the Loffredo, del Tufo, di Capua, Cavaniglia, di Somma, Minutolo, Gesualdo, della Marra, Carafa, Seripando, di Sangro, and della Leonessa, all but one of which were members of the *Seggi* of Capuana or Nido, and all of which were mentioned in the most important contemporary books on the Neapolitan nobility. Most of the husbands had lordships, and many were titled themselves, or belonged to titled families. Considering that at this time the large inflation of titles was just beginning, the marquisate of Brienza was very recent, and Ascanio's branch still untitled, these alliances show the weight the Caracciolo had within the aristocracy. A sample of the patrimonies of the men these women married, taken from royal fiscal documents, shows that several of them belonged to wealthy families, at times wealthier than the Caracciolo Brienza, and indeed a few, such as the di Capua dukes of Termoli or the Carafa counts of Montorio, considerably wealthier.[43] Few data exist on the dowries of these Caracciolo daughters. The dowries of the daughters of Ascanio and Aurelia Caracciolo – who had herself brought 10,500 ducats to her husband in

---

[41] Cornelia Caracciolo, wife – eventually – of Carlo Caracciolo Sant'Eramo, and Imara Ruffo and her mother, Teodora Alberti, in the eighteenth century.

[42] Visceglia, "Linee," pp. 448–49.

[43] See the contemporary bibliography on the Neapolitan nobility, especially Ammirato and Aldimari, as well as the descriptions of Naples containing lists of *Seggi* members, such as Contarino, Mazzella, Costo, Beltrano, Capecelatro, and Tutini, all cited in chapter 1. The del Tufo did not belong to a *Seggio*, but both Costo (1613) and Capecelatro, *Origine*, count them among the old titled families. The sample is based on ASN Petizioni dei relevi, Significatorie dei relevi, and Taxis Adohae; for the di Capua Significatorie 1–I, fols. 78r–79r (1513); Taxis Adohae 105–I, fols. 112r–v (1540); 109, fols. 169v–70r (1560); 112, fol. 160v (1595); 113, fols. 22v–23r (1599); D'Ambrosio, "La feudalità," pp. 42–47; for the Carafa, see ASN Petizioni 30–I, fols. 48v–50v (1569). There are almost no examples of marriages between daughters of high feudal families and men of the provincial nobility: see Caridi, *Uno "stato" feudale nel Mezzogiorno spagnolo* (Rome, 1988), p. 115, when the sister and cousin of the impoverished Vespasiano Carafa received dowries of only 1,000 and 2,000 ducats for their marriages to provincial notables.

1540 – were slightly below 10,000 ducats, but there were five of them, and four sons, to take care of.[44]

In the seventeenth century, fewer women of the Caracciolo Brienza married, but they received larger dowries. Faustina, daughter of Giovan Battista, second marquis of Brienza, married Carlo Gambacorta, marquis of Celenza, and later also prince of Macchia, in 1621. She brought a dowry of 30,000 ducats, slightly smaller than her mother Diana's, thirty-one years before; and she received very favorable conditions in her contract from Andrea Gambacorta, the groom's father, who donated all of his patrimony to his son on his marriage except for an annual revenue. This arrangement, though not too rare, shows the interest of the Gambacorta – a family recently titled, and of vague Pisan origins – in an alliance with the Caracciolo.[45] Faustina's own daughter, Cristina, and the importance of her dowry will be discussed below. In 1683, Faustina, daughter of Domenico, seventh marquis of Brienza, married Orazio Tuttavilla, duke of Calabritto, of a family of remote French origin and old membership in the *Seggio* of Porto. The groom, whose grandfather had led the royal army in 1647–48, had a higher title than the Caracciolo Brienza and a larger patrimony. The price for this prestigious match was 40,000 ducats, the highest dowry the Caracciolo Brienza paid before the late eighteenth century. The fact that Faustina was an only daughter probably explains this extravagant alliance.[46]

Four daughters of Giuseppe, eighth marquis of Brienza, reached adulthood, and they all married between 1709 and 1718, each with a dowry of 39,000 ducats, only part of which came directly from their father. The main dowry fund of the clan paid the four brides 27,000 to 31,000 ducats each. The husbands included two dukes, a marquis (of the Caracciolo clan), and the prince of Ischitella. In 1765, Teresa, daughter of Litterio, tenth marquis of Brienza,

---

[44] ACB 2.4, a report, dated 1579, to the *Sommaria* from Aurelia detailing her husband's services to the crown and the heavy burdens of her large family, and asking for support. Around 1580, 10,000 ducats was a fairly common dowry for women also of the *togati* elite, see Pilati, "La dialettica," p. 213.

[45] Visceglia, "Linee," for donations from fathers; the marriage contract is in ACB 3.2.3. Carlo's father's estate passed to Carlo on his marriage, according to the fiscal document drawn at his father's death, ASN Petizioni 49–I, fols. 202r–6v (1624). The Gambacorta were not in the *Seggi*, although Costo and Capecelatro mention them among the titled families; the latter, *Origine*, pp. 83 and 169, extols their greatness and lists them among the non-*Seggio* foreign families. According to Mazzella (*Descrittione*, p. 545), they were made marquis of Celenza in 1598. Their elevation to the title of prince of Macchia in 1641 is mentioned by A. Bulifon, *Giornali di Napoli dal MDXLVII al MDCCVI* (Naples, 1932), p. 177, and in ASN Museo 99B135 (a list of the titles given by the Spanish government). On the Gambacorta, see also G. Intorcia, *Magistrature del regno di Napoli. Analisi prosopografica, secoli XVI–XVII* (Naples, 1987), p. 315, which lists the provincial governorships held by the family (and where the marquisate of Celenza is dated to 1589); AGS Secretarías provinciales Nápoles 200, fols. 96vff. and 140vff. of 17 April and 18 July 1641, with the bestowing of the principate of Macchia.

[46] On the long lawsuit over the payment of this dowry, see ACB 10.3. On the patrimony of the Tuttavilla, see ASN Significatorie relevi 30–I, fols. 58v–60v (1592); 85, fols. 209r–15r (1699); Relevi 247 (1678; a large volume of over 500 fols.).

married Gaetano Sforza Cesarini, duke of Segni, a Roman aristocrat. Teresa received at least 60,000 ducats from the dowry funds to which she was eligible, in addition to 8,000 ducats from her father. This short-lived marriage – Teresa died two years later – was the only instance of marriage outside the Neapolitan aristocracy, except for Litterio's own two marriages. Marriage with non-Neapolitans presumably became more common in the eighteenth century, as the aristocracy travelled abroad more often and acquired a more cosmopolitan lifestyle. Litterio's other daughter, Carmela, married in 1793 the duke Pignatelli Monteleone, possibly the wealthiest nobleman in the kingdom, with a dowry of 88,000 ducats, only 8,000 of which her father paid himself. To give an idea of the enormous value of these dowries, the oligarchs of Puglia's royal towns, with all of their aristocratic claims, could only afford dowries of 2,000 ducats in the late eighteenth century.[47]

With the exception of three or four decades in the mid-seventeenth century, therefore, the family managed to marry all of its daughters. The alliances were always formed with families of high status. The complex stratification within the aristocracy meant, however, that membership in a clan and in the *Seggi* – and also in which *Seggio* – as well as the specific demographic circumstances of each family, were at least as important as the actual wealth of a family in influencing the parties' decision. Though the actual process of selection of a prospective spouse is not known to us, the city of Naples, like Paris, constituted the appropriate marriage market for the high aristocracy of the kingdom, and we have seen that the Caracciolo Brienza moved to Naples from the fiefs when their children reached marriageable age. In the city, the position and prestige associated with the various clans and *Seggi* was made more evident and therefore relevant to family choices. Their position within the large and powerful Caracciolo clan enabled the Caracciolo Brienza to have a profitable marriage policy, marked by receiving larger dowries than the family paid.[48]

But the clan also proved useful in more tangible ways. Although the incoming dowries were often larger than the outgoing ones, it is remarkable that the Caracciolo Brienza could afford to marry off almost all of their daughters, whereas they disposed of only one incoming dowry per generation. This feat was achieved through institutions that the Caracciolo clan, like others in Naples, established to allow its members to pursue a successful and effective policy of alliances. The reality and strength of solidarity within the clan appears not only

---

[47] The contracts are in ACB 3.2.9, 10, 11, 13, 14, and 25; for Teresa's wedding, see also ACB 141.62; Carmela's wedding is in ACB 161, unnumbered fol.; the *Monte di Ciarletta*'s contributions to these dowries appear in ACB App. 1. On Puglia, see Spagnoletti, "Forme di autocoscienza e vita nobiliare: il caso della Puglia barese" *Società e storia* 6 (1983), pp. 49–76. On many of these questions, see Cowan, *The Urban Patriciate*, chapters 5 and 6.

[48] Paris, Turin, and undoubtedly all other capitals played the same role as marriage markets, see Forster, *Saulx-Tavanes*, chapter 3; Woolf, *Studi*, pp. 153–58; Chaussinand–Nogaret, *French Nobility*, pp. 117–29.

through the dowry funds, but also through other common initiatives dedicated to devotion or to the education of members of the clan.

THE CLAN'S WELFARE INSTITUTIONS

Stuart Woolf, in his study of the Piedmontese nobility in the early modern period, has pointed to the heavy burden of dowries as the main cause of the economic decline of the aristocracy, and the same problem faced the aristocracy of all European countries. Though the Neapolitan aristocracy did not have access to the court dowries available to its Piedmontese counterparts, it gave large dowries to its daughters and this endangered its economic situation. Particularly in the second half of the sixteenth century, when new groups were beginning, with royal encouragement, to seek entrance into the landed and titled elite, it became necessary for the old aristocracy to protect its social pre-eminence. Its feudal and military traditions, its lack of involvement to any significant degree in commercial or manufacturing ventures, and the emphasis on purity of blood in line with Spanish ideas, help explain why the Neapolitan aristocracy was reluctant to admit new blood into its ranks. A strong concern with insincere vocation, and the colorful scandals taking place in Neapolitan convents throughout the sixteenth and seventeenth centuries, would have helped convince many aristocratic fathers of the unadvisability of placing daughters in convents. Since, however, it was undesirable for a woman of any social class to remain lay and nubile, aristocrats had to lower the cost of dowries. In order to do this they used an institution common in the kingdom by the sixteenth century, the *Monte di maritaggi*, or dowry fund.[49]

Confraternities, guilds, villages, and kinship groups established corporate dowry funds, known as *Monti*, and money for dowries was a very common form of charitable bequest. In fact, many aristocrats left money for dowries for poor women of their fiefs, usually in amounts of twelve to twenty-five ducats. The hospital of the Annunziata, an old and large charitable institution in Naples associated with the *Seggio* of Capuana, and also a public bank from 1587 to 1702, received and managed bequests to dower some of its poor inmates so that they might find suitable husbands. The provincial aristocracy also established *Monti* in the sixteenth century, as for example did the *Seggio* of Porta in the town of Sorrento. Chapels and congregations even in small towns, as well as the

---

[49] Woolf, *Studi*, pp. 153–58; Marchisio ("Ideologia," pp. 74–77) refers to the same problem, and on p. 71 she briefly mentions dowry funds, but the topic is not touched on again in her article; Forster, *Toulouse*, chapter 6, and *Saulx-Tavanes*, chapter 3. The attitude towards spinsterhood was different in France, where nubile aristocratic daughters were numerous, though the subject of satire (Forster, *Toulouse*, p. 126); Heers, *Le clan*, pp. 244–46, on the use of clan funds for poor relatives in Genoa; G. W. Pedlow, *The Survival of the Hessian Nobility* (Princeton, 1988), pp. 33–34, reports the creation, after the abolition of convents, of a foundation of dower aristocratic daughters.

università themselves, distributed contributions for marriages or nuns' dowries. Many family *Monti* existed also in small towns, and there were at least two in Brienza in 1668.[50] These *Monti* bore no relation to the *Monte delle doti* of Florence, which was a form of public debt, and indeed they seem to have been an institution peculiar to the kingdom of Naples. Although the *Monti* often began to make loans to subscribers and outsiders, they remained private institutions until their eventual dissolution under the Napoleonic monarchy, and some actually survived even that unfortunate moment.[51]

In the early sixteenth century, the high aristocracy of the kingdom began to establish its own *Monti*, on the basis of the clan or *Seggio*. By the seventeenth century, one or more *Monti* existed for almost every clan. The indexes of the banks' records, for example, show at least one *Monte* for the Carafa, several for the Capece, many *Monti* for the Caracciolo, and the *Monte dei Giunti* and the *Monte delle ventinove famiglie*. These two last united members of different clans. A *Monte* was founded in 1639 by a hundred noblemen of different clans "as since a long time many others have been founded." Other sources mention a *Monte dei Ruffi*, a *Monte* of the Muscettola, and the *Monte di Manso*.[52]

The *Monti* allowed, if managed with a modicum of honesty and efficiency,

---

50 For examples of bequests for dowries in the fiefs, see ACB 4.1, the wills. On the Annunziata, see G. B. D'Addosio, *Origine, vicende storiche e progressi della Real Santa Casa dell'Annunziata di Napoli* (Naples, 1883). For Sorrento, see ASN Museo 99B121 (my thanks to Patrizia Aversa for this reference). Also C. Belli, "Famiglia, proprietà e classi sociali a Montefusco nella prima metà del secolo XVII" *MEFRM* 95 (1983), pp. 357–58, footnote 40; G. Delille, "Un esempio di assistenza privata: i Monti di maritaggio nel regno di Napoli (secoli XVI–XVIII)" in *Timore e carità: i poveri nell'Italia moderna*, acts of the conference *Pauperismo e assistenza negli antichi stati italiani* held in Cremona in March 1980 (Cremona, 1982); Delille, "L'ordine dei villaggi e l'ordine dei campi. Per uno studio antropologico del paesaggio agrario nel regno di Napoli (secoli XV–XVIII)" in *Storia d'Italia Einaudi. Annali VIII Insediamenti e territorio* (Turin, 1978), p. 515. For the *Monti* in Brienza, see ACB 50.1.1 and ASV, Sacra Congregazione del Concilio, *Relationes ad limina* 491, Marsicen, for 1714, unnumbered fol.

51 A. Molho, "Investimenti nel Monte delle doti di Firenze, un'analisi sociale e geografica" *QS* 21 (1986), pp. 147–70; in Siena, the *Monti* were quasi-political institutions, see D. Marrara, *Riseduti e nobiltà. Profilo storico-istituzionale di un'oligarchia toscana nei secoli XVI–XVIII* (Pisa, 1976); a sort of *Monte* to give subsidies to poorer nobles existed in Siena, see O. Di Simplicio, "Sulla 'nobiltà povera' a Siena nel Seicento" *Bullettino senese di storia patria* 88 (1982), pp. 71–94. Several Caracciolo Brienza received loans from the *Monti*: for the *Monti*'s budgets, see ACB 7, 11.1 (loans to Carlo Caracciolo Sant'Eramo), and App. 21.

52 ASBN, Pandette (see Appendix on sources); the *Monte dei Ruffi* is mentioned in ACB 18.89 and 8.44–46; the *Monte Muscettola* was established in 1613, see Visceglia, "Formazione," p. 563. On the *Monte di Manso*, founded in 1608 by Giovan Battista Manso, marquis of Villa, see M. Manfredi, *Giovan Battista Manso nella vita e nelle opere* (Naples, 1919); the *Monte di Manso* was the only institution in the city of Naples which had, among its administrators, both noblemen of the *Seggi* and noblemen of other families. The founder had, in fact, designated forty families from the non-*Seggio* aristocracy who had a right to be governors of his *Monte* and to enjoy its benefits, see V. Di Sangro, *Famiglie del patriziato napoletano e delle nobili fuori Seggio ascritte al Real Monte di G. B. Manso marchese di Villa dall'anno 1608 ad oggi* (Naples, 1886); for the 1639 *Monte* see Capecelatro, *Annali*, p. 144; on the *Monti* see also G. Muto, "Gestione del potere e classi sociali nel Mezzogiorno spagnolo" in A. Tagliaferri, ed. *I ceti dirigenti in Italia in età moderna e contemporanea* (Udine, 1984), p. 292.

many aristocratic women to receive a dowry consistent with their families' status in society. In general, a *Monte* was founded by a group of aristocratic fathers. More rarely it was established by an individual in his or her will. The founders all pledged to deposit a fixed sum (usually not very high, commonly 1,000 ducats) in a bank account. Usually three to five governors were chosen among the members; each year one of them stepped down and a new one was elected to join the others. They invested the original capital mostly in tax-farms or loans and reinvested the yield for a set number of years, usually about twenty. After that period, the yield from this trust fund in each year constituted the dowry for a daughter of one of the members. The founders established rules to decide who should receive the dowry in case more than one eligible woman married each year. If, in any given year, no eligible woman married, that year's yield was reinvested. If a woman who had received a dowry from the *Monte* died without heirs, the *Monte* claimed her dowry back, just as any aristocratic father would, and reinvested it. Provisions were set to regulate the amount of the dowry, the election of governors, and possible litigation between members. Male descendants of the founders inherited membership in the *Monti*, some of which expressly excluded married cadet sons from enjoying the benefits. In general, the *Monti* also provided *monacaggi* (nuns' dowries) and life annuities to members' daughters who chose a religious life. In the seventeenth century, aristocratic *monacaggi* were 1,000 to 1,500 ducats.[53]

The main purpose of the *Monti* was clearly affirmed in the statutes. The founders of the *Monte dei Giunti*, for instance, remarked that

noble women, if they are not provided with some subsidy in dowry, are forced to enter into religious life, or convents, not because they are moved by a fervent spirit to serve God, but because they cannot see any possibility of marrying their peers. From this arises a disservice to Our Lord God, and a small advantage to religion. Other women who wanted to marry, have been forced to take husbands of conditions different from their own, thereby denigrating their blood and confounding nobility.[54]

Some *Monti* stipulated that the governors had to approve all weddings, while others required at least the approval of the male members of each woman's

---

[53] I have seen the statutes of the *Monte dei Giunti* (1585) in ASN Archivio del Monte dei Giunti, part I rubrica I categoria I 1/1; for the *Monte delle ventinove famiglie* (1585), see *ibid.* 12; for the *Monte Carafa* (1582), see ASN Archivio Carafa di Castel San Lorenzo 21.1–2; *Monte Caracciolo detto della Cassa Grande* (1578) is in ACB 7.6.5 and in ASN Archivio Giudice Caracciolo 118 bis.2.2.; *Monte del conte d'Oppido* (1546) is in *ibid.*, 2.1; *Monte Caracciolo di Ciarletta* (1584), various copies in ACB, for example, 7.3.7, pp. 15–22 (vol. 7 consists entirely of documents relating to the *Monti*); *Monte Capece* (1584) is in BNN ms. San Martino 144. Vols. 1–21 of the Appendix to ACB also consist mainly in documents relating to family *Monti*. See also, notwithstanding its several inexactitudes, A. Caracciolo di Torchiarolo, "I Monti di previdenza della famiglia Caracciolo" *Atti dell'Accademia Pontaniana* new series 6 (n.d.), pp. 337–61. In the ASN there is an entire series consisting of numerous documents from the *Monte Caracciolo detto della Cassa Grande*. Russo, *Monasteri*, pp. 53–54, on *monacaggi*.
[54] Statutes of the *Monte dei Giunti*, already cited, fol. 1v.

family. Many statutes had special clauses defining who would be acceptable as a husband. The statute of the *Monte Ciarletta*, for example, limited its benefits to those women who married *Seggio* noblemen, or "public and noted noblemen, who have been held as noblemen for many years, excluding *penitus* those women who will marry ignoble people, or new noblemen who may have been made noble or declared to be such by decree."[55]

Aristocratic theorists of the time, as we have seen, stated that a woman automatically gained, or descended to, her husband's status, and so usually tolerated a nobleman's marriage to a non-noble woman. There was, however, in reality strong opposition to this type of alliance, as we have seen even with Giuseppe Caracciolo's marriage to Teresa Pinto, hardly a *parvenue*. Some *Monti* had provisions against such marriages. For instance, the *Monte Cassa Grande* excluded from its benefits the daughters of "plebeian and vile" mothers, although the sons of such mothers, if they married properly, could regain the benefits of the *Monte* for their own daughters.[56] The case of women who would remain in their families, lay and unmarried, was contemplated by a few *Monti*, and these women were granted life annuities. But this was a very rare and distressing occurrence. The *Monte dei Giunti* and that of the *ventinove famiglie*, for example, granted these benefits only when the woman "because of some defect or illness is not able to marry or be a nun"; and the *Monte Carafa* considered it a "most rare [event], so that now there is no such woman, nor do we know whether there has ever been any."[57]

The Caracciolo Brienza had claims to four *Monti*. They had a hereditary right to the *Monte* created by the count of Brienza, Alfonso Caracciolo, in 1543, which gave dowry contributions of 3,000 ducats. They had a claim to a second *Monte*, founded by Giovan Antonio Caracciolo, count of Oppido, in his will of 1546, which also provided dowries of 3,000 ducats. Concerned about the unity of his clan, Giovan Antonio had written that

although the family [*famiglia*] of the Caracciolo house [*casa*], all noblemen of the *Seggio* of Capuana, is under only one family name, nonetheless the aforesaid noblemen of the said family have different coats of arms ... My desire is that the said family, as *in substantia* it is all one and they all enjoy in unity the honors of the *Seggio* of Capuana and of the city, so they should have the same insignia and coats of arms ... so that the said family be perpetually united and not divided, *quia virtus unita crescit*.

He therefore ruled that the Caracciolo, who inserted in their coats of arms both the symbols of the Caracciolo Rossi and those of the Caracciolo Pisquizi, would be eligible to enjoy his inheritance. Ascanio Caracciolo, one of the ancestors of

---

[55] ACB 7.3.7, p. 19.
[56] ACB 7.6.5., clause no. 16. On women's status, see de Luca, *Il cavaliere*. A slightly different view is in C. Rota, *Legalis Androgynus, sive tractatus de privilegiis mulierum* (Naples, 1665).
[57] *Monte dei Giunti*, fol. 6r; *Monte delle ventinove famiglie*, p. 28; *Monte Carafa*, 2 (additional statutes of 1586). The *Monte Capece* granted nubile women a generous annuity of 280 ducats a year.

The continuity of feudal power

the Caracciolo Brienza, did so in 1555. A third *Monte* for which the Caracciolo Brienza were also eligible, was the *Monte Cassa Grande*, which had been founded in 1578 by various members of the clan, including Giulia Caracciolo, marquise of Brienza, in the name of her son, Giovan Battista. It gave dowries of 4,000 ducats.[58]

These three *Monti* were all managed rather poorly, especially those of Brienza and Oppido. By the eighteenth century, many of their debtors did not pay all or any of their debts, which were labeled "unreceivable" (*inesigibili*). This meant that the dowries provided by these *Monti* were at best uncertain. In the marriage contracts of his daughters, Giuseppe Caracciolo, eighth marquis of Brienza, disclaimed any responsibility in case his sons-in-law could not actually receive all of the promised dowries.

But the Caracciolo Brienza were also eligible for a fourth and more successful *Monte*, the one founded by Scipione Caracciolo di Ciarletta in his will of 1584. Scipione left his entire estate to the Annunziata, and he enjoined that the revenues be reinvested until the estate yielded 11,200 ducats per year. Then 1,000 ducats should be used to give dowries to five inmates of the hospital, 200 ducats for administrative expenses, and 10,000 ducats to dower daughters descended from either Ciarletta Caracciolo Viola (d. 1450), Scipione's great-great-grandfather, or Ciarletta' brother Gualtiero (d. 1447). This group, by the end of the sixteenth century, consisted mainly of the Caracciolo families of Avellino, Brienza, Vico, Torrecuso, and San Vito. Membership in this *Monte* created an additional subdivision within the Caracciolo clan. In 1800, for example, Litterio Caracciolo, marquis of Brienza, ruled in his will that in case of lack of male heirs, his entailed patrimony could go to a woman, but only if she be married to a man from one of the families which enjoyed the benefits of the *Monte Ciarletta*.[59]

This *Monte* only began its operations in the 1650s. Since several member families became extinct, and in many years no eligible woman married, the frequent reinvestment of yearly dividends led to very large dowries by the early eighteenth century. The dowries were so large, in fact, that in 1774 the eight families still belonging to the *Monte* agreed to change the original statutes, concerned that the "entire family" was being damaged by dowries much larger than any the Caracciolo men could hope to receive. The dowries were therefore

---

58 Giovan Antonio's will is quoted in ASN Archivio Giudice Caracciolo 118 bis.2.1. I have not seen the original will, which is in the Archivio Caracciolo Martina in the Biblioteca Comunale of Martina Franca (Taranto). We have seen above that the *Monte Oppido* also provided contributions to cadets aged forty or more. Ascanio's notarized new coat of arms is mentioned in ACB 148, unnumbered fol., which also details the right of the Caracciolo Brienza on the *Monte* of the count of Brienza. *Monte Cassa Grande*, statutes, already cited.
59 Scipione's will is in ACB 7.3.7. Litterio's will of 1800 is in ACB App. 22, unnumbered fol.; in 1805, an addition to the will allowed marriage to any Caracciolo man, because of concern that the previous limitation may have been too strict, and that a forced marriage may be a risky enterprise; see also ACB 9.50. See Figure 4.

limited to 70,000 ducats, with which Caracciolo women "could at any time be sure to see magnates of their own status desire to marry them." The remaining yield of the *Monte*, which was still growing, would be divided among cadet sons. Detailed rules set the contributions available for cadet sons in the different careers the families saw open to them. These careers were, in order of importance, the magistracies, the army, the knighthood of Malta, the church, the government (as provincial governors or ambassadors), and the Roman curia. Cataldo Caracciolo Brienza, for example, began receiving 600 ducats a year in 1782, when, at the age of fourteen, he became a second lieutenant in the royal cadets. All the rules excluding daughters who married non-noblemen, or the sons of non-noble mothers, from the benefits of the *Monte* were maintained, as well as the prohibition for cadet sons to marry. Similar provisions in favor of cadet sons were enacted in 1789 by another well-managed *Monte*, that of the *ventinove famiglie*, which had also been strengthened by the extinction of several member families. In the eighteenth century, various aristocratic families established special funds, also called *Monti*, designed to support cadet sons in their endeavors.[60]

In the changed circumstances of the eighteenth century, as we have seen above for the entails, the *Monti* themselves could become a danger if too successful. But the growth of dowries could not be halted. In 1801, Ferdinand IV tried to limit all dowries to 15,000 ducats by law, and to divert any *Monte* contribution higher than 15,000 ducats to the benefit of the sons, in order to reduce differences between noble families with successful *Monti* and those without them. This attempt failed, and many dowries remained far above 15,000 ducats. The Napoleonic government abolished the *Monti* in its antifeudal policy, but some were reestablished after 1815. The dissolution of the *Monte di Ciarletta* and the division of its properties among the thirteen member families in the 1810s, brought each of them real estate and credit worth more than 100,000 ducats.[61]

The *Monti* were the most visible and effective institution binding the several families within the clan, also because the management of the *Monti* obviously brought members of the clan together. Clans also had a few common devotional institutions. Although they had no church or monastery of the clan like San Giuseppe dei Ruffi, there was a Caracciolo chapel in the archbishopric. The *Monte Ciarletta* had a chapel under its own patronage, and various Caracciolo

[60] On *Monte Ciarletta*, see ACB App. 5, unnumbered fol.; on the *Monte delle ventinove famiglie*, see ASN Archivio del Monte dei Giunti, 12; on funds for cadets, see Visceglia, "Linee"; on Cataldo's provision, see ACB 2.39. The Cassa Grande had shrunk from forty-four to seventeen families, but was nonetheless burdened with a heavy deficit, see ASN Archivio Giudice Caracciolo, 118bis.2.3.

[61] The 1801 law is in L. Giustiniani, ed. *Nuova collezione delle prammatiche del regno di Napoli*, VI, *De iure dotium prammatica* I, pp. 283–87. The division of the *Monte Ciarletta* is the object of many documents in ACB 7 and App. 1–21, as well as in ASN Archivio Caracciolo Torchiarolo 90 and 91.

Plate 6 Church of San Giovanni a Carbonara, Naples

families had patronage over chapels in the church of San Giovanni a Carbonara. The marquis of Brienza and the marquis of Sant'Eramo had joint patronage over the old sacristy of that church, as joint heirs of Ascanio and Aurelia Caracciolo who had acquired the chapel in 1567 for 300 ducats, and they buried their dead in the crypt there. The Caracciolo Brienza wills and notarial acts show that members of the clan were the most common choice as executors, and often acted as proxies for their relatives.[62]

But, besides the *Monti*, the most important field of intervention of the clan was the education of its members' children. In the seventeenth and eighteenth centuries, colleges for the aristocracy were established in many cities in Italy and in all of Europe, both in the form of military academies and as colleges for general education. Religious orders like the Jesuits, Theatines, and Somaschians specialized in the education of the elite. In Naples there was at least one aristocratic college, the *Seminarium Nobilium*, founded in 1608 by the *Monte di Manso* and open to all aristocratic sons. But in Naples again, unlike other European countries, the clan played a prominent role, and at least two of the major clans established their own colleges.

In 1620, the Caracciolo founded a college for their sons' education. They used part of the estate left by the count of Oppido in the previous century, and in addition each titled member of the clan gave 1,000 ducats and each untitled head of a family gave 500 for the establishment. The college was to have a maximum of fourteen boarders below the age of eighteen (though Celano says there were up to twenty-five students at some point) who received annuities of fifty-five to seventy ducats depending on their number. The expenses for the teachers, the food, and the upkeep of the building were estimated at 967 ducats a year. The teaching was entrusted to the Somaschians, but the college was ruled by five lay governors (three beginning in 1712), who were all members of the clan. The subjects taught were Catholic doctrine, grammar, rhetoric, philosophy, mathematics, civil law ("so necessary to noblemen"), chivalric arts, and languages. Lay instructors were hired to teach French, fencing, dance, and riding. The college was housed in a building next to the church of San Giovanni a

---

62 The Brienza–Sant'Eramo chapel is described in R. Filangieri di Candida, "La chiesa e il monastero di San Giovanni a Carbonara" *ASPN* 48 (1923), 114–17; in it were eighteen paintings by Vasari. Filangieri's description is alas outdated. The chapel has long been used as a storage room for the restorers; though lately improving in shape, San Giovanni a Carbonara has been under restoration since 1945, and can only be visited on rare occasions of which one is made aware through secret avenues and mysterious connections. I visited it in 1986 through a friend's friend's friend; very little of the original appearance of the chapel can be reconstructed, although, after a good deal of sweeping, I could identify Ascanio's tombal stone. The Vasari are gone. I have no idea of the state of the crypt. Documents on the chapel are in ACB App. 23, unnumbered fol.; see ACB 9.52 for the 1567 purchase; the chapel is also described in C. de Lellis, *Supplimento a Napoli sacra di Don Cesare d'Engenio Caracciolo* (Naples, 1654), pp. 91–96 (the book, constituting part II of d'Engenio's 1624 *Napoli sacra*, is dedicated to Giuseppe Caracciolo, marquis of Brienza). For the governorships of the *Monte Ciarletta*, see ACB 34, for the wills, see ACB 4.1., and for a sample of notarial acts, see ACB 8 and 9.

Carbonara, in the old Caracciolo neighborhood. Detailed rules were issued to decide the clothing, the food, and the services that the college would offer. The lay staff included a cook, servants, barbers, a pharmacist, and a doctor. The college was probably formed on the model of the *Seminarium nobilium*, which had been entrusted to the Jesuits in 1629. The *Seminarium* was designed to teach "civil and canon laws, and chivalric exercises," together with Christian piety and *belles-lettres*. Giulio Cesare Capaccio remarked that the Caracciolo college "shows the true way to raise noblemen," and Celano noted that "the boys are educated in the fear of God, in *belles-lettres*, and in exercises that are fitting ornament to noblemen, such as fencing, music, etc."[63]

In the mid-eighteenth century, the Caracciolo college had a patrimony of around 75,000 ducats, with an effective yield of about 1,300 ducats per year, which covered the expenses. The number of boarders declined with the extinction of many families, and was below ten for most of the century. In 1798, the college joined with the college of the Capece to create the "College of the two families of Capuana." The administration was joint, but the patrimonies were kept separate. The Capece paid 200 ducats a year for the use of the Caracciolo building. Each boarder was now paying 108 ducats a year in fees. The teaching staff, besides the priests, consisted in a teacher of philosophy with a salary of 120 ducats a year, a teacher of humanities and rhetoric (ninety-six ducats), a teacher of grammar (eighty-four ducats), a fencing teacher (forty ducats), a dance and violin teacher (thirty ducats), and a teacher of French (thirty-six ducats). Expenses for salaries, laundry, and furniture totalled ducats 1,720.4.10 a year. In 1824, the college was dissolved and the palace sold for ducats 4,907.1.18, which were divided among the families.[64]

The Neapolitan aristocracy, therefore, still found in the old clan a powerful institution that bound together all member families and could be used to support the weaker among them. To some extent, the clans might also have made the extinction of individual families more acceptable to the aristocracy, since the

---

[63] ASN Archivio Giudice Caracciolo 118bis.2.5 has the statutes and the acts of foundation, as well as other documents pertaining to the college. The building, appropriately, is today a school. For the *Seminarium* see Manfredi, *Manso*. Its founder had wanted the Theatines to run this college but, following a long lawsuit, it remained with the Jesuits. The building which housed the *Seminarium* is still extant, and the initial inscription is still on the entrance door. G. C. Capaccio, *Il forastiero dialogi* (Naples, 1634), p. 923; C. Celano, *Notizie del bello, dell'antico e del curioso della città di Napoli* (1692) (7 vols.; Naples, 1974), I, p. 228. Vitale, "Modelli," pp. 42–64, analyzes the changing values in aristocratic education in sixteenth-century Naples, from a feudal–military emphasis to courtly and Humanistic values.

[64] ASN Archivio Giudice Caracciolo, already cited; the new establishment is in ACB APP. 18, unnumbered fol. As a sobering evaluation of the relative value of some teachers, it may be noted that the porter earned sixty ducats a year, the menservants seventy-eight each, the washingwoman thirty-six, and the cook, with his helper, one hundred and twenty. On the 1824 sale, see ACB 165, unnumbered fol. On colleges for the aristocracy, see G. P. Brizzi, *La formazione della classe dirigente nel Sei-Settecento, i Seminaria nobilium nell'Italia centrosettentrionale* (Bologna, 1976), p. 26 and footnote 70 for information in Naples; see also Marchisio, "Ideologia," pp. 82–83; for France, see Schalk, *From Valor*, chapter 8.

extended family represented by the clan would continue and perpetuate the family's name and traditions. As said before, the persistent feudal and military nature of the Neapolitan aristocracy, as well as Spanish cultural influences, helps explain the continuing importance of clans. The aristocracy was ready to respond to social, political, and economic changes by adapting its old institutions to new circumstances, in order to preserve its families and its social prevalence. The *Monti*, and to a smaller extent the colleges, were designed to alleviate the burden of family expenses, and their main result was to buttress the aristocracy's wealth. But the *Monti* also served to limit intermarriage with the ascending robe and financial families, and to strengthen the will of the clan over that of the family and that of the family over that of individuals. The *Monti* were very effective and contributed to preserve the aristocracy's sense of social superiority and to make *mésalliance*, at least until the eighteenth century, a rather rare occurrence. They also eased the conscience of aristocratic fathers, especially after the 1560s, when Tridentine prelates and ideas brought a reformist attitude to Naples and its religious institutions. These forms of clan solidarity, peculiar to the kingdom of Naples, stress the significance ascribed by the old barons of the kingdom to horizontal bonds of kinship and to their military and feudal traditions, and the strength of the common interests they felt they shared with all those bearing the same family name.[65]

WOMEN AND THE PRESERVATION OF FAMILY PATRIMONY

These horizontal solidarities were useful in preserving the prestige and patrimony of all aristocratic families, with the purpose of passing them safely to the following generations. Large dowries also enabled women to play a significant role in both the preservation and the transmission of aristocratic wealth. The protected legal status of dowries left space for litigation over women's inheritances. When their husbands predeceased them, women could use their claim to their dowries for their own benefit and that of either their natal or marital family. In some cases, litigation within a family represented more a concerted effort to protect the patrimony than an actual conflict. The last section of this chapter will look at the importance of women and of litigation over their wealth in insuring the passage of aristocratic estates from one generation to the next.

Aristocratic dowries were protected by various legal guarantees, and the

[65] Delille, *Famille*, stresses the importance extended clans held for most social groups in the kingdom throughout the old regime, and places it in the context of his anthropological interpretation of the kingdom's "otherness," see above, introduction. The solidarity of the clans did not always die out with the old regime. The Caracciolo came together in the so-called "Pia Unione della famiglia Caracciolo," founded in 1925 to propagate devotion to St. Francesco Caracciolo, and to cooperate with the religious order of the Regular Minor Clerics (also known as "Caracciolini") founded by the Saint in 1558. In 1988, more than 100 Caracciolo (of the estimated 420 living ones) attended a Mass in Rome to celebrate the reconstitution of the Pious Union; I thank Prince Alfonso Caracciolo di Forino for this information.

separation of the patrimonies of the two spouses' families was enforced in Naples much more strictly than elsewhere in Italy. The high aristocracy of the kingdom had a set of customs, called the *Uso dei Proceri e Magnati*, which regulated the restitution of the dowry to the wife's family at the death of one of the spouses. By the sixteenth century, however, many aristocratic marriage contracts adopted a private pact, known as the *Patto di Capuana e Nido*, but not applying only to members of those two *Seggi*, which separated ever more rigidly the wife's estate from her husband's. The new pact did not allow a woman to inherit her husband's estate, while on the other hand barring the husband from inheriting his wife's dowry from their children, should these die heirless after their mother. The dowry had always to return, in the absence of children, to the woman's natal family. The new pact also limited the amount of her dowry that a woman could dispose of freely to ten percent if she had children and to fifty percent if she did not. The new pact, in short, aimed to limit drastically the possibility that women might transfer wealth from their natal families to those of their husbands.[66]

The *antefato* (the husband's donation to his wife at marriage) was also strictly regulated in 1617 to a set percentage of the dowry, though often this limitation was circumvented in the marriage contract. The *antefato*, though declared in the marriage contract, went to the woman only at her husband's death, but at her death it returned to his heirs. In the sixteenth and seventeenth centuries, many steps were taken to maintain the separation of the two families' patrimonies. Dowries could rarely be used for anything except the purchase of annuities or real estate, which offered guarantees to the wife's family. This separation also meant that in general, although mothers could donate additional gifts to their daughters, mothers' dowries were not used to help form those of the daughters, since the dowry was considered strictly a responsibility of the father's patrimony. Only in the eighteenth century, when the aristocracy began to break entails and to change the rules of the *Monti*, did some families renounce, in the marriage contracts, their right to redeem dowry money, so that it might by used more freely.[67]

Visceglia has seen the growing separation between the patrimonies, and the limitations on women's power to dispose of their wealth, in the light of her

---

[66] More information and bibliography in chapter 6. In Piedmont, the dowry did not revert to the wife's family, see Woolf, *Studi*, pp. 31–35.

[67] Visceglia, "Linee," pp. 459–70; the 1617 law is in Giustiniani, *Nuova collezione*, II, *De antefato sive donatione propter nuptias prammatica* I, pp. 257–58. F. P. de Stefano, *Romani, Longobardi e Normanno-Franchi della Puglia nei secoli XV–XVII; ricerche sui rapporti patrimoniali tra coniugi fino alla prammatica de antefato del 1617* (Naples, 1979). In Piedmont, the *aumento dotale* (counter-dowry) was equivalent to one third of noble dowries, one fourth of all others (Woolf, *Studi*, pp. 31–35). In Piedmont and in France, it was quite common for daughters' dowries to be formed in part with their mothers' dotal money, see Forster, *Toulouse*, chapter 6; on the legal situation of dowries, see Owen Hughes, "Strutture familiari e sistemi di successione ereditaria nei testamenti dell'Europa medievale" *QS* 11 (1976), pp. 929–52; the jointures of English widows were also strictly protected, examples in Stone, *Family and Fortune* (Oxford, 1973).

Aristocratic family strategies

Giulio Cesare (d. 1544) m. Ippolita Filomarino (d. 1571)
|
Marco Antonio (d. 1573) m. Diana Caracciolo
                    m. Giulia Caracciolo (d. 1620)
|
Giovan Battista (d. 1620) m. (1590) Diana Caracciolo (d. 1649)
|
Faustina Caracciolo (1602/5–73) m. (1621) Carlo Gambacorta (d. 1648)
|
Cristina Gambacorta (d. 1717) m. (1658) Domenico Caracciolo (1643–81)
|
Giuseppe II (1660–1720) m. (1688) Teresa Pinto (1668–1755)
|
Domenico II (1690–1726) m. (1722) Imara Ruffo (d. 1754)
|
Litterio Caracciolo (1725–1807)

Figure 5 The Caracciolo Brienza's marriages

general interpretation of aristocratic family policy. This policy, she argues, became more formalized and authoritarian in the sixteenth and seventeenth centuries. In the seventeenth century, women owed their main loyalty to their natal families. Fewer men left their wives as guardians of their children and estate, and those who did limited their widows' power. The number of bequests to wives also allegedly decreased. She denies that the changes in the eighteenth century, when the aristocracy acted to break entails and to reform *Monti*, had a real impact on women's position in the aristocratic family.[68] I shall claim that a closer look at specific situations shows the reality to have been more complex. The fact that most Neapolitan aristocratic daughters were able to marry already placed them in a favored position in comparison to aristocratic women in other European countries. Moreover, women's rights to their dowries and their power to dispose of their wealth, at least during their lifetime, could play an essential role in the transmission and preservation of their families' patrimony. Women's loyalties were not predetermined, and the specific situation could orient their decisions in favor of one or the other of their families. Without claiming that women were wholly free economic agents, I shall argue that they enjoyed a considerable amount of freedom and were ready to use it to further their own purposes, which did not necessarily conform to those of their families.[69]

This freedom was particularly noticeable in the case of widows. There has been no demographic study of the Neapolitan aristocracy to address questions such as the age of spouses at their marriage. In the family considered here it does

---

[68] Visceglia, "Linee," especially pp. 468–70, and Visceglia, "Ideologia nobiliare e rappresentazione della donna" *Prospettive Settanta* 7 (1985), pp. 88–110.

[69] Some of these positions about Venetian women are taken by Chojnacky in his articles cited in footnote 3. See also B. Diefendorf, "Widowhood and Remarriage in Sixteenth-century Paris" *Journal of Family History* 7 (1982), pp. 379–95, which stresses widows' activities and abilities as managers of their wealth.

not seem that the age difference between spouses was very great. The death of many Caracciolo Brienza men at a relatively young age – much younger than the age at death of their wives – however, produced a series of widows who survived their husbands by several decades. Ippolita Filomarino (d. 1571) survived Giulio Cesare Caracciolo by twenty-seven years. Giulia Caracciolo (d. 1620) survived Marco Antonio by forty-seven years, Diana (d. 1649) survived Giovan Battista by twenty-nine years, Faustina (d. 1673) survived Carlo Gambacorta by twenty-five years, Cristina (d. 1717) survived Domenico I by thirty-six years, Teresa (d. 1755) survived Giuseppe II by thirty-five years, and Imara (d. 1754) survived Domenico II by twenty-eight years. This last was the only one to remarry.[70]

Several of these widows were active financial managers. As we have seen, Ippolita and Giulia bought the four family fiefs, probably with their own dowry money, and then passed them to their sons. Giulia, in 1592, also bought the town of Diano which she donated to her son three years later. Giulia, Diana, and Faustina were guardians for all or some of their children, and Teresa stepped in as guardian of her grandson when her daughter-in-law, Imara, remarried. Notarial records and two account books show their involvement in tax-farms and loans, mainly to other members of the aristocracy. In particular, Diana lent several thousand ducats of her own money to various people, sometimes even before her husband's death, and also invested in tax-farms, with yields of six and a half to nine percent on her capital. She bought grain and animals, and expressed concern that her money should not be kept "in laziness." Cristina seems to have invested in loans as well. She kept her household separate from her son's and received the income from the family palace. She disposed of enough property of her own to establish a chaplaincy in Atena with an endowment of almost 2,000 ducats in 1702. Teresa, besides her long guardianship of her grandson, managed her own capital, invested in tax-farms, and had at least 10,000 ducats of her own to dispose of at her death. Teresa's own mother, Geronima Capece Bozzuto, also engaged in lending activities. In the early seventeenth century, it was another aristocratic widow, Costanza Gesualdo, duchess of Gravina, who sold to Giuseppe Caracciolo her credit of 10,300 ducats on the *università* of Atena.[71]

---

[70] I am not counting here Teodora Alberti (d. 1758), who survived her third husband by thirty years, because as an heiress she had full and undisputed rights to the enjoyment of her entire fortune. See Figure 5.

[71] On Giulia, see ACB 9.15–16; on Diana, particularly ACB 9.23 (a loan, and 9, throughout), 12.3 (a bundle of papers relating to her investments – the quote is from 12.3.1), 22 (an account book), and ASN Assensi feudali 4, unnumbered fol., act of 19 February 1622; Cristina's account book is in ACB 23, and her chaplaincy in ACB 76.4.3; for Teresa, see ACB 9.35 (a loan), and 6.2, 6.3, and 6.4 (bundles of documents on her wealth), her will in ACB 4.1.55, and in 6.2.9 details on the 10,000 ducats; on Geronima, see ACB 77.1.20; on Costanza Orsini, see ACB 77.1. For similar examples of financial shrewdness on the part of aristocratic widows, see D. Dessert, *Argent, pouvoir et société au Grand Siècle* (Paris, 1984), pp. 363–65.

But the economic importance these women had for the Caracciolo Brienza was based less on their own private wealth, than on the use they made of their dowry claims in litigation involving the family and its creditors. There was a considerable amount of litigation within the family. Often, in the case of mothers' dowry claims, the litigation was probably fictitious, and the family may actually have been acting together to preserve the patrimony against outside pressures. This can be seen in the disputes over the dowries of Diana and Cristina, which were crucial in the survival of the Caracciolo Brienza fortune.

In 1590, Giovan Battista, marquis of Brienza, married Diana Caracciolo, sister of the duke of Sicignano, who offered the large dowry of 33,000 ducats (plus a trousseau worth 2,000 ducats), 16,000 of which were to be paid immediately, and 17,000 within four years. Giovan Battista donated 3,500 ducats to his wife and promised an *antefato* of 11,000 ducats. Diana was also promised other gifts from members of his family. In 1623, when Giovan Battista's estate could not meet its creditors, Diana sued her son, Giacomo Caracciolo, the new marquis of Brienza, for restitution of her dowry and *antefato*. Giacomo gave his mother Atena and Sasso, to guarantee her dowry claim to 44,000 ducats and her other claims, just before the rest of the estate was confiscated by the royal courts to pay the creditors. Giacomo could do this because his mother's claim dated back to 1590, therefore gaining precedence over many of Giovan Battista's other debts, and on 3 June 1624, the Sacred Royal Council of Naples recognized Diana as lord of Atena and Sasso.[72]

Diana managed Atena and Sasso freely until her death; as guardian of her younger son, Giuseppe, she further requested from Giacomo Giuseppe's legacies from their father, uncle, and aunt, for a total of 20,000 ducats. In 1634, Diana sold Atena to Giuseppe for 19,000 ducats, so that he might obtain a princely title on it – which he did in 1636. In 1637, she sold Sasso to him for 20,000 ducats. He did not pay her, however, and she continued to collect the revenues of the two fiefs, issuing a fictitious receipt for the payment in order to give Giuseppe full right to his title. Notwithstanding the public litigation between Diana and Giuseppe on the one side and Giacomo on the other, Giacomo donated the baronial palace in Atena in 1633, which he had kept in 1623, to Giuseppe, and in 1626 Diana made Giacomo her proxy to administer Giuseppe's properties in Sala. Two of Diana's daughters entered convents, and both renounced all their claims to the family estate in favor of their mother. When Diana died in 1649, therefore, she was able to leave Giacomo only his

[72] Documents on these events in ACB 73.2, and 43.2, especially 48. The 1624 decree is in ACB 73.2.27 (a large bundle of unnumbered documents). The royal assent is also in ASN Cedolari Nuovi 37, fol. 32r, and Repertori dei Quinternioni 14-III, fols. 11r–v.

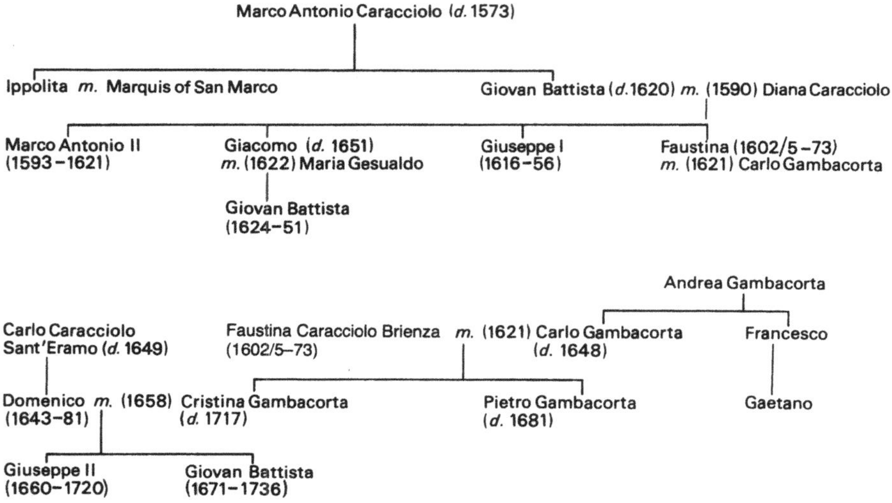

Marco Antonio Caracciolo (d. 1573)

Ippolita *m.* Marquis of San Marco

Giovan Battista (d. 1620) *m.* (1590) Diana Caracciolo

Marco Antonio II (1593–1621)

Giacomo (d. 1651) *m.* (1622) Maria Gesualdo

Giuseppe I (1616–56)

Faustina (1602/5–73) *m.* (1621) Carlo Gambacorta

Giovan Battista (1624–51)

Andrea Gambacorta

Carlo Caracciolo Sant'Eramo (d. 1649)

Faustina Caracciolo Brienza (1602/5–73) *m.* (1621) Carlo Gambacorta (d. 1648)

Francesco

Domenico *m.* (1658) (1643–81)

Cristina Gambacorta (d. 1717)

Pietro Gambacorta (d. 1681)

Gaetano

Giuseppe II (1660–1720)

Giovan Battista (1671–1736)

Figure 6a Family of Giovan Battista Caracciolo
b Family of Faustina Caracciolo

legal share, amounting to 4,500 ducats, and, with the exception of a few small bequests, the bulk of her estate was left to Giuseppe.[73]

This course of action was pursued as a remedy to the precarious economic situation of the family head, Giacomo. That Giuseppe never married provides further evidence that this situation was the result of concerted action by the family. Since Giacomo had a son, who could have inherited his uncle's estate and title, there is a legitimate suspicion that Giuseppe planned to leave his estate to him, in effect bypassing Giacomo and thereby saving at least part of their father's patrimony. In 1651, however, both Giacomo and his son died, and in his will of 1654 Giuseppe speaks of his likely marriage, though he does not seem to have married by the time of his death in the plague of 1656. The family's intention to bypass Giacomo is suggested also by the donation that Ippolita Caracciolo, widow of the marquis of San Marco and sister of Giovan Battista, marquis of Brienza, made of her claim to 2,000 ducats with interests over the estate of her late brother, whose heir Giacomo was. In 1636, Ippolita donated her claim to Giacomo's son, Giovan Battista, and to his heirs. Giovan Battista's guardian in

---

[73] See previous footnote. The sale of Atena and Sasso to Giuseppe is in ACB 81.1.5, ASN Cedolari nuovi 88, fols. 42r–v and 37, fol. 93v, ASN Repertori Quinternioni 9, fol. 287v, and in ASN notai del '600, 912/12 Pietro Antonio dell'Aversano, fols. 420r–428r (5 October 1634), and 912/13, fols. 101v–3r (5 March 1635, Diana's receipt). Giuseppe's title is mentioned in the repertories of titles in ASN Museo 99B137 (*titoli vicereali*), 99B135 (*titulorum Neapolis*), and 99B138 (*privilegi napoletani a Simancas*). The proxy is in ACB 46.1.4 (a large bundle of unnumbered documents); in 1621, Giacomo had given his mother full proxy powers on his entire patrimony, *ibid.*

the administration of this donation was to be his mother, and in no case should Giacomo, or his creditors, be permitted any claim on this donation.[74]

Diana's claim on her 44,000 ducats, in any event, served to keep Atena and Sasso separate from the rest of the patrimony, and successive marquis of Brienza presented themselves, *qua* heirs to Diana, as claimants on their own patrimony. Even when, in 1738, under pressure from very tenacious creditors, the Sacred Council annulled the 1623 concession of Atena and Sasso to Diana, it still recognized Litterio Caracciolo's claim to 44,000 ducats on the two fiefs and his enjoyment of their revenues as interest. The creditors maintained that Diana's dowry had been unjustifiably large and that it had never been actually paid, serving from the beginning as a protection for Giovan Battista's already fragile estate. The lawsuit went on into the 1770s, and only in 1778 was Litterio definitely recognized as lord of Atena and Sasso, thanks to the dowry claim he held as heir to his ancestor Diana.[75]

Before the eighteenth century, however, the Brienza patrimony went through another, more complex, set of vicissitudes, in which again a woman's dowry served to protect it and preserve it for the family. Constrained by feudal law, Giuseppe Caracciolo, fifth marquis of Brienza, willed all his estate to his sister Faustina, widow of Carlo Gambacorta. However, he charged her to keep only 1,000 ducats and to pay the balance to Domenico, first son of their cousin Carlo Caracciolo Sant'Eramo. In the event of Domenico's demise, the estate should go to the Caracciolo Torella or, in third place, to the Caracciolo Avellino, since Giuseppe desired "that my estate should not leave my clan [*casa*] and its males, to preserve it in my family the Caracciolo Rossi." Faustina, supposedly, concealed the will, claimed Giuseppe's entire heritage for herself as heir *ab intestato*, but then proceeded in 1658 to marry her daughter, Cristina, to Domenico Caracciolo, giving her a dowry of 46,000 ducats, 25,000 ducats represented by the fief of Atena, and 6,000 by the titles of marquis of Brienza and prince of Atena. At her death in 1673, Faustina entailed her own estate to her son, Pietro Gambacorta, marquis of Celenza and prince of Macchia, and to his male heirs. If Pietro had no male heirs, the entail should go to his female heirs if they married in the Caracciolo, not the Gambacorta, clan. Only in the absence

---

[74] ASN notai del '600, 1038 Giovan Giacomo Stilo, vol. for 1635–36, fols. 86v–89r (6 June 1636). Giuseppe's will is discussed in ACB 4.1.33–34; a copy of it is in ASN Pandetta Corrente 570, vol. IV, fols. 5r–16r. See Figure 6a.

[75] ACB App. 22, unnumbered fol., and 77.2 for documents on the lawsuit in the eighteenth century. The creditors maintained that since Diana came of a ducal family and had a few drops of royal blood in her veins, her marriage to the indebted second marquis of Brienza was hardly deserving of a large dowry. From another point of view, a 1599 report on the Neapolitan aristocracy described the duke of Sicignano, Diana's brother, as heavily indebted and poor, so that the actual dowry may indeed have been smaller, see Ceci, "I feudatari napoletani alla fine del secolo XVI" *ASPN* 24 (1899), pp. 122–38. Be that as it may, either way this seems a good example of clan solidarity to a family in difficulty.

of any heir from Pietro should the entail go to Cristina, and, in third place, to the Caracciolo Avellino.[76]

In 1663, however, Domenico and Cristina, on the basis of Giuseppe's rediscovered will, sued Faustina and Pietro for Cristina's dowry. In fact, both Atena and the titles should have gone to Domenico anyway, according to Giuseppe's will, so that he could claim his wife's dowry. In 1673, an appointed arbiter assigned Atena to Domenico with the two titles and ordered Pietro to pay his brother-in-law 25,000 ducats. In the meantime, Sasso had been confiscated by the royal courts for other debts of the estate, and was only redeemed by Domenico's son, Giuseppe II, in 1703. In 1674 and 1675, the arbiter's decision was confirmed by the royal courts. Pietro, therefore, never enjoyed possession of his mother's fiefs, although he did pay the feudal succession taxes on them. The litigation continued until 1681, when both Pietro and Domenico died.[77]

Although Pietro, who had no children, left his estate firstly to his uncle, secondly to various other distant Gambacorta, and only as a last resort to Cristina, she began a long lawsuit to gain at least a share of the Gambacorta patrimony. The Caracciolo patrimony, in any case, could not be taken away from Faustina's descendants, and so it was safely in the hands of Cristina and her heirs. After 1681, Atena and the palace in Naples, which Faustina had bought, were assigned to Cristina as a guarantee for her dowry, which she still claimed from Pietro's heirs, since of course it was the Gambacorta, not the Caracciolo, estate that was responsible for her dowry. Cristina then embarked on a long widowhood in possession of a considerable fortune. A Gambacorta by birth, she did not seem inclined to favor her father's relatives in any way, and her final decisions followed her own feelings more than any attachment to a clan. Overcoming previous disagreements between them, she made a large donation to her second son, Giovan Battista, and thereby forced her first son, Giuseppe, and his heirs to abide by a court decision of 1723 and pay an annuity of 500 ducats to Giovan Battista and his heirs in order to keep possession of Atena and the family palace.[78]

It is impossible to prove that Faustina, her daughter, and her son-in-law were acting together to keep the patrimony in the hands of the Caracciolo. The

---

[76] Giuseppe's will is quoted in ACB 12.3.5, unnumbered fol., and in the sources cited in footnote 74. Faustina's is in ACB 4.1.37–38.

[77] ACB 10.3.5, 14.1 (especially 3, 4, 13, 14, 15 and 17), 15.10, unnumbered fol., 77.2.2, 5 and throughout, and 139.27. On the *relevio* paid by Pietro for Faustina, see ASN Significatorie dei relevi 77, fols. 237r–46v, and 78, fols. 59r–60r; ASN Relevi 239, fols. 1r–394r, and 257, fols. 965rff.

[78] Pietro's final decisions are quoted in ACB 14.1.17; for Cristina's inheritance, see ACB 14.2, ACB 15 (especially 4, 10, and 11), and ACB 139–27, particularly fol. 234r. Her disagreements with Giovan Battista in 1691 are in ACB 77.2.7. The Gambacorta estate was confiscated by the government in 1701, after Gaetano Gambacorta, Pietro's cousin and heir, was involved in the aristocratic conspiracy against the Bourbon government which took its name, "congiura di Macchia," from Gaetano's principality in Puglia. See Figure 6b.

concealment of Giuseppe's will, followed soon by Cristina's marriage to Domenico with a large dowry, however, certainly had the effect of giving the couple a
doubly strong claim on Faustina's estate, which would have been necessary had
Pietro had children. Indeed, one can infer from Pietro's payment of the succession taxes for his mother on all of her properties that he had a strong right to her
estate, stronger than the documents, most of which were written for the Caracciolo, would show. Moreover, Faustina's request in her will that Pietro's female
heirs be allowed to inherit her property only if married to a Caracciolo, however
consonant with her loyalty to her natal clan, would certainly have been a reason
for much tension with the Gambacorta. Pietro, like his father before him, had
willed that if he only had a female heir, his estate could go to her only if she
married in his clan. Besides loyalty to Faustina's clan, what was at issue here was
probably the greater prestige, power, and influence of the Caracciolo over the
Gambacorta: still a provincial family, who only came to live in Naples during
Faustina's widowhood, they were not yet a member of any *Seggio* and were likely
to have less leverage on the crucial decisions of the royal courts. In fact, so weak
must have been Pietro Gambacorta's impact on the Caracciolo patrimony, that
one chronicler, reporting his sudden death in 1681, referred to him as "the
prince of Macchia, of the Caracciolo clan [*casa*]."[79]

Besides the specific peculiarities of their demographic history, there is no
reason to believe that the Caracciolo Brienza granted the women of their family a
role any different from that of other aristocratic women. The aristocracy certainly closed its ranks during the sixteenth century, and, by barring access to the
Seggi and by instituting *Monti* and entails, tried to preserve its status in the face of
new ascending groups in society. But these moves on the part of the aristocracy
did not necessarily imply a more rigid, formal, and constrictive life within the
aristocratic family. Of course aristocratic ideas and society were, and remained,
patriarchal; but the accidents of demography, and the very laws designed to
protect aristocratic wealth, made women not the passive figures they are often
thought to have been, but actually gave them substantial power and space to
influence their families' fortunes. The rules were set by men, but it was often
women who applied them, and at least as much credit and responsibility for their
families' survival and success goes to them as to their husbands and sons. It was
probably not without consequence that only three of the nine marquis of Brienza
whose lives are here analyzed survived their mothers by longer than three years.

Nor did these women's endeavors meet with ingratitude. When Diana Caracciolo died in 1649 she requested in her will that her funeral take place in the
church of Santi Apostoli with no pomp, her body closed in a black sack. But her
son and heir, Giuseppe, who owed the conservation of what was left of his
father's estate to his mother's sagacious management of her dowry claims, had
other ideas. Parrino reports that when the marquise of Brienza died

---

[79] Confuorto, *Giornali*, I, p. 76. Pietro's father's will is in ACB 4.1.20.

her son don Giuseppe Caracciolo, prince of Atena, gave his mother a very solemn funeral celebrated in the church of the house of the fathers of the Company of Jesus. A splendid Mausoleum was erected in the church, surrounded by 250 images of the most famous personages of her clan [*casato*], among whom were those women who, overcoming the weakness of their sex, had made themselves praiseworthy for posterity; around it were also thirty-six sepulchral pyramids embellished with hieroglyphs and beautiful inscriptions in Hebrew, Chaldaean, Syrian, Arabic, Chinese, Greek, and Latin; the whole work was entitled 'The Eclipsed Moon.'

Although displays of humility in wills were not rare and may not always have been meant seriously, there is no doubt that Diana received preferential treatment. Her funeral, her granddaughter's husband complained thirty years later, cost more than 10,000 ducats; by comparison, the funeral of Diana's daughter, Faustina, in 1673 cost her disappointed son Pietro ducats 123.2.--.[80]

A study of only one family can obviously make no more than tentative hypotheses on the entire aristocracy. In the matter of family policy in particular, however, a detailed reconstruction of one family's situation is perhaps the best way to test the validity of generalizations put forward by studies of larger segments of the aristocracy, and to analyze more closely the complex motivations and circumstances that played a role in determining a family's decisions.

Although the fundamental problem that faced Neapolitan aristocratic families was common to aristocracies throughout Europe – how to transmit the patrimony intact from one generation to the next without risking the extinction of the family – the solutions they found responded to specific local conditions and resulted at times in the creation of original institutions. The very legal restrictions placed on their money enabled women to play a crucial role in the success of their families. The old clans remained an essential frame of reference for the identity of each aristocratic family, both by influencing the family's own self-perception, and by contributing to the definition of each family's status within the aristocracy. This is evident from an analysis of the Caracciolo Brienza's marriage policy, which shows how more elements than just a family's wealth and prestige entered the choice of marriage partners and the decisions as to the amount and mode of payment of dowries. The old clans also gained renewed

---

[80] The will is in ACB 4.1.22 bis. D. A. Parrino, *Teatro eroico e politico de' governi de' viceré del regno di Napoli* (2 vols.; Naples, 1770; first edit. 1692), II, p. 156. There may have been more to Giuseppe's filial devotion than gratitude. Born when his mother was around forty years of age, and orphaned of his father at the age of four, Giuseppe spent most of his life with her, until she was in her seventies. He never married, and at his death he not only asked to be buried beside her, but he requested that his heart be taken from his corpse and placed in a metal box at his mother's feet; see his will cited in footnote 74. Giuseppe's sorrow at his mother's death even inspired the rather weak Muse of a local poet, G. Battista, *Poesie meliche* (Naples, 1650), p. 113 (I thank Thomas Willette for this reference). For the costs, see ASN Pandetta Corrente 570, vol. marked 2, fols. 690r–v, and vol. marked 3, fols. 237r–v. On funerals, see Visceglia, "Corpo," and Vitale, "Modelli," especially pp. 39–40.

importance as the families were subject to two opposing pressures: on the one hand, to limit their sons' marriages because of the new political and economic situation which made the proliferation of aristocratic branches politically useless and economically injudicious; on the other hand, not to jeopardize, in a society heavily influenced by Counter-Reformation ideals, their daughters' spiritual welfare by forcing them into the religious life. Through the old clans and their new institutions the aristocracy was able to escape this predicament.[81]

[81] Two works addressing the issues have reached me too late for full consideration: G. Muto, "I trattati napoletani cinquecenteschi in tema di nobiltà" in acts of the conference *Sapere e/è potere. Discipline, dispute e professioni nell'Università medievale e moderna* held in Bologna in 1989 (Bologna: Mulino, 1990), and Muto, "I 'segni d'honore.' Rappresentazioni della dinamica nobiliare a Napoli in età moderna," paper presented at the conference *La nobiltà in età moderna. Composizione ed ideologia nobiliare in Italia centromeridionale* held in Rome in 1990. Muto stresses the attraction exercised by aristocratic lifestyle and culture on the new elite groups of magistrates, lawyers, and financiers.

6

Offices, courts, and taxes; the aristocracy and the Spanish rule

Francia o Spagna, purché se magna.
(France or Spain, as long as we can eat.)

Neapolitan proverb

The supposed growth of state power was long considered as one of the defining elements of the early modern period. Whether it be Burckhardt's state as a work of art or Weber's bureaucratic impersonal state, historians up to a generation ago saw the rise of a centralized, absolutist state as a central characteristic of the sixteenth to eighteenth centuries in most of Europe. The works of Federico Chabod are perhaps the best application of these ideas to Italian history. In the last twenty-five years or so, however, historians have begun to doubt the actual extent of state power; while the state apparatus certainly grew in bulk, its effectiveness in replacing or weakening other centers of power has been called into question. Historians have studied phenomena like patronage and clientage networks, and Italian historians in particular have stressed the persisting importance of local elite groups and traditional institutions in Italy's regional states, and the dialectic relationship between center and periphery within them. State power grew, when it did, in fits and bounds, and often in the service of the vested interests of particularistic groups. The concept of absolutism does little justice to a complex process that witnessed the continuing thriving of traditional centers of power and social groups. The relationship between the Neapolitan feudal aristocracy and the Spanish monarchy reflects the ambiguities of the so-called process of state-building.[1]

The old aristocracy was quite successful in protecting its social and economic position in the kingdom from the ascent of new financial and robe families.

---

[1] The bibliography on these issues includes F. Chabod, *Scritti sul Rinascimento* (Turin, 1981), and Chabod, *Lo stato e la vita religiosa a Milano nell'epoca di Carlo V* (2 vols.; Turin, 1971), both collections of essays; G. Chittolini, *La formazione dello stato regionale e le istituzioni del contado, secoli XIV e XV* (Turin, 1979), and Chittolini, ed. *La crisi degli ordinamenti comunali e le origini dello stato del Rinascimento* (Bologna, 1979); E. Fasano Guarini, "Principe e oligarchie nella Toscana del Cinquecento" *Annali della Facoltà di Scienze Politiche dell'Università di Perugia* 16 (1979–80), pp. 105–26, and Fasano Guarini, ed. *Potere e società negli stati regionali italiani fra Cinquecento e Seicento* (Bologna, 1978); on these issues from a Marxist perspective, see P. Anderson, *Lo stato assoluto* (Milan, 1980; English edit. 1974).

Along with most European aristocracies, Neapolitan barons also faced, however, the development of a bureaucratic monarchical state that not only encouraged the growth of new families, but sought as well to limit, and at times eliminate, the old aristocracy's political power at the center and its control over the provinces. Unlike other early modern Western European states, however, monarchical authority in Naples was wielded for over two centuries by a foreign dynasty that had in other, larger, countries the main foundations of its power. This had at least two essential consequences.

The first was the absence of a court at the center of government; although the viceroys surrounded themselves with several of the traditional ornaments of a royal court, and although the kingdom retained the ceremonial status of a monarchy without suffering any institutional impoverishment, the viceroys were only chief magistrates with relatively short tenures – between 1553 and 1734 none governed for more than nine years – and limited opportunity for the magnificence and munificence of courts graced with a resident sovereign. The *Seggi* brought the aristocracy together in the city government and forged its internal links, but their function as social centers was largely outside the control of the viceroy and Naples was the scene of a rather polycentric social life, as prominent families rivaled the social and cultural ambitions of individual viceroys. The lack of a royal court in Naples also meant a higher degree of fragmentation of the patronage networks, both between the sovereign and the aristocracy and between the latter and its own clients. The viceroys believed that their job of bringing the feudal aristocracy into the state would be made easier by its integration into the royal court, and, in 1640, Viceroy Medina suggested to King Philip IV that Neapolitan aristocrats be called to participate in the Madrid court life.[2]

The second related consequence of Spain's rule was the integration of the kingdom in an imperial system that assigned a specific role to Naples. Particularly after the 1570s, when Spain's rule was secure and Spanish interests geared northwards from the Mediterranean, what the kings wanted from Naples were contributions in money, supplies, and manpower for their enterprises elsewhere. The monarchy, therefore, abandoned even the Aragonese kings'

---

[2] In Piedmont, for example, the Savoy court played a much larger role in aristocratic life, see S. J. Woolf, *Studi sulla nobiltà piemontese nell'epoca dell'assolutismo*, (Turin, 1963), especially the introduction. On the consequences of the absence of a royal court in Naples for artistic developments, see G. Labrot and R. Ruotolo, "Pour une étude historique de la commande aristocratique dans le royaume de Naples espagnol" *Revue historique* 104, no. 264 (1980), pp. 25–48; social life in seventeenth-century Naples is described in the cited chronicles of Bulifon, Confuorto, and Fuidoro; see also G. Galasso, *Napoli spagnola dopo Masaniello* (2 vols.; Florence, 1982); courtly values were in any case present in Neapolitan aristocratic culture, see G. Vitale, "Modelli culturali nobiliari a Napoli tra Quattro e Cinquecento" *ASPN* 105 (1987), pp. 42–64. See A. Musi, *La rivolta di Masaniello nella scena politica barocca* (Naples, 1989), pp. 69–72 for Medina's suggestion; on these issues, see also H. G. Koenigsberger, *The Practice of Empire* (Ithaca, 1969; first edit. 1951).

limited policy of favoring urban and trading interests, and accepted compromises regarding the power structure within the kingdom so long as the kingdom's tasks within the imperial system were fulfilled. The feudal aristocracy could most easily guarantee order, stability, and compliance with Spain's needs, and therefore its social and economic privileges were preserved. The monarchy's needs also meant that, in a situation in which the exact boundaries between the viceroy's power and royal control were never clearly defined and depended to a large extent on personalities and circumstances, the kingdom's aristocracy and bureaucracy enjoyed more freedom of action and could, at times, play Madrid against the viceroy and vice versa.[3]

The consequences of Spain's rule have long been the subject of debate among historians of the South of Italy. Until the 1950s, Spanish bad government was often blamed for many of the evils that plagued the Mezzogiorno. Since the 1960s, the judgment on the Spanish monarchy in Naples has been tied to the debate on "refeudalization." Rosario Villari has spoken of a crisis of the state in the five or six decades preceding the 1647–48 revolt: the monarchical government abdicated its role of arbiter of social tension and allowed aristocratic pressure on the population to increase significantly, so that during the revolt large segments of the population abandoned the traditional monarchical loyalty of the kingdom for the first and only time in the early modern period. Although Villari has recognized the Spanish contribution to the establishment of a bureaucratic state in the Mezzogiorno, he has argued that the indispensable support the aristocracy offered to the monarchy during the revolt meant that, from 1648 until the mid-eighteenth century, the government failed to be a balancing power, and social conflicts and the general "backwardness" of the kingdom were actually accentuated.

In opposition to Villari, Giuseppe Galasso has emphasized – reelaborating Croce's ideas – the importance of Spain's rule for the process of state-building in the kingdom. The Spanish monarchy, Galasso believes, had such superior political and military strength that Neapolitan aristocrats had to give up all claims to an autonomous political role as possible kingmakers. Those who refused to do so, like the partisans of the French in 1528 or later the prince of Salerno, lost their possessions. Galasso has denied that the decades preceding the revolt saw a complete crisis of the state; he has argued that the revolt left the aristocracy weaker, since it showed how much the aristocracy's position in the provinces had to rely on the government's support, and that therefore the state's power in the

---

[3] The situation in Piedmont was quite different (Woolf, *Studi*, introduction); in Milan, the political situation was similar to that in Naples, and there too it resulted in the persisting strength of traditional local institutions and power groups, see U. Petronio, *Il Senato di Milano, istituzioni giuridiche ed esercizio del potere nel Ducato di Milano da Carlo V a Giuseppe II* (Milan, 1972); G. Vigo, *Fisco e società nella Lombardia del Cinquecento* (Bologna, 1979); on the rationale of the Spanish rule in Naples, see J. Marino, *Pastoral Economics* (Baltimore, 1988), pp. 160–62.

kingdom expanded in the second half of the seventeenth century. Most recently, Aurelio Musi, while denying Villari's class interpretation of the revolt, has stressed the political, economic, and social divisions between the provinces and the capital, and the resulting complex web of microconflicts that made up the revolt of 1647–48. Among the causes of these divisions, Musi has emphasized the growing power of the feudal aristocracy in the provinces and the failure of the state's bureaucratic alternative to feudal power.[4]

As we have seen, it seems now beyond doubt that the first half of the seventeenth century was a time of increasing aristocratic pressure on the vassal population. Feudal rule, however, became more lenient or at least acceptable to its subjects after the revolt, and recent studies have shown an increase in the power and influence of the state apparatus, particularly of the tribunals and councils of the capital, in the second half of the century. The present study, as we have seen, confirms the increase in aristocratic power in the provinces in the first part of the seventeenth century, a power that was not seriously threatened until the end of the following century. But the aristocracy drew economic and social advantages from the Spanish government's policies also outside of its fiefs, and in this chapter we shall analyze specific examples of how the aristocracy could profit from the entrance of Naples into the Spanish empire, and from the development of a bureaucratic monarchy.[5]

For the aristocracy, loss of direct political power as a possible alternative to royal power, a phenomenon common to all Western European dynastic states, was more than compensated by several advantages. Membership in a vast empire increased the opportunities for aristocratic military and administrative service. In addition, the aristocracy could often find ways to turn the laws to its advantage; and even the courts, composed as they were of lawyers whose main customers were aristocrats and of magistrates who aspired to – or already enjoyed – noble status, proved very sympathetic. If on the one hand the lawsuits, and the need to be present in Naples, entailed expenses, on the other hand service to the crown gave the right to appeal to royal protection and generosity.

---

[4] B. Croce, *Storia del regno di Napoli* (Bari, 1924; second edit. 1931); G. Pepe, *Il Mezzogiorno d'Italia sotto gli Spagnuoli* (Florence, 1952); Galasso's and Villari's works are cited in chapter 3; see also Villari, "La Spagna, l'Italia e l'assolutismo" *Studi storici* 18 (1977), 4, pp. 5–22 (also in Villari, *Ribelli e riformatori dal XVI al XVIII secolo* (Rome, 1979), pp. 43–67); G. D'Agostino, *La capitale ambigua, Napoli dal 1458 al 1580* (Naples, 1979); A. Lepre has observed that, while individual barons were weakened, the baronage as a class became stronger, *Storia del Mezzogiorno d'Italia* (2 vols.; Naples, 1986), I, p. 50; Musi, *La rivolta*, especially pp. 72–82; P. L. Rovito, "Strutture cetuali, riformismo ed eversione nelle rivolte apulo-lucane di metà Seicento" *ASPN* 106 (1988), pp. 241–308, sees rather a connection between the revolt in Naples and those in the provinces in the leadership role exercised by "civil" notables such as lawyers, doctors, and magistrates, at least in the first phase of the revolutionary events.

[5] On the growth of the state bureaucracy, particularly after the revolt, see Galasso, *Napoli spagnola*; R. Ajello, ed. *Giuristi e società al tempo di Pietro Giannone* (Naples, 1980); R. Colapietra, *Vita pubblica e classi politiche del viceregno napoletano (1656–1734)* (Rome, 1961); Rovito, *Respublica dei togati. Giuristi e società nella Napoli del '600* (Naples, 1981).

Furthermore, the financial needs of the crown forced it to sell lands, jurisdictions, titles, and shares of the public fiscal revenues, all of which the aristocracy was happy to buy. Its fiscal exemptions and dominant position within the representative institutions of the kingdom allowed the aristocracy to shift fiscal pressure onto others, and to take upon itself only a limited fiscal burden.

OFFICES AND SERVICES

The Spanish government needed a large and increasing number of men to serve as administrators, diplomats, and soldiers. Although the venality of offices was not as widespread in Naples as in France or Castile, most lower- and middle-rank offices in the kingdom were sold, as were some upper-rank ones. The legal career and the magistracies were the main avenue for upward social mobility, and many noble families of the seventeenth century had their origins in sixteenth-century *togati* (lawyers and magistrates). The old feudal aristocracy, however, enjoyed its share of offices, some venal but mainly not venal, and could serve the king of Spain in any of his many realms. In the sixteenth century, it was in fact service to the king and the church that enabled some members of old, noble families to acquire wealth and titles. Like the purchase of feudal jurisdictions or shares of the public debt, the acquisition of offices was not only a sound economic investment, but also a way to strengthen a family's position in respect both to its vassals and to other aristocrats.[6]

Some offices, like the traditional seven Grand Offices of the court, had always been, and were to remain, a precinct of the old aristocracy. These seven *Grandi Uffici* no longer entailed any power, but in the sixteenth century they carried a healthy annual salary of 2,190 ducats plus various gifts and privileges, with no obligations of any kind. We have already seen that aristocratic cadets pursued careers in the Spanish armies throughout Europe, and, later, in the church. The old aristocracy also occupied several positions in the councils and magistracies in Naples and Madrid, both those reserved for lawyers and those which did not require legal training. In the first half of the seventeenth century, for example,

---

[6] Discussion and examples abound in Rovito, *Respublica*; V.I. Comparato, *Uffici e società a Napoli (1600–1647)* (Florence, 1974); Villari, *La rivolta antispagnola a Napoli. Le origini (1585–1647)* (Bari, 1967); R. Mantelli, *Burocrazia e finanze pubbliche nel regno di Napoli a metà del Cinquecento* (Naples, 1981), especially pp. 66–78; Mantelli, *Il pubblico impiego nell'economia del regno di Napoli* (Naples, 1986), argues that while the high aristocracy occupied only about ten percent of venal offices, it received a large share of non-venal ones, especially in the military, pp. 311–28, 338–42; on offices at the provincial level, see Musi, "Amministrazione, potere locale e società in una provincia del Mezzogiorno moderno: il Principato Citra nel secolo XVII" *Quaderni sardi di storia* 4 (1984), pp. 81–118, and Musi "La venalità degli uffici in Principato Citra. Contributo allo studio del sistema dell'amministrazione periferica in età spagnola" *Rassegna storica salernitana* new series, 3 (1986), pp. 77–91, where he argues that there was a strong degree of compenetration between offices and feudal power in the provinces; on Sicily, see V. Sciuti Russi, "Aspetti della venalità degli uffici in Sicilia (XVII–XVIII secolo)" *RSI* 88 (1976), pp. 342–55. On the issue in general, see Anderson, *Lo stato*, pp. 42–56, and 382.

nine of the fifteen Neapolitans who became regents of the Collateral Council, the very pinnacle of a career in the magistracies, were *Seggio* aristocrats. The aristocracy also occupied positions of provincial government within the kingdom, especially in areas and times in which those positions entailed the use of the governors' military powers. The positions which could most enduringly affect an aristocratic family, however, were those outside of the kingdom itself. The Neapolitan aristocracy provided the kings of Spain with generals, ambassadors, viceroys, and counselors. A memoir written in the mid-seventeenth century for the Caracciolo Avellino, for instance, lists, for the Caracciolo clan alone, twenty-eight viceroys and governors, twenty generals, twenty-five state counselors, and twenty-six ambassadors, plus twenty-two Grand Masters of religious orders, eleven archbishops, and two cardinals.[7]

The fortunes of the Caracciolo Brienza began, in fact, with royal service at the highest level. It was Marino Caracciolo who, having passed from Leo X's ambassador to Charles V into imperial service as ambassador, cardinal, and eventually governor of Milan, acquired the prestige, wealth, and power upon which were based the fortunes of the Caracciolo Brienza, Avellino, and Sant'Eramo. The sale of the county of Gallarate in Lombardy, which duke Francesco Sforza had bestowed on Marino in 1530, provided the means for the acquisition of the family's fiefs in the kingdom of Naples, and Marino's ecclesiastic career served to grant bishoprics and abbeys to several of his nephews. In the following generation, Ascanio Caracciolo served in Charles V's armies, was a prominent personal friend of both viceroy Toledo and his son, and served Philip II in the kingdom and in Rome. His son, Giovan Battista Caracciolo, marquis of Sant'Eramo, was a member of the Collateral Council. After this time the Caracciolo Brienza, sure of their status, only rarely entered royal service, and none of them is known to have served outside the kingdom of Naples.[8]

The interest of the Caracciolo Brienza in royal offices as an investment did not, however, disappear. In particular, an analysis of two offices will show the ways in which offices were acquired, and the possibilities they offered for profits. The family, at different moments of its history, held two venal offices, those of Lieutenant Master of the Royal Stables (*Cavallerizzo Maggiore*), and Guardian of the Royal Hunting (*Montiero Maggiore*).

In 1557, Philip II made Ascanio Caracciolo Lieutenant Master of the Royal

---

[7] ACB 1.2 (this memoir also covers the period preceding the Spanish conquest). Comparato, *Uffici*, chapter 2; Villari, *La rivolta*, pp. 125–29; Villari, "Note sulla rifeudalizzazione del regno di Napoli alla vigilia della rivoluzione di Masaniello" *Studi storici* 6 (1965), especially pp. 306–15; Musi, *La rivolta*, pp. 81–82; on Piedmont, see Woolf, *Studi*, pp. 61–69, and 159–64.

[8] ACB 1 and 2. No other Caracciolo Brienza seems to have been a member of any royal tribunal in Naples, with the exception of Giuseppe II, who was regent of the Vicaria in 1715, see ACB 2.29 and G. A. Summonte, *Historia della città e regno di Napoli* (6 vols.; third edit., Naples, 1748–50; first edit. 1599–1601, 1640–43), VI, Appendix 3, p. 43.

Stables, with a salary of 400 ducats a year. This seems to have been a royal grace and not a sale. The office consisted in the management of the royal *razze*, or breeds, of horses, that were kept in Puglia and Calabria. It entailed jurisdiction on the stable staff, and the power to levy fines on those who damaged the royal breeds. The office passed to Ascanio's son, Giovan Battista, and to his two sons Marino and Carlo. In the early seventeenth century, the salary was 562 ducats a year, and the office was valued at 24,000 ducats. Although Carlo Caracciolo offered to levy 500 infantrymen to obtain the passage of the office to his son, at Carlo's death in 1648 the office went to another branch of the Caracciolo, the marquis of Cervinara. In 1636, Carlo Caracciolo also made a bid to buy the office of Treasurer General of the kingdom for 36,000 ducats, but his offer was not accepted.[9]

The office of *Montiero Maggiore* passed through several hands in the seventeenth century. Its value grew at each purchase, from 10,000 ducats in 1620 to 20,000 ducats in 1637. In 1647, Carlo Gambacorta, prince of Macchia and marquis of Celenza, husband of Faustina Caracciolo, bought it from the prince of Sant'Agata for 22,000 ducats. These sales had to be approved by the royal government, which kept the *jus luendi* on the office (that is, the right to repurchase it at any time) in order to avoid the complete privatization of public revenues. In 1654, Pietro Gambacorta, Carlo's heir, sold the office to his mother, Faustina Caracciolo, for 23,000 ducats. Two years after her death, in 1675, the government gave up its *jus luendi* and sold the office in full property to Pietro Gambacorta for 42,050 ducats, from which were deducted the 22,000 ducats that Pietro's father had paid for the office almost thirty years earlier. The rise in price shows not only the continuing increase in the office's value, but also the value added by full ownership. The government's needs for the war in Messina explain its decision to sell its *jus luendi* at that time. The act of sale expressly recognized Pietro's right to sell, bequeath, or entail the office. After Pietro's death, the office remained in the Gambacorta family, and in 1707 its value was set at 52,000 ducats.[10]

This office was responsible for the protection of the royal hunting grounds near Naples, and the *Montiero Maggiore* had the power to grant hunting licenses for a large area around the capital. He enjoyed the profits from the sale of all products of the royal hunting grounds (grass, nuts, wood, acorns), the rents of two palaces in Naples, plus a fourth of the value of all game entering the Naples

[9] ACB 2.1–9. G. D. Tassone, *Observationes jurisdictionales politicae ac practicae* ... (Naples, 1632; second edit. 1716), p. 137; Mantelli, *Burocrazia*, pp. 295–99; Mantelli, *Il pubblico impiego*, p. 435, notes that in 1689 the office was back in the hands of the marquis of Sant'Eramo; Summonte, *Historia*, I, p. 199.

[10] ASN, Archivio Carafa Castel San Lorenzo 5, particularly no. 2; notai del '600, 281/19, Alessandro Grimaldi, 1654, fols. 195r–208r; BNN ms. XI-B-19, fols. 88r–108v (the sale of 1675). A copy of this latter document probably exists also in the protocols of the notary, Giacinto de Monte, in ASN, but I was unable to locate it there.

market, and ceremonial privileges equal to those of a titled nobleman. Moreover, he exerted full civil and criminal jurisdiction over his staff, levied fines on all unlicensed hunters, and had the power to appoint judges and actuaries, and to keep armed men and his own jail, a right that the government vainly tried to take away from the office in 1653. The *Montiero* received a salary of 200 ducats a year, while the government also paid 418 ducats a year for the six guardians of the hunting grounds. The licenses were deemed to yield 1,200 ducats a year in the mid-seventeenth century, and the jurisdictional powers another 300. The total revenues of the office were estimated at 2,500 ducats a year in the mid-seventeenth century, which represented a yield of over eleven percent on the price Carlo Gambacorta paid for it in 1647.[11]

In the late sixteenth century, the Caracciolo Brienza also owned the *Mastro-dattia* (Actuary office) of the city of Taranto in Puglia, which was valued at 11,000 ducats in 1582. In 1597 it was rented for 700 ducats a year, and it gave the same yield in the early 1600s. The office was, however, sold by the royal courts around 1608 for 14,000 ducats to pay for some of Giovan Battista Caracciolo's debts. This office collected a fee for each legal act concluded in the city.[12] The nominal holders had no actual role in the management of any of these offices. Their role was limited to the collection of the revenues of rents, and the actual authority was delegated. These offices were obviously a form of *rentier* investment, and their high and secure yields made them very attractive to the aristocracy.

The appointment of Giuseppe Caracciolo, prince of Atena, as *maestre de campo* of a *tercio* of Neapolitan infantry in December 1647 proved less profitable economically. Giuseppe had been a very prominent defender of the viceroy in the days of the revolt, and the appointment was meant as a compensation. Giuseppe's *tercio* remained in existence at least until 1654, though we do not know where it served after the revolt. In 1658, the *Sommaria* (the financial tribunal) asked Giuseppe's sister and heir, Faustina, to pay ducats 2,594.2.--½ for money advances Giuseppe had received but neither used nor returned. Faustina replied that Giuseppe had credit for ducats 2,278.2--½ towards the captains of his *tercio*, and asked for a delay. In 1663, the government agreed to take over Giuseppe's credit and cancel his debt in exchange for 200 ducats and the claims Faustina herself had on the government for her tenure as *Montrice*

---

[11] Besides the cited sources, ASN, Attuari diversi 1043/12 on the jail; Tassone, *Observationes*, p. 137, Summonte, *Historia*, I, p. 200. The yield of venal offices was lower in France, where the nobility also bought many of them, see R. Forster, *The Nobility of Toulouse in the Eighteenth Century, a Social and Economic Study* (Baltimore, 1960; second edit. 1971), pp. 102–6.

[12] ASN, notai del '600, 508/14, Giuseppe Ragucci, 1681, fols. 42r–53r, and ACB 43.3.5 and 17.1 (a list of unnumbered notarial acts); 133.2, fols. 120r–21r for the 1597 rent; 45.7.2 for the 1600s rent. The office was sold to Francesco Cavaniglia, Giovan Battista's brother-in-law. Mantelli, *Pubblico impiego*, pp. 392, and 433–35, notes that the office had been rented for 100 ducats in 1560, and for 550 in 1594; in 1689, the office was in the hands of the Caracciolo prince of Avellino.

Maggiore. The transaction was concluded in 1668. It is not clear whether the Caracciolo profited economically from Giuseppe's military office, but his *tercio* proved essential to them in other ways. It was in fact with these troops, paid by the royal government, that Giuseppe repressed the revolt of his and his brother's vassals in 1648.[13]

As in many other early modern states, the Spanish government expanded the ranks of its officials and sold many of its offices. The aristocracy figures prominently among both the appointees and the purchasers of these positions, both in the capital and the provinces. Many of the offices simply represented sources of revenue and did not imply any intervention of the owner in the administration, although the increasing indebtedness of the government led to the gradual privatization, also through the offices, of the largest part of public revenues.[14]

ROYAL LAWS AND COURTS

The royal government had the power to regulate the membership of the feudal aristocracy and the extent of feudal jurisdiction through its laws and the decisions of its courts, and in the Spanish period the government attempted to do so more than had hitherto been done in Naples. There were, in fact, no less than twenty-seven *prammatiche* (royal laws) *De baronibus et eorum officio* (*On barons and their office*), and forty-eight *De feudis* (*On fiefs*), twenty-two and thirty-five respectively issued during the Spanish period.[15] Very often, however, these laws had a limited effect. The aristocracy could establish its own customs to regulate family alliances, and, to a certain extent, even inheritance practices. Moreover, the composition of the royal courts often made them unwilling to rule against the aristocracy, as we shall see later, particularly in respect of the aristocracy's relations with its vassals and creditors.

Royal laws, as we have seen in a previous chapter, attempted, often vainly, to control the barons' exercise of feudal powers. Several other laws regulated the degree of family relations within which feudal successions was permitted, not only in order to control who held the fiefs, but also to insure the crown's right of devolution. Although parts of feudal law were based on old traditions which

[13] ACB 1.3, 2.22–26, 8.19, 17.5, and 44.1.11; ASN, Processi civili Sommaria, ordinamento Zeni 138/4.
[14] On the aristocracy and the state in other parts of Italy, see E. Stumpo, "I ceti dirigenti in Italia in età moderna. Due modelli diversi: nobiltà piemontese e patriziato toscano" in A. Tagliaferri, ed. *I ceti dirigenti in Italia in età moderna e contemporanea* (Udine, 1984), pp. 151–97; C. Mozzarelli, "Strutture sociali e formazioni statuali a Milano e Napoli tra '500 e '600" *Società e storia* 1 (1978), pp. 431–63; Mozzarelli, "Stato, patriziato e organizzazione della società nell'età moderna" *Annali dell'Istituto Storico Italo-Germanico di Trento* 2 (1976), pp. 421–512.
[15] L. Giustiniani, ed. *Nuova collezione delle prammatiche del regno di Napoli* (15 vols.; Naples, 1803–8), III, *De baronibus et eorum officio*, and IV, *De feudis*. Seven other *prammatiche De feudis* were issued by the Austrian viceroys.

bound the king himself, the barons were keenly aware of his power to regulate feudal succession. Almost each General Parliament of the kingdom included the extension of feudal succession among the graces it asked the sovereign to grant. Unlike the kingdom of Sicily, where already in the fifteenth century feudal succession was extended to the seventh degree, in the kingdom of Naples it was only in 1655, partially as a compensation for aristocratic loyalty in the revolt, that Philip IV granted the full extension of feudal succession to the fourth degree. The king also exercised strict control over the alienation of fiefs. Whereas the viceroy could grant royal assent to many transactions involving feudal property, there were nine cases in which the assent could only be given by the king himself. These included all transactions concerning titled and ecclesiastic fiefs. Throughout the Spanish period, the crown resisted all attempts by the Neapolitan aristocracy and the viceroys themselves to make it change its stance on this point.[16]

The aristocracy, nonetheless, controlled the transmission of property within the immediate family with little or no intervention by the government. The one *prammatica De antefato* (*On the marriage settlement*) of 1617, was the only one issued during the Spanish period to regulate matters of family policy. Until 1806, customs and traditions dating from Lombard or Norman times regulated institutions like the *vita milizia* and the *paraggio* dowry, which set the claims of cadets and daughters on feudal property, while Roman law governed the *legittima* (legal share) of all children on allodial property. These customs and traditions could vary depending on the people involved or on the location of any property; their variety, antiquity, and ambiguities gave rise to a large body of juridical literature produced both in response to specific cases in the courts, and as independent scholarly treatises.[17]

The aristocracy, moreover, had recourse to private decisions, both individual and corporate, regulating the transmission of its property, particularly in the area of marriages. Since the customs were often unclear or debatable, each testator

[16] A. Cernigliaro, *Sovranità e feudo nel regno di Napoli, 1505–1557* (2 vols.; Naples, 1983), part II and pp. 673–714; N. Santamaria, *I feudi, il diritto feudale e la loro storia nell'Italia meridionale* (Naples, 1881; reprint Bologna, 1978); G. A. Lanario, *Repetitiones feudales* (Naples, 1630); S. Rovito, *Luculenta commentaria* (Naples, 1649); G. A. de Giorgio, *Repetitiones feudales ineditae* (Naples, 1724); G. Sorge, *Jurisprudentia forensis* (10 vols.; V, *De feudis*, Naples, 1742) D. Civitella, *Delle consuetudini di Napoli sotto i titoli De successionibus ab intestato et ex testamento commentario* (Naples, 1785); on the Neapolitan school of feudal jurisprudence, see G. D'Amelio, "Polemica antifeudale, feudistica napoletana e diritto longobardo" *QS* 9 (1974), pp. 337–50. On Sicily, see G. Dragonetti, *Origine de' feudi ne' regni di Napoli e Sicilia* (Naples, 1788). On the fourth degree, see *prammatica XXXV De feudis*, on the nine cases, see *prammatica IV De feudis*, in Giustiniani, *Nuova collezione*.

[17] A. Capano, *De vita militia tractatus* (Naples, 1642); P. De Gregorio, *Tractatus de vita et militia, de dote de paragio* (Palermo, 1596; second edit. Naples, 1642, as appendix to Capano's work); G. Abignente, *Il diritto successorio nelle province napoletane dal 500 al 1800* (Nola, 1881); ACB 161, unnumbered fol., contains the calculations of the *vita milizia* for Litterio Caracciolo's cadet sons in the 1780s. The main subject of Tassone, *Observationes*, is the *prammatica De antefato*.

could rule over future passages of his estate. Although the wording of entails was often the ground for disputes, Neapolitan jurists recognized the very wide powers of decision of the individual testator in the establishment of entails.[18]

Most threatening to the aristocracy were the Lombard customs by which a spouse could inherit from the other, even in the absence of children. The aristocracy tended to avoid the passage of property from one family to another through marriages, and possibly already in Norman times most aristocratic marriage agreements had recourse to the so-called *Usages of the Magnates* (*Usi dei Proceri e Magnati*), a set of rules regulating the succession of spouses and the restitution of dowries. In the Angevin period, an even stricter set of rules, the *Pact of Capuana and Nido*, was formed, whereby the mixing of the spouses' patrimonies was made well-nigh impossible. The *Pact* also went further than the *Usages* in limiting a woman's right to will her estate, as we have seen. By the Spanish period, all aristocratic marriages were contracted according to the *Pact*. Both the *Usages* and the *Pact*, although included later in the sixteenth century in the customs of the city of Naples, were entirely private rules by which the parties involved in the marriage contracts spontaneously agreed to abide. The crown recognized the validity of these agreements, and they were taken into account in royal laws and upheld in royal courts.[19]

Royal legislation could, therefore, to a large extent be circumvented by the aristocracy. The ambiguities of customs and laws, and the wide possibilities for interpretation of the wording of entails, marriage contracts and wills, however, might give considerable power to the royal courts whenever lawsuits were initiated. Spanish Naples was as litigious as any other early modern European society, and lawsuits went on for many years, often for centuries. The Caracciolo Brienza kept lawyers permanently at their service, as did other aristocrats and most *università* of the kingdom.

The frequency of litigation in the royal courts did not, however, prove harmful to the aristocracy. The legal complexities of family policy could be successfully used in litigation with creditors. As we have seen, it was through a clever handling of her dowry claim that Diana Caracciolo preserved Atena and Sasso from the confiscation demanded by her husband's creditors in the 1620s. In the

---

[18] Capano, *De fideicommisso masculino* (Naples, 1649); O. Barbato, *Modestinus elucidatus sive de fideicommisso, maioratu ac primogenitura* (Naples, 1643).

[19] A. di Letizia, *Degli usi dei Proceri e Magnati e di Capuana e Nido commentari* (Naples, 1786); F. Ciccaglione, *Le leggi e le più note consuetudini che regolarono i patti nuziali nelle province napoletane innanzi alla pubblicazione del codice francese* (Naples, 1881); G. M. Monti, "Il patto dotale napoletano di Capuana e Nido" in Monti, *Dal '200 al '700* (Naples, 1925), pp. 3–39; C. Rota, *Legalis Androgynus, sive tractatus de privilegiis mulierum* (Naples, 1665); M. A. Visceglia, "Linee per uno studio unitario dei testamenti e dei contratti matrimoniali dell'aristocrazia feudale napoletana tra fine Quattrocento e Settecento" *MEFRM* 94 (1982), pp. 393–470; G. Muto, "Lo 'stile antiquo': consuetudini e prassi amministrative a Napoli nella prima età moderna" *MEFRM* 100 (1988), pp. 317–30; on the usages in lower-class contracts, see G. Caridi, "Capitoli matrimoniali, dote e dotario in Calabria (XVI–XVII secolo)" *ASCL* 54 (1987), pp. 11–44.

The aristocracy and the Spanish rule

1680s, Giuseppe II adopted, in his defense against his father Domenico's creditors and his own brother's claims, the line that he did not hold his patrimony as heir to Domenico, but rather as claimant to various entails established in the family in previous generations. Again in the late eighteenth century, the longstanding claims of creditors over Atena and Sasso were offset by Litterio Caracciolo's rights as heir to an entailed dowry established almost 200 years before.[20]

The clever use of the intricacies of family policy were only one of the ways in which royal courts' decisions favorable to the aristocracy could be obtained. In general, besides the skills of its lawyers, the aristocracy could count on a high degree of support from the courts themselves. The *Sommaria* and the Sacred Council were the most common courts for civil lawsuits involving the aristocracy and its creditors, and they were staffed by magistrates with pretensions to nobility, and lawyers who often numbered many aristocrats among their clients. In fact, family relations between the judges and one of the parties were common ground – in a society very sensitive to ideas of family solidarity – for the rejection of the judge by the other party, as examples from trials involving the Caracciolo Brienza show. In memoirs addressed to his nephews, Francesco D'Andrea, possibly the best and most noted lawyer in late seventeenth-century Naples, extolled the law career as the best and safest way for men of good birth to ascend socially and acquire wealth. The prestige of lawyers, higher in Naples than elsewhere according to D'Andrea, was due mainly to the many lawsuits involving "great patrimonies and very wealthy estates." The aristocracy needed the support of the lawyers, and

the foremost lords of the kingdom try to win their favor, and some pay a regular salary to many lawyers to avoid having them as opponents ... they treat them with utmost respect ... even if the lawyers be of low birth ... they recognize them as their equals or even betters.[21]

Because of this situation, lawyers who had become magistrates would quite likely be sympathetic to the aristocracy's litigation with its vassals or creditors. Moreover, the aristocracy could, and did, strengthen its ties with the courts' staff through more direct means. It is hard to come by evidence of outright corruption, but the problem was widespread in Naples, many lamented it, and the royal government sent several investigators (known as visitors) to the kingdom to try and remedy the situation. Giovan Battista Caracciolo Brienza bequeathed 300 ducats to the lawyer and magistrate Scipione Rovito and named

[20] ACB 16.8b; 73.2, especially 20; 77.2.23–25.
[21] F. D'Andrea, *I ricordi di un avvocato napoletano del '600*, ed. N. Cortese (Naples, 1923), p. 66 (the work previously appeared in *ASPN* 44–46 (1919–21) as "Avvertimenti ai nipoti"); on D'Andrea and the rise of the *togati*, see also S. Mastellone, *Francesco D'Andrea politico e giurista* (Florence, 1969). See ASN Processi civili Sacro Consiglio ord. Zeni 121/25 and 121/48 for examples of the rejection of judges; see also Rovito, *Respublica*, chapter 4.

him as his executor, though this is no proof of any foul play on Rovito's part. In 1684–86, the priest Lorenzo de Colutiis, agent for Giuseppe II, marked in his accounts for the marquis many small sums paid to clerks and lower-rank officers of the courts, some of which may have been fees, but a few of which are identified as "gifts." Around 1740, the lawyers of the Caracciolo Brienza suggested that the marquis come to Naples, because the lawsuit with creditors over Atena and Sasso had come to a decisive point. They added that "before this lawsuit is concluded some maneuvering is necessary; for this some money has to be spent under cover, and the best way to do this is through Your Excellency's own hands." Payments to judges and lower court staff were common and open in the eighteenth century. In the 1760s, Litterio Caracciolo asked his agent in Naples to present gifts to the servants of lawyers and judges.[22]

The royal courts proved quite favorable to the Caracciolo Brienza in their trials with both vassals and creditors. Although the government was concerned, especially in the seventeenth century, with the *università*'s indebtedness and tried to assist them, baronial jurisdiction was protected by the royal tribunals, and the expansion of feudal powers in the decades around 1600 was often abetted by the royal courts. Still in the eighteenth century, when feudal powers came under attack from reformers, the courts defended the Caracciolo Brienza's old powers over their vassals. In the 1730s, for instance, the Sacred Council and the Collateral Council upheld the marquis' second-degree jurisdiction against the *università* of Brienza, the *Sommaria* did likewise for the marquis' right of *zecca*, and the Sacred Council recognized the marquis' right of *piazza* and his power to appoint the master for Brienza's fair. Also in 1730, and again ten years later, the *Sommaria* upheld the Caracciolo's right to the *portolania* of Atena. The Caracciolo also profited from several decisions of the Sacred Council throughout the seventeenth century in their lawsuit with the *università* of Sala over the latter's debts to the family.[23]

The best example of the advantages the aristocracy drew from sympathetic royal courts is the solutions of the trials initiated by creditors. Since oftentimes the creditors themselves were noble, the courts did not directly aim to protect one class against another. But in general the legal system itself, not unlike that of

[22] ACB 16.8a, unnumbered fol.; 138.24, fols. 29r–40r; 77.2.21; 140.40, fol. 29r. Corruption is discussed in all the cited books on the bureaucracy, and in A. M. Rao, "La questione feudale nell'età tanucciana" paper presented at the conference *Bernardo Tanucci, la corte, il paese 1730–80,* held in Catania in October 1985, pp. 5–7 of the typescript. In Sicily, too, the budget of an eighteenth-century aristocratic family included gifts to judges and lawyers, A. Guarneri, "Alcune notizie sovra la gestione di una casa baronale" *Archivio Storico Siciliano* 17 (1892), pp. 117–50.

[23] ACB 45.1.14, 17, 18, 20, and 32; 45.6.2; 75.1.14 and 20; for Sala, see 89.3; similar examples are in Lepre, *Feudi e masserie, problemi della società meridionale nel '600 e nel '700* (Naples, 1973), especially p. 45, and in R. Merzario, *Signori e contadini di Calabria. Corigliano Calabro dal XVI al XIX secolo* (Milan, 1975), pp. 56–64; Visceglia, "Comunità, signori feudali e *officiales* in Terra d'Otranto fra XVI e XVII secolo" *ASPN* 104 (1986), pp. 259–85; a detailed study of feudal jurisdiction and the courts' attitude towards it is in A. Cernigliaro, "Giurisdizione baronale e prassi delle avocazioni nel Cinquecento napoletano" *ibid.,* pp. 159–241.

Spain or Sicily, was so designed as to favor aristocratic debtors. They could not be arrested, and, especially if they were members of the titled nobility, they could count on royal munificence and support, as can be seen in the case of the Caracciolo Brienza patrimony in the seventeenth century. At the death of Giovan Battista Caracciolo, his debts amounted most probably to more than the total value of his estate, and in the early 1620s, the Sacred Council, pressured by the creditors, decided to confiscate the entire patrimony.[24]

In 1625, an appraiser for the government valued the four Caracciolo fiefs, plus the properties in neighboring Sala, at ducats 192,678.4.14½. Atena and Sasso were, however, detached from the estate and assigned to Diana Caracciolo and to her third son, Giuseppe, in satisfaction of her dowry claim, while the properties at Sala – the Caracciolo claimed – had been bought by marquis Marco Antonio II with his uncle Marino's inheritance, and had therefore never been part of Giovan Battista's estate. A list of creditors by seniority of claim was formed, and Diana's dowry claim was given fourth place, since the court considered it as dating from 1590 when she had married Giovan Battista. A caretaker was assigned to the estate, or what was left of it, and the Sacred Council began procedures to rent Brienza and Pietrafesa and pay the creditors with the proceeds. This process was known as the "deduction" (*deduzione*) of the patrimony.[25]

The rent of the "deducted" fiefs was awarded through an auction in court, theoretically open to all and repeated every three or four years. The Caracciolo Brienza held the rent, however, from 1625 to 1690, when, as we have seen, Giuseppe II repurchased Brienza and Pietrafesa in full property. Renting the fiefs to the old feudal lords – who still kept their title of marquis of Brienza – may have made good sense, since the vassals were likely to accept the situation more easily. However, the fact that so many years went by without anybody success-fully challenging the Caracciolo Brienza's offers to rent the fiefs seems to show that the Caracciolo were being favored in some ways.

This is confirmed by the similar examples of Montenegro in the 1650s and 1660s, and of Sasso in the last third of the seventeenth century. Both fiefs, after their "deduction," were rented out through auctions; and in both cases the Caracciolo Brienza's was the winning offer. The same happened in the late seventeenth century with the confiscation of the Caracciolo Brienza palace in Naples. Moreover, in the examples of Brienza and Montenegro, the Caracciolo obtained rebates on the rents, undoubtedly because of the economic hard times

---

[24] Many documents in ACB refer to these events and the ensuing centuries of litigation, that have also been discussed in previous chapters. In what follows, therefore, I have given references only to specific documents cited in the text. For the whole lawsuit, see also ASN Pandetta Corrente 2026 and 570, which repeat much of the information scattered in ACB with some additional documents.

[25] The appraisal is in ACB 43.3.1; for Sala, see ASN Pandetta Corrente 2026, vol. III, fols. 454r–55v.

of the mid-seventeenth century, but certainly with the effect of further reducing the amount of money going to the creditors. In the case of Brienza, a part of the rent went to the Caracciolo Brienza themselves in payment of credits they claimed on the estate of Giovan Battista Caracciolo because of various entails and bequests: for example, 970 ducats a year in the 1640s, or between a third and a fourth of the rent, were discounted to satisfy various Caracciolo claims.[26]

The *deduzione* of a patrimony was similar to what happened in Sicily when an aristocratic estate was managed by the *Deputazione degli Stati*. It seems, however, that in Naples the courts, through rents and auctions, were willing for all practical purposes to leave the fiefs in the hands of their old lords. Moreover, the Caracciolo could appeal to royal munificence. Around 1570, Aurelia Caracciolo obtained 4,000 ducats as a royal gift for the services of her late husband, Ascanio. From the 1620s, when his patrimony was confiscated, and for more than twenty years after that, the Sacred Council awarded Giacomo Caracciolo, marquis of Brienza, 1,000 ducats a year for his support, notwithstanding the fact that Giacomo himself was, through an agent, renting his two confiscated fiefs of Brienza and Pietrafesa. This form of grants to bankrupt aristocrats from their own confiscated possessions was also common in Habsburg Spain.[27] Through direct munificence or through the workings of the legal system, therefore, the indebted Caracciolo Brienza received the support of the royal government against their creditors, be they commoners or other aristocrats; and hence they succeeded in surviving the economic difficulties of the mid-seventeenth century with all of their possessions intact.

The Spanish government, therefore, failed in its attempts to exercise and increase its control over the aristocracy's relations with its vassals and creditors. The greater power of the Spanish kings, compared to that of their predecessors, resulted in the expansion of royal legislation and of the numbers and powers of royal tribunals. But aristocratic family policy remained largely outside the sphere of royal laws, and the intricate legal position of aristocratic patrimonies helped protect them against creditors' claims. Furthermore, the presence in the royal tribunals of lawyers and magistrates with aspirations to nobility, and the

---

[26] For Brienza and Pietrafesa, see ACB, and ASN Pandetta Corrente 2026, vol. III (particularly fols. 125r–v for the 970 ducats), and IV. For Sasso, see ASN Pandetta Corrente 570, vol. I and vol. marked 2, and ACB 14, 77.1 and 73.2.5. For Montenegro, see ACB 11.1 and 2. For the palace, see ACB 16.8i and ASN Pandetta Corrente 570, vol. marked 3.

[27] On Sicily, see the detailed, though not at all satisfactory, work of G. Tricoli, *La Deputazione degli Stati e la crisi del baronaggio siciliano dal XVI al XIX secolo* (Palermo, 1966); E. Pontieri, *Il tramonto del baronaggio siciliano* (Florence, 1943), discusses the *Deputazione* and the ties between the barons and lawyers and magistrates; on Spain, see C. Jago, "The Influence of Debt on the Relations between Crown and Aristocracy in Seventeenth-Century Castile" *Economic History Review* series 2, 26 (1973), pp. 218–36; B. Yun Casalilla, *Sobre la transición al capitalismo en Castilla. Economía y sociedad en Tierra de Campos (1500–1830)* (León, 1987); on the issue of litigiousness, see R. L. Kagan, *Lawsuits and Litigants in Castile, 1500–1700* (Chapel Hill, 1981). For Aurelia, see ACB 2.4.

frequency of corruption, meant that the royal courts most often ruled in favor of the aristocracy in lawsuits opposing it to its vassals or creditors.

THE CROWN'S FINANCIAL NEEDS

The financial needs of the crown grew rapidly and constantly from the early sixteenth century at least until the mid-seventeenth century revolt, and an increasing toll in money, men, and supplies, was demanded of the kingdom of Naples. As was happening in Castile and elsewhere in early modern Europe, the government had recourse to a variety of means to augment its revenues besides the raising of heavier taxes. We have already seen how offices were sold and how they could be profitable investments for the aristocracy. The crown also sold lands, titles, and jurisdictions, and the old aristocracy took a lion's share of these too, in effect strengthening the feudal structure of the kingdom. Moreover, the aristocracy acquired a large share of the public debt in the form of the many fiscal revenues the government sold to private citizens in exchange for cash anticipations. The growing state debt resulted in a series of opportunities to enlarge aristocratic wealth.

The government resorted first to the sale of lands. Possibly because – as Galasso writes – the Spanish government felt its domination safer than its predecessors had, in the first half of the sixteenth century it sold many towns and villages that had been kept in the royal domain by the Aragonese kings. This was also the result of an attempt to establish a new group of feudatories more directly tied to the new monarchy, and, especially after the French invasion of 1528, to compensate faithful Neapolitans and Spaniards. Gennaro Incarnato has shown the rapid changes in the structure of feudal property in Abruzzo Ultra between 1500 and 1540. The most notable of these changes was the drastic diminution of the number of royal towns from fifteen (including the large *contado* of Aquila) to six (including now only a small territory around Aquila). In the following 130 years, Incarnato shows that only two more royal towns were enfeoffed, probably in the 1630s and 1640s when the royal government sold all it could to pay for the expenses of the Thirty Years War. Similar data are available for Calabria, and in general the number of royal towns had shrunk to about fifty throughout the kingdom by 1550. The number of royal towns remained very small until the Bourbon years, since fiefs devolved to the crown were invariably given again in fief, and *università* who bought themselves back into the royal domain were soon sold again by the government, as was the case with Atena in the 1560s.[28]

---

[28] Galasso, *Economia e società nella Calabria del Cinquecento* (Naples, 1967; second edit. Milan, 1975), chapter I; Galasso, "Momenti e problemi di storia napoletana nell'età di Carlo V" in Galasso, *Mezzogiorno medievale e moderno* (Turin, 1965; second edit. 1975), pp. 139–97, especially pp. 167–86; G. Incarnato, "L'evoluzione del possesso feudale in Abruzzo Ultra dal 1500 al 1670" *ASPN* 96 (1971), pp. 219–87. Villari, "Baronaggio e finanze a Napoli alla vigilia della rivoluzione del 1647–48" *Studi storici* 3 (1962), pp. 259–305, especially pp. 298–305 for the sales

The continuity of feudal power

From data provided by Incarnato and other sources, it seems that the old aristocracy of the kingdom did not always profit directly from these sales of fiefs, and in some cases it actually provided the crown with more lands to sell, particularly after 1528 when the fiefs of prominent pro-French aristocrats were confiscated. But the old aristocracy succeeded in buying fiefs from the original recipients of the royal sales. Incarnato has shown how the many Spaniards who acquired fiefs in Abruzzo in the 1530s quickly lost them to the large feudal complexes of the Acquaviva, Piccolomini or Colonna. In any case, the sixteenth century brought a general increase in the degree of commercialization of fiefs. We have seen that the Caracciolo Brienza bought Brienza and Pietrafesa from the Caracciolo dukes of Martina, Sasso from an untitled Caracciolo branch, and Atena from the Carafa counts of Morcone.

After about 1550, the sale of fiefs could therefore no longer yield significant revenues for the crown. In the late sixteenth and especially in the seventeenth centuries, the government began to sell first jurisdiction and then titles. Incarnato mentions the frequent sales of feudal jurisdiction in Abruzzo Ultra in the late sixteenth century. It was natural for feudatories who had recently bought a fief to enlarge their authority on it by acquiring, through purchases and often through usurpations, new privileges and rights. Each new source of revenue increased the capital value of the fief. The royal government tried to control usurpations of feudal rights, and the Caracciolo Brienza papers contain numerous fiscal documents, known as *risulte*, which discuss the validity of specific feudal claims. The Caracciolo Brienza also regularly purchased additional rights.

When the family bought its four fiefs they already included several feudal rights, most notably first-degree jurisdiction. In 1557, Ippolita Filomarino, mother of Marco Antonio I, bought from the government second-degree jurisdiction and the rights of *portolania* and *zecca* for the fief of Salvia. In 1560 she bought the same jurisdiction and rights for the fiefs of Brienza and Pietrafesa, for a total price of 1,535 ducats, calculated on the basis of five ducats per vassal household. In 1573, the Caracciolo bought second-degree jurisdiction and the *portolania* of Atena and the *portolania* of Sala. Eighteen years earlier the royal government had sold the right of *zecca* of Atena to its then-owner, Luigi Carafa, prince of Stigliano. In 1589, Giulia and Giovan Battista Caracciolo bought the monopoly right on ovens in Atena for 740 ducats from the baron of nearby San Rufo. In 1588, lastly, the Caracciolo purchased from the crown the *portolania* of Sasso for 260 ducats. The concentration of these purchases in the very first years of the Caracciolo's domination points not only to the expansion of the family's economic means in the favorable years between

in the seventeenth century; F. Del Vecchio, "La vendita delle terre demaniali nel regno di Napoli dal 1628 al 1648" *ASPN* 103 (1985), pp. 163–211, denies that the government engaged in large sales of domanial lands before the revolt.

1550 and 1590, but also to the need they felt for wider authority over their new vassals.[29]

The sale of titles was another source of revenue for the crown, especially in the viceroyal period. In the early fifteenth century, the last Angevin sovereigns had begun to bestow noble titles on their vassals. The first non-royal prince and duke of the kingdom date from that time. In 1428, Petriccone Caracciolo bought Brienza and Sasso from Queen Giovanna II with the title of count of Brienza for 1,000 gold ounces. But the number of titled feudatories remained relatively low in the kingdom until well into the sixteenth century. Table 6.1 shows the remarkable increase in the number of titles bestowed by the kings of Spain on Neapolitan feudatories from the second half of the sixteenth century onwards. It also shows the gradual decline in prestige of the lower title of count. Although not all the sources for Table 6.1 are entirely reliable, the trend is very clear and resembles the situation in Habsburg Spain itself.[30] Titles were based on the possession of an inhabited fief. Many went to new nobles of commercial or bureaucratic origins, but many, too, were bestowed on members of old, noble families.

The crown did not officially sell titles, and the documents rarely mention any payment. But in most instances there can be little doubt that the titles were purchased. While very little is known about the bestowal of the marchional title on Brienza to Marco Antonio Caracciolo in 1569, the princely title given to his grandson, Giuseppe, on Atena in 1636 is well documented. Since 1623, Atena and Sasso belonged to Diana Caracciolo. In 1634, when her son, Giuseppe, turned eighteen, Diana sold Atena to him in full property for 19,000 ducats, which Diana allowed him to pay within ten years. Giuseppe left all revenue from Atena to his mother as interest on the price. Giuseppe, that is, acquired only nominal possession of Atena, but he hastened to go through the ritual ceremonies of the *presa di possesso*. The next year Giuseppe, "wishing ... to obtain from His Majesty the title and dignity of prince" on Atena, asked his mother to sign a fictitious receipt for the 19,000 ducats, which Giuseppe promised to use for the sole purpose of demonstrating his actual possession of Atena and therefore obtaining the title. In October 1636, Giuseppe became the prince of Atena. The procedure shows that the initiative lay entirely with the

---

29 ASN Refute Quinternioni 202, fols. 35r–38r; ACB 43.1.28 and 45.1.1; 75.6, 7, and 10; 74.2.3 and 75.1.1–4; 81.1.12; ASN Repertori dei Quinternioni 14-III, fols. 11r–v. In the 1560s, Atena had briefly succeeded in repurchasing itself into the royal domain. However, when a *università* reentered the royal domain, alienated feudal rights did not revert to the crown, but were exercised by the *università* itself. Therefore the *zecca* of Atena, bought by the prince of Stigliano in 1555, passed to the Caracciolo Brienza when they bought Atena in fief.

30 Examples for Spain are in A. Dominguez Ortiz, *El Antiguo Régimen: los Reyes Catholicos y los Austrias* (Madrid, 1973), p. 118; for Sicily, see O. Cancila, *Baroni e popolo nella Sicilia del grano* (Palermo, 1983), p. 163; for Northern Italian states, see C. Donati, *L'idea di nobiltà in Italia* (Bari, 1988), pp. 280–81; for France, see Schalk, "Ennoblement in France from 1350 to 1660" *Journal of Social History* 16 (1982), pp. 101–10.

Table 6.1. *Noble titles in the kingdom of Naples*
(1444–1750)

year	princes	dukes	marquis	counts	totals
1444	2	10	2	42	56
1528	6	19	15	59	99
1599	23	33	65	44	165
1601	23	36	66	57	182
1607–8	27	48	76	62	213
1613	38	57	85	59	239
1620	47	72	108	69	296
1646–71	84	124	159	71	438
1672	119	144	158+	25	446+
1750	149	239	227	34	649

Sources: C. Foucard, "Fonti di storia napoletana nell'Archivio di Stato di Modena" *ASPN* 2 (1877), pp. 725–57 (one of the ten dukes here is the duke of Calabria, a title belonging to the heir to the throne); T. Pedio, *Napoli e Spagna nella prima metà del Cinquecento* (Bari, 1971), pp. 166–73 (quoting a Venetian list dating from 1528); G. Ceci, "I feudatari napoletani alla fine del secolo XVI" *ASPN* 24 (1899), pp. 122–38; S. Mazzella, *Descrittione del regno di Napoli*... (Naples, 1601, reprint Bologna, 1981; first edit. 1586); B. Capasso, ed. "Napoli descritta nei principi del secolo XVII da G. C. Capaccio" *ASPN* 7 (1882), p. 534; T. Costo *et al.*, *Compendio dell'historia del regno di Napoli*... (Venice, 1591; second edit. Naples, 1613); H. Bacco Alemanno, *Il regno di Napoli in dodici provincie*... (Naples, 1609; second edit. 1620); O. Beltrano, *Breve descrittione del regno di Napoli diviso in dodici provincie*... (Naples, 1646; second edit. 1671, reprint Bologna, 1969); G. Campanile, *Notizie di nobiltà* (Naples, 1672); Summonte, *Historia*, 6, Appendix 2. Particularly in the later lists, several titles belonged to the same family; for example, already in 1613 thirty-six of the fifty-nine counts held other, higher, titles, or were heirs to them, and so did forty-one of the seventy-one counts in 1671. I have, however, in this table counted the number of titles existing in the kingdom, not that of their holders. The figures from Beltrano increase very little between the 1646 and the 1671 edition, so that they probably refer to the years around the earlier date; the figures for the marquis in 1672 are low, because six pages of the book were missing from the copy in BNN; since each page holds between two and three titles, the total should probably be about 170 to 176 marchional titles. Many of these sources were published several times in the seventeenth century, and the differences between the various editions are at times very confusing; this explains why my figures do not always match Villari's (*Rivolta*, pp. 189–91).

Caracciolo, so that it is most likely that the title was actually purchased. As we have seen, the family was trying in those years to establish Giuseppe's claim on the entire Caracciolo Brienza patrimony as a solution to the debts that weighed on Giuseppe's brother, the marquis Giacomo. In these circumstances, obtaining a title for Giuseppe was probably another way to insure the safe passage of most of the patrimony to him.[31]

A further example of the practice of acquiring nominal possession of a fief in order to purchase a title is the fictitious sale of Sasso from Giuseppe Caracciolo to Achille Capece Minutolo, a close friend, nobleman of the same *Seggio* of Capuana, and a neighbor of Giuseppe in Naples. The sale, declared by both parties in a secret act to be fictitious, took place in 1645 at Achille's request, so that he could obtain a ducal title from the king. The price of Sasso was set at 20,000 ducats, but again none of it was paid and Giuseppe kept the revenues of the fief as interest on the price. Achille obtained his title in the same year, and he and Giuseppe were very close in the days of the revolt. Although the purchase was only formally annulled in 1737, neither Achille nor any of his successors ever had anything to do with Sasso and its revenues.[32]

The last and main device the Spanish government used to raise the funds it needed was the sale of public revenues. In the kingdom of Naples, the government sold the revenues of both direct taxes, such as the *fiscali* on the *università* or the *adoe* on the barons, and indirect taxes, such as the *gabelle* and *arrendamenti* (tax-farms). Only a part of the taxes levied by the provincial fiscal agents and of the tax-farms paid by the *arrendatori*, therefore, reached the royal treasury. Purchase of these shares of the public revenues was open to all, and aristocrats showed a strong interest in investing in them on their own or through intermediary financiers, whenever their economic situation allowed them to do so. The large network of aristocratic backers of Bartolomeo d'Aquino's financial

[31] ASN notai '600,Pietro Antonio dell'Aversano, 912/12, 1634, fols. 420r–29r, and 912/13, 1635, fols. 101v–3r (copies of these documents were also in ACB, but they have disappeared; ACB 90, under 73.1.1–5 and 9, for summaries of the acts). The title is listed in ASN Museo 99B135 *Titulorum Neapolis* and 99B137, indexes to a series of volumes destroyed in 1943. It is also listed in ASN Museo 99B138, an index of Neapolitan privileges in the Simancas archives. A ducal title in 1595 cost 4,000 Castilian ducats, see Marino, *Pastoral Economics*, p. 170; see also F. Caracciolo, *Uffici, difesa e corpi rappresentativi nel Mezzogiorno in età spagnola* (Reggio Calabria, 1974), pp. 32–34; further examples of sales of titles are in A. Calabria, "Finanzieri genovesi nel regno di Napoli nel Cinquecento" *RSI* 101 (1989), p. 611, footnote 112, and, without references, in R. Colapietra, *Dal Magnanimo a Masaniello* (2 vols.; Salerno, 1973), II, pp. 369–70.
[32] ASN Museo; ACB 81.1.10 and 12. On Giuseppe's and Achille's relations, see F. Capecelatro, *Diario 1647–1650* (3 vols.; Naples, 1850–54), I, pp. 233–35; II, pp. 477–79, and 508–12, and see index. Achille had an important role during the revolt, see Musi, *La rivolta*, pp. 171–73, 252, and 269; he was a member of the Collateral Council in 1641, see G. Intorcia, *Magistrature del regno di Napoli. Analisi prosopografica* (Naples, 1987), p. 341.

speculations in the 1630s and 1640s was the most prominent instance of this phenomenon.[33]

The Caracciolo Brienza invested early on in *fiscali*. Between 1541 and 1559, Ascanio Caracciolo had a capital of 2,000 ducats invested at ten percent on the *fiscali*, and Ippolita Filomarino, wife of Giulio Cesare Caracciolo, had a capital of 6,644 ducats in *fiscali*, also at ten percent, though we do not know on which *università* these *fiscali* were assigned. Villari has argued that the aristocracy tended to purchase *fiscali* on its own fiefs, so as to strengthen its grip on its vassals in yet another way, excluding the government from any interference in its "states." This tendency certainly existed and was not limited to the years Villari identifies as the heyday of "refeudalization." Like the purchase of additional jurisdiction, buying *fiscali* on one's own fiefs was also a way to strengthen a new lordship. Marco Antonio I, for example, owned 150 ducats a year on the *fiscali* of Brienza, which he gave to the monastery he established there in the 1560s. In 1577, his mother, Ippolita Filomarino, owned ducats 270.2.07 a year, or about seventy-five percent of the *fiscali* paid by Brienza. These represented a nine percent yield on a capital of ducats 3,004.4.10, but they had already been sold by 1584. Ippolita had also bought ducats 119.3.-- a year on the *fiscali* of Salvia for a capital of ducats 1,328.4.--, which were sold by her grandson, Giovan Battista, by 1590. In the mid-seventeenth century, the Caracciolo Brienza owned *fiscali* for a capital value of 6,000 ducats on their new fief of Montenegro. In later years, though some members of the family owned *fiscali* on other *università* of the kingdom, their precarious economic situation prevented the Caracciolo Brienza from holding on to the *fiscali* on their fiefs, which passed to other creditors of the government. Still in 1750, only about twenty-five percent of the *fiscali* paid by Brienza reached the royal treasury. The same strategy of buying the *fiscali* on newly acquired fiefs was enacted by the Doria princes of Angri and dukes of Eboli in the 1640s.[34]

[33] The issue is discussed in Mantelli, *Burocrazia*, especially chapter 9; L. de Rosa, *Studi sugli arrendamenti del regno di Napoli, aspetti della distribuzione della ricchezza mobiliare nel Mezzogiorno continentale (1649–1806)* (Naples, 1958); Villari, "Note" and "Baronaggio"; Galasso, "Le riforme del conte di Lemos e le finanze napoletane nella prima metà del Seicento" in Galasso, *Mezzogiorno*, pp. 199–229. The feudal *adoa* on Brienza was alienated to creditors of the government in the seventeenth century, see ASBN, AGP, 1640, Giornale Cassa 202, fol. 31r, and ASN Pandetta Corrente 2026, vol. III, fol. 628r (1656). On d'Aquino and the aristocracy's role in the fiscal system, see Villari, *Rivolta*, especially pp. 167–68, Musi, *Finanze e politica nella Napoli del '600: Bartolomeo d'Aquino* (Naples, 1976), and Musi, *La rivolta*, pp. 97–107; on the situation in the neighboring papal state, see E. Stumpo, *Il capitale finanziario a Roma fra '500 e '600* (Milan, 1985); on the ties between aristocracy and financiers in France, see D. Dessert, *Argent, pouvoir et société au Grand Siècle* (Paris, 1984), pp. 341–78.

[34] Villari, *Rivolta*, chapter 5. ASN Taxis Adohae 115–I, a list of barons and their revenues for 1636, shows many feudatories to have indeed owned the *fiscali* on their fiefs. ACB 8.8; 9.8; 49.1.16; 45.7.16; ASN Fiscali e Adoe 29, fol. 51r for Ippolita; the data for 1541–59 in Calabria, "State Finance in the Kingdom of Naples in the Age of Philip II" Ph.D. Dissertation, University of California, Berkeley, 1978, App. D (a revised version of this work is to appear as *The Cost of Empire* with Cambridge University Press in 1991). In the mid-seventeenth century, the Genoese

The aristocracy and the Spanish rule

Roberto Mantelli and Luigi de Rosa have tried to break down the holders of shares of public revenues in social categories. However useful their data are, it is difficult to establish clear social categories on the basis of the indications in the documents. Particularly in the case of the mid-sixteenth-century data available to Mantelli, his separation of "titled nobles" from "others" – supposedly *borghesi* – raises several problems. Many of the individuals he classifies as non-noble belonged to prominent families of the city aristocracy, though they were not titled. For example, in 1563 Ippolita Filomarino, her son, Marco Antonio Caracciolo, and his cousin, Ascanio Caracciolo, are all counted by Mantelli among the "others," although their noble status is undoubted. Therefore his percentages for the share of the public debt owned by the aristocracy, thirty-one percent for 1563 and forty-one percent for 1571–72, are certainly a low estimate, and the aristocracy's share must have been considerably larger. Similar problems make comparison of Mantelli's data with those of de Rosa for the late seventeenth and eighteenth century difficult. It seems, however, that, after a phase of heavy investment in tax-farms on the part of the aristocracy, its share of the public revenues in the later seventeenth century was down at only ten to twenty percent. In the eighteenth century it increased again, as did that of ecclesiastical institutions.[35]

For an individual family, its degree of involvement in public finances depended on its specific economic situation. Shares of *arrendamenti* or *fiscali* were, as we have seen, the part of the aristocratic patrimony easiest to sell or buy, so that the Caracciolo Brienza's investments in them underwent wide fluctuations. Ippolita Filomarino owned 597.4.17 and Ascanio Caracciolo 282 ducats a year on the hearth tax in 1563, and the same in 1571–72. Soon, however, the family's economic troubles caused them to sell some of these investments. In 1592, Giovan Battista Caracciolo sold an annual income of 210 ducats that he had from the *gabella* of Calabrian silk. Throughout most of the seventeenth century, the Brienza seem only rarely to have had money invested in public revenue. Carlo Caracciolo Sant'Eramo had a small annual income from *arrendamenti*. In 1668, his son, Domenico I, owned an annual income of 150 ducats a year from the *Dogana* of Foggia. Domenico's daughter, Faustina,

Agostino Centurione held an annual 108.2.17 ducats on four *università* in Basilicata, including Pietrafesa, see Colapietra, *Dal Magnanimo*, II, p. 497. In 1736, only ducats 33.4.07+5/6 of the 487.1.– – that the *università* of Pentidattilo paid in *fiscali* went to the royal treasury (ACB 19.87). For Montenegro, see ACB 89.3.20; 11.1.16 and 30, unnumbered fol.; 11.2.5 no. 4; 16.8c and 8d; in 1647, Carlo Gambacorta had 300 ducats a year for a capital of 4,285 ducats on the *fiscali* of his fief of Celenza, see ASN Notai del '600, 912/25, P. A. Aversano (1647–48), fols. 66r–73v; examples for other families are in Lepre, *Feudi*, pp. 42, 49–50, and 58. For the Doria, see A. Villone, *Privilegi giurisdizionali e dominio feudale: lo stato dei Doria d'Angri nella seconda metà del secolo XVII* (Naples, 1980), p. 13.

35 Mantelli, *Burocrazia*, pp. 307–26 and 377–426; de Rosa, *Studi*, especially Appendix. Ecclesiastical institutions owned less than two percent of the public revenue in the mid-sixteenth century, but their share grew constantly after that time.

received a capital of 1,200 ducats on the *arrendemanto* of the *zecca* as part of her dowry. The same fluctuations in the degree of involvement in public revenue have been observed for other aristocratic families, such as the Muscettola Leporano.[36]

As we have seen before, aristocratic women, especially widows, often disposed of considerable wealth; and the *arrendamenti* and *fiscali* represented a perfect investment for them, thanks to their high yield – between seven and ten percent – relative safety, and easy marketability. In the early seventeenth century, in fact, Giulia and Diana Caracciolo both invested in public revenues. In 1610, Giulia owned seventy ducats a year on the *gabelle* of the city of Naples. In 1623, her daughter-in-law owned ducats 10.4.05 a year for a capital of 155 ducats on the *quattro fondaci del sale* (a *gabella*), and in 1640 she had ducats 466.3.10 a year on the tax on Calabrian silk. In the 1620s, she owned annuities for ducats 342.1.13 on two *università* in Terra di Lavoro and one in Molise. At the end of the seventeenth and in the eighteenth century, Teresa Pinto managed the part of her dowry represented by a capital of 12,542 ducats on three *arrendamenti*, and in the 1720s she had a personal revenue from five *arrendamenti* and some *fiscali* of ducats 415.3.08 a year. Her investments then became part of her grandson's patrimony.[37]

The sale of lands, titles, jurisdictions, and shares of public revenue on the part of the government was common to many early modern states, and often the aristocracy secured a large part of the loot.[38] In Naples in particular, the aristocracy stood to profit as much as, and probably more than, any other group in the kingdom from the government's financial needs. New fiefs and titles were acquired, the barons' power was augmented through purchases of jurisdiction and *fiscali*, and the *arrendamenti* offered profitable, convenient investment opportunities which did not violate, and actually reinforced, the aristocracy's *rentier* mentality. We must, however, look at other effects of the government's hunger for money, notably the increase in fiscal pressure, in order to evaluate these advantages. It seems clear that the feudal aristocracy was one of the privileged groups less severely hurt by royal fiscal policies.

[36] Mantelli, *Burocrazia*, pp. 312 and 385–86 (on p. 387 he lists a Giulia Caracciolo for 720 ducats, but I have no way of knowing whether she was the wife of Marco Antonio Caracciolo). ASN Pandetta Corrente 2026, vol. III, fols. 149r–v for Giovan Battista, and ACB 11.2.5 no. 4 for Carlo; 137.16, fols. 113v–29r for Domenico; 89.3.17 for Faustina. For the Muscettola, see Visceglia, "Formazione e dissoluzione di un patrimonio aristocratico: la famiglia Muscettola tra XVI e XIX secolo" *MEFRM* 92 (1980), pp. 569, 574, 583, 590, and Table 3.
[37] See above, Chapter 2. ASBN, Popolo, 1610, Giornale Banco 80, p. 485 for Giulia; ACB 22, fols. 40r, 65r–67v, 83r–v, 90r–98v (also ACB 12.3.6), and ASBN, S. Giacomo, 1640, Giornale Banco 195, p. 148 for Diana; ACB 3.2.7 and 24, unnumbered fols. at end of volume, for Teresa (also ASBN, Salvatore, 1690, Giornale Cassa 339, fol. 87v, and Giornale Cassa 340, fol. 142r).
[38] For Piedmont, see Woolf, *Studi*, introduction and pp. 141–45.

The aristocracy and the Spanish rule

FISCAL PRESSURE

In the early nineteenth century, Bianchini showed in detail the great increase in government taxation which had taken place in the kingdom of Naples during the Spanish period. Later historians have confirmed and augmented Bianchini's data. Both direct and indirect taxes grew, particularly between 1530 and 1647. To give only one example, the nominal hearth tax rose from ducats 1.2.11 in the early sixteenth century to almost five ducats soon before the revolt. The number and entity of indirect taxes grew too, and both exports and internal consumption were taxed, a policy which resulted, by the late seventeenth century, in the almost complete disappearance of Neapolitan exports. Extreme disparity existed in the distribution of the fiscal burden on the kingdom. The church and clergy enjoyed their traditional exemptions, and the inhabitants of the city of Naples paid no direct taxes, an immunity which was the main reason for Naples' demographic explosion in the Spanish period. The feudal aristocracy also managed to pay very little in tax, using fully, and extending all of, its legal privileges. Even in the later eighteenth century, when privileges had been abolished and abuses corrected, Galanti estimated that the total fiscal pressure on aristocratic income amounted at most to seven percent.[39]

The feudal aristocracy paid different taxes on its feudal and allodial income. Any aristocrat who was a Neapolitan citizen – and this included all *Seggio* aristocrats, even if not residing in Naples – paid no taxes on any property in the capital. In fact, the taxes on feudal income decreased with time, and many aristocrats succeeded in paying no taxes at all on allodial property, at least until the Bourbon reign. The example of the Caracciolo Brienza will show how fiscal pressure on the aristocracy actually decreased between the mid-sixteenth and the early eighteenth century. The aristocracy had the further advantage of being the only group with a right to represent the entire kingdom in its dealings with the king. Most taxes had to be approved by the General Parliament of the kingdom, which consisted, by the later sixteenth century, in only the barons and the representatives of the city of Naples. After 1642, the Parliament was never

[39] L. Bianchini, *Per la storia delle finanze del regno di Napoli* (Naples, 1835; second edit. 1859); Galasso, "L'ultimo feudalesimo meridionale nell'analisi di Giuseppe Maria Galanti" *RSI* 95 (1983), pp. 262–81. The literature on taxation is vast, most recently, de Rosa, *Il Mezzogiorno spagnolo tra crescita e decadenza* (Milan, 1987), a collection of reelaborated articles; a good introduction to the fiscal system is in Calabria, "State Finance"; Musi, *La rivolta*, p. 278, argues that after the revolt, the burden of direct taxes on the provinces increased to make up for the abolition of many *gabelle*, resulting in further division between the capital and the countryside. In the eighteenth century, the French dukes of Saulx-Tavanes also paid about seven percent of their revenue in taxes, while the nobles of Toulouse paid more than twice as much, see Forster, *The House of Saulx-Tavanes. Versailles and Burgundy, 1700–1830* (Baltimore, 1971), p. 105; Forster, *Toulouse*, p. 38; taxes represented five and a half percent of the expenses of the Strozzi in seventeenth-century Florence, see A. Manikowski, "Aspetti economici del mecenatismo di una famiglia aristocratica fiorentina nel XVII secolo" *Ricerche storiche* 16 (1986), pp. 81–94; on Spanish Lombardy, see Vigo, *Fisco e società*.

again called; and political representation for the whole kingdom fell on the *Seggi* of Naples and therefore, again, mainly on the old aristocracy.[40]

Two taxes were levied on feudal revenues, including anything granted in fief, be it lands, rights, or shares of the public revenue. The first was the traditional feudal succession tax of the relief (*relevio*), which in the kingdom of Naples was calculated at half the net revenue in the year of the feudatory's death. Within one year the new feudatory himself declared to the *Sommaria* how much he had to pay, and the *Sommaria* could choose to investigate his declaration and augment the size of the relief. An additional tax, the so-called *jus tapeti*, equal to thirteen and a third percent of the relief, went to the *Gran Camerario* of the kingdom. The average annual revenue to the crown from the relief was probably around 30,000 ducats.

The second feudal tax was the annual *adoa*, which by the fourteenth century had replaced the annual forty days of armed service owed by each feudatory to his king. The *adoa* was equal to fifty-two and a half percent of the fief's revenues, but by the Spanish period, half of it had been charged to each baron's vassals in the form of *fiscali*. Moreover, in 1505 the *adoa* was frozen at what it then was. The *adoa* on feudal rights enfeoffed separately was also first calculated at specific rates, and then fixed according to the *tassa vecchia* (old rate). Though the *adoe* on a few feudal revenues were fixed in 1564 – the *tassa nuova* – most feudal income in the kingdom paid the *adoa* according to the 1505 figures. This meant that fiefs that increased in value during the Spanish period still paid lower feudal taxes than others that had produced more revenue in 1505. The *adoa*, however, was not due when the kingdom paid a *donativo* (gift) to the king. In 1566, the *donativi* were made into ordinary taxes, for 600,000 ducats a year, one third of which was paid by the barons. In 1600, the share of the barons was reduced to one fourth. The *adoa* figures, from then on, served merely as the basis for dividing the annual 150,000 ducats of the barons' *donativo* – and any possible extraordinary *donativi*, of which there were many – among all feudatories of the kingdom. As Capano put it, "hodie barones non solvunt adoham, sed ad taxam adohae solvunt donativum." For the ordinary *donativo*, this meant that each baron owed an annual tax equal, in the first third of the seventeenth century, to 1.39 times the *adoa* for which he was registered.[41]

[40] G. D'Agostino, *Parlamento e società nel regno di Napoli, sec. XV–XVII* (Naples, 1979), part I. On taxes, see F. Caracciolo, "Fisco e contribuenti in Calabria nel secolo XVI" *Nuova rivista storica* 47 (1963), pp. 504–38.

[41] The best and most detailed discussions of relief and *adoa* are A. Capano, *De jure relevi* (Naples, 1630), and Capano, *De jure adohae* (Naples, 1636) (the quote is on p. 4). Naturally all extraordinary *donativi* had to be approved by the Parliament, which decided both their size and their distribution between barons and *università*. For the change in the share of the *donativo* paid by the barons, see Caracciolo, *Uffici*, pp. 225–26. Fiscal documents pertaining to feudal property were kept in regular series by the *Sommaria*; many have survived and are now in ASN. For examples of the rates fixed for the *adoa* on several types of feudal rights, see ASN Cedolari nuovi 89, fol. 218v. For the 1.39 figure, see ASN Taxis Adohae 115–I (1636), fols. 1r–6v. The relief was

As the sixteenth century progressed, therefore, what had originally been a yearly tax of 26.25 percent on feudal revenues decreased steadily in value. The same happened with fixed feudal taxes in other states, particularly in Piedmont. Since a large share of feudal income in the kingdom of Naples was in kind, sixteenth-century inflation alone would have resulted in a widening gap between actual feudal income and the *adoa*. Perhaps the most egregious example of this gap is the case of Avellino, which grew in population and wealth thanks to the textile industry developed by the Caracciolo princes. In 1632, feudal revenues from Avellino amounted to ducats 14,829.1.14+1/3, on which the *adoa* was a slim ducats 93.-.13+1/6, or about 0.6 percent. In general, the *adoa* by the early seventeenth century represented one to five percent of feudal revenues, which meant, in a year without extraordinary *donativi*, a tax of about two to seven percent. In the mid-seventeenth century, the situation may have been slightly more difficult for the aristocracy, but after 1648 fiscal pressure (in terms of the *donativi*) declined, and in the eighteenth century the ever-constant *adoa* represented a very small burden for the barons.[42]

The initial *adoe* on Brienza and Pietrafesa were set at ducats 66.4.06 and 7.1.07 respectively, while in 1573 the two fiefs gave net revenues of ducats 2,532.4.14 and 956.1.08. The *adoa* represented, therefore, about two and a half and less than one percent respectively of the yearly feudal income. After the government sold new jurisdictions to the Caracciolo the *adoe* rose, and in the seventeenth century the total *adoa* for the four Caracciolo fiefs was set at ducats 177.-.05+3/4, resulting in a contribution to the *donativo* of about 285 ducats a year, or between six and ten percent of the Caracciolo's feudal income in the central troubled decades of the century. In the eighteenth century, the *adoe* were at ducats 83.3.05 for Brienza, 16.1.18¼ for Pietrafesa, 68.4.02+1/12 for Atena, and 21.4.13½ for Sasso, for a total of ducats 190.3.18+5/6, which by then was what the Caracciolo actually paid, since *donativi* were no longer levied every year. Although their income was rising, the Caracciolo paid feudal taxes representing only about two thirds of what they had paid in the previous century.[43]

The relief was obviously a more random tax, and its impact on a family depended on genealogical events. The close deaths, in 1620–21, of Giovan Battista and Marco Antonio II, for instance, were certainly the *coup de grace* on

---

equal to half the net revenues minus the *adoa*. No *adoa* was due in a year when a baron had to pay his relief.

[42] For examples in the fiscal documents see ASN, especially Taxis Adohae (see Appendix on sources). For Avellino, see ASN Significatorie dei relevi 53–I, fols. 131v–40r (on his other fiefs, the prince paid much more). L. Bulferetti, "La feudalità e il patriziato nel Piemonte di Carlo Emanuele II (1663–1675)" *Annali della Facoltà di Lettere, Filosofia e Magistero dell'Università di Cagliari* 21 (1953), pp. 367–623; the Sicilian aristocracy paid slightly higher *adoe* (about eleven percent in 1573), see Cancila, *Baroni*, p. 129.

[43] ASN Petizioni dei relevi 35, fols. 38r–39v (1573); Relevi 236, fols. 557r–608v (1658); Significatorie dei relevi 77, fols. 237r–46v (1680), and ACB 44.1.2; ACB 44.2.7, 61.1.5, and 74.1.11.

Giacomo Caracciolo's patrimony. The aristocracy, however, often succeeded in paying less than its lawful due of the relief. First of all, the relief was never paid within the allotted year from the original assessment. Especially in the seventeenth century, the Caracciolo Brienza spread payments over periods of five to fifteen years. The *Sommaria* not only never charged them the double relief the law inflicted on any feudatory who took longer than a year to declare his relief, but also never exacted in full the interests on the late payments, agreeing instead to compromises that favored the family. Moreover, the *Sommaria* took its time with the investigations of the barons' declared revenues. Most barons declared fewer and smaller revenues than they actually had, and esteemed products at very low prices.

The collusion between the *Sommaria* and the barons was perhaps not yet as widespread as Angelo Massafra has observed for the late eighteenth century, and in fact in most instances the *Sommaria* did order investigations that resulted in additions to the reliefs paid by the Caracciolo Brienza, in one case even for 300 ducats (or more than twenty-five percent). But the delays often led to transactions, and certainly the reliefs paid seem to have decreased more quickly and dramatically than the family's revenues, going from the ducats 3,658.3.15 paid in 1623 for the death of Marco Antonio II to the ducats 1,429.1.17+5/12 paid following the death of Giuseppe I (1656), and the ducats 1,128.2.05½ paid for Faustina's death (1673). In 1708, an anticipated relief was levied from all barons by the new Austrian government, and therefore no relief was due twelve years later on the death of Giuseppe II. In 1728, after the death of Domenico II, the *Sommaria* agreed to accept 1,750 ducats and spare itself, and the Caracciolo Brienza, the trouble of an investigation, although the family's revenue was increasing steadily at that point. Due to Litterio's long life, this was to be the last relief the Caracciolo Brienza paid.[44]

If the aristocracy could pay relatively little on its feudal property, it often succeeded in paying even less on allodial property. As citizens of the capital, many feudatories were classified in their fiefs as non-resident property-owners; their allodial goods, therefore, paid only the *bonatenenza*, a tax designed to pay for only a few general expenses of the *università*. Unlike feudal taxes, which were paid to the government, the *bonatenenza* was levied by the *università* themselves. This meant that the actual payment depended on the law-abiding impulses of the barons, and on the strength of municipal autonomy. In most cases, before and after the Bourbon *Catasto* of 1741, the barons persuaded their *università* to accept compromises and fixed sums for the *bonatenenza*. A common practice was

[44] A. Massafra, "Fisco e baroni nel regno di Napoli alla fine del secolo XVIII" in *Studi storici in onore di Gabriele Pepe* (Bari, 1969), pp. 625–75. ASN Certificatorie dei relevi 151, fols. 65r–81r (1686); Relevi 166, inc. 2, fols. 11r–12r, and Petizioni 57, fols. 105v–8v (1651–55); Significatorie 77, cited above; Significatorie 81, fols. 117r–19v, and 162r–63v, and ACB 44.1.14 (1686); Relevi 236, cited above; Relevi 239 (1670s); ACB 44.1.22 (1728). In a sense, Marco Antonio II died too late. In fact, if a baron's successor died within a year of his predecessor's death only one relief was due.

to pass off parcels of allodial land as feudal, so as to avoid or reduce the *bonatenenza*; few *università* had the power or resistance to argue. "When the *università* fight with the barons for the *catasto*," Galanti observed, "everything is feudal; when the government asks for a relief, everything is allodial."[45]

In the late sixteenth century, as we have seen, the Caracciolo Brienza concluded agreements with their *università* for perpetual rents of most baronial revenues. In these agreements, the *università* exempted the baron from any present or future *bonatenenza*. By the late seventeenth century, the *università* had succeeded in reclaiming their right to the *bonatenenza*. In 1677, the Caracciolo paid thirty ducats a year for their allodial property in Pietrafesa, which yielded a net income of 917 ducats, and fifty for Brienza, where their allodial property yielded ducats 614.-.04+3/4, or about three and eight percent respectively. The right of the *università* of Pietrafesa to levy the *bonatenenza* was confirmed by the *Sommaria* in 1718. In the early eighteenth century, the *bonatenenza* for Brienza was down to thirty ducats a year. Atena still did not receive any *bonatenenza* in 1729, while in Sasso in 1728 the marquis paid only four ducats a year.[46]

The Austrian government failed to achieve much success in its plans for fiscal reform. The Bourbon *Catasto* of 1741 caused long investigations and litigations in order to determine the amount of the barons' *bonatenenza*. But the results were not very effective, and the Caracciolo Brienza continued to pay fixed sums for their *bonatenenza* in the later eighteenth century, even while their revenues were growing. The *bonatenenza* for Brienza was set at ducats 34.3.-- a year and remained so until the nineteenth century. In Pietrafesa between 1743 and 1770, the *bonatenenza* was offset by some payments the *università* owed the marquis. In Sasso and Atena, where allodial property was scarce, the *bonatenenza* amounted to a relatively high tax in rate, but there too it declined with time. In 1748, the *bonatenenza* was ducats 47.2.10 in Atena on revenues of ducats 359.2.09, and twelve ducats on revenues of ducats 37.-.15 in Sasso, or about thirteen and thirty percent respectively. In 1776, however, it was fifty ducats on revenues of ducats 555.1.-- in Atena, and 14.2.10 on revenues of 82.3.12 in Sasso, or about nine and eighteen percent respectively. Moreover, these revenues do not include the value of allodial buildings used by the marquis himself.[47]

So not even the vaunted Bourbon reforms managed to attack the aristocracy's fiscal privileges. The *Catasto* was far, in this respect, from having the wideranging effects of fiscal reform demonstrated in Northern Italian states. Even when

---

[45] Cited in Galasso, "L'ultimo," p. 276, footnote 49, and Massafra, "Fisco," p. 659.
[46] The agreements, dating from 1592–93, are in ACB 133.2, fols. 104r–15r (Brienza), 61.2.4 (Pietrafesa), and 74.2.3 (Atena). The 1677 figures are in ACB 43.3.7. In 1615, the marquis still did not pay any *bonatenenza* in Brienza, but the issue was under litigation (ACB 48.1.1, fols. 2059r–65r). Pietrafesa was already receiving thirty ducats a year in *bonatenenza* in 1668 (ACB 61.2.8). ACB 61.2.10 (1718); 45.7.9 (1729 for Brienza); 75.2.1 (1729 for Atena); 82.6.3 (1728).
[47] ACB 48.1.14, 45.7.21, 61.2.47, 77.1.32–33, 81.1.17–18, and 45.7.17. On the Austrian period (1707–34), see A. Di Vittorio, *Gli Austriaci e il regno di Napoli* (2 vols.; Naples, 1969–73).

reform attempts were made in Naples, the royal tribunals, and especially the *Sommaria*, supported the barons' privileges and tolerated their evasion against the interests of the royal treasury. Only in the 1790s, when the pressure of war expenses forced the government to extreme action, did fiscal pressure on aristocratic wealth become heavier by two to four times. Beginning in 1793, feudal income was taxed at ten percent, often at much more, and taxes were levied on aristocratic property also in Naples. Since this sudden rise in fiscal pressure came at a time of increasing difficulty in collecting aristocratic revenues, particularly feudal ones, it resulted in a severe financial crisis for the aristocracy and in the detachment of many aristocrats from the Bourbon monarchy, especially in 1799 and then in 1806.[48]

If, therefore, the Spanish presence in the kingdom of Naples by the 1530s was solid and internationally secure and meant that the institutions of a bureaucratic state were developed in the Mezzogiorno, the growth of the government's power to tax and try its subjects did not seriously limit the old aristocracy's control over its fiefs or damage its privileged position in Neapolitan society. Certainly the viceroyalty of don Pedro de Toledo (1532–53) marked a decline in the political autonomy of the aristocracy, and the definitive acceptance of the Spanish position in Naples; but the Spanish monarchy did not use its political power to enact any change in the kingdom's social structure or economy, withdrawing in effect even from the limited antifeudal policies of the Aragonese kings. The feudal aristocracy had to accept a monarchy whose hold on the kingdom it could no longer seriously challenge, and to submit formally to the authority of royal tribunals, but this was a small price to pay for the preservation of its traditional privileges and for the opportunities to strengthen its position in the kingdom that the Spanish rule created.[49]

We have seen that the mid-sixteenth century brought significant adaptations and changes in aristocratic family policy that were, on the whole, quite successful in defending the aristocracy's social preeminence. In this chapter, more specifically, we have seen how the feudal aristocracy profited from the Spanish government's needs and policies. Royal service, in the kingdom and in the Spanish imperial system, provided the aristocracy with wealth, power, and prestige; the purchase of offices offered secure and high revenues. The power and influence of royal tribunals did not prove harmful to the aristocracy: lawyers and magistrates were sympathetic and easily corruptible, and the legal system

[48] Massafra, "Fisco"; Woolf, *Studi*, pp. 69–75, 97–102, and 119–22, on the effects of Vittorio Amedeo II's fiscal reforms. On the antifeudal polemics and policies of the 1790s, see Rao, *L'"Amaro della Feudalità"* (Naples, 1984); Galasso, "La legge feudale napoletana del 1799" *RSI* 76 (1964), pp. 507–29.
[49] Galasso, "Momenti"; in the absence of any coherent set of policies for the kingdom on the part of the Spanish government, it seems, therefore, excessive to hail the Toledan period as a final victory of the state apparatus, as at times does Cernigliaro, *Sovranità*, especially part III.

worked against the vassals and the creditors of the aristocracy. Royal laws failed effectively to control the exercise of feudal powers or the transmission of aristocratic patrimonies. The crown's needs led it to sell fiefs, titles, jurisdictions, and public revenue to the aristocracy, reinforcing the latter's grip on the provinces and on the kingdom's economy. Aristocratic fiscal exemptions, finally, were not seriously called into question. Unlike Piedmont, where by the late seventeenth century the government succeeded in challenging aristocratic powers and privileges, in Naples, as in Sicily, it was only at the very end of the old regime that any significant attack was wrought by the government on the feudal aristocracy.[50]

In this situation, loyalty to the monarchy and careful self-interest coincided for the Caracciolo Brienza as for most Neapolitan aristocrats. Giuseppe Caracciolo, although one of three sponsors of a minority resolution opposing a new general tax in the last Parliament called in Naples in 1642, was a prominent supporter from the earliest days of the revolt of 1647 of Viceroy Arcos, whose life he helped save, together with his brother Giacomo and their cousin Carlo Caracciolo Sant'Eramo. Probably because of this, his Naples house was sacked by the rebels, and his mother's house was threatened. He later served on the Spanish fleet against the French ships in front of Naples, and in the war against the rebels' army.[51]

The family remained loyal to the government through the dynastic changes of the early eighteenth century, without, however, playing any important public role, though Giovan Battista, brother of Giuseppe II, was appointed an infantry captain by the viceroy in October 1701 after the so-called conspiracy of Macchia. In 1744, the marquis of Brienza was one of the aristocrats who successfully pressured the king, after the battle of Velletri in which the aristocracy's support of the crown had once again been decisive, to annul the 1738 law limiting the barons' criminal jurisdiction, a further example of how loyalty was both a response to favors and a means to obtain them.[52] Only the troubled last decade of the eighteenth century brought a serious break between factions of the

---

[50] Woolf, *Studi*, introduction and conclusion; P. Villani, *Mezzogiorno tra riforme e rivoluzione* (Bari, 1977; first edit. 1962), chapter 4; on Sicily, see O. Cancila, "Introduzione" to F. di Napoli, principe di Resuttano, *Noi il Padrone* (Palermo, 1982).

[51] ACB 1.3, 2.7–8 and 26. See Capecelatro, *Diario*, I, for Giuseppe, and *ibid.*, p. 198 for Diana's house; on Giuseppe's role in the early days of the revolt, see A. Fiordelisi, *Gl'incendii in Napoli ai tempi di Masaniello* (Naples, 1895), p. 27; for Giuseppe's service on the ships, see his will in ASN Pandetta Corrente 570, vol. IV, fols. 5r–16r; on his cousin Sant'Eramo, see Rovito, "Strutture," pp. 297–98. G. Carignani, "L'ultimo Parlamento Generale del regno di Napoli nel 1642"*ASPN* 8 (1883), pp. 34–57. Carignani noted that the other two sponsors of the 1642 defeated resolution and their property were not attacked by the rebels.

[52] ACB 2.32; Rao, "La questione," pp. 15–18; Galasso, *Napoli spagnola*, II, p. 624 on Giovan Battista. On the political strength of the aristocracy in the early Bourbon period, see also I. Del Bagno, "Governo borbonico e reintegrazione nei *Seggi* napoletani intorno alla metà del Settecento" *ASPN* 103 (1985), pp. 377–99, and F. Cammisa, "Un atto di accusa contro la giurisdizione feudale, redatto a Napoli nel 1764" *ASPN* 105 (1987), pp. 493–520.

aristocracy and the Bourbon monarchy. Whatever its effects on the general situation of the kingdom and its inhabitants, Spanish rule benefited the old feudal aristocracy. At the end of Spain's rule, and for quite a while after that, the aristocracy had not suffered any considerable diminution in its economic and social power within the kingdom.[53]

[53] A recent work on the relations between the early modern state and the aristocracy in Italy is A. Spagnoletti, *Stato, aristocrazie e Ordine di Malta nell'Italia moderna* (Rome: Ecole française de Rome, 1988).

Conclusion

In a recent article, Eric Cochrane has analyzed the field of Neapolitan historiography over the past few decades. Although some of his comments are polemical, he points out correctly that the attention of historians has been unevenly distributed, and that large gaps remain in our understanding of the history of Spanish Naples. Demography, popular religion, literature, law, and administration have all been the object of historical analysis. Several studies have treated the social and economic history of the kingdom, though the general context and broader interpretations provided by Galasso and Villari in the 1960s have not been significantly challenged or revised.[1]

Several recent studies on the social and economic history of Spanish Naples have discussed the position of the aristocracy, and stressed the persistence of aristocratic power and privilege in the kingdom throughout the Spanish period and into the eighteenth century. Most of this work, however, has focused primarily on agrarian history and has presented only a limited picture of aristocratic wealth and power. It has often neglected the broader social and political aspects of aristocratic power and the non-landed elements of aristocratic wealth. The feudal nature of the Neapolitan aristocracy and the pervasiveness of feudal institutions in the kingdom have been acknowledged by these writers, but they usually regard feudalism only as the root of aristocratic lawlessness and of social conflict at the local level. Their analysis, therefore, is often little more than an elaboration of old attacks on feudal abuses.

The main aim of the present work has been to broaden our understanding of how the continuity of aristocratic feudal power was achieved, through an examination of a wide range of behavior of an aristocratic family from the mid-sixteenth to the early eighteenth centuries. A study of this type allows us to place the aristocratic patrimony, its composition and management, and the relations of the aristocracy with the rural communities, in the broader context of the aristocracy's preeminent social and political position, both in the provinces and in the capital. It illustrates the connections between the local power of the aristocracy, its relations with the Spanish government and other privileged social groups, and the strategies it devised to preserve its elite status in Neapolitan society.

[1] E. Cochrane, "Southern Italy in the Age of the Spanish Viceroys: Some Recent Titles" *Journal of Modern History* 58 (1986), pp. 194–217.

A family case-study, moreover, makes it possible to assess the role of the aristocracy's feudal nature in determining its wealth, social status, and political power. The feudal character of a large part of the aristocracy's wealth complicated its relations with the royal government. The transmission of feudal property was regulated by special laws which even the king himself could only shape to a limited extent. These same feudal laws also set the conditions of aristocratic family policy, regulating the rights of cadet sons and daughters, and the claims of widows to their husbands' estates.

Fiefs were the core of the aristocratic patrimony, and the analysis of the non-feudal components of aristocratic wealth shows how different investments were aimed at preserving the full ownership of the fiefs and at insuring, through diversification of assets, the solidity of the patrimony as a whole. The many baronial rights were certainly used to maintain political influence within the fiefs, but they were also an essential part of feudal revenue. Because land remained only one among many sources of income, the Neapolitan aristocrats were never reduced to a class of privileged landowners. Moreover, the continuing importance of feudal rights influenced the ways in which the aristocracy and its vassals perceived their mutual ties. True, feudal rights were often a source of abuses and made it easier for the baron to act as an oppressive landlord, but they also made him a representative of the community, a mediator between the villagers and the outside world, the patron and lord – sometimes harsh, sometimes benevolent – of his vassals.

The paternalistic aspects of feudal rule are often neglected by historians, although they relate to the traditionalism of aristocratic land management: in a sense, paternalism and entrepreneurship were mutually exclusive, and the rewards of the former were not necessarily inferior to those of the latter. This neglect is due in large part to the emphasis placed by most historians on the so-called urbanization of the Neapolitan aristocracy. While it is true that in the Spanish period most feudal families began to live in the capital and to acquire or build palaces there, the move to Naples was rarely complete. Often, aristocratic families lived in Naples only when children were of marriageable age or when important legal acts, such as divisions of inheritance or lawsuits, necessitated their presence. The feudal aristocracy continued to reside frequently in its fiefs, and to maintain a strong physical presence there.

The little attention given by most historians of the Mezzogiorno to feudal rights as sources of revenue, and to the aristocracy's residence in the fiefs and ties to the local communities, is due not only to their choice of sources, but also to the fact that most studies have concentrated on the more prosperous regions of the kingdom, such as Puglia, Terra di Lavoro, or the plain of the Sele. These regions were often characterized by agricultural specialization, by a relatively high level of agricultural commercialization, and (particularly in Puglia) by large estates employing landless or migrant rural labor. These regions, however, were far from characteristic of the Mezzogiorno.

The fiefs of the Caracciolo Brienza, and most of Basilicata, Abruzzi, or Calabria, were mountainous, relatively isolated, and marked by fragmented peasant landownership. In these regions, the feudal lords could not easily increase their landed revenues without breaking resilient local traditions, and feudal rights remained an essential source of revenue. Unlike the *università* of more prosperous regions, smaller, poorer communities, like those ruled by the Caracciolo Brienza, also preserved their ancient representative institutions to the end of the old regime. A local notability developed, but was not large or wealthy enough to become an oligarchy, as most historians assume on the evidence of the large towns of Puglia. Baronial paternalism and traditional management served, therefore, also to maintain the ties between the lords and the mass of their vassals, resisting changes that would primarily have benefited a narrow segment of the local population.

The continuity of feudal rule at the local level, its traditionalism, and the lack of innovation in aristocratic land management, do not mean that the history of the Neapolitan aristocracy was a static one. While the feudal aristocracy lost little of its economic power and social status, the kingdom of Naples in 1750 was not the same as in 1550. The aristocracy had adapted to changes in its political position and in the society and economy of the kingdom at large. Probably more than any other social group, it was able to profit from the Spanish government's needs and policies, thereby strengthening its control over the provinces and acquiring a large share of the assets (titles, lands, new taxes) that the monarchy was forced to sell. The aristocracy also met the challenge posed by the ascent of new families, and succeeded in keeping its ranks and membership closed to newcomers to a larger extent than many other Western European aristocracies. It achieved this goal by exploiting the characteristics of feudal law, and especially by using the old institution of the clan in innovative ways. Neither the rise nor the fall of the Spanish monarchy eliminated the power of the Neapolitan aristocracy. One could transpose to the Neapolitan aristocracy at the end of the old regime the final, proud words of Consalvo Uzeda in Federico De Roberto's *I Viceré*:

I remember that in 1861, when my uncle the duke was elected to Parliament the first time, my father told me: "You see? When we had viceroys, the Uzeda were viceroys; now we have deputies, and uncle goes to Parliament" ... Once the power of our family came from the kings; now it comes from the people ... The difference is more apparent than real ... Certainly, there seems to be an abyss between the Sicily of before 1860, still almost feudal, and the Sicily of today; but the difference is all external. The first person elected by almost universal suffrage is neither a man of the people, not a bourgeois, nor a democrat: it is I, because I am the prince of Francalanza. The prestige of the nobility is not and cannot be extinguished ... Certainly, absolute monarchy better protected the interests of our caste; but a superior force, an irresistible stream has carried it away ... Do we too have to surrender? Our duty, instead of despising the new laws, seems to me to use them! ... No, our race is not degenerate: it is always the same.

Glossary

adoa feudal annual tax replacing the barons' military service; originally equal to fifty-two and a half percent of feudal revenues, but fixed in most cases in the early sixteenth century.

Annona the grain dole of the city of Naples managed by the city government.

antefato in the marriage settlement, the money the husband assigns to the wife; its relation to the amount of the dowry was regulated in 1617, but the law was rarely obeyed by the aristocracy; for the aristocracy, the *antefato* went to the wife at her husband's death but returned to his heirs when the widow died.

arciprete head priest of a parish.

arrendamento tax-farm.

arrendatore holder of an *arrendamento*.

bagliva old regalian right that was often enfeoffed; in the Spanish period it consisted in most places of jurisdiction over minor misdemeanors.

baglivo holder of the *bagliva*.

battendiero structure built on rivers' shores, used for the preparing and washing of cloth; often a feudal monopoly.

benestante in eighteenth-century fiscal documents, a wealthy person.

bonatenenza tax on allodial property paid by all property-owners to the community.

cantaro measure of weight, equal to eighty-nine kg.

carlino the tenth part of a ducat.

casale a small village without full administrative autonomy.

catapania the right to set prices for the goods sold in a community; usually exercised by the communities.

catasto a direct tax, or the land survey drawn for fiscal purposes; the 1741 *Catasto* was a fiscal survey of the entire kingdom ordered by the new Bourbon government.

Cavallerizzo Maggiore Master of the Royal Stables, a venal office.

chiusa enclosed parcel of land.

città administrative term to define a large, usually walled, *università*.

colta feudal right consisting in a fee intended to cover the expense of guarding the feudal castle.

Glossary

Commissione Feudale Feudal Committee, operating under the French government (1806–15), in charge of the abolition of the feudal regime.

comune term replacing *università* after 1806.

conservatore person in charge of collecting baronial revenues in kind.

Consiglio Collaterale highest political–administrative organ of the Kingdom of Naples. Instituted by Ferdinand of Aragon in 1507, it had administrative, legislative, and judiciary functions.

deduzione legal action by which a patrimony was confiscated and administered by government delegates in order to pay the debtors.

difesa closed or hedged field; access was often only limited during part of the year.

Dogana delle pecore royal office in charge of the large-scale transhumant livestock breeding in the northeastern part of the kingdom; centered in Foggia and founded in the mid-fifteenth century (modeled on the Spanish *Mesta*).

donativo fiscal contribution to the king; originally voluntary and voted anew by each Parliament, by the late sixteenth century it had become an ordinary tax of 600,000 ducats per year, to which extraordinary *donativi* were often added.

Eletto in Naples the title of the elected representatives of the five aristocratic *Seggi*, plus the representative of the People (*Popolo*); in other *università* the title of the aldermen.

erario person in charge of collecting baronial revenues in money.

fida feudal right consisting of fees levied on livestock grazing the feudal domain or other feudal territories.

fiscalario holder of *fiscali*.

fiscali taxes paid by the *università* to the government, often farmed out or sold by the government to its creditors.

gabella any of several indirect taxes.

Grandi Uffici the seven traditional Grand Offices of the royal court.

grano the hundredth part of a ducat.

Grassiero the viceroy's representative with the Naples city government in matters concerning the *Annona*.

jus luendi the right to repurchase whatever was sold at the same sale price; usually it applied to real estate; the seller could choose to renounce this right, to keep it, or to sell it separately.

jus prohibendi any of the feudal monopoly rights (such as the mill, the oven, the inn, the *battendiero*).

jus serendi traditional right of the residents of a fief to sow any uncultivated land in the feudal or community domain.

jus tapeti feudal succession tax equal to thirteen and a third percent of the relief.

legittima legal share of any allodial property pertaining to all children of the deceased.

maritaggio dowry contribution assigned by any public or private *Monte*.

massaro di campo tenant farmer; in the eighteenth century the term referred to wealthy farmers.

masseria usually a relatively large farm.

mastrodatti holder of the *mastrodattia*.

mastrodattia actuary office, with the right to charge fees for all acts issued.

meridionalismo tradition of interest in the economic and social problems of the South of Italy; movement of study of those problems, especially in the late nineteenth century.

mischio a mixture of wheat and rye.

moltiplico reinvestment fund usually established on revenues from entailed assets.

monacaggio nun's dowry.

Monte di maritaggi dowry fund established by an individual, a family, a clan, a community, a guild, or any other institution.

Montiero Maggiore Guardian of the Royal Hunting, a venal office.

nobile vivente fiscal category; literally "living nobly."

paraggio minimum dowry guaranteed by feudal law to all barons' daughters who married.

paramenti di camera room ornaments.

pesi e misure see *zecca*.

Piazza see *Seggio*.

piazza feudal right consisting of fees levied on all merchandise sold or bought by outsiders in the fiefs.

portolania feudal right consisting of fines levied on those who broke the laws regulating the state of public roads.

portolano holder of the *portolania*.

porzionarii the clergy participating in a *ricettizia* parish church.

prammatica royal law.

presa di possesso ritual marking the official taking of possession of a fief by its new holder.

Relationes ad limina reports to Rome of episcopal visits.

relevio feudal succession tax (relief).

ricettizia type of parish church organization common in the Mezzogiorno: each parish owned land and revenues that were shared by the participant clergy (*porzionarii*).

risulta fiscal investigation into the legitimacy of feudal rights.

rotolo measure of weight, equal to 0.89 kg.

Sacro Regio Consiglio royal tribunal of Aragonese origins, highest court of appeal in the kingdom; also the first court for civil cases involving feudal patrimonies.

Seggio (or *Sedile*) one of the five subdivisions of the aristocracy of the city of Naples, originally districts of the city; their membership became closed at the beginning of the sixteenth century.

seminativo arborato tree-covered arable land.

seminativo nudo cleared arable land.

sindacato following the end of any officer's tenure, the investigation of his accounts.

sindaco chief officer of each *università*, mayor.

società di campo company formed for the cultivation of one or more farms.

soma measure of capacity for wine, equal to 58.16 l.

Sommaria highest financial and fiscal court of the kingdom.

stato global feudal patrimony of any baronial family, the ensemble of its (generally contiguous) fiefs.

tarì the fifth part of the ducat.

terra administrative term to define any small *università*.

terraggio share of the harvest of feudal land owed by the peasant to the feudal lord.

togati lawyers and magistrates, mostly of the Naples tribunals (equivalent to the French robins or the Spanish *letrados*).

tomolo measure of surface, equal to 0.33 ha.; measure of capacity for grains, equal to 0.55 hl.

università any city or village in the kingdom having the legal status of a community.

valchiera see *battendiero*.

vaticale traveling merchant.

Vicaria central civil and criminal court in Naples; its decisions could be appealed to the Sacred Royal Council.

vita milizia annual subsidy, consisting in a share of the feudal revenues, to which all cadet sons were entitled.

zecca feudal right consisting in the enforcement of laws regulating standard weights and measures, and of the resulting fees and fines.

Appendix on sources

Archival research for this work has been conducted in four archives: the Archivio Segreto Vaticano (ASV) in the Vatican; the Archivio di Stato di Potenza (ASP), in Potenza, the regional capital of Basilicata; the Archivio Storico del Banco di Napoli (ASBN) in Naples; and the Archivio di Stato di Napoli (ASN), also in Naples. A few manuscripts have been consulted in the Biblioteca Nazionale di Napoli (BNN). Microfilms have been obtained of several documents in the Archivo General de Simancas (AGS), Spain.

In the Vatican Archives I have consulted the *Relationes ad limina* from the records of the Sacra Congregazione del Concilio (the reports to Rome of the episcopal visits prescribed by the Council of Trent) for the three dioceses that comprised the fiefs of the Caracciolo Brienza. These all begin in the last two decades of the sixteenth century and are:

vol. 177   Satriano-Campagna
vol. 185   Capaccio
vol. 491   Marsico Nuovo

In the Potenza Archive I have consulted the series *Notai di Potenza, Intendenza di Basilicata*, and *Corporazioni religiose*. Of the *Notai*, I have seen all the extant registers of the notaries residing in the four fiefs of the Caracciolo Brienza, plus the registers of the notaries of neighboring villages who had drawn acts for the family. I have followed these records up to 1720. Often copies of these documents were either in the family archive or in trial records in Naples (ASN).

The *Intendenza* consists mostly in administrative acts dating from the French period (1806–15); I have seen vols. 578–79 (for Brienza), 695 (for Pietrafesa), and 746 (for Sasso). The ecclesiastical documents of the series *Corporazioni* date in large part from the nineteenth century; I have seen vols. 116 (Pietrafesa), 155 (Sasso), and 173 (Brienza).

Most of the equivalent documentation for Atena should be in the district archive of Sala Consilina, in the province of Salerno, but, because of the continuing post-earthquake situation of the region, it is all but impossible to gain access to the Sala archive.

Appendix on sources

The Bank of Naples Archive includes all the documents originating from the eight public banks of the city of Naples. These banks (Banco dei Poveri, Banco della Pietà, Banco di Sant'Eligio, Banco dello Spirito Santo, Banco del Salvatore, Banco di San Giacomo e Vittoria, Banco del Popolo, and Banco della Santissima Annunziata)[1] were established between the last years of the sixteenth and the early decades of the seventeenth century, and with the exception of the AGP that failed in 1702, survived to the end of the old regime. They functioned in many ways like modern banks; customers – public and private – kept accounts and could draw *polizze* that were similar to checks. The banks did not offer any interest, but allowed their customers to engage in a variety of transactions without having to involve any actual species. The *polizza* could be signed by numerous consecutive individuals, passing the credit along; it would only be finally paid in species when a customer decided to cash it at the bank. Banks invested their funds in tax-farms and various loans, and were often forced to lend money to the government; the system was not without abuses and corruption, but overall it worked with remarkable efficiency throughout the seventeenth and eighteenth centuries.[2]

These activities resulted in an enormous mass of documents that are mostly preserved. Each bank kept an index of its customers for each semester; the index (called *Pandetta*), in alphabetical order by first names, provides a reference number for each customer (men, women, or institutions). The so-called *Libro Maggiore* then reports a summary of all the activities of each customer in each semester; the entries for each customer are numbered (with the numbers one finds indexed in the *Pandetta* next to each customer's name). The entries give the name of the customer and the date of each transfer involving the account, the amount of money in question, and, often, a one-word name for the other party in the transaction. Whenever that other party also had an account with the bank, there is a cross-reference to the relevant account. Knowing now the date, the amount of money that changed hands, and the name of at least one of the two parties in the transaction, one can find the *polizza* in the *Libri Giornali* (which consist in several volumes for each semester); the *polizza* will, often, provide a detailed description of the transaction. In general, *Giornali di Banco* include *polizze* for which only one of the parties had an account with the bank, whereas *Giornali di Cassa* include the records of transactions involving two customers of the bank. *Giornali* include full copies of all *polizze*; the original *polizze* – of which there are an estimated 250 million – cannot be consulted.

Although families and individuals tended to keep their accounts in only one or two banks at any given time, they were of course involved in transactions with other individuals who had accounts in other banks, so that records referring to

[1] Also known as AGP, from the Annunciation words *Ave Gratia Plena*.
[2] L. de Rosa, *Il Mezzogiorno spagnolo tra crescita e decadenza* (Milan, 1987) describes and discusses in detail the functioning and the history of the Neapolitan banks. On the ASBN, see also *L'Archivio Storico del Banco di Napoli, una fonte preziosa per la storia economica, sociale e artistica del Mezzogiorno d'Italia* (Naples, 1972).

any one person or family might be found in the records of any of the eight banks. Given the organization of the material (most of which is remarkably well preserved), unless one is looking for a specific *polizza* the date of which is known, finding the record for any transaction involves a three-step search through the *Pandetta*, the *Libro Maggiore*, and the *Giornali*. Since, moreover, scholars have access to a limited number of documents each day, this rich archive has so far been rarely used by historians.

In order to examine at least a small sample of these documents, I have decided to see only the records of all the banks for one semester in every decade; whenever possible, I have seen the records of the second semester of each year ending with a 0, beginning from the earliest records of the banks (1590 or 1600 for most of the eight banks) up to 1720. I have seen the accounts of all the members of the Caracciolo Brienza family, plus the accounts of any individual whom I could identify as an agent for the family. Besides documenting some specific transactions, the records in the *Libri maggiori* confirm the picture of the history of the family's finances as it appears from the documents in the family archive; after the early seventeenth century, the involvement of the Caracciolo Brienza in financial transactions, and the movement of money in general to and from their accounts, decreases significantly, and only increases again after the 1680s, as discussed in chapter 2.

The bulk of the research for this study has been conducted in the State Archive of Naples, the ASN. I shall here describe first the general documents I have consulted and then the family archive of the Caracciolo Brienza.

THE ASN

F. Trinchera's *Degli archivi napoletani relazione* (Napes, 1872) provides a good introduction to the ASN, but much of its specific information was rendered obsolete by the Nazi fire of 1943 that destroyed some of the most valuable documents in the ASN. The *Guida dell'Archivio di Stato di Napoli* by Jole Mazzoleni (2 vols.; Naples, 1972), constitutes a valuable introduction to the ASN and refers to the specific inventories existing for most series of documents. The ASN is divided in three main sections: *Amministrativa, Diplomatica*, and *Giustizia*, each of which is divided in subsections and includes numerous series of documents. Only the most important series used in this study will be discussed here.

Sezione Amministrativa

Of the documents included in the *Sezione Amministrativa* I have seen in particular the series:

Appendix on sources

Conti delle Università, which contains accounts and documents relating to the *università*'s finances, mostly for the eighteenth century

Catasto Onciario, the records of the fiscal survey of the entire kingdom drawn by the Bourbon government beginning in 1741

Fiscali e Adoe, records of the fiscal payments made by the *università* and the barons

Frammenti dei Fuochi and

Catasti Antichi, the surviving demographic records of various *università*

Dipendenze della Sommaria and

Diversi della Sommaria, all sorts of administrative documents, relating often to censuses or royal properties

Ministero dell'Interno and

Affari demaniali Winspeare, the documents relating to the activity of the *Commissione Feudale* in the French period (1806–15) and afterwards

The *Sezione Amministrativa* also holds the printed documentation of the *Commissione Feudale*, in particular the *Bollettino delle sentenze della Commissione Feudale*, with its *Supplemento*, and the *Bollettino delle ordinanze dei commissari ripartitori dei demani*.

All of these series are well indexed, and I have seen all the documents pertaining to the four fiefs of the Caracciolo Brienza or to the family itself.

Sezione Giustizia

The Sezione Giustizia consists primarily in trial records and notarial registers. Very numerous trial records survive for the Spanish period, indexed in thirty or so inventories drawn in large part in the late nineteenth century. The inventories include the names of the two parties, a date, and, often, a very summary description of the issue at stake. I have consulted the trial records that seemed of particular interest involving members of the Caracciolo Brienza family. The records vary in size from a single sheet to several volumes. Apart from the records cited in the main text, an explanation is required for the often-cited records inventoried as ASN Pandetta Corrente 570 and 2026: these two bundles each consist of numerous volumes, loosely tied together with strings and placed one on top of the other in no apparent order. A few of the volumes are marked with a (non-consecutive) number, and these I have cited as "vol. marked X"; most of the volumes, however, are not marked, and I have assigned them Roman numerals, according to the order in which I found them when I consulted them in the spring of 1987; most volumes provide folio numbers, and I have reported them when appropriate.

Consultation of notarial registers also poses problems. The registers of most notaries consist in a volume for each year, sometimes accompanied by a few specialized volumes for wills, marriage contracts, or other types of acts. The inventories simply give the notary's name, and the number of surviving volumes with their dates. Many, but by no means all, of the volumes include their own index in the first few folios. Considering that there were hundreds of notaries in seventeenth-century Naples, each leaving up to fifty volumes of registers, it is impossible – particularly when provided with a maximum of three volumes per day by the strict rules of the ASN – to search for all the notarial documents involving a family across more than a century. I have, therefore, only seen notarial acts to which other documents referred; in fact, trial records and many of the records in the family archive often mention notarized events in the history of the family, and provide the name of the notary and the date of the document. The seventeenth-century acts (series *notai del '600*) are relatively accessible; the sixteenth-century acts (series *notai del '500*), on the other hand, are still – and have been for quite a few years now – in the process of being reinventoried, and are therefore in large part not available (they include the registers of any notary who began his career in the sixteenth century); the registers of notaries who carried their activity past 1750 are not in the ASN but in the Archivio Notarile, which is closed to the public since the 1980 earthquake.

Sezione Diplomatica

Most of the documents relating to feudal matters are in the *Sezione Diplomatica*. In particular, all the documentation relating to the feudal taxes (the relief and the *adoa*) survives in various series of documents, that often repeat the same information. There are inventories for all these series, but only a few series are indexed (and in some cases the indexes date back to the eighteenth century).[3] These series all consist in volumes. They are:

Refute dei Quinternioni
Intestazioni feudali
Cedolari Nuovi (these three are all indexed, and I have consulted the
    documents referring to all the fiefs the Caracciolo Brienza ever owned)
Taxis Adohae
Certificatorie per l'intestazione nel cedolario
Petizioni dei relevi (no indexes exist for these series, and I have consulted all the
    extant volumes; some volumes include their own index, but many do not,
    though often the parties to the document are named on top of each
    document; I have seen the documents referring to the Caracciolo Brienza
    and to the families with which they were contracting marriage alliances)
Significatorie dei relevi (for this series a three-volume eighteenth-century index

---

[3] By inventory, I mean a list of all the contents of the series (volumes or bundles) with an indication in general of which years are covered in each, but nothing else; by index, I mean lists by name of all the parties (or fiefs) involved in the documents, with the appropriate page or folio references.

survives, providing summaries of all documents; I have seen the surviving documents referring to the family)

Relevi are the most complete of the fiscal documents dealing with feudal patrimonies; they are arranged by provinces, and the *relevi nuovi* are indexed, while for the *relevi originali* there is only an inventory; I have seen the relevant volumes of the *nuovi* and all the volumes of the *originali* for the provinces of Principato Citra and Basilicata, where the Caracciolo Brienza had their fiefs

Registri dei Quinternioni and

Repertori dei Quinternioni, for which general inventories exist, contain the remains of a once very rich series that discussed all passages of feudal property from one owner to the next

Assensi feudali consists in eleven bundles of documents reporting the royal assent to transactions involving feudal property; there is no index and I have seen all the bundles

Aside from feudal matters, the *Sezione Diplomatica* includes the *Provvisioni del Collaterale*, an indexed series consisting in the replies of the Collateral Council to petitions addressed to it by the *università*, mostly relating to community finances; I have seen the documents referring to the *università* enfeoffed to the Caracciolo Brienza.

The *Sezione Diplomatica* also includes the hundred or so private archives (*Archivi privati*) that have, over the years, been deposited in the ASN; I have seen the inventories of most of them and selected documents from a few of them.

THE FAMILY ARCHIVE OF THE CARACCIOLO DI BRIENZA

Not least among the reasons why the Caracciolo Brienza were chosen as the object of this study was the state of their papers in the ASN. The Archivio Privato Caracciolo di Brienza (ACB) has both old and modern inventories, consists mostly in documents in a good state of conservation, and includes large series of documents relating to several aspects of the family's history; a large share of its documents also dates back to the Spanish period. Before describing the contents of the ACB, I will discuss its origins.[4]

Origins of the archive

In 1773, Litterio Giuseppe Caracciolo, tenth marquis of Brienza, sixth prince of Atena, lord of Pietrafesa and Sasso, completed the organization of his family archive and wrote the foreword to its majestic inventory. In it he stressed that

---

[4] The modern inventory is in the printed work *Archivi privati* (2 vols.; Rome, 1967), II, pp. 91–149, and was prepared by A. Silvestri of the ASN.

whereas "since not few lustres and centuries my house has acquired fiefs and heritages, prestigious offices have been bestowed on my ancestors, lawsuits have been fought, transactions concluded, debts extinguished etc., never care has been taken to form an archive"; he therefore found himself "in too dense a darkness, among lawsuits, doubts, and uncertainties," and decided to organize an archive with the documents he could still find pertaining to the history of his family. After remarking that the incompleteness of the archive was due to the lack of "preliminary lights [*lumi*]," he urged his successors to continue "such a necessary work, profitable to their maintenance."[5]

The marquis had copies made of many notarial acts which involved his family. Notaries in the kingdom of Naples kept and bequeathed their registers, and, by paying a fee, any party could ask for notarized copies of any surviving act. Many of the notarial acts existing in the ACB today are copies made in the 1770s. In 1774, then, the marquis paid 240 ducats to Vincenzo Eccellente "master deskmaker" for four walnut "bureaux" to hold the documents, and on April 22 of that year he entrusted the whole archive to Michelangelo Pacifici, a clergyman from Solofra, who remained the family archivist at least until 1805. Pacifici, who received eight ducats per month, in addition to food and lodging in the marquis' palace in Naples, also wrote a genealogical treatise on the family, which was included in all the bound inventories.[6]

The ancestors of Litterio Caracciolo had not totally lacked "lights," nor had they been fully unaware of the need for an aristocratic family to keep records of its rights and properties, for involvement in lawsuits was hardly a new feature of aristocratic life. Litterio and his archivist could, therefore, collect a few original account books dating from as early as the 1620s, as well as some inventories drawn in the sixteenth and seventeenth centuries. More important, the notarial registers proved to be a very fruitful source of documents of all kinds. Since the late 1740s, when Litterio had assumed his full responsibilities as head of the family, account books of general and daily expenses, of travel and kitchen expenses, and of various types of revenue had been kept, though not at all systematically. An archive had existed in the castle in Brienza at least since 1764. Notwithstanding the losses reported as early as the 1770s, and those which occurred later, particularly in the course of the many lawsuits which involved Giulia Caracciolo, granddaughter of Litterio and last heir to the family, the archive which passed from the Società Napoletana di Storia Patria into the ASN in 1939 is a very valuable one, and its inventories and internal organization are an

[5] ACB, foreword to the three main inventories contained in the archive, with their copies, vols. 39, 40, 69, 70, 90, and 91. Vols. 41, 42, 71, 72, 92, and 93 are indexes to the inventories.
[6] See ACB 8.108 and 9.40 for the payment to Eccellente, and the contract with Pacifici. Vol. 117, which contains papers relating to the archive, mentions Pacifici as the archivist through 1805. The genealogical treatise is accompanied by an attractive large family tree.

impressive witness to the influence of eighteenth-century *lumi* on the Neapolitan aristocracy.[7]

Although the foreword written by Litterio Caracciolo is the only example known to me of a discussion by a Neapolitan aristocrat of his reasons for keeping an archive, the Brienza were not alone among the aristocracy in eighteenth-century Naples in organizing their family papers. A small sample of inventories surviving in other aristocratic archives shows that the Doria princes of Angri, the Tocco princes of Montemiletto, the Ruffo princes of Scilla, the Palma d'Artois and di Sant'Elia, and the Giudice di Cellamare dukes of Giovinazzo, were all arranging and inventorying their papers, hiring archivists, and establishing archives in their palaces in the eighteenth century, especially in the second half of the century. The Roman and Florentine families of the Salviati and Corsini also arranged their archives in these years.[8]

The fact that aristocratic archives were put together primarily to help the families in the many lawsuits in which they were involved, in the kingdom of Naples as in Piedmont and elsewhere, influenced the types of documents that were preserved.[9] The ACB, like most other Neapolitan aristocratic archives, includes primarily records of sales and purchases, family documents regulating inheritances or marriages, trial records or documents prepared to support the family's case in court, fiscal records, assessments of property, and notarial acts. Account books, if indeed they were kept, would probably not be preserved unless they could show the family's right to certain contested sources of revenue. Papers of a very private nature, such as diaries or letters, would also probably not be included, and in fact no inventory of a family archive that I have seen mentions any correspondence other than the official letters of family members who occupied public positions. Since the Caracciolo Brienza resided in the kingdom and spent a large amount of their time in their fiefs, administrative correspondence with local agents is also very limited. In general, the types of documents included in the ACB seem to have been very similar to those of other Neapolitan aristocratic archives.

The organization of the ACB

The ACB includes volumes and bundles. Most volumes have folio numbers. The bundles consist in many documents, often arranged in two or more

[7] On the archive in Brienza, see ACB 48.9, the appointment of Francesco Mazzei as general agent of the marquis in the fiefs. For the lost books, see the inventories in vols. 109, and 110.

[8] The inventories are in ASN, Doria d'Angri 18/5, Tocco 228, Giudice Caracciolo 97 bis (Palma), and 88 (Giudice), Ruffo Scilla 710, 711, and 712. Other family archives, such as the Caracciolo di Torchiarolo and Carafa di Castel San Lorenzo, do not include old inventories. P. Hurtubise, OMI, *Une famille-témoin* (Vatican City, 1985), introd.; Moroni, "Le ricchezze dei Corsini," p. 262.

[9] For Piedmont, see S. J. Woolf, *Studi sulla nobiltà piemontese nell'epoca dell'assolutismo* (Turin, 1963), p. 37.

numbered subsections. Each subsection consists of several loose documents, each of which, in most cases, is inserted in a folder. The folders, all prepared in the 1770s, carry a short summary of the content of the document and give the number of the bundle, of the subsection, and of the document itself. References to documents in the bundles, therefore, consist of three numbers separated by periods. Whenever the documents cited are longer than one or two folios, I have given the folio number or marked it as "unnumbered fol." In bundles that have no internal arrangement it is often impossible to give a precise reference, since the documents are simply piled on top of each other and loosely tied together with centuries-old strings; again, I have marked these "unnumbered fol." All translations from documents (as from secondary literature) are mine.

The ACB is divided into several sections. They are:

1 *Scritture di Napoli* contain documents relating to the family history in the capital. They are arranged in forty-two volumes and bundles. They include the following papers:

1–2 genealogical materials, and papers relating to offices held by the family, and to various personal privileges and honors of family members
3–4 baptism and death records, marriage contracts and wills
5 papers relating to the family's residences in the capital
6 papers relating to allodial properties and tax-farms
7 records of the family *Monti*
8 debts, credits, and bank records
9 purchases, sales, and donations
10–15 lawsuits involving family inheritances
16 inventories, expenses, and appointments of agents
17 trial records
18–20 papers relating to properties in Sicily and Calabria
21 trial records
22–32 account books, lists of payments, and accounts of agents
33 inventory of jewels (1773)
34 papers relating to the *Monte Ciarletta*
35 inventory of property and papers
36–38 account books
39–42 inventory of part 1 of the archive and indexes

2 *Scritture di Brienza e Pietrafesa* contain documents relating to these two fiefs. They are arranged in thirty volumes and bundles. They include the following papers:

43–47 purchases, sales, feudal rights, rents, and taxes for Brienza
48 litigation with the *università* of Brienza

49–50 ecclesiastic foundations in Brienza
51–59 volumes of rents, accounts, lists of properties, and vassals' obligations for Brienza
60 inventory of all revenues (1620)
61–63 purchases, and the like for Pietrafesa
64–68 volumes of accounts, and the like for Pietrafesa
69–72 inventory of part 2 of the archive and indexes

3 *Scritture di Atena* contain papers for this fief, in eight volumes and bundles, arranged as follows:

73–77 purchases, litigations and the like for Atena
78–80 volumes of accounts, and the like for Atena

4 *Scritture di Sasso* contain papers for this fief, in eight volumes and bundles, arranged as follows:

81–82 purchases, and the like for Sasso
83–88 volumes of accounts, and the like for Sasso

5 *Scritture di Sala e Padula* consist in five volumes and bundles arranged as follows:

89 papers relating to properties in Sala and Padula
90–93 inventory of parts 3, 4, and 5 of the archive and indexes

The remaining sections of the archive were put together after the 1770s and are not as neatly arranged; many of the bundles are not numbered or subdivided. They are:

6 *Processi criminali delle corti baronali* consist in fifteen bundles of trial records for the baronial courts of the four fiefs, beginning in the last quarter of the eighteenth century, and arranged as follows:

94–96 Atena
97–101 Brienza
102–3 Pietrafesa
104–7 Sasso
108 inventory

7 *Volumi diveri* consist in twenty-four volumes (numbers 109–32) with inventories, lists of revenues or rents, vassals' obligations, accounts, and fiscal payments, mostly dating from the 1770s onwards up to the mid-nineteenth century.

8 *Scritture varie* consist in two bundles:

133 statutes of Atena, registers of a notary from the fiefs, and records of a trial

134 records of a trial, and papers relating to a chapel in Brienza

9 *Processi civili* contain many papers, mostly of judicial origins, and divided in thirty-two bundles, arranged as follows:

135–42 records of eighty-four trials involving the family from the early seventeenth to the mid-nineteenth centuries

143–66 papers of various types, mostly prepared to support the family's case in trials, dating mostly from the eighteenth and nineteenth centuries; many refer to the affairs of Giula Caracciolo (d. 1875), last heir to the family

The ACB also includes an Appendix of twenty-three volumes and bundles, numbered separately, containing papers relating in large part to the *Monti* to which the Caracciolo Brienza had rights, in particular to the *Monte Ciarletta*, for which see chapter 5.

Bibliography

This bibliography consists of all the titles cited in the text. Articles and books are listed together.

Abignente, G. *Il diritto successorio nelle province napoletane dal 500 al 1800* (Nola: San Felice, 1881).

"Aggiunta alli Diurnali di Scipione Guerra" *ASPN* 36 (1911), pp. 124–205, 329–82, 507–80, 751–98.

Ago, R. "Braccianti, contadini e grandi proprietari in un villaggio laziale nel primo '700" *QS* 16 (1981), pp. 60–91.

Ajello, R., ed. *Giuristi e società al tempo di Pietro Giannone* (Naples: Jovene, 1980).

Aldimari, B. *Memorie historiche di diverse famiglie nobili* (Naples: Giacomo Raillard, 1691).

Alianelli, N. *Delle consuetudini e degli statuti municipali nelle province napoletane* (Naples: publisher unknown, 1873).

Aliberti, G. *Potere e società locale nel Mezzogiorno dell'Ottocento* (Bari: Laterza, 1987).

Ammirato, S. *Delle famiglie nobili napoletane* (Florence: Giorgio Marescotti, 1580; second vol. Florence: Amadore Maffi, 1651).

Anatra, B. "I rapporti tra corona e ceti privilegiati nella Sardegna del XVII secolo" in S. di Bella, ed. *La rivolta di Messina (1674–78) e il mondo mediterraneo nella seconda metà del Seicento*, acts of the conference held in Messina in October 1975 (Cosenza, 1979), pp. 71–80.

Anatra, B., Puddu, R., and Serri, G. *Problemi di storia della Sardegna spagnola* (Cagliari: Editrice Democratica Sarda, 1975).

Anderson, P. *Lo stato assoluto* (Milan: Mondadori, 1980; English edit. 1974).

Anes, G. *El Antiguo Régimen. Los Borbones* (Madrid: Alianza Editorial Alfaguara, 1975).

Angiolini, F. "Le basi economiche del potere aristocratico nell'Italia centrosettentrionale tra XVI e XVIII secolo" *Società e storia* 1 (1978), pp. 317–31.

Archivi privati (2 vols.; Rome: Archivi di Stato, 1967).

L'Archivio Storico del Banco di Napoli, una fonte preziosa per la storia economica, sociale e artistica del Mezzogiorno d'Italia (Naples: ASBN, 1972).

Ariès, P. *L'enfant et la vie familiale sous l'Ancien Régime* (Paris: Plon, 1960).

Aston, T. H., and Philpin, C. H. E., eds. *The Brenner Debate. Agrarian Class Structure and Economic Development in Preindustrial Europe* (Cambridge: Cambridge University Press, 1987; first edit. 1985).

Atienza Hernandez, I. *Aristocracia, poder y riqueza en la España moderna. La casa de Osuna, siglos XV-XIX* (Madrid: Siglo Veintiuno, 1987).

Aymard, M. "L'abolition de la féodalité en Sicile: le sens d'une réforme" *Annuario*

Bibliography

dell'Istituto Storico Italiano per l'età moderna e contemporanea 23–24 (1971–72), pp. 67–85.

"En Sicile, dîmes et comptabilité agricole" in Le Roy Ladurie–Goy, eds. *Les fluctuations du produit de la dîme* (Paris–The Hague, 1972), pp. 294–303.

"Une famille de l'aristocratie sicilienne aux XVIe et XVIIe siècles: les ducs de Terranova, un bel example d'ascension seigneuriale" *Revue historique* 96, no. 247 (1972), pp. 29–66.

"Rendements et productivité agricole dans l'Italie moderne" *Annales ESC* 28 (1973), pp. 475–98.

"Amministrazione feudale e trasformazioni strutturali tra '500 e '700" *Archivio Storico per la Sicilia Orientale* 71 (1975), pp. 17–42.

"La transizione dal feudalesimo al capitalismo" in *Storia d'Italia Einaudi. Annali I Dal feudalesimo al capitalismo* (Turin: Einaudi, 1978), pp. 1131–92.

"L'Europe moderne: féodalité ou féodalités?" *Annales ESC* 36 (1981), pp. 426–35.

"Strutture delle aziende e studio della produzione e della produttività agricola in Italia meridionale nell'età moderna: prospettive di ricerca" in Massafra, ed. *Problemi di storia* (Bari, 1981), pp. 17–24.

Bacco Alemanno, H. *Il regno di Napoli in dodici provincie . . .* (Naples, 1609; second edit. ed. C. d'Engenio, Naples: Lazaro Scoriggio, 1620).

Baker, G. R. F. "Nobiltà in declino: il caso di Siena sotto i Medici e gli Asburgo-Lorena" *RSI* 84 (1972), pp. 584–616.

Barbagallo, F. *Mezzogiorno e questione meridionale (1860–1980)* (Naples: Guida, 1980).

Barbagli, M. *Sotto lo stesso tetto. Mutamenti della famiglia in Italia dal XV al XX secolo* (Bologna: Mulino, 1984).

Barbato, O. *Modestinus elucidatus sive de fideicommisso, maioratu ac primogenitura . . .* (Naples: Giacomo Gaffari, 1643).

Barbone Puglise, N. "Due tavole di Silvestro Buono a Brienza" *Napoli nobilissima* new series, 24 (1985), pp. 93–99.

Battista, G. *Poesie meliche* (Naples: Ettore Cicconio, 1650).

Beckett, J. V. *The Aristocracy in England, 1660–1914* (New York: Basil Blackwell, 1986).

Belli, C. "Famiglia, proprietà e classi sociali a Montefusco nella prima metà del secolo XVII" *MEFRM* 95 (1983), pp. 339–92.

Belmonte, T. *The Broken Fountain* (New York: Columbia University Press, 1989; first edit. 1979).

Beltrano, O. *Breve descrittione del regno di Napoli diviso in dodici provincie . . .* (Naples: Beltrano, 1646; second edit. 1671; reprint Bologna: Forni, 1969).

Benaiteau, M. "La rendita feudale nel regno di Napoli attraverso i relevi: il Principato Ultra (1550–1806)" *Società e storia* 9 (1980), pp. 561–611.

"L'agricoltura nella provincia di Principato Ultra nell'età moderna (secoli XVII e XVIII)" in Massafra, ed. *Problemi di storia* (Bari, 1981), pp. 201–19.

"Les dépendances féodales des di Tocco en Calabre Citérieure: 1788–1810" in acts of the Sixth Congreso Storico Calabrese *La Calabria dalle riforme alla restaurazione* (2 vols.; Catanzaro: Società Editrice Meridionale, 1981), II, pp. 15–26.

Bennassar, B. *Il secolo d'oro spagnolo* (Milan: Rizzoli, 1985; French edit. 1982).

Bentley, J. H. *Politics and Culture in Renaissance Naples* (Princeton: Princeton University Press, 1987).

Bibliography

Berengo, M. *Nobili e mercanti nella Lucca del '500* (Turin: Einaudi, 1965).

Bianchini, L. *Per la storia delle finanze del regno di Napoli* (Naples: Stamperia Reale, 1859; first edit. 1835).

Billacois, F. "La crise de la noblesse européenne (1550–1650), une mise au point" *Revue d'histoire moderne et contemporaine* 23 (1976), pp. 258–77.

Bizzocchi, R. "La dissoluzione di un clan familiare: i Buondelmonti di Firenze nei secoli XVI e XVII" *ASI* 140 (1982), pp. 3–45.

Bois, G. *The Crisis of Feudalism. Economy and Society in Eastern Normandy, c. 1300–1550* (Cambridge: Cambridge University Press, 1984; French edit. 1976).

Boldini, L. "Bomarzo, sopravvivenze e trasformazioni di un microcosmo feudale dell'Alto Lazio tra il'700 e l'"800" *Studi romani* 34 (1986), pp. 107–18.

Borrelli, C. *Vindex Neapolitanae Nobilitatis* (Naples: Egidio Longo, 1653).

Borelli, G. "Nozze e doti in una famiglia nobiliare durante la prima metà del XVIII secolo" *Economia e storia* 8 (1971), pp. 321–42.

Un patriziato della Terraferma veneta tra XVII e XVIII secolo. Ricerche sulla nobiltà veronese (Milan: Giuffrè, 1974).

Boutier, J. "Les 'Notizie diverse' de Niccolò Gondi (1652–1720). A propos de la mémoire et des stratégies familiales d'un noble florentin" *MEFRM* 98 (1986), pp. 1097–151.

Brizzi, G. P. *La formazione della classe dirigente nel Sei-Settecento, i Seminaria nobilium nell'Italia centrosettentrionale* (Bologna: Mulino, 1976).

Brunner, O. *Vita nobiliare e cultura europea* (Bologna: Mulino, 1972; German edit. 1949).

Bulferetti, L. "La feudalità e il patriziato nel Piemonte di Carlo Emanuele II (1653–1675)" *Annali della Facoltà di Lettere, Filosofia e Magistero dell'Università di Cagliari* 21 (1953), pp. 367–623.

"L'oro, la terra e la società; un'interpretazione del nostro Seicento" *Archivio Storico Lombardo* 80 (1953), pp. 5–66.

Bulgarelli Lukacs, A. "Le 'Universitates' meridionali all'inizio del regno di Carlo di Borbone, la struttura amministrativa" *Clio* 17 (1981), pp. 5–25.

"Le 'Universitates' meridionali all'inizio del regno di Carlo di Borbone" *Clio* 18 (1982), pp. 208–26.

Bulifon, A. *Giornali di Napoli dal MDXLVII al MDCCVI* (Naples: Società Napoletana di Storia Patria, 1932).

Burke, P. "Southern Italy in the 1590s: Hard Times or Crisis?" in P. Clark, ed. *The European Crisis of the 1590s. Essays in Comparative History* (London: Allen and Unwin, 1985), pp. 177–90.

The Historical Anthropology of Early Modern Italy. Essays on Perception and Communication (Cambridge: Cambridge University Press, 1987).

Bush, M. L. *The European Nobility*, I, *Noble Privilege* (New York: Holmes and Meyer, 1983); II, *Rich Noble, Poor Noble* (Manchester: Manchester University Press, 1988).

Calabria, A. "State Finance in the Kingdom of Naples in the Age of Philip II" Ph.D. Dissertation, University of California, Berkeley, 1978.

"Finanzieri genovesi nel regno di Napoli nel Cinquecento" *RSI* 101 (1989), pp. 578–613.

Cammisa, F. "Un atto di accusa contro la giurisdizione feudale, redatto a Napoli nel 1764" *ASPN* 105 (1987), pp. 493–520.

253

Bibliography

Campanelli, M. "Note sul patrimonio dei Teatini in Italia alla vigilia dell'inchiesta innocenziana" in Galasso and Russo, eds. *Per la storia sociale e religiosa del Mezzogiorno d'Italia* (2 vols.; Naples: Guida, 1980–82), I, pp. 179–238.

Campanile, G. *Notizie di nobiltà* (Naples: publisher unknown, 1672).

Cancila, O. "Introduzione" to F. di Napoli, principe di Resuttano, *Noi il Padrone* (Palermo: Sellerio, 1982).

Baroni e popolo nella Sicilia del grano (Palermo: Palumbo, 1983).

Cannon, J. *Aristocratic Century. The Peerage of Eighteenth-Century England* (Cambridge: Cambridge University Press, 1987; first edit. 1984).

Capaccio, G. C. *Il forastiero dialogi* (Naples: Giovan Domenico Roncagliolo, 1634).

Capano, A. *De jure relevi* (Naples: Secondino Roncaglioli, 1630).

De jure adohae (Naples: Francesco Savii, 1636).

De vita militia tractatus (Naples: Giacomo Gaffari, 1642).

De fideicommisso masculino ... (Naples: Onofrio Savii, 1649).

Capasso, B., ed. "Napoli descritta nei principi del secolo XVII da G. C. Capaccio" *ASPN* 7 (1882), pp. 68–103, 531–54, 776–97.

Capecelatro, F. *Degli annali della città di Napoli 1631–1640* (Naples: Tipografia di Reale, 1849).

Diario, 1647–1650, ed. A. Granito di Belmonte (3 vols.; Naples, 1850–54).

Origine della città e delle famiglie nobili di Napoli in vol. II of Capecelatro, *Istoria della città e del regno di Napoli detto di Sicilia* (Naples: Gravier, 1769; written in the 1630s; reprint Cosenza: Brenner, 1989).

Capobianco, G. G. *Tractatus de iure et officio baronum erga vasallos burgenses* (Naples: Tarquinio Longo, 1622; first edit. 1614).

Caracciolo, F. "Fisco e contribuenti in Calabria nel secolo XVI" *Nuova rivista storica* 47 (1963), pp. 504–38.

Il regno di Napoli nei secoli XVI e XVII (Rome: Magistero Università di Messina, 1966).

Uffici, difesa e corpi rappresentativi nel Mezzogiorno in età spagnola (Reggio Calabria: Editori Meridionali Riuniti, 1974).

"Finanze e gravami cittadini in Calabria e nel regno di Napoli al tempo di Filippo II" *Nuova rivista storica* 66 (1982), pp. 37–58.

Sud, debiti e gabelle. Gravami, potere e società nel Mezzogiorno in età moderna (Naples: ESI, 1983).

Caracciolo, T. *Nobilitatis Neapolitanae Defensio* in L. A. Muratori, ed. *Rerum Italicarum Scriptores*, new edit. by G. Carducci, V. Fiorini, and P. Fedele, vol. XXII, I (Bologna: Zanichelli, 1935), pp. 141–48.

Caracciolo di Torchiarolo, A. *Una famiglia italianissima: i Caracciolo di Napoli nella storia e nella leggenda* (Naples, 1939).

"Un feudatario di Gallarate: il cardinale Marino Caracciolo," offprint from *Rassegna Gallaratese di storia e d'arte* 12 (1953).

"Alcune notizie sulla famiglia Francone e l'arredamento di una case patrizia napoletana al principio del secolo XVIII" *Studi in onore di Riccardo Filangieri* (3 vols.; Naples, 1959), III, pp. 29–50.

"I Caracciolo di Avellino in un inventario del XVII secolo," offprint from *Samnium* 35 (1962).

Bibliography

"I Monti di previdenza della famiglia Caracciolo" *Atti dell'Accademia Pontaniana* new series, 6 (n.d.), pp. 337–61.

Caridi, G. "Capitoli matrimoniali, dote e dotario in Calabria (XVI–XVII secolo)" *ASCL* 54 (1987), pp. 11–44.

Uno "stato" feudale nel Mezzogiorno spagnolo (Rome: Gangemi, 1988).

Carignani, G. "L'ultimo Parlamento Generale del regno di Napoli nel 1642" *ASPN* 8 (1883), pp. 34–57.

Carpanetto, D. and Recuperati, G. *Italy in the Age of Reason, 1685–1789* (New York: Longman, 1987).

Casey, J. *The Kingdom of Valencia in the Seventeenth Century* (Cambridge: Cambridge University Press, 1979).

Cassandro, G. I. *Storia delle terre comuni e degli usi civici nell'Italia meridionale* (Bari: Laterza, 1943).

Storia di una terra del Mezzogiorno: Atena Lucana (Rome, 1946; originally in *Rivista di storia del diritto italiano* 16 (1943)).

Catalani, L. *I palazzi di Napoli* (Naples, 1845; new edit. Naples: Colonnese, 1979).

Ceci, G. "Pizzofalcone" *Napoli nobilissima* 1 (1892), pp. 60–62, 85–89, 105–9, and 129–33.

"I feudatari napoletani alla fine del secolo XVI" *ASPN* 24 (1899), pp. 122–38.

Celano, C. *Notizie del bello, dell'antico e del curioso della città di Napoli . . .*, ed. G. B. Chiarini (7 vols.; Naples: ESI, 1974; first edit. 1692).

Cernigliaro, A. *Sovranità e feudo nel regno di Napoli 1505–1557* (2 vols.; Naples: Jovene, 1983).

"Giurisdizione baronale e prassi delle avocazioni nel Cinquecento napoletano" *ASPN* 104 (1986), pp. 159–241.

Cervellino, L. *Direttione overo guida dell'Università . . .* (Naples: Giovan Francesco Paci, 1686).

Cestaro, G. "Il feudo ecclesiastico di Castellano e Perolla" in De Rosa–Malgeri, eds. *Società e religione*, II, pp. 121–35.

Chabod, F. *Lo stato e la vita religiosa a Milano nell'epoca di Carlo V* (2 vols.; Turin: Einaudi, 1971).

Scritti sul Rinascimento (Turin: Einaudi, 1981).

Chaussinand-Nogaret, G. *The French Nobility in the Eighteenth Century, from Feudalism to Enlightenment* (Cambridge: Cambridge University Press, 1985; French edit. 1976).

Chittolini, G. *La formazione dello stato regionale e le istituzioni del contado, secoli XIV e XV* (Turin: Einaudi, 1979).

ed. *La crisi degli ordinamenti comunali e le origini dello stato del Rinascimento* (Bologna: Mulino, 1979).

Chojnacky, S. "Patrician Women in Early Renaissance Venice" *Studies in the Renaissance* 21 (1974), pp. 176–203.

"Dowries and Kinsmen in Early Renaissance Venice" *Journal of Interdisciplinary History* 5 (1975), pp. 571–600.

"Kinship Ties and Young Patricians in Fifteenth-Century Venice" *Renaissance Quarterly* 38 (1985), pp. 240–70.

Chorley, P. *Oil, Silk and the Enlightenment. Economic Problems in Eighteenth-Century Naples* (Naples: Istituto Italiano per gli Studi Storici, 1965).

Bibliography

Ciccaglione, F. *Le leggi e le più note consuetudini che regolarono i patti nuziali nelle provincie napoletane innanzi alla pubblicazione del codice francese* (Naples: Vaglio, 1881).

Cipolla, C. M. "Note sulla storia del saggio d'interesse" *Economia internazionale* 5 (1957), pp. 255–74.

Civitella, D. *Delle consuetudini di Napoli sotto i titoli De successionibus ab intestato et ex testamento commentario* (Naples: Vincenzo Moccola-Vocola, 1785).

Cochrane, E. "Southern Italy in the Age of the Spanish Viceroys: Some Recent Titles" *Journal of Modern History* 58 (1986), pp. 194–217.

Italy, 1530–1630 (New York: Longman, 1988).

Colangelo, G. "La diocesi di Marisco dal concilio di Trento al 1656," in De Rosa–Malgeri, eds. *Società e religione*, II, pp. 163–98.

Colapietra, R. *Vita pubblica e classi politiche del viceregno napoletano (1656–1734)* (Rome: Edizioni di storia e letteratura, 1961).

Dal Magnanimo a Masaniello. Studi di storia meridionale nell'età moderna (2 vols.; Salerno: BETA, 1973).

Collenuccio, P., Roseo, M., and Costo, T. *Compendio dell'historia del regno di Napoli ...* (Venice: Barezzo Barezzi, 1591; second edit. 1613).

Comparato, V. I. *Uffici e società a Napoli (1660–1647), aspetti dell'ideologia del magistrato nell'età moderna* (Florence: Olschki, 1974).

Confuorto, D. *Il torto o vero il dritto della nobiltà napoletana*, BNN ms. X-A-25 (1690s).

Giornali di Napoli dal MDCLXXIX al MDCIC (2 vols.; Naples: Lubrano, 1930).

Coniglio, G. *Il regno di Napoli al tempo di Carlo V. Amministrazione e vita economico-sociale* (Naples: ESI, 1951).

Contarino, L. *Dell'antiquità, sito, chiese, corpi santi, reliquie et statue di Roma, con l'origine e nobiltà di Napoli* (Naples: Giuseppe Cacchii, 1569).

Cooper, J. P. "Patterns of Inheritance and Settlement by Great Landowners from the Fifteenth to the Eighteenth Century" in J. Goody, *et al.*, eds. *Family and Inheritance. Rural Society in Western Europe, 1200–1800* (Cambridge: Cambridge University Press, 1976), pp. 192–327.

Coppola, M. "Distribuzione del reddito e squilibri socio-economici nel Vallo di Diano durante il Decennio francese" *Rassegna storica salernitana* new series, 3 (1986), pp. 91–102.

Cortese, N. *Feudi e feudatari napoletani della prima metà del Cinquecento da documenti dell'AGS* (Naples: Società Napoletana di Storia Patria, 1931; first appeared in *ASPN* 54–56 (1929–31)).

Costo, T. See Collenuccio, P.

Cowan, A. F. *The Urban Patriciate. Lübeck and Venice, 1580–1700* (Köln: Böhlau, 1986).

Craig, G. "Witness" *The New York Review of Books*, 6 December, 1990, pp. 2–7.

Croce, B. *Storia del regno di Napoli* (Bari: Laterza, 1931; first edit. 1924).

Uomini e cose della vecchia Italia (2 vols.; Bari: Laterza, 1956; first edit. 1926).

"Il marchese di Vico Galeazzo Caracciolo" in Croce, *Vite di avventure, di fede, di passione* (Bari: Laterza, 1936).

Cuozzo, E. *Commentario* to E. Jamison, ed. *Catalogus baronum* (Rome: Istituto Storico Italiano per il Medio Evo, 1984).

D'Addosio, G. B. *Origine, vicende storiche e progressi della Real Santa Casa dell'Annunziata di Napoli* (Naples: A. Cons, 1883).

Bibliography

D'Agostino, G. *La capitale ambigua, Napoli dal 1458 al 1580* (Naples: Società Editrice Napoletana, 1979).

Parlamento e società nel regno di Napoli, secoli XV–XVII (Naples: Guida, 1979).

D'Ambrosio, G. "La feudalità in Terra di Lavoro nella seconda metà del secolo XVII", tesi di laurea, University of Naples, 1984–85.

D'Amelio, G. "Polemica antifeudale, feudistica napoletana e diritto longobardo" *QS* 9 (1974), pp. 337–50.

D'Andrea, F. *I ricordi di un avvocato napoletano del '600*, ed. N. Cortese (Naples: Lubrano, 1923; originally in *ASPN* 44–46 (1919–21) as "Avvertimenti ai nipoti").

Davies, T. "La colonizzazione feudale della Sicilia nella prima età moderna" in *Storia d'Italia Einaudi. Annali VIII Insediamenti e territorio* (Turin: Einaudi, 1978), pp. 415–72.

Famiglie feudali siciliane. Patrimoni redditi investimenti tra '500 e '600 (Caltanissetta–Rome: Salvatore Sciascia, 1985).

"Village-Building in Sicily: An Aristocratic Remedy for the Crisis of the 1590s" in P. Clark, ed. *The European Crisis of the 1590s. Essays in Comparative History* (London: Allen and Unwin, 1985), pp. 191–208.

Davis, J. C. *The Decline of the Venetian Aristocracy as a Ruling Class* (Baltimore: Johns Hopkins University Press, 1962).

A Venetian Family and its Fortune 1500–1900: The Donà and the Conservation of their Wealth (Philadelphia: American Philosophical Society, 1975).

de Angelis, F. G. *Tractatus de officialibus baronum* (Naples: Francesco Benzi, 1689).

De Felice, R. *Aspetti e momenti della vita economica di Roma e del Lazio nei secoli XVIII e XIX* (Rome: Edizioni di storia e letteratura, 1965).

de Frede, C. *Rivolte antifeudali nel Mezzogiorno e altri studi cinquecenteschi* (Naples: De Simone, 1984; first edit. 1977).

de Giorgio, *Repetitiones feudales ineditae...* (Naples: Felice Mosca, 1724).

de Gregorio, P. *Tractatus de vita et militia, de dote de paragio...* (Palermo: Giovan Antonio de Franciscis, 1596; second edit. as appendix to Capano, A., *De vita militia* (Naples, 1642).

de la Ville sur-Yllon, L. "Strada di San Giovanni a Carbonara" *Napoli nobilissima* 15 (1906), pp. 17–23.

Del Bagno, I. "Reintegrazione nei Seggi napoletani e dialettica degli 'status'" *ASPN* 102 (1984), pp. 189–204.

"Governo borbonico e reintegrazione nei Seggi napoletani intorno alla metà del Settecento" *ASPN* 103 (1985), pp. 377–99.

de Lellis, C. *Supplimento a Napoli sacra di Don Cesare d'Engenio Caracciolo* (Naples: Roberto Mollo, 1654).

Discorsi delle famiglie nobili del regno di Napoli (3 vols.; Naples, 1654, 1663, 1671; reprint Bologna: Forni, 1968).

de Leonardis, G. F. *Prattica degli officiali regii e baronali del regno di Napoli* (Naples: Costantino Vitale, 1619; first edit. 1599).

Delille, G. *Croissance d'une société rurale: Montesarchio et la Vallée Caudine aux XVIIe et XVIIIe siècles* (Naples: Istituto Italiano per gli Studi Storici, 1973).

Agricoltura e demografia nel regno di Napoli nei secoli XVIII e XIX (Naples: Guida, 1977).

"L'ordine dei villaggi e l'ordine dei campi. Per uno studio antropologico del paesaggio agrario nel regno di Napoli (secoli XV-XVIII)" in *Storia d'Italia Einaudi. Annali* VIII *Insediamenti e territorio* (Turin: Einaudi, 1978), pp. 499–560.

"Un esempio di assistenza privata: i Monti di maritaggio nel regno di Napoli (secoli XVI–XVIII)" in *Timore e carità: i poveri nell'Italia moderna*, acts of the conference *Pauperismo e assistenza negli antichi stati italiani* held in Cremona in March 1980 (Cremona: Biblioteca Statale e Libreria Civica, 1982).

Famille et propriété dans le royaume de Naples (XVe–XIXe siècles) (Rome: Ecole Française de Rome, 1985).

della Marra, F. "Ruina di case napoletane del suo tempo scritta da don Ferrante della Marra duca della Guardia (1641)" *ASPN* 25 (1900), pp. 355–86.

de Luca, G. B. *Il cavaliere e la dama* (Rome: Dragandelli, 1675).

de Lutio di Castelguidone, L. *I Sedili di Napoli* (Naples: Morano, 1973).

Del Vecchio, F. "La vendita delle terre demaniali nel regno di Napoli dal 1628 al 1648" *ASPN* 103 (1985), pp. 163–211.

De Maddalena, A. *Dalla città al borgo, avvio di una metamorfosi economica e sociale nella Lombardia spagnola* (Milan: Franco Angeli, 1982).

De Matteis, A. *L'Aquila e il contado. Demografia e fiscalità (secoli XV–XVIII)* (Naples: Giannini, 1973).

de Pietri, F. *Cronologia della famiglia Caracciolo* (second edit. Naples: Stamperia Simoniana, 1803; first edit. 1605).

De Rosa, G. *Vescovi, popolo e magia nel Sud* (Naples: Guida, 1971).

"Per una storia della parrocchia nel Mezzogiorno" in De Rosa, *Chiesa e religione popolare nel Mezzogiorno* (Bari: Laterza, 1978). pp. 21–46

"Pertinenze ecclesiastiche e santità nella storia sociale e religiosa della Basilicata dal XVIII al XIX secolo" in De Rosa, *Chiesa e religione popolare nel Mezzogiorno* (Bari: Laterza, 1978), pp. 47–101.

De Rosa, G., and Cestaro, A. *Territorio e società nella storia del Mezzogiorno* (Naples: Guida, 1973).

De Rosa, G., and Malgeri, F., eds. *Società e religione in Basilicata* (2 vols.; n.p.: D'Elia, 1978).

de Rosa, L. *Studi sugli arrendamenti del regno di Napoli, aspetti della distribuzione della ricchezza mobiliare nel Mezzogiorno continentale (1649–1806)* (Naples: Arte Tipografica, 1958).

Il Mezzogiorno spagnolo tra crescita e decadenza (Milan: Mondadori, 1987).

de Seta, C. *Napoli* (Bari: Laterza, 1981).

Dessert, D. *Argent, pouvoir et société au Grand Siècle* (Paris: Fayard, 1984).

de Stefano, F. P. *Romani, Longobardi e Normanno-Franchi della Puglia nei secoli XV–XVII; ricerche sui rapporti patrimoniali tra coniugi fino alla prammatica de antefato del 1617* (Naples: Jovene, 1979).

Dewald, J. *The Formation of a Provincial Nobility. The Magistrates of the Parlement of Rouen, 1499–1610* (Princeton: Princeton University Press, 1980).

Pont-St-Pierre 1398–1789. Lordship, Community, and Capitalism in Early Modern France (Berkeley–Los Angeles: University of California Press, 1987).

Diefendorf, B. "Widowhood and Remarriage in Sixteenth-Century Paris" *Journal of Family History* 7 (1982), pp. 379–95.

di Letizia, A. *Degli usi dei Proceri e Magnati e di Capuana e Nido commentari* (Naples: Pietro Perger, 1786).

Bibliography

di Sangro, V. *Famiglie del patriziato napoletano e delle nobili fuori Seggio ascritte al Real Monte di G. B. Manso marchese di Villa dall'anno 1608 ad oggi* (Naples: V. Morano, 1886).

Di Simplicio, O. "Sulla 'nobiltà povera' a Siena nel Seicento" *Bullettino senese di storia patria* 88 (1982), pp. 71–94.

Di Vittorio, A. *Gli Austriaci e il regno di Napoli, 1707–1734*, I, *Le finanze pubbliche*; II, *Ideologia e politica di sviluppo* (Naples: Giannini, 1969–73).

Dominguez Ortiz, A. *La sociedad española en el siglo XVII*, I (Madrid: Instituto "Balmes" de sociología, 1963).

El Antiguo Régimen: los Reyes Catholicos y los Austrias (Madrid: Alianza Editorial Alfaguara, 1973).

Donati, C. *L'idea di nobiltà in Italia (secoli XIV–XVIII)* (Bari: Laterza, 1988).

Doria, G. "Investimenti della nobiltà genovese nell'edilizia di prestigio (1530–1630)" *Studi storici* 27 (1986), pp. 5–55.

Dragonetti, G. *Origine de' feudi ne' regni di Napoli e Sicilia* (Naples: Stamperia Reale, 1788).

Ebner, P. *Storia di un feudo del Mezzogiorno. La baronia di Novi* (Rome: Edizioni di storia e letteratura, 1973).

Chiesa, baroni e popolo nel Cilento (2 vols.; Rome: Edizioni di storia e letteratura, 1982).

Elliott, J. H. *Imperial Spain, 1469–1716* (New York: Meridian–St. Martin's Press, 1977; first edit. 1963).

Fabris, F. *La genealogia della famiglia Caracciolo*, revised by A. Caracciolo di Torchiarolo (Naples, 1966; originally in Litta, P., *Famiglie celebri italiane* (Milan, 1819 on)).

Fanfani, T. *Potere e nobiltà nell'Italia minore tra XVI e XVII secolo, i Taglieschi d'Anghiari* (Milan: Giuffrè, 1983).

Faraglia, N. F. *Il comune nell'Italia meridionale (1100–1806)* (Naples: Regia University, 1883).

Fasano Guarini, E. "Principe e oligarchie nella Toscana del Cinquecento" *Annali della Facoltà di Scienza Politiche dell'Università di Perugia* 16 (1979–80), pp. 105–26.

ed. *Potere e società negli stati regionali italiani fra Cinquecento e Seicento* (Bologna: Mulino, 1978).

Febvre, L. "Ce que peuvent nous apprendre les monographies familiales" *Annales d'histoire sociale* 4 (1942), pp. 31–34 (also in Febvre, *Pour une histoire à part entière* (Paris: SEVPEN, 1962), pp. 404–9).

Felloni, G. *Gli inventimenti finanziari genovesi in Europa tra il Seicento e la Restaurazione* (Milan: Giuffrè, 1971).

Filamondo, R. M. *Il genio bellicoso di Napoli* (Napes: Parrino, 1694).

Filangieri di Candida, R. "La chiesa e il monastero di San Giovanni a Carbonara" *ASPN* 48 (1923), pp. 5–135.

Fiordelisi, A. *Gl'incendii in Napoli ai tempi di Masaniello* (Naples: L. Pierro, 1895).

Forster, R. "Obstacles to Agricultural Growth in Eighteenth-Century France" *American Historical Review* 75 (1970), pp. 1600–15.

The House of Saulx-Tavanes. Versailles and Burgundy, 1700–1830 (Baltimore: Johns Hopkins University Press, 1971).

The Nobility of Toulouse in the Eighteenth Century, A Social and Economic Study (Baltimore: Johns Hopkins University Press, 1960; second edit. 1971).

Bibliography

"The 'World' between Seigneur and Peasant" *Studies in Eighteenth-Century Culture* 5 (1976), pp. 401–21.

Merchants, Landlords, Magistrates. The Depont Family in Eighteenth-Century France (Baltimore: Johns Hopkins University Press, 1980).

Foucard, C. "Fonti di storia napoletana nell'Archivio di Stato de Moderna" *ASPN* 2 (1877), pp. 725–57.

"Frammento d'un diario inedito napoletano" *ASPN* 13 (1888), pp. 788–820; 14 (1899), pp. 34–68, 265–352.

Fuidoro, I. *Giornali di Napoli dal MDCLX al MDCLXXX* (3 vols.; Naples: Lubrano, 1934–39).

Galasso, G. "La legge feudale napoletana del 1799" *RSI* 76 (1964), pp. 507–29.

"La feudalità napoletana nel secolo XVI" *Clio* I (1965), pp. 535–54.

Economia e società nella Calabria del Cinquecento (Milan: Feltrinelli, 1975; first edit. Naples, 1967)

"Le riforme del conte di Lemos e le finanze napoletane nella prima metà del Seicento" in Galasso, *Mezzogiorno medievale e moderno* (Turin: Einaudi, 1975; first edit. 1965), pp. 199–229.

"Momenti e problemi di storia napoletana nell'età di Carlo V" in Galasso, *Mezzogiorno medievale e moderno* (Turin: Einaudi, 1975; first edit. 1965), pp. 139–97.

"Aspetti e problemi della società feudale napoletana attraverso l'inventario dei beni dei principi di Bisignano (1594)" in *Studi in memoria di Federigo Melis* (Naples: Giannini, 1978), IV, pp. 255–77.

"Un'ipotesi di 'blocco storico' oligarchico–borghese nella Napoli del '600: i *Seggi* di Camillo Tutini tra politica e storiografia" *RSI* 90 (1978), pp. 507–29.

"Ideologia e Sociologia del patronato di San Tommaso d'Aquino su Napoli (1605)" in Galasso and C. Russo, eds. *Per la storia sociale e religiosa del Mezzogiorno d'Italia* (2 vols.; Naples: Guida, 1980–82), II pp. 213–49.

"Strutture sociali e produttive, assetti colturali e mercato dal secolo XVI all'Unità" in Massafra, ed. *Problemi di storia* (Bari, 1981), pp. 159–72.

"Cultura materiale e vita nobiliare in un inventario calabrese del '500" in Galasso, *L'altra Europa, per un'antropologia storica del Mezzogiorno d'Italia* (Milan: Mondadori, 1982), pp. 284–311.

Napoli spagnola dopo Masaniello, politica, cultura, società (2 vols.; Florence: Sansoni, 1982; previously in Pontieri, ed. *Storia di Napoli*).

"L'ultimo feudalesimo meridionale nell'analisi di Giuseppe Maria Galanti" *RSI* 95 (1983), pp. 262–81.

Il Mezzogiorno nella storia d'Italia (Florence: Le Monnier, 1977; revised edit. 1984).

"Prefazione" to Musi, *La rivolta di Masaniello* (Naples, 1989).

Galasso, G., and Romeo, R., eds. *Storia del Mezzogiorno* (16 vols.; Naples: Edizioni del Sole, 1987 on).

Giannetti, A. "La strada dalla città al territorio: la riorganizzazione spaziale del Regno di Napoli nel Cinquecento" in *Storia d'Italia Einaudi. Annali* VIII *Insediamenti e territorio* (Turin: Einaudi, 1978), pp. 241–85.

Giorgetti, G. *Contadini e proprietari nell'Italia moderna. Rapporti di produzione e contratti agrari dal secolo XVI a oggi* (Turin: Einaudi, 1974).

Bibliography

Giustiniani, L. *Dizionario geografico ragionato del regno di Napoli* (12 vols.; Naples: Vincenzo Manfredi, 1797–1805).

ed. *Nuova collezione delle prammatiche del regno di Napoli* (15 vols.; Naples: Stamperie Simoniana, 1803–08).

Goldsmith, J. L. *Les Salers et les d'Escorailles, seigneurs de Haute Auvergne, 1500–1789* (Clermont-Ferrand: Institut d'études du Massif Central, 1984).

Goldthwaite, R. A. *Private Wealth in Renaissance Florence. A Study of Four Families* (Princeton: Princeton University Press, 1968).

"Organizzazione economica e struttura famigliare" in acts of the Third Convegno di studi sulla storia dei ceti dirigenti in Toscana *I ceti dirigenti nella Toscana tardo comunale* (Florence: Francesco Papafava Editore, 1980).

"The 'Empire of Things': Consumer Demand in Renaissance Italy" in F. W. Kent, and P. Simons, with J. C. Eade, eds. *Patronage, Art and Society in Renaissance Italy* (Canberra–Oxford: Oxford University Press, 1987), pp. 153–75.

Goodwin, A., ed. *The European Nobility in the Eighteenth Century, Studies in the Nobilities of the Major European States in the Pre-Reform Era* (New York: Harper and Row, 1967; first edit. London, 1953).

Gothein, E. *Il Rinascimento nell'Italia meridionale* (Italian transl. Florence: Sansoni, 1915).

Granata, L. *Economia rustica per lo regno di Napoli* (2 vols.; Naples: Nunzio Pasca, 1830).

Grassby, R. B. "Social Status and Commercial Enterprise under Louis XIV" in R. F. Kierstead, ed. *State and Society in Seventeenth-Century France* (New York: New Viewpoints, 1975), pp. 200–32.

Grelle Iusco, A., ed. *Arte in Basilicata, rinvenimenti e restauri* (Matera: De Luca, 1981).

Grendi, E. "Profilo storico degli Alberghi genovesi" *MEFRM* 87 (1975), pp. 241–302.

Guarneri, A. "Alcune notizie sovra la gestione di una casa baronale" *Archivio Storico Siciliano* 17 (1892), pp. 117–50.

Gullino, G. "I patrizi veneti di fronte alla proprietà feudale (secoli XVI–XVIII), materiale per una ricerca" *QS* 15 (1980), pp. 162–93.

Heers, J. *Le clan familial au Moyen Age. Etude sur les structures politiques et sociales des milieux urbains* (Paris: Presses Universitaires de France, 1974).

Hollingsworth, T. H. *The Demography of the British Peerage*, supplement to *Population Studies* 18 (1964–65).

Hurtubise, P., OMI *Une famille-témoin: les Salviati* (Vatican City: Biblioteca Apostolica Vaticana, 1985).

Imperato, F. *Discorso politico intorno al regimento delle piazze della città di Napoli* (Naples: Felice Stigliola, 1604).

Incarnato, G. "L'evoluzione del possesso feudale in Abruzzo Ultra dal 1500 al 1670" *ASPN* 96 (1971), pp. 219–87.

Intorcia, G. "Problemi del governo provinciale: l'Udienza di Basilicata nel Seicento" *ASPN* 102 (1984), pp. 139–55.

Magistrature del regno di Napoli. Analisi prosopografica, secoli XVI–XVII (Naples: Jovene, 1987).

Italia, A. *La Sicilia feudale. Saggi* (Rome: Società Editrice Dante Alighieri, 1940).

Jago, C. "The Influence of Debt on the Relations between Crown and Aristocracy in Seventeenth-Century Castile" *Economic History Review* series 2, 26 (1973), pp. 218–36.

Bibliography

"The 'Crisis' of the Aristocracy in Seventeenth-Century Castile" *Past and Present* 84 (1979), pp. 60–90.

Jamison, E., ed. *Catalogus baronum* (Rome: Istituto Storico Italiano per il Medio Evo, 1972).

Jones, P. "Economia e società nell'Italia medievale: la leggenda della borghesia" in *Storia d'Italia Einaudi. Annali I Dal feudalesimo al capitalismo* (Turin: Einaudi, 1978), pp. 185–372.

Kagan, R. L. *Lawsuits and Litigants in Castile, 1500–1700* (Chapel Hill: North Carolina University Press, 1981).

Kent, F. W. *Household and Lineage in Renaissance Florence. The Family Life of the Capponi, Ginori, and Rucellai* (Princeton: Princeton University Press, 1977).

Kettering, S. *Patrons, Brokers and Clients in Seventeenth-Century France* (Oxford: Oxford University Press, 1986).

Koenigsberger, H. G. *The Practice of Empire* (Ithaca: Cornell University Press, 1969; first edit. 1951).

Kula, W. *Teoria economica del sistema feudale. Proposta di un modello* (Turin: Einaudi, 1980; first edit 1970; Polish edit. 1962).

Labatut, J.-P. *Les ducs et pairs de France au XVIIe siècle, étude sociale* (Paris, Presses Universitaires de France, 1972).

Les noblesses européennes (Paris: Presses Universitaires de France, 1978).

Labrot, G. "Le comportement collectif de l'aristocratie napolitaine du seizième au dix-huitième siècle" *Revue historique* 101, no. 258 (1977), pp. 45–71.

"Un esempio di strategia artistica: il palazzo del nobile napoletano," paper presented at Villa Pignatelli in Naples on 12 January, 1978.

Baroni in città. Residenze e comportamenti dell'aristocrazia napoletana, 1530–1734 (Naples: Società Editrice Napoletana, 1979).

"Naissance et croisssance d'un quartier de Naples: Pizzofalcone, 1530–1689" *Urbi* 1 (1979), pp. 47–66.

"Images, tableaux et statuaire dans les testaments napolitains" *Revue historique* 106, no. 268 (1982), pp. 131–66.

"Trend économique et mécénat dans le royaume de Naples, 1530–1750" in acts of the Seventeenth Settimana di Studio dell'Istituto Internazionale di Storia Economica "Francesco Datini" di Prato, *Gli aspetti economici del mecenatismo in Europa (Secoli XIV–XVIII)* (Prato, 1985; now also in *MEFRM* 98 (1986), pp. 329–81).

Labrot, G., and Ruotolo, R. "Pour une étude historique de la commande aristocratique dans le royaume de Naples espagnol" *Revue historique* 104, no. 264 (1980), pp. 25–48.

Lacava, M. *Istoria di Atena Lucana* (Naples: publisher unknown, 1893).

La Malfa, U. "Mezzogiorno nell'Occidente" *Nord e Sud* 1 (1954), pp. 11–22.

Lanario, G. A. *Repetitiones feudales...* (Naples: Lazzaro Scoriggio, 1630).

Laporta, G. "Agricoltura e pastorizia nel feudo di Monteserico nei secoli XVI e XVII" in Massafra, ed. *Problemi di storia*, pp. 291–308.

Lepre, A. "Rendite di monasteri nel Napoletano e crisi economica del '600" *QS* 5 (1970), pp. 844–65.

Feudi e masserie, problemi della società meridionale nel '600 e nel '700 (Naples: Guida, 1973).

Bibliography

"I beni dei Muscettola di Leporano nel '600 e '700" in *Studi in memoria di Nino Cortese* (Rome: Istituto per la storia del Risorgimento italiano, 1976), pp. 275–307.

Terra di Lavoro nell'età moderna (Naples: Guida, 1978).

Il Mezzogiorno dal feudalesimo al capitalismo (Naples: Società Editrice Napoletana, 1979).

"Azienda feudale e azienda agraria nel Mezzogiono continentale tra Cinquecento e Ottocento" in Massafra, ed. *Problemi di storia* (Bari, 1981), pp. 27–40.

"Le campagne pugliesi nell'età moderna" in *La Puglia tra medio evo ed età moderna, città e campagna* (Milan: Electa, 1981), pp. 273–331.

Storia del Mezzogiorno d'Italia (2 vols.; Naples: Liguori, 1986).

Le Roy Ladurie, E., and Goy, J., eds. *Les fluctuations du produit de la dîme, conjuncture décimale et domaniale de la fin du Moyen Age au XVIIIe siècle* (Paris–The Hague: Mouton, 1972).

Levi, G. *L'eredità immateriale. Carriera di un esorcista nel Piemonte del Seicento* (Turin: Einaudi, 1985).

Lévy, C., and Henry, L. "Ducs et pairs sous l'Ancien Régime: caractéristiques démographique d'une caste" *Population* 15 (1960), pp. 807–30.

Ligresti, D. *Sicilia moderna: le città e gli uomini* (Naples: Guida, 1984).

Litchfield, R. B. "Demographic Characteristics of Florentine Patrician Families, Sixteenth to Nineteenth Century" *Journal of Economic History* 29 (1969), pp. 191–205.

Emergence of a Bureaucracy: The Florentine Patricians 1530–1790 (Princeton: Princeton University Press, 1986).

Macry, P. *Mercato e società nel regno di Napoli; commercio del granno e politica economica nel Settecento* (Naples: Guida, 1974).

Ottocento. Famiglie, elites e patrimoni a Napoli (Turin, Einaudi, 1988).

Malanima, P. *I Riccardi di Firenze, una famiglia e un patrimonio nella Toscana dei Medici* (Florence: Olschki, 1977).

"Patrimonio, reddito, investimenti, spese di una famiglia dell'aristocrazia fiorentina nel '700" in Mirri, ed. *Ricerche di storia moderna* (Pisa, 1979), pp. 225–60.

Mandelli, L. *La Lucania sconosciuta*, 2 vols.; BNN ms. X–D–1/2 (mid-seventeenth century).

Manfredi, M. *Giovan Battista Manso nella vita e nelle opere* (Naples; N. Jovene, 1919).

Manikowski, A. "Aspetti economici del mecenatismo di una famiglia aristocratica fiorentina nel XVII secolo" *Ricerche storiche* 16 (1986), pp. 81–94.

Mantelli, R. *Burocrazia e finanze pubbliche nel regno di Napoli a metà del Cinquecento* (Naples: Pironti, 1981).

Il pubblico impiego nell'economia del regno di Napoli: retribuzioni, reclutamento e ricambio sociale nell'epoca spagnola (secoli XVI–XVII) (Naples: Istituto Italiano per gli Studi Filosofici, 1986).

Marchisio, S. "Ideologia e problemi dell'economia familiare nelle lettere della nobiltà piemontese (XVII–XVIII secolo)" *Bollettino storico–bibliografico subalpino* (1985), pp. 67–130.

Marino, J. "I meccanismi della crisi nella Dogana di Foggia nel XVII secolo" in Massafra, ed. *Problemi di storia* (Bari, 1981), pp. 309–20.

Pastoral Economics in the Kingdom of Naples (Baltimore: Johns Hopkins University Press, 1988).

Bibliography

Marrara, D. *Riseduti e nobiltà. Profilo storico-istituzionale di un'oligarchia toscana nei secoli XVI-XVIII* (Pisa: Pacini, 1976).

Marshall, S. *The Dutch Gentry, 1500–1650. Faith, Family, and Fortune* (New York: Greenwood Press, 1987).

Martinez Ferrando, J. E. *Privilegios otorgados por el emperador Carlos V en el Reyno de Nápoles* (Barcelona: Archivo de la Corona de Aragón, 1943).

Masella, L. "Mercato fondiario e prezzi della terra nella Puglia barese tra XVII e XVIII secolo" *MEFRM* 88 (1976), pp. 261–96.

Massafra, A. "Un problème ouvert à la recherche: la 'crise' du baronnage napolitain à la fin du XVIIIe siècle" in *L'abolition de la féodalité dans le monde occidental*, Actes du colloque international (Toulouse, November 1968), I, pp. 245–62.

"Fisco e baroni nel regno di Napoli alla fine del secolo XVIII" in *Studi storici in onore di Gabriele Pepe* (Bari: Dedalo, 1969), pp. 625–75.

"Giurisdizione feudale e rendita fondiaria nel Settecento napoletano: un contributo alla ricerca" *QS* 7 (1972), pp. 187–252.

ed. *Problemi di storia delle campagne meridionali nell'età moderna e contemporanea* (Bari: Dedalo, 1981).

"Déséquilibres régionaux et réseaux de transport en Italie méridionale du milieu du XVIIIe siècle à l'Unité italienne" *Annales ESC* 43 (1988), pp. 1045–80.

Mastellone, S. *Francesco D'Andrea politico e giurista (1648–1698), l'ascesa del ceto civile* (Florence: Olschki, 1969).

Mazzella, S. *Descrittione del regno di Napoli...* (Naples, 1601; reprint Bologna: Forni, 1981; first edit. 1586).

Mezzoleni, J. *Guida dell'Archivio di Stato di Napoli* (2 vols.; Naples: ASN, 1972).

McArdle, F. *Altopascio. A Study in Tuscan Rural Society, 1587–1784* (Cambridge: Cambridge University Press, 1978).

Merzario, R. *Signori e contadini di Calabria. Corigliano Calabro dal XVI al XIX secolo* (Milan: Giuffrè, 1975).

Meyer, J. *Noblesses et pouvoirs dans l'Europe d'Ancien Régime* (Paris: Hachette, 1973).

Miceli, M. "La giurisdizione civile e criminale nel regno di Napoli" *Rivista araldica* 65 (1967), pp. 159–65, 300–09; 66 (1968), pp. 62–66, 87–96, 159–62, 257–61; 67 (1969), pp. 142–45, 306–09; 68 (1970), pp. 55–58.

Mingay, G. E. *The Gentry. The Rise and Fall of a Ruling Class* (London: Longman, 1976).

Mira, G. *Vicende economiche di una famiglia italiana dal XIV al XVII secolo* (Milan: Vita e pensiero, 1940).

Mirri, M., ed. *Ricerche di storia moderna, II, Aziende e patrimoni di grandi famiglie (secoli XV-XIX)* (2 vols.; Pisa: Pacini, 1979).

Molho, A. "Investimenti nel Monte delle doti di Firenze, un'analisi sociale e geografica" *QS* 21 (1986), pp. 147–70.

Monti, G. M. "Il patto dotale napoletano di Capuana e Nido" in Monti, *Dal '200 al '700* (Naples: ITEA, 1925), pp. 3–39.

Montroni, G. "Alcune riflessioni sulle storie di famiglia in età contemporanea" *Studi storici* 27 (1986), pp. 901–13.

"Aristocrazia fondiaria e modelli di trasferimento della ricchezza in Inghilterra tra XVII e XIX secolo: lo 'Strict Settlement'" *Studi storici* 30 (1989), pp. 579–602.

Bibliography

Moro, R. *Il tempo dei signori. Mentalità, ideologia, dottrine della nobiltà francese d'Antico Regime* (Rome: Savelli, 1981).

Moroni, A. "Le ricchezze dei Corsini. Struttura patrimoniale e vicende familiari tra Sette e Ottocento" *Società e storia* 9 (1986), pp. 255–92.

Moscati, R. *Una famiglia "borghese" del Mezzogiorno* (Naples: ESI, 1964).

"Le Università meridionali nel viceregno spagnolo" *Clio* 3 (1967), pp. 25–40.

Mozzarelli, C. "Stato, patriziato e organizzazione della società nell'età moderna" *Annali dell'Istituto Storico Italo-Germanico di Trento* 2 (1976), pp. 421–512.

"Strutture sociali e formazioni statuali a Milano e Napoli tra '500 e '600" *Società e storia* 1 (1978), pp. 431–63.

Musi, A. *Finanze e politica nella Napoli del '600: Bartolomeo d'Aquino* (Naples: Guida, 1976).

"La spinta baronale e i suoi antagonisti nella crisi del Seicento" in F. Barbagallo, ed. *Storia della Campania* (2 vols.; Naples: Guida, 1978), I, pp. 223–44.

"Regione storica, provincia e società nel Mezzogiorno moderno" *Quaderni sardi di storia* 1 (1980), pp. 83–100.

"Il Principato Citeriore nella crisi agraria del XVII secolo" in Massafra, ed. *Problemi di storia* (Bari, 1981), pp. 173–88.

"Amministrazione, potere locale e società in una provincia del Mezzogiorno moderno: il Principato Citra nel secolo XVII" *Quaderni sardi di storia* 4 (1984), pp. 81–118.

"La venalità degli uffici in Principato Citra. Contributo allo studio del sistema dell'amministrazione periferica in età spagnola" *Rassegna storica salernitana* new series, 3 (1986), pp. 77–91.

La rivolta di Masaniello nella scena politica barocca (Naples: Giuda, 1989).

Muto, G. *Le finanze pubbliche napoletane tra riforme e restaurazione (1520–1634)* (Naples: ESI, 1980).

"Strutture e funzioni finanziarie delle 'università' del Mezzogiorno tra '500 e '600" *Quaderni sardi di storia* 1 (1980), pp. 101–22.

"Una struttura periferica del governo dell'economia nel Mezzogiorno spagnolo: i percettori provinciali" *Società e storia* 6 (1983), pp. 1–36.

"Gestione del potere e classi sociali nel Mezzogiorno spagnolo" in A. Tagliaferri, ed. *I ceti dirigenti in Italia in età moderna e contemporanea* (Udine: del Bianco, 1984), pp. 287–301.

"Gestione politica e controllo sociale nella Napoli spagnola" in C. de Seta, ed. *Le città capitali* (Bari: Laterza, 1985), pp. 67–94.

"Lo 'stile antiquo': consuetudini e prassi amministrativa a Napoli nella prima età moderna" *MEFRM* 100 (1988), pp. 317–30.

Nader, H. "Noble Income in Sixteenth-Century Castile: The Case of the Marquises of Mondéjar, 1480–1580" *Economic History Review* series 2, 30 (1977), pp. 411–28.

Neuschel, K. *Word of Honor. Interpreting Noble Culture in Sixteenth-Century France* (Ithaca: Cornell, 1989).

Novario, G. M. *De vassallorum gravaminibus tractatus* (Naples: Tipografia Moriana, 1774; first edit. 1634).

Owen Hughes, D. "Strutture familiari e sistemi di successione ereditaria nei testamenti dell'Europa medievale" *QS* 11 (1976), pp. 929–52.

"From Brideprice to Dowry in Mediterranean Europe" in M. A. Kaplan, ed. *Women*

265

Bibliography

and History, X, *The Marriage Bargain: Women and Dowries in European History* (1985) (originally in *Journal of Family History* 3 (1978)).

"Sumptuary Laws and Social Relations in Renaissance Italy" in J. Bossy, ed. *Disputes and Settlements. Law and Human Relations in the West* (Cambridge: Cambridge University Press, 1983), pp. 69–99.

"Representing the Family: Portraits and Purpose in Early Modern Italy" *Journal of Interdisciplinary History* 17 (1986), pp. 7–38.

Pacca, C. A. *Discorso circa li seggi di questa città di Napoli*, BNN ms. San Martino 73 (late sixteenth century).

Historia della famiglia Caracciola, BNN ms. San Martino 379 (*c.* 1580–85).

Pacelli, V. "La collezione di Francesco Emanuele Pinto, principe di Ischitella" *Storia dell'arte* 11 (1979), 36–37, pp. 165–204.

Palermo, F., ed. "Narrazioni e documenti sulla storia del regno di Napoli dall'anno 1522 al 1667" *ASI* 9 (1846), pp. 147–90.

— ed. "Narrazioni tratte dai giornali del governo di Don Pietro Girone duca d'Ossuna vicerè di Napoli, scritti da Francesco Zazzera" *ASI* 9 (1846), pp. 473–617.

— ed. "Relazioni varie dall'anno 1561 al 1596" *ASI* 9 (1846), pp. 193–99.

Palumbo, M. *I comuni meridionali prima e dopo le leggi eversive della feudalità* (2 vols.; Montecorvino Rovella-Cerignola, 1910–16; reprint Bologna: Forni, 1979).

Pansini, G. "Per una storia del feudalesimo nel granducato di Toscana durante il periodo mediceo" *QS* 7 (1972), pp. 131–86.

Parrino, D. A. *Teatro eroico e politico de' governi de' vicerè del regno di Napoli...* (2 vols.; Naples: Gravier, 1770; first edit. Naples: Parrino, 1692).

Paternoster, G. *Ritratto di paese, Brienza 1872*, G. A. Colangelo, ed. (Venosa, 1984).

Pecori, R. *Del privato governo delle università* (2 vols.; Naples: Donato Camp, 1770–73).

Pedio, T. "Condizioni economiche generali e stato dell'artigianato e delle manifatture in Basilicata attraverso la statistica murattiana del regno di Napoli" *ASCL* 32 (1963), pp. 235–73; 33 (1964), pp. 5–53.

Napoli e Spagna nella prima metà del Cinquecento (Bari: Cacucci, 1971).

Pedlow, G. W. *The Survival of the Hessian Nobility, 1770–1870* (Princeton: Princeton University Press, 1988).

Pelizzari, M. R. "Per una storia dell'agricoltura irpina nell'età moderna" in Massafra, ed. *Problemi di storia* (Bari, 1981), pp. 189–200.

Pepe, G. *Il Mezzogiorno d'Italia sotto gli Spagnuoli* (Florence: Sansoni, 1952).

Pescosolido, G. *Terra e nobilità; i Borghese (secoli XVIII e XIX)* (Rome: Jouvence, 1979).

Petraccone, C. *Napoli dal '500 all''800, problemi di storia demografica e sociale* (Naples: Guida, 1974).

Petronio, U. *Il Senato di Milano, istituzioni giuridiche ed esercizio del potere nel Ducato di Milano da Carlo V a Giuseppe II* (Milan: Giuffrè, 1972).

"Giurisdizione feudale e ideologia giuridica nel Ducato di Milano" *QS* 9 (1974), pp. 351–402.

Pezzana, A. "Note sui suffeudi nell'Italia meridionale nel secolo XVIII" *Rivista araldica* 67 (1969), pp. 37–48.

Pilati, R. "La dialettica politica a Napoli durante la visita di Lope de Guzmán" *ASPN* 105 (1987), pp. 145–221.

Bibliography

Placanica, A. *Uomini, strutture, economia in Calabria nei secoli XVI-XVII* (Reggio Calabria: Editori Meridionali Riuniti, 1974).

Moneta, prestiti, usura nel Mezzogiorno moderno (Naples: Società Editrice Napoletana, 1982).

Pomian, K. "review" of A. Manikowski, *Spoleczeristvo elitarnej konsumpcij* in *Annales ESC* 44 (1989), pp. 1153-55.

Pontieri, E. *Il tramonto del baronaggio siciliano* (Florence: Sansoni, 1943).

"A proposito della 'Crociata' contro i Valdesi della Calabria nel 1561" in Pontieri, *Nei tempi grigi della storia d'Italia* (Naples, 1966; first edit. 1949), pp. 159-96.

ed. *Storia di Napoli* (10 vols.; Naples: ESI 1967-72; second edit. 1975-81).

Powis, J. *Aristocracy* (Oxford: Basil Blackwell, 1984).

Queller, D. E. *The Venetian Patriciate. Reality versus Myth* (Urbana–Chicago: University of Illinois Press, 1986).

Racioppi, G. "Gli statuti della bagliva delle antiche comunità del Napoletano" *ASPN* 6 (1881), pp. 347-77, 508-30.

Ranieri, L. *Le regioni d'Italia*, XIII, *La Basilicata* (Turin: UTET, 1961).

Rao, A. M. *L'"Amaro della Feudalità": la devoluzione di Arnone e la questione feudale a Napoli alla fine del '700* (Naples: Guida, 1984).

"La questione feudale nell'età tanucciana" paper presented at the conference *Bernardo Tanucci, la corte, il paese 1730–1780*, held in Catania in October 1985, typescript.

Reinhardt, V. *Kardinal Scipione Borghese (1605–1633). Vermögen, Finanzen und sozialer Aufstieg eines Papstnepoten* (Tübingen; Max Niemeyer, 1984).

Rendella, P. *Tractatus de pascuis, defensis, forestis et aquis...* (Trani: Lorenzo Valerio, 1630).

Reumont, A. von *The Carafas of Maddaloni. Naples under Spanish Dominion* (London: Bohn, 1854; German edit. 1850).

Romano, D. *Patricians and Popolani. The Social Foundations of the Venetian Renaissance State* (Baltimore: Johns Hopkins University Press, 1987).

Romano, R. *Tra due crisi: l'Italia del Rinascimento* (Turin: Einaudi, 1982; first edit. 1971).

Napoli: dal viceregno al regno, storia economica (Turin: Einaudi, 1976).

Rössler, H., ed. *Deutscher Adel, 1430–1740* (2 vols.; Darmstadt: Wissenschaftliche Buchgesellschaft, 1965).

ed. *Deutsches Patriziat, 1430–1740* (Limburg: C. A. Starke, 1968).

Rota, C. *Legalis Androgynus, sive tractatus de privilegiis mulierum* (Naples: Giovan Francesco Pace, 1665).

Roveda, E. "Una grande possessione lodigiana dei Trivulzio tra '500 e '700" in Mirri, ed. *Ricerche di storia moderna*, II, pp. 25-139.

Rovito, P. L. *Republica dei togati. Giuristi e società nella Napoli del '600* (Naples: Jovene, 1981).

"La rivoluzione costituzionale di Napoli (1647–1648)" *RSI* 98 (1986), pp. 367-462.

"Strutture cetuali, riformismo ed eversione nelle rivolte apulo-lucane di metà Seicento" *ASPN* 106 (1988), pp. 241-308.

Rovito, S. *Luculenta commentaria...* (Sixth edit.; Naples: Giacomo Gaffaro, 1649).

Ruocco, D. *Le regioni d'Italia*, XV, *La Campania* (Turin: UTET, 1965).

Russo, C. *I monasteri femminili di clausura a Napoli nel secolo XVII* (Naples: Istituto di storia medievale e moderna, n.d.).

"Poteri istituzionali e poteri di fatto nelle campagne meridionali in età moderna: chiesa e comunità" *ASPN* 104 (1986), pp. 159-76.

Bibliography

Ryder, A. *The Kingdom of Naples under Alfonso the Magnanimous. The Making of a Modern State* (Oxford: Oxford University Press, 1976).

Sabbatini, R. *I Guinigi tra '500 e '600; il fallimento mercantile e il rifugio nei campi* (Lucca: Pacini Fazzi, 1979).

Salomon, N. *La campagne de Nouvelle Castile à la fin du XVIe siècle* (Paris: SEVPEN, 1964).

Santamaria, N. *I feudi, il diritto feudale e la loro storia nell'Italia meridionale* (Naples: Marghieri, 1881; reprint Bologna: Forni, 1978).

Schalk, E. "Ennoblement in France from 1350 to 1660" *Journal of Social History* 16 (1982), pp. 101–10.

From Valor to Pedigree. Ideas of Nobility in France in the Sixteenth and Seventeenth Centuries (Princeton: Princeton University Press, 1986).

Schipa, M. *Il regno di Napoli al tempo di Carlo di Borbone* (Naples, 1904; first published in *ASPN* 27–28 (1902–3)).

Sciuti Russi, V. "Aspetti della venalità degli uffici in Sicilia (XVII-XVIII secolo)" *RSI* 88 (1976), pp. 342–55.

Sella, D. *Crisis and Continuity. The Economy of Spanish Lombardy in the Seventeenth Century* (Cambridge, Mass.: Harvard University Press, 1979).

Sereni, E. *Storia del paesaggio agrario italiano* (Bari: Laterza, 1982; first edit. 1961).

Sheppard, T. *Lourmarin in the Eighteenth Century* (Baltimore: Johns Hopkins University Press, 1971).

Sinisi, A. "Una famiglia mercantile napoletana del XVIII secolo, i Maresca di Serracapriola" *Economia e storia*, second series, 3 (1982), pp. 139–203.

Sorge, G. *Jurisprudentia forensis* (10 vols.; V, *De feudis*, Naples, 1742).

Spagnoletti, A. "Le aggregazioni alla nobiltà nelle università di Terra di Bari nel XVIII secolo" *Società e storia* 3 (1980), pp. 35–59.

"L'incostanza delle umane cose": il patriziato di Terra di Bari tra egemonia e crisi (XVI-XVIII secolo)" (Bari: Edizioni del Sud, 1981).

"Forme di autocoscienza e vita nobiliare: il caso della Puglia barese" *Società e storia* 6 (1983), pp. 49–76.

"Giudici e governatori regi nelle università meridionali (XVIII secolo)" *ASPN* 105 (1987), pp. 415–54.

Spring, D., ed. *European Landed Elites in the Nineteenth Century* (Baltimore: Johns Hopkins University Press, 1977).

Stone, L. "Marriage among the English Nobility in the Sixteenth and Seventeenth Centuries" *Comparative Studies in Society and History* 3 (1960), pp. 182–206.

Family and Fortune. Studies in Aristocratic Finance in the Sixteenth and Seventeenth Centuries (Oxford: Oxford University Press, 1973).

"Family History in the 1980s: Past Achievements and Future Trends" *Journal of Interdisciplinary History* 12 (1981), pp. 51–87.

"Inheritance Strategies among the English Landed Elite, 1540–1880" in G. Delille and F. Rizzi, eds. *Le modèle familial européen; normes, déviances, contrôle du pouvoir* (Rome: Ecole Française de Rome, 1986), pp. 267–90.

Stone, L., and Fawtier Stone, J. C. *An Open Elite? England, 1540–1880* (Oxford: Oxford University Press, 1984).

Storchi, M. L. "Un'azienda agricola della piana del Sele tra il 1842 ed il 1855" in Massafra, ed. *Problemi di storia*, pp. 117–39.

Bibliography

Storia del Vallo di Diano (3 vols.; Salerno: Laveglia, 1982–85).

Stumpo, E. "I ceti dirigenti in Italia nell'età moderna. Due modelli diversi: nobiltà piemontese e patriziato toscano" in A. Tagliaferri, ed. *I ceti dirigenti in Italia in età moderna e contemporanea* (Udine: del Bianco, 1984), pp. 151–97.

Il capitale finanziario a Roma fra '500 e '600. Contributo alla storia della fiscalità pontificia in età moderna (1570–1660) (Milan: Giuffrè, 1985).

Sturdy, D. J. *The D'Aligres de la Rivière, Servants of the Bourbon State in the Seventeenth Century* (Woodbridge: The Boydell Press, 1986).

Summonte, G. A. *Historia della città e regno di Napoli* (6 vols.; third edit., Naples: Domenico Vivenzio, 1748–50; first edit. 1599–1601, 1640–43).

Tamassia, N. *La famiglia italiana nei secoli XV e XVI* (Rome: Multigrafica Editrice, 1971; first edit. 1910).

Tassone, G. D. *Observationes jurisdictionales politicae ac practicae ad regiam pragmaticam sanctionem editam de anno 1617 quae dicitur de antefato* (Naples: Michele Luigi Mutio, 1716; first edit. 1632).

Teall, E. "The Seigneur of Renaissance France: Advocate or Opressor?" *Journal of Modern History* 37 (1965), pp. 131–50.

Torras i Ribé, J. M. *Evolució social i econòmica d'una família catalana de l'antic règim. Els Padró d'Igualada (1642–1862)* (Barcelona: FSVC, 1976).

Trasselli, C. *Lo stato di Gerace e Terranova nel Cinquecento* (Vibo Valentia: Edizioni Parallelo 38, 1978).

Tricoli, G. *La Deputazione degli Stati e la crisi del baronaggio siciliano dal XVI al XIX secolo* (Palermo: Fondazione Culturale Lauro Chiazzese, 1966).

Trifone, R. *Feudi e demani. L'eversione della feudalità nell'Italia meridionale* (Milan: Società Editrice Libiana, 1909).

Trinchera, F. *Degli archivi napoletani relazione* (Naples: ASN, 1872).

Tutini, C. *Del origine e fundatione de' Seggi di Napoli* (Naples: Beltrano, 1644).

Vazquez de Prada, V. *Historia económica y social de España*, III, *Los siglos XVI y XVII* (Madrid: Confederación española de cajas de ahorros, 1978).

Verga, M. "Un esempio di colonizzazione interna nella Sicilia del XVIII secolo: i Notarbartolo duchi di Villarosa" in Mirri, ed. *Ricerche di storia moderna* (Pisa, 1979), 11, pp. 261–95.

"Rapporti di produzione e gestione dei feudi nella Sicilia centro-occidentale" in Massafra, ed. *Problemi di storia* (Bari, 1981), pp. 73–89.

Vicens Vives, J., ed. *Historia social y económica de España y América* (5 vols.; Barcelona: Editorial Teide, 1957; new edit. as *Historia de España y América*, Barcelona: Editorial Vicens Vives, 1971).

Vierhaus, R., ed. *Der Adel vor der Revolution, zur sozialer und politischer Funktion des Adels in vorrevolutionärem Europa* (Göttingen: Vandenhoeck und Ruprecht, 1971).

Vigo, G. *Fisco e società nella Lombardia del Cinquecento* (Bologna: Mulino, 1979).

Villani, P. ed. "Eboli nel 1640" *Rassegna storica salernitana* (1953), pp. 196–207.

"Vicende della proprietà fondiaria in un comune latifondistico del Mezzogiorno" *Annuario dell'Istituto Storico Italiano per l'età moderna e contemporanea* 12 (1960), pp. 17–96.

"Ricerche sulla proprietà e sul regime fondiario nel Lazio" *Annuario dell'Istituto Storico Italiano per l'età moderna e contemporanea* 12 (1960), pp. 97–263.

Bibliography

"La feudalità dalle riforme all'eversione" *Clio* 1 (1965), pp. 599–622.

"Signoria rurale, feudalità, capitalismo nelle campagne" *QS* 7 (1972), pp. 5–26.

ed. *Economia e classi sociali nella Puglia moderna* (Naples: Guida, 1974).

Mezzogiorno tra riforme e rivoluzione (Bari: Laterza, 1977; first edit. 1962).

Villani, P., *et al.*, eds. *Nunziature di Napoli* (3 vols.; Rome: Istituto Storico Italiano per l'età moderna e contemporanea, 1962–70).

Villari, R. *Mezzogiorno e contadini nell'età moderna* (Bari: Laterza, 1961; new edit. 1977).

"Baronaggio e finanze a Napoli alla vigilia della rivoluzione del 1647–48" *Studi storici* 3 (1962), pp. 259–305.

"Note sulla rifeudalizzazione del regno di Napoli alla vigilia della rivoluzione di Masaniello" *Studi storici* 4 (1963), pp. 637–68; 6 (1965), pp. 295–328; 8 (1967), pp. 37–112.

"La feudalità e lo stato napoletano nel secolo XVII" *Clio* 1 (1965), pp. 555–75.

La rivolta antispagnola a Napoli. Le origini (1585–1647) (Bari: Laterza, 1967).

ed. *Il Sud nella storia d'Italia* (2 vols.; Bari: Laterza, 1974; first edit. 1961).

"La Spagna, l'Italia e l'assolutismo" *Studi storici* 18 (1977), 4, pp. 5–22 (also with minor changes in Villari, *Ribelli e riformatori dal XVI al XVIII secolo* (Rome: Editori Riuniti, 1979), pp. 43–67).

"Masaniello: Contemporary and Recent Interpretations" *Past and Present*, 108 (1985), pp. 117–32.

Elogio della dissimulazione. La lotta politica nel Seicento (Bari: Laterza, 1987).

Villone, A. *Privilegi giurisdizionali e dominio feudale: lo stato dei Doria d'Angri nella seconda metà del secolo XVII* (Naples: Guida, 1980).

Visceglia, M. A. "Formazione e dissoluzione di un patrimonio aristocratico: la famiglia Muscettola tra XVI e XIX secolo" *MEFRM* 92 (1980), pp. 555–624.

"Rendita feudale e agricoltura in Puglia nell'età moderna (XVI-XVIII secolo)" *Società e storia* 9 (1980), pp. 527–60.

"L'azienda signorile in Terra d'Otranto nell'età moderna (secoli XVI-XVIII)" in Massafra, ed. *Problemi di storia* (Bari, 1981), pp. 41–71.

"Corpo e sepoltura nei testamenti della nobiltà napoletana (secoli XVI-XVIII)" *QS* 17 (1982), pp. 583–614.

"Linee per uno studio unitario dei testamenti e dei contratti matrimoniali dell'aristo-crazia feudale napoletana tra fine Quattrocento e Settecento" *MEFRM* 95 (1983), pp. 393–470.

"Ideologia nobiliare e rappresentazione della donna" *Prospettive Settanta* 7 (1985), pp. 88–110.

"Sistema feudale e mercato internazionale: la periferizzazione del paese" *Prospettive Settanta* 7 (1985), pp. 69–88.

"Comunità, signori feudali e *officiales* in Terra d'Otranto fra XVI e XVII secolo" *ASPN* 104 (1986), pp. 259–85.

"Durata e rinnovamento delle famiglie feudali in Terra d'Otranto tra Medioevo ed età moderna" paper presented at the department of history in the University of Naples on 11 June 1986.

Il bisogno di eternità. Comportamenti aristocratici a Napoli in età moderna (Naples: Guida, 1988).

Bibliography

Territorio, feudo e potere locale. Terra d'Otranto tra Medioevo ed età moderna (Naples: Guida, 1988).

Vitale, G. "Modelli culturali nobiliari a Napoli tra Quattro e Cinquecento" *ASPN* 105 (1987), pp. 27–103.

"La nobiltà di Seggio a Napoli nel basso Medioevo: aspetti della dinamica interna" *ASPN* 106 (1988), pp. 151–69.

Volpe, F. *Il Cilento nel secolo XVII* (Naples: Ferraro, 1981).

Winspeare, D. *Storia degli abusi feudali* (Naples: Angelo Trani, 1811).

Woolf, S. J. *Studi sulla nobiltà piemontese nell'epoca dell'assolutismo*, Memoria dell'Accademia delle Scienze di Torino, Classe di Scienze Morali, Storiche e Filologiche (Turin, 1963).

Wright, A. D. *The Counter-Reformation. Catholic Europe and the Non-Christian World* (New York: St Martin's Press, 1982).

Yun Casalilla, B. *Sobre la transición al capitalismo en Castilla. Economía y sociedad en Tierra de Campos (1500–1830)* (León: Junta de Castilla y León, 1987).

Zanetti, D. *La demografia del patriziato milanese nei secoli XVII-XVIII-XIX* (Pavia: University of Pavia, 1972).

Zotta, S. "Momenti e problemi di una crisi agraria in uno 'stato' feudale napoletano (1585–1615)" *MEFRM* 90 (1978), pp. 715–96.

"Rapporti di produzione e cicli produttivi in regime di autoconsumo e di produzione speculativa. Le vicende agrarie dello 'stato' di Melfi nel lungo periodo (1530–1730)" in Massafra, ed. *Problemi di storia* (Bari, 1981), pp. 221–89.

Index

Index

Index

Index

Index

Index

Ruffo, Paolo, prince of Castelcicala, 174
Ruffo, Sofia, 175
rural bourgeoisie, 109, 139, 146
rural community (see also *università*), 2, 5, 15,
  26, 32, 38, 92, 100, 108, 109, 116, 126,
  129, 132, 135, 139, 147, 155, 156, 233, 234
rural labor, 69, 73, 83, 85, 114, 235
rural population, 3, 6, 9
rustic fiefs, 110
rye, 91, 92

Sacred Royal Council, 138, 195, 197, 213–16
St. James, order of, 173
St. Michel, order of, 26
Sala, 30, 42, 52, 61, 62, 64, 65, 147, 149, 195,
  214, 215
salaries, 65–66, 73, 118, 123, 190, 206, 208,
  209
Salerno, 27, 93, 94, 96, 97, 112, 114
Salerno, archbishop of, 137
Saluzzo dukes of Corigliano, 125
Salvia, 30, 31, 42, 44, 53, 218, 222
Sanfelice family, 177
San Giovanni a Carbonara church, 24n., 29,
  48, 49, 66, 120, 165, 166, 189
San Giuseppe dei Ruffi church, 187
San Gregorio Armeno convent, 176
San Rufo, 218
Sanseverino princes of Bisignano, 31, 53, 66,
  120, 164
Sanseverino prince of Salerno, 164, 204
Sant'Agata, prince of, 208
Santamaria, N., 108
Santa Maria degli Angeli monastery, 49, 121
Sant'Anastasia, 50
Sant'Angelo a Fasanella abbey, 27, 29–31, 169
Sant'Elmo castle, 27
Sant'Eramo, 127, 163
Santi Apostoli church, 49, 199
Sardinia, 13, 19
Sasso, 1, 21, 31, 32, 37, 38, 42, 44, 45, 63,
  75, 76, 91, 92, 93, 94, 96, 97, 102, 112,
  113, 114, 118, 122, 123, 128, 132, 133,
  135, 136, 140, 142, 143, 144, 145, 147,
  148, 150, 151, 165, 171, 195, 197, 198,
  212, 213, 214, 215, 218, 219, 221, 227,
  229
saving, 69
Savona, 33
schools, in the fiefs, 129, 136, 156
Scrivania di Razione, 172
Seggi, 24–25, 36, 47, 119, 162, 171, 175, 177,
  181, 183, 199, 203, 225
Seggi, aggregations to, 24
Seggio aristocracy, 24–25, 31, 36n., 177, 183n.,
  185, 207, 225

Seggio of Capuana, 24, 25, 119, 165, 172, 177,
  179, 182, 185, 192, 221
Seggio of Montagna, 24, 177
Seggio of Nido, 24, 25, 179, 192
Seggio of the People, 24
Seggio of Porta in Sorrento, 182
Seggio of Portanova, 24
Seggio of Porto, 24, 173, 174, 180
seigneurie, 9
Selci, duke of, 174
Sele river, 43, 83, 97, 234
Seminara, duke of, 53
Seminarium nobilium, 189–90
Seripando family, 177, 179
Serra family, 20, 175
Serra, Luigi, prince of Cassano, 175
Serra, Teresa, 175
Sforza, Ascanio, cardinal, 27
Sforza, Francesco, duke of Milan, 207
Sforza, Cesarini, Gaetano, prince of Segni, 181
sharecropping, 82
shepherds, 66, 97
Sicily, 1, 13, 15n., 19, 27, 37, 40n., 41, 80, 81,
  85, 92, 101, 106, 130, 168, 169, 174, 211,
  215, 216, 231
Siena, 28, 168
silk, 94, 114, 143
sindaco, 114–15, 145
Società Napoletana di Storia Patria, 35
Somaschians, 189
Sommaria, 209, 213, 214, 226, 228–30
Sorrento, 182
Southern Italy (or Mezzogiorno), 1, 7–15, 20,
  103, 109, 112, 131, 139, 204, 230, 234, 235
Spain (and the Spanish), 4, 5, 13, 14, 15n., 19,
  20, 52, 86, 94, 103, 164, 165, 168, 169,
  203, 204, 206, 207, 215–19
Spanish army, 29, 31, 168, 169, 206
Spanish customs and ideas, 11, 182, 191
Spanish empire, 13, 27, 168, 203–05
Spanish government, 20, 27, 47, 53, 93, 103,
  115–17, 157, 149, 157, 202, 204, 205, 206,
  208, 210, 216–24, 230, 233–35
Spanish grandees, 26
Spanish rule in Naples, 12–17, 20, 21,
  103–04, 159, 162, 164, 202–32, 233, 235
state (and state apparatus), 2, 3, 5–7, 14, 19,
  103, 119, 146, 147, 159, 202–05, 230
statutes of *università*, 82, 108, 110, 147
strict settlement, 4
structure of patrimony, 36–67
subfeudatories, 142
subfiefs, 86, 113, 142
Suor Orsola Benincasa convent, 49

Tanagro river, 113

Index

CAMBRIDGE STUDIES IN EARLY MODERN HISTORY

Lille and the Dutch Revolt: Urban Stability in an Era of Revolution
ROBERT S. DUPLESSIS
The Armada of Flanders: Spanish Maritime Policy and European War, 1568–1668
R. A. STRADLING

For EU product safety concerns, contact us at Calle de José Abascal, 56–1°,
28003 Madrid, Spain or eugpsr@cambridge.org.

www.ingramcontent.com/pod-product-compliance
Ingram Content Group UK Ltd.
Pitfield, Milton Keynes, MK11 3LW, UK
UKHW010033140625
459647UK00012BA/1364